My Life as
a Teenage POW

BILLY

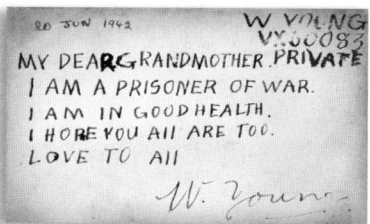

MY LIFE AS A TEENAGE POW
BILLY

Lynette Silver and Billy Young

SALLY MILNER
PUBLISHING

First published in 2016 by
Sally Milner Publishing Pty Ltd
734 Woodville Road
Binda NSW 2583 AUSTRALIA

© Lynette Silver and K W (Billy) Young 2016

National Library of Australia Cataloguing-in-Publication data:

Creator: Silver, Lynette Ramsay, 1945- author.

Title: Billy : My life as a teenage POW / Lynette Silver, Keith (Billy) Young.

ISBN: 9781863514958 (paperback)

Notes: Includes bibliographical references and index.

Subjects: Young, Keith.
  Prisoners of war—Australia—Biography
  Prisoners of war—Sabah—Sandakan.
  Prisoners of war—Singapore—Outram.
  World War, 1939-1945—Prisoners and prisons.
  World War, 1939-1945—Personal narratives, Australian

Other Creators/Contributors:
  Young, Keith, author.

Dewey Number: 940.547252

Design: Natalie Bowra
Editing: Anne Savage
Printed in China

All rights reserved. No part of this publication may be reproduced, stored in a retrieval system, or transmitted in any form or by any means, electronic, mechanical, photocopying, recording or otherwise, without prior permission of the copyright owners and publishers.

10 9 8 7 6 5 4 3 2 1

CONTENTS

Acknowledgements vii
Author's Note ix
Prologue xi

1 In the beginning: 1925–1941   1
2 Fending for myself: 1934 – July 1941   23
3 You'll be sorry: July – November 1941   51
4 War games: 8 December 1941 – 13 February 1942   75
5 Reluctant guests of the Emperor: 13 February – 7 July 1942   95
6 To Sandakan: 7 July – November 1942   119
7 Camp life: September 1942 – February 1943   143
8 On borrowed time: 19 February – early April 1943   175
9 Out of the frying pan … : mid-April – 23 August 1943   201
10 … and into the fire: 23 August 1943 – early 1944   213
11 Riding a receding tide: Early 1944 – early 1945   247
12 Out of the shadows: early 1945 – 19 August 1945   273

Epilogue: Afterwards   307
The Australian dead of Sandakan   321
Bibliography   337

"Sandakan" by Billy Young

ACKNOWLEDGEMENTS

Lynette Silver would like to thank Billy Young's family members who kindly supplied photographs from their private collections; her friends Di Elliott in Canberra and Robbert van der Rijdt of Dutch War Graves, for assisting with additional background research and for visiting and photographing the grave of Pieter van Hemert in Java on Billy's behalf; and her husband Neil Silver for his unstinting enthusiasm and support throughout the writing of this book.

Billy and Lynette also thank all the members of the 'Sandakan Family' who encouraged him to tell his story.

DEDICATION

To all those who did not come home, especially the Dead End Kids

AUTHOR'S NOTE

Billy: My Life as a Teenage POW has been compiled from a personal chronicle penned by Billy Young throughout the 1970s, supplemented by hundreds of conversations that we have shared in the course of a close friendship spanning more than two decades. It is the only first-hand published account by an ordinary soldier imprisoned by the Japanese at the infamous Sandakan POW Camp, and one of only three books by a survivor of the Kempeitai's equally notorious Outram Road Gaol. Billy is now the only soldier left alive from Sandakan, and the only Australian prisoner still alive from Outram Road.

As a historian who has invested almost thirty years researching all the wartime events that took place in this book – including those in Malaya, Singapore and Borneo in which Billy took part – I have been privileged to be invited not only to share his memories but in many ways to become an integral part of them.

I didn't realise how special this rapport between us was until January 2004, when we were interviewed together by *The Sydney Morning Herald*'s Tony Stephens after each being awarded an OAM in the Australia Day Honours list for our work in relation to the Sandakan POW story.

'Billy Young', Tony wrote, 'talks to Lynette Silver as if she had been in the Sandakan prisoner-of-war camp with him and his mates; as if she knew them like he knew them while they were young. Ms Silver knows more than probably anyone about Sandakan and the 2428 who died in the camp, on the "death march" to Ranau, or at their wretched destination.'

It's true. I do feel as if I know them; that I was there with Billy throughout his captivity as an invisible observer. And Billy recognises this by talking to me as if I were actually there, a mate to share his joys and sorrows, to discuss and mull over the ins and outs of everyday life in a prison camp. That we have a 'shared memory' has become more evident in recent years as he relies on me to provide input into his recollections by supplying the name of a mate, or a date, or some other small fact that has temporarily slipped his mind.

We have used this unusual and precious partnership to create *Billy: My Life as a Teenage POW*, with me providing historical details gleaned from years of combing archival documents, and Billy giving its unique narrative immense vibrancy and life as he takes us on a very personal journey. Through the eyes of a tearaway teenaged soldier, Billy shares with us his thoughts and experiences, some of which have never before been revealed – secrets that he has kept even from his closest family.

The autobiographical narrative has been compiled by me, using Billy's own words whenever possible but occasionally supplemented with small historical details to give added depth. Interspersed throughout this first-hand account is a 'second voice', which I supply solely as the historical narrator. These sections, easily identifiable as they are in italics, contain information that fall outside the scope of Billy's personal experiences. This historical narrative is secondary, but read in tandem with the autobiographical strand it expands the story in a way not possible otherwise.

Billy Young is a remarkable human being and a national treasure. I am proud and humbled to have him as my friend.

Lynette Silver
October 2015

PROLOGUE

Time. It is not only relative, it can also be deceptive. Fooling us through our adolescence with its change of pace. Urging us on with its promise of great expectations. Dragging its feet at the pull of our impatience.

We daydream, make plans and schemes, on what and how we will spend that time. Then, suddenly, wham! It's gone. Time has done a bunk. The reins lie limp in our hands and we are left looking back at misty shadows – shadows fast disappearing into a distant fogbank of memories.

For me, they are galloping away much too quickly: a mob of brumbies heading for the hills. I need to round them up, put my brand on them before they fade away altogether and are lost in the wilds of beyond, gone forever.

The day I joined the army is such a shadow. A shadow camouflaged in time.

Billy Young
October 2015

CHAPTER 1

IN THE BEGINNING

1925 – 1941

It is July 1941, and Australia is at war. Australian troops are fighting the Germans in North Africa and the Middle East and the Japanese, starved of oil, rubber and other commodities, are threatening to make a move into resource-rich South-East Asia. The threat is not taken seriously but, as a precaution, the Australian Government has agreed to strengthen the British garrison in Malaya and Singapore with two brigades of its 8th Division. Although no one perceives any real danger to Australia, there are plenty of patriotic young men willing to volunteer to fight for the King and the Empire. Others, out of work, down on their luck, or perhaps wanting to escape a difficult family situation, also answer the call – the pay is good, three meals a day are guaranteed, and there is every chance of a posting overseas. Keith William Young, just fifteen years old, orphaned, unemployed, broke and on the run from the law, is making his way to an Army recruiting office in Melbourne with Phil, a similarly youthful and wayward acquaintance.

A surly early morning breeze pushed its way through a bank of winter fog, enveloping in whirling, damp, grey cotton-balls of mist anyone foolish enough to be out and about at that ridiculously early hour of the day. Its icy blast had pounced, catching us off guard. Bodies blue and shivering, we hopped, frog like, from one foot to the other in time with our chattering teeth.

These long-ago shadows are still very much alive, sustained over their long haul from teenaged kid to old age by the vigour and fire of youth: the old coal-fired train engine, billowing shafts of black smoke from its long pipe-stack, whistling a sharp shrill warning of its departure, before huffing and puffing great lungsful of steam through the throat of Melbourne's Spencer Street Railway Station; people hunched, packed down inside hats and overcoats, pushing and shoving, harassed by time and necessity, far too much concerned with it all to give any heed to two young blokes about to join the army and fight for 'God, King and Country' and, hopefully, get on the right side of a good feed.

Jumping onto the back of the first tram of the day, we managed to almost reach Flinders Street Railway Station before the connie (conductor) came along. Our lack of tuppence for the fare, as both of us were absolutely flat stony broke, forced us to skedaddle, but we continued on foot the short distance to the flag-bedecked Town Hall recruiting centre. It was closed. Could you credit it? And with a great big war going on and the two of us outside looking in, just bursting to enlist? Not only closed, but shut tight, and in almost broad daylight. Temporarily thwarted, but determined to join up, we crouched together in the doorway of the porch, hungry, cold and hungry; impatient, cold and hungry. We waited, and waited.

A good deal later, as the morning defrosted and the sun wore holes in the fog, the Army finally arrived and opened up. 'Not before time', we said to the lieutenant as he unlocked the door. 'Another five minutes and we were off to give our business to the Air Force.' Our words were wasted. Neither he nor his two offsiders had slightest interest in anything we had to say.

Once inside, they took their sweet time setting up, and were more interested in talking about football than getting down to business. After what seemed an age, one of them dragged himself away, wandered over to the counter where we were waiting and asked, 'Which force are you blokes interested in? AIF or Militia?'

'The one that goes overseas.'

'Right. AIF. Are you old enough?'

'How old is old enough?'

'Nineteen.'

'Great. That's us then.'

'You'll need your parents' consent'.'

'Got none.'

'What, both of you?'

'Yep.'

'Then you'll need your next-of-kin's consent. Um, you do have a next-of-kin?'

'Yep, an aunt.'

'An aunt. Well, take these forms and get your aunt's signature. Right?'

'Right. Great. Good-oh', we chorused.

CHAPTER 1 In the beginning

I really was an orphan. I was born in 1925 in Tasmania, at 'Alva', my Nana Young's Federation-style cottage at 7 Tower Road, New Town, a suburb of Hobart. The actual date was 4 November and, if I'd waited another ten minutes, I could have been a Guy Fawkes baby. Sister Cotton, who ran a well-known maternity hospital and also attended private patients, delivered me in Nana's front room.

My dad's family came to Tasmania from England in the 1840s and settled at a little place called Sandfly, near Margate, which is south of Hobart. He was born in 1900. I have a photo of Dad, standing proudly in front of the local school with his bike, about to ride away for the last time. As he pedalled off, the headmistress was heard to say, 'Well, there he goes. He'll either end up prime minister or in prison.'

He was still at school when the Great War began. In 1915, the Anzac story and the landings on Gallipoli must have inspired him, because he decided to join the army. He was way, way too young to enlist – only fifteen – but he was tall and

'Big Bill' with his bike

strapping and big for his age, which is why he was known as Big Bill. He went to the recruiting office, passed the medical and next thing was in the army. Of course, he didn't say a word to anyone at home, because he knew the family would put a stop to it.

The ship was ready to sail for Egypt, ultimate destination Gallipoli, when someone dobbed him in to my grandmother, Susan. Bad move. She controlled the household with an iron hand and her word was law. Not even my grandfather Doug could stand up to her. She demanded that someone in the family drive her immediately to the wharf and stormed aboard the crowded transport. Spotting him easily because of his height, she dragged him off by his ear, big as he was, down the gangway, into the car and home. This action, which made my father a laughing stock and humiliated him to his very core, earned her the nickname of The Admiral.

Nana's tough, rough action had such an effect on my teenaged father that he left home shortly afterwards and took off for Sydney. I have no idea what he did in the big smoke, but the return of the Prodigal Son to Hobart came as a bombshell. In 1925, after ten years away, he turned up on Nana's doorstep with my unmarried and obviously pregnant mother in tow, along with her small son from a previous relationship.

Nana might have wanted her son back, but she certainly didn't want the extra and very unwelcome baggage he had brought with him. My grandmother was a real virago, a despotic tartar, described by my cousin as an 'old bitch'. Not only did she rule the family roost with an iron and unforgiving hand, but she was of a strict Methodist persuasion, which at that time did not tolerate dancing, gambling, drinking, anything slightly racy, sex outside marriage, or Papists.

My poor mother didn't stand a chance. Not only was she pregnant as a result of extramarital relations but even worse she was Irish Catholic. To aggravate the situation, just after Dad arrived home, one of his sisters, my Aunty Gladys, was tragically killed in a car crash. My mum was no substitute for the now sainted, Protestant, decently married Gladys. According to my Aunt Elsie, from the minute my mother set foot in the Young family home, Nana made her life a nightmare. And Aunty Elsie should know. She only lived with Nana because her bigamist husband, my 'Uncle' Edward, had abandoned her and returned to his wife. Nana, who never let poor Elsie forget that she had been duped and dumped, treated her like an unpaid slave.

'Your Mum was a lovely lady', Aunty Elsie once told me, 'but she was stuck out there at Moonah on her own with two small kids, with Nana giving her a hard time. One day she just disappeared.'

I don't remember her at all. All I know is that one day she just upped and went and took Kevin, my half-brother, with her. I was told she was dead. Maybe they didn't want to tell a small boy the truth. My only real link to her at all is her name on my birth certificate, which states that she was formerly Adora Shaw.

Above: The Young Family, from left to right, Cocky (Harold), Nana, Ada, Elsie, Doug. Below: Susan (Nana), Irene, Elsie, before the war

Billy's mother is a real mystery. There is no trace of the birth, death or marriage of anyone in Australia by the name of Adora Shaw, nor of any marriage to Big Bill Young, or to anyone, at all. The date of 'marriage' recorded on Billy's birth certificate, 4 May 1925, is most probably the date on which the couple began living together as man and wife. As Nana was the informant, it could also be a completely fictitious date, but 4 May seems an odd choice by the morally righteous Nana, since Adora was well and truly pregnant by then. Somewhat unusually, Billy's 'premature' birth was publicised, with a notice in November 1925 that referred to his parents as the very circumspect 'Mr and Mrs W J Young'.

In 1928, Big Bill and Adora, as Bill and Dora, were included in a memorial notice for the saintly Gladys. The 1928 electoral roll listed an Adora Young as home duties and William John Young as a stripper, living in the house owned by the zinc company at Moonah. Stripping was a tough physical job that involved removing the zinc deposits from electrodes after the electrolysis process had been completed. The Hobart paper also reported that in late 1927 a woman named Dora Young had attended at charity fair at New Town, not far from the Young family home in Tower Road. Apart from these instances, there is no trace of anyone named Adora/Dora Shaw or Young in Tasmania after 1928.

Shortly after my mum vanished, my father, whom I adored to the point of hero worship, moved to Sydney, taking three-year-old me with him. As he had a good job at the zinc works, where Uncle Doug was a superintendent, a nice house and a family to help look after me in Hobart, I reckon he must have gone to Sydney to look for Mum. I also reckon he found her. I can remember being taken to see a pile of earth, which I was told was her grave, in a cemetery with big, spear-pointed wrought-iron gates. When I grew up, I tried to find that cemetery and visit my mum's grave, but you know something? Every old cemetery in Sydney has wrought-iron gates and fences, so I'm still looking.

Despite exhaustive searches, no trace of Adora can be found in New South Wales. It is likely that she kept in touch with Big Bill, if only to keep a link with their son. Even if she did, it appears that she changed her name, for there is no record of any death or marriage for her as either Shaw or Young.

Dad's brother, Uncle Harold, who had a good job with a construction firm, lived in Sydney. Harold was Nana's favourite child and was known as Cocky, because he was. Uncle Cocky lived with my Aunt Ilma, her husband Vince and their daughter, my cousin, who had been given the high-falutin' name Wilhelmina.

She never used it and always answered to Billie. This didn't create any confusion in the family as everyone called me by my first name, Keith, or else Keithy.

Nana, of course, did not approve of Vince, who was Roman Catholic. This was bad enough, but tensions became much worse when Aunty Ilma changed sides and became a Papist to marry him, in a Catholic church in Hobart. Everyone knew she gone over to the RCs – there was a notice in the paper about the wedding. So, as far as Nana was concerned, Vince was very definitely persona non grata, even though he was well off and lived in Waverley, in the posh eastern suburbs of Sydney. It was probably just as well they didn't live in Hobart, because Nana would have made their lives a misery. Aunty Ilma offered us a home with her when we arrived from Hobart but Dad turned her down. He had nothing against Catholics, because my mother was one, but he was also very left-wing, and in his eyes Uncle Vince was a filthy capitalist.

Billy, aged six, with his father 'Big Bill', c. 1928 in Surry Hills

Uncle Cocky had no such qualms and was happy to live in comfort in a spacious well-appointed house, with hot and cold running water and a proper indoor WC, a room to himself, three home-cooked meals a day and Aunty Ilma to wait on him hand and foot. It was a thousand light years away from our place, a rented room in a terrace house in Albion Street, Surry Hills, a very poor slum area. For a while Uncle Cocky and Dad ran a billiard parlour in nearby Redfern, which was also a front for an SP bookie's operation. As the only kind of betting allowed in those days was at the racecourse, this was all highly illegal, so someone always had to act as a cockatoo and keep an eye out for the cops.

Somehow we managed, with Dad earning a bit here and a bit there and the local corner store allowing him to put goods on tick. Once, when I was sent off to chalk up a tin of condensed milk, I punched a hole in it and hid behind the bedroom door while I scoffed down as much as I could before I was caught.

Work was hard to find and people living a hand-to-mouth existence took whatever jobs were available, always on the lookout for some way to make an extra bob. To help make ends meet, Dad worked as a street photographer for a while. He set up his tripod in nearby Elizabeth Street, outside the Sydney Hotel, which was a popular watering hole for well-heeled drinkers. On the ground beside him was his gear, which included a bucket full of hypo and another with water, to process the photographic plates. One day as he was touting for business a well-dressed bloke, who was a bit under the weather, came out of the pub and tripped, knocking over the water bucket. 'Hey', said Dad. 'You've just spilt all me chemicals – that cost me thirty bob.' To compensate for this 'loss', the bloke, who was most apologetic, handed over two one-pound notes.

After that my father got a job as an ironworker in a nearby foundry. He hadn't been doing it for very long when he suddenly disappeared. He was gone for a few months. With no mother to care for me, I was sent to a Catholic Children's Home on the western outskirts of Sydney.

Billy was told that his father's prolonged absences, for there was more than one, were due to his working away from Sydney, supposedly as a shearer in outback New South Wales and as a cane cutter in Queensland. However Big Bill, an unskilled labourer, was not away shearing sheep or cane cutting, both skilled occupations for which he had no training. He was 'doing time'. Like many others, William Young, now aged 30, had run afoul of the law in his efforts to provide for himself and Billy during a world-wide depression that saw thousands of jobless roaming the streets and children malnourished, even dying, from lack of food.

In April 1931 he appeared in Redfern Court, arrested for forging and uttering a cheque in the name of Mr W B Carey, a prosperous tea broker whose office was in Bridge

Street, Sydney. It was a serious charge. The prosecution alleged that, after obtaining a cheque book in Carey's name, Big Bill had tried to cash a cheque for 100 pounds at the Redfern branch of the Commercial Banking Company of Sydney. When challenged by the suspicious bank manager, a scuffle broke out and Big Bill made good his escape.

However, there was no hiding from the long arm of the law. Apprehended and arrested, he was charged on 20 April. On 18 May, he was found guilty by Judge Edwards of uttering (the forgery having been carried out by another) and remanded for sentencing until the following day.

In an attempt to mitigate what would certainly be a custodial sentence, Big Bill told the court that his wife was dead and he had a small son, aged five, to care for. 'I haven't got twopence to my name', he pleaded. 'I do not go around with any gang.'

Judge Curlewis, who presided over the sentencing hearing, took into consideration the plea that Big Bill was not part of one of the city's gangs, which had been preying on small shopkeepers, especially women, by passing forged cheques. However, this and the fact that he was a single parent with a small dependent son were not enough to keep him out of gaol. He was sentenced to six months' imprisonment.

With Big Bill cooling his heels at His Majesty's pleasure, provision had to be made for Billy, lest 'the welfare' place him in a state institution. It appears that at this point Aunty Ilma and Uncle Vince stepped in, and arranged for him to live in the children's home, run by an order of Catholic nuns, where there was plenty of fresh air, open space and strict discipline. Billy, who was not yet six and had just started school, hated it.

The orphanage was built on stilts, with the basement area screened with wooden lattice, like the tropical houses you see in Queensland. When it was time for lunch, we'd sit against the lattice on stools, waiting for the big boys to arrive with a baby bath filled with slices of bread and treacle. They were called dodgers, and each kid was allowed two slices. Try and cadge another piece and you'd get a clout.

Fortunately, I was rescued from my misery one day when a lady, a complete and utter stranger, turned up with a letter from my father, authorising the nuns to hand me over. While she was no spring chicken, she looked kind enough and had a nice voice, but I was not too sure about the dead fox draped around her neck, with its glassy bright eyes staring at me. I was getting ready to run when she told me my dad had asked her to take me home with her. The nuns didn't seem to have any problem with this and since I couldn't wait to get out of the place, I didn't either.

It was a bit of a walk up a steep hill to the railway station, where she asked if I'd like a drink while we waited for the train. She had a cup of tea, but I had raspberry cordial and a big piece of Chester cake, which was a kind of fruit-mince slice, with pastry and icing on the top.

Billy's newfound and most unlikely protector was Christina Aird, known as Jepson. Born in Sydney in 1870, she had been found, at the age of fourteen, wandering the streets in the company of thieves and prostitutes by Emma Clithero, a friend of Christina's parents. Mrs Clithero had taken her to her own house, where Christina repaid the kindness by decamping with a silver watch, a pair of boots, a hat, yards of fine fabric, ribbon and lace, and two dozen pearl buttons. Found guilty of theft, she was sent to Shaftsbury Reformatory School for Girls at Watsons Bay for five years.

Out of reform school, at the age of nineteen and unmarried, she gave birth to a son, whom she named after her brother, George William Aird. She married in 1890, but the marriage failed, despite the efforts of her husband, Thomas Gogerty, to make a go of it. Within four months of the wedding Christina was in court, complaining about her dress allowance, a complaint dismissed by the judge, who told her to go home, as her labourer husband had barely enough money to feed himself.

For the next few months, to Thomas Gogerty's distress, his wife stayed out late at night, frequented dances, and was seen in the company of men, one of whom knocked him down when he tried to persuade her to come home. Despite Christina's behaviour, Thomas was prepared to forgive her, even to the extent of offering to pay her one pound fine when, lacking the funds, she was jailed for fourteen days for using indecent language in Oxford Street. His unrepentant wife rejected the offer, unless he also paid the fine of her sixteen-year-old female companion, convicted of the same offence. Thomas refused, so they both stayed in gaol. After five years Thomas, who had 'a great leaning' for Christina, finally gave her up as 'a bad job' and divorced her on the grounds of desertion in 1903. Sometime after 1914 Christina formed a de facto relationship with Cockney-born George Jepson, whose wife Mary had died in February that year.

By 1929 Christina and George Jepson were living as a couple at 506 Jones Street, in the inner city suburb of Ultimo. They ran a fruit and vegetable stand in nearby Paddy's Markets and were known to all and sundry as Ma and Pop. It is very likely that Big Bill was introduced to them in 1931 by Pop's brother Sam, a habitual criminal. He lived in Redfern, not far from Big Bill's Albion Street home, the billiard parlour/SP bookie establishment and the CBC Bank where Bill had tried to pass the forged cheque.

Samuel Jepson was very well known to the local constabulary. He had been arrested on numerous occasions dating back to 1907 on various charges of consorting, assault, stealing and inflicting grievous bodily harm. Four months after Big Bill went to gaol, Samuel and three other like-minded felons were arrested when the police raided a house in Elizabeth Street, Sydney, where they were counterfeiting two-shilling coins. The court

Paddy's Market, Sydney, c. late 1930s

showed no mercy and sent them to gaol for eighteen months. It seems likely that that Big Bill, also in gaol at that time, was worried about his small son being in the orphanage, and arranged for Christina Jepson to give Billy a home

Christina, despite her misspent youth, was Billy's salvation. She took him to a large, rambling building on Jones Street, Ultimo, where the bewildered five-year-old quickly warmed to her. It wasn't long before the motherless little Billy was regarding Ma and Pop as his surrogate grandparents.

The Jepsons may have been a bit long in the tooth but when they were younger and more agile they had both worked in a circus. The circus went broke during a tour of Australia, leaving Pop stranded. Pop had started off his working life as a jockey in England, but after too many falls and broken bones he had retired from the racing game to train horses and lions at the circus. Because of a poorly mended leg, which left him with an awkward gait, he was also known as Stiffy. Ma, a woman of multiple talents, was very versatile, performing as a bareback rider, a fortune teller and a tattooed lady. The last occupation wasn't as dramatic as it sounds. The tattoos were only temporary and could easily be removed.

The Jepsons' showbiz careers had come to an end when the circus went bust, but Ma still kept her hand in by telling fortunes and reading tea-leaves. Her tea-leaf talents were taken very seriously, especially by her old circus friend Millie – an older, quite tiny lady, whose grey hair was so over-peroxided that it was falling out. Apart from being vain about her fading appearance, Millie was also extremely superstitious. If a death occurred among their acquaintances, she would declare that it had been foretold to her, because she had seen a black moth.

Ma, an accomplished actress, made the most of Millie's firmly held beliefs. Swilling the leaves around the cup, she would look at them intently this way and that, and solemnly warn Millie that, as the leaves had formed a cloud, it would be best not to go out that day. Millie, whose faith in the leaves and Ma's power was absolute, would not venture from her chair for the entire day.

When my dad hooked up with Ma and Pop they were living in Ultimo, a slum area of Sydney near Darling Harbour that had seen better times. The gentry had long gone, their once fine houses now occupied by the impoverished working class. The Jepsons had leased a big sandstone house with stables and a large courtyard, where they hired out horses and carts, mainly to other stall holders at Paddy's Market. The Big House, as we called it, was like a rabbit warren, with multiple rooms, so they also took in boarders, mostly lame ducks they'd taken pity on. This included men who had been maimed in the Great War: like Les the soldier who'd been gassed, and lived with his wife and daughter, Shirley, in one room. Les had only one leg, and was company for Wingy, who had only one arm. There was also a lady called Sissy, who was some kind of Jepson relation, and Harry the sailor, but I can't remember what was the matter with him.

Wingy's real name was Stephen Gould. One of ten children, he was born in 1894 into a Labor-voting Irish Catholic family on a farm at Clybucca, near Kempsey on the New South Wales north coast. After leaving home at fifteen, he worked as a cane cutter and on the trams in Brisbane, where he became a staunch unionist. He enlisted in the AIF in January 1916 at the age of 22, was posted to the infantry and served on the Western Front. His war came to an abrupt end in June 1918 when he was hit by shrapnel from an exploding shell that wiped out two of his mates and left him with a shattered left arm, broken right femur and multiple other wounds. His leg mended, more or less, but his arm was too mangled to save and was amputated.

Returning home, Wingy decided to become a teacher. Taking up studies under the repatriation scheme, he obtained a scholarship to Sydney Teachers College which at that time was located in Hereford House, Glebe. With a Bachelor of Arts under his belt, he taught for several years in northern New South Wales before moving to Ultimo, where in 1928 he was elected Secretary of the Glebe Branch of the Labor Party. After holding the post for five years he married in 1934. His son John, who founded the popular Gould's Bookstore, was a well-known political activist.

People came and went at the Big House, but the most exciting person I can remember was a fella I was told was the Jepsons' son – a dark, mysterious type who looked a bit like a fading, middle-aged Rudolph Valentino. For all that, he was a pretty handsome devil, and snappily dressed with it. He said his name was Randy, and Ma doted on him.

He arrived out of the blue when I was about six years old, bringing with him a studio portrait of himself and the news that he was playing the role of a villain in a film. Being in showbiz herself, Ma was very taken with the idea of having an actor son, and tacked his photo, which wasn't framed, to the wall of the kitchen where she could brag about it to everyone who called. Randy must have decided to join Pop in the fruit and veg business because, when I was invited in for some cordial one day by a very pretty and much younger lady who was with him, I could hardly squeeze down the passageway past all the turnips and carrots sticking out of the boxes. However, the life of a barrowman, trundling a cart up and down the streets selling greengroceries, mustn't have been to Randy's liking because he didn't stay very long, and vanished just as mysteriously as he had arrived.

The mysterious visitor whom Billy had met as Randy was George William Aird, now known as Ranji Jepson, just one of his many aliases. Although Ma appears to have avoided any further confrontations with the law, the same could not be said for her son.

He had embarked on a criminal career at the age of sixteen and for the next 24 years was in and out of gaol in three states for crimes ranging from housebreaking, being drunk and disorderly, offensive language, theft, larceny, fraud, false pretences, stealing firearms, assault and manslaughter. When he became too well known to police as George William Aird, he adopted several aliases – George (William) Owen/Owens/ Howard/Ryan and Jepson, and also the exotic-sounding Ranji Jepson/Ryan. Swarthy and sultry, with matinee-idol good looks, he appeared in court dressed in a suit, hat and, on one occasion, patent leather shoes. As a con man, he had the gift of the gab and talked his way out of two or three charges with apparent ease.

His crime wave in New South Wales stopped between 1915 and 1919 – not because he had reformed but because he had joined the army. Falsifying his date of birth, his next-of-kin and his place of birth, he enlisted as George William Percival Owen in Brisbane on 26 July 1915. In addition to the remarks about his physical appearance, the army noted that he had two flags tattooed on his forearms, the legacy of a brief stint as a merchant seaman.

After the usual training period in Egypt, Private Owen went to England where managed to stay out of the war by being constantly AWL, disobeying orders, resisting arrest and passing himself off as a sergeant and a war hero, by not only wearing three sergeant's stripes but also awarding himself a Distinguished Conduct Medal and a Military Medal. With each court martial, the sentences increased, culminating in hard labour for five years. His only break during his final incarceration was a trip to hospital to be treated for venereal disease.

To celebrate his early release from prison in June 1919, following the Armistice the previous November, he promptly went AWL, an action that resulted in 'admonishment' and immediate departure for Australia on 1 July. Disembarking in Melbourne, he made his way north to Sydney where, on 26 September, he signed his name, under his current alias of George Owen, on two legal documents. The first was re-enlistment in the AIF for Special Duty – escorting German internees to Europe. The second was on a marriage certificate, following a civil service at the Sydney Registry Office with Delilah (Leila) Sarah Colless.

He set sail almost immediately to carry out his special duties. He lasted just one month. In defiance of explicit orders, he bought goods from the army's shipboard canteen which he then traded with the internees. His remark that he had come on board 'to make what he could out of the internees' was overheard by an officer, resulting in his removal from the ship at Fremantle.

It does not appear that he had any contact with his wife, who was pregnant, for the next three years. In 1922, evidently believing that he was still carrying out 'special duties', she wrote to the army enquiring about the non-receipt of her non-existent allowance. George ignored a court order for maintenance for Delilah and his child and in 1928 she tried to divorce him on the grounds of desertion. George failed to appear in court, and the action evidently did not proceed.

Now back in Civvy Street, George committed a string of offences during the 1920s as George/William Owen. Occasionally, he worked as a tram conductor, a fruiterer and a salesman in a jewellery store – a three-day stint that ended when he allegedly made off with a watch and rings to the value of sixty pounds.

It appears that George made use of his mother's collection of ornate and temporary tattoos to avoid a gaol term for this theft, after his former employer had recognised him on a tram in Oxford Street. When another employee of the firm also positively identified George as the missing salesman, the case looked to be cut and dried. At George's committal hearing, his alibi – that he was in bed with a broken toe at the time, something to which his 'wife' attested – may not have saved him from being indicted had he not rolled up his sleeves, revealing not two simple flags, but 'extraordinary' tattoos on his forearms that the two witnesses, inexplicably, had failed to notice. On the basis that George's intended defence was to be a case of mistaken identity, the prosecution decided not to proceed.

Finding New South Wales now far too hot, George moved into Victoria in the late 1920s where, as George Owens, he avoided being prosecuted for the theft of a bag of wheat as he had 'a clean record'. By August he was in Western Australia where, posing as Basil Mervyn Faulkner, a salesman 'from the east', he used a forged cheque to defraud Ollie Olson, the licensee of The Globe Hotel, of ten pounds. The magistrate, glancing at George's record which now covered crimes in three states, remarked, 'Since 1906 you have occupied your time very fully in going to gaol. I must not let you make a start here.' To which the accused replied, 'I am leaving this state right away.'

The magistrate had other ideas. 'Oh no you're not', he countered. 'Six months hard labour.' Released in early March the following year, George returned to Sydney and his obviously very forgiving mother, who idolised her handsome son with his brooding movie-star looks.

The crime of uttering that landed Big Bill in gaol in 1931 for the first time has George Aird/Owen/Jepson's fingerprints all over it. Bill Young was an affable, warm-hearted and generous soul, unworldly to the point of gullibility, who could never deny anyone who asked a favour. To conceive, let alone carry out such an enterprise as uttering a forged cheque, was way out of his league. With George's well-established history of forgery and false pretences, it seems highly likely that he arrived back from Western Australia in March 1931 just in time to test out a new scam, with Bill doing a trial run as his patsy. George definitely knew where the CBC Head Office, the closest branch to Mr Carey's tea importing business in Bridge Street, was located. He later used it as a false address in 1935, when he tried to con the army into giving him a set of war medals which they had evidently seen fit to withhold. He claimed that his discharge document, his medals and his 'returned from active service badge' had been stolen from his previous lodgings at 345 George Street, the address of the palatial, marble-bedecked CBC Bank.

The visit by the exotic Ranji Jepson coincided with the period when Billy first went to live at the Big House, just after Big Bill's unfortunate experience with the forged cheque. As Billy noticed, Ranji soon became disenchanted with the thought of honest work, and in early 1932 was back in Western Australia, where he once more tried his hand at passing dud cheques. Still masquerading as the salesman named Faulkner, he obtained goods and services to the value of several hundred pounds from businesses and individuals in Kalgoorlie and Perth. After appearing in court on multiple charges relating to fraud and false pretences, he was sentenced in March 1932 to two-and-a-half years in gaol. He re-offended on his release and spent a further two months in prison.

Randy Jepson had no interest in helping Pop, whose horse-and-cart hire business was going down the gurgler. Poor Pop's timing was bad. As cars replaced horse-drawn transport and money tightened during the Depression, he was forced to sell off some of his horses and carts to make ends meet. As the business shrank, so did our accommodation. Ma and Pop had to give up the Big House, and the cart-hire business, and shift to progressively smaller places. The first move was just down the road a bit to a large terrace house.

Typical inner city Sydney slum, 1930s

Despite Ma's irresponsible youth, she seems to have settled down in old age, providing much-needed stability for Billy, whose father was in constant trouble with the police. He didn't help matters by being seen with Sam Jepson, who had moved into 488 Jones Street, the address of the Big House occupied by his brother and the Youngs. In May 1932, Big Bill, not long out of gaol, was arrested on a charge of consorting with known criminals. The judge was unmoved by Big Bill's plea that he 'practically lived next door' to Sam, and 'chatted to him in a vacant lot'. Verdict: guilty as charge. Sentence: three months' gaol.

He was out of prison by September that year, but by November was once more before the court, along with two others, this time on a charge of breaking and entering a store in Redfern, with intent to steal. Big Bill and one of the others, who had been arrested after being hit by police with a baton, had not gone quietly. However, despite his recent run-ins with the law, the prosecution case was not strong enough to gain a conviction. The accused were acquitted on a technicality by Judge White, enabling Bill to return home a free man.

A fortnight later Sam Jepson died. His demise and the removal of an undoubtedly bad influence did not exactly keep Big Bill out of strife, because Pop Jepson also sailed close to the wind on occasion. During the next eighteen months, Big Bill was back in court on charges of having goods in custody and stealing.

When my dad turned up again to claim me, he stuck close by the Jepsons. It was quite a handy arrangement, because he often worked as a fruit-and-veg barrowman for them. Being a pretty big bloke, and fit, he was also quite a good heavyweight boxer. Whenever funds ran a bit low, he'd do some prize-fighting for Billy Sharman in his travelling tent show. The pay was good: at least a pound a fight, more if it was at the Easter Show. There was also money to be made by betting on the side. Dad gave the punters their money's worth by letting his challengers get a few punches in and stringing the flight out until almost the last minute, when he'd go for the kill.

Sideshow banner promoting the Sharman Boxing Troupe

It was fortunate that Billy had Ma to look after him the during his father's brushes with the law, or he may well have found himself back in the orphanage. To protect him from the harsh realities of life, the Jepsons continued with the charade that Big Bill's sudden and lengthy absences were due to his working away from Sydney. Big Bill himself kept up the pretence, telling Billy that the shiny new two-bob piece, presented to him on his return home, had been found at the market, 'under a cabbage'.

However, Big Bill and the Jepsons did not take into account the sharp ears of a small boy. He sometimes overheard 'kitchen talk' among the adults, who asked visitors just released from gaol how Big Bill was getting on, and how 'the 'screws' were treating him. Billy, who knew better than to ask questions, lest he get a good clip over the ear, pushed any unwanted thoughts and suspicions to the back of his mind, preferring instead to go along with it, in much the same way that a child, who suspects that the Tooth Fairy or Santa Claus may not be real, maintains the fantasy.

Even when not in gaol or boxing with Sharman's Show, Big Bill depended on Ma to help care for Billy, so much so that when they were all forced to move out of 488 Jones Street and into nearby Pyrmont, they were fortunate to find rented accommodation in Burlinson Street in two adjoining houses. However, after twelve months they were on the move again, this time to a smaller house in nearby Bulwarra Street.

In 1935, while they were still at 488 Jones Street, George Aird/Owen etc turned up again, having been released from gaol in Western Australia, but Billy does not have any particular recollection of him. He stayed long enough to try and obtain the war medals from the army before moving to Brisbane. In 1938, after enlisting the aid of the RSAILA (Returned Serviceman's League) he finally obtained the medals on the grounds that he needed them to obtain work. He died in Queensland in 1960 as William George Owen. Whether he continued with his criminal activity is not known, but if he did, it was under a new alias.

As Ma and Pop took the boarders with them with each move, it was a tight squeeze in the final house – a small terrace in Bulwarra Street, a back lane that was cheek-by-jowl with a stinking tannery and tallow works and not much more than a slum.

Everyone in Ultimo was in the same boat, so people helped each other out in times of crisis. Next door to our big terrace house in Burlinson Street, where we lived before moving to Bulwarra, there was a nice young woman called Miss Salmon, who had a small boy about my age. She loved him very much but, as she was unmarried and very poor, the Child Welfare Department made unannounced inspections to make sure she was looking after him properly. Luckily, someone she knew at the welfare office was able to tip her off and, as soon as she heard that she would receive a visit, she'd collect all my clothes, which didn't amount to all that much, and take them to her place so that she'd pass muster.

When we needed assistance, people also helped us out. On one memorable occasion, Pop bought a load of mullet at auction. Under the terms of the sale, the fish could be kept frozen at the ice works until the owner was ready to dispose of them. On the day that Pop chose to sell the defrosted fish at the markets, the weather was atrocious. It bucketed down raining, and the buyers stayed away in droves.

Now, most people stuck with a pile of fish they had paid for and couldn't unload would have gone into a decline. Not Pop. With my Dad as a willing accomplice, he borrowed a wooden rowing boat and an old T-model Ford truck from Mr Selway, who lived down the road a bit and made a living from selling wood, ice and coal. He was a kind fella, who also let Wingy come along on his deliveries to flog off rabbits that he'd bought from trappers.

Driving the truck, and with the boat and the defrosted fish in the back, Dad and Pop headed for Botany Bay. After filling the boat with fish, they quietly rowed it out into the bay and then rowed back in, where they sold all their 'freshly caught' catch to gullible punters waiting on the beach.

Many people besides us did it tough. Thousands. Evictions were common in Ultimo, with neighbours who couldn't afford the rent being thrown out onto the street. My dad, who had a well-developed social conscience, went in to bat for them by remonstrating with landlords and persuading shopkeepers to help out with food and essential commodities, which he collected in a hand-cart. He even put up canvas shelters on vacant lots, persuading the authorities to let the newly homeless stay for a couple of days until they found somewhere to go.

As things got worse financially Pop couldn't afford to pay for his barrow licence at the markets, so I'd keep cockatoo for him. As soon as I saw the inspector coming I'd warn Pop, who'd pick up his barrow and start walking slowly along. As long as the barrow wasn't stationary he couldn't get booked. Sometimes he'd be midway through serving someone when the inspector came into sight, so he'd just tell the customer to 'Follow me' and keep counting out the oranges and apples.

During the very lean years everyone did whatever they could to turn a bob or two. Wingy, despite having only one real arm, had quite a few enterprises on the go. Besides making wooden clothes pegs, he manufactured mothballs in the tin bath in the bathroom, which he commandeered for hours on end. Besides his rabbits, Wingy also sold wooden clothes props door-to-door.

As there were no trees growing round Ultimo for Wingy's clothes prop business, Ma Jepson would organise us to go for a picnic in the bush, where we cut saplings to size and plundered the native flora. Once we had enough, we'd catch the train back to the city, ignoring complaints from other passengers about clogging up the aisles with wooden poles and masses of maiden-hair fern, boronia and waratahs, stuffed into sopping wet chaff bags to keep them fresh.

In the winter, Wingy flogged hot chestnuts that he roasted on a portable brazier. He didn't have a licence or a spot at the markets, so he stuck close by us. When Pop could afford it, he hired a good pitch outside the public toilets, right beside the big iron gates at the markets, where he could catch the passing trade going in and out of the markets and in and out of the loo. If I saw an inspector coming our way I'd give Wingy a whistle and he'd trundle off, pretending he was a mobile street peddler.

Once, when things were very tight, we hiked into the bush near Lilyfield and picked bunches of boronia to sell at the markets. As Pop didn't have the money to pay for a trader's licence or a spot, I hung around near a stall that was selling soap, pretending I was part of that operation. The flowers were selling for one penny a bunch and I was doing quite well, so well that when a very nicely dressed and well-spoken lady customer asked if I could change a two-bob bit, I proudly handed her 1/11 in change in coppers. When Pop turned up to see how I was doing I said, 'Real good Pop. I've sold more than two bob's worth', and showed him. 'Oh Keithy', he said, looking at the two-bob bit, 'it's a dud.' I thought I'd be in real trouble, but Pop just put it in his pocket, ready to pass onto the next sucker.

Counterfeiting florins or two-bob bits from lead coated in a thin layer of silver was common. The police were always raiding some place or other. One day there was a hit on the terrace house next door, which was empty as the Salmons had been evicted. There was a hell of a commotion, with cops yelling and banging on the door. As the gang scattered and made a run for it out the back lane they threw their dies, lead and chemicals over the fence into our yard. I don't know what the chemicals were but they sure stank. The cops of course came in to retrieve the equipment, and also to question Pop, who wasn't all that thrilled to get a visit from the law.

Not long afterwards a young bloke sleeping in the upstairs part of the Salmons' empty house was woken up by something. Thinking it was the cops, he tried to get away by jumping over the spikes of the iron verandah railing and onto the footpath below. However, he didn't lift his leg high enough and impaled himself. Of course, everyone in our place heard the screams and went rushing out but to my great disappointment Ma said it was too bloodthirsty for a kid to see and sent me back inside.

The unfortunate victim was George Stephens, aged 21 who, in March 1933, was squatting in the vacant house abandoned by the counterfeiters. He was asleep in the upstairs front bedroom when he was woken by an estate agent entering the house to make an inspection. In his dash for freedom, to avoid arrest for vagrancy, he caught his leg on the spike, and hung there for some time, head down, until his flesh gave way and he crashed onto the footpath, twenty feet below. He was taken to hospital with concussion and severe lacerations to his leg and elbow.

Overall, the Depression didn't have much impact on me. When you're little you don't realise what your situation is, as long as you have enough to eat, have a roof over your head and someone to look after you. I was just a kid, happy to be alive, and to enjoy simple ways of passing the time, like riding my fruit-box billycart round the streets, helping Dad peddle fruit and veggies and kicking cans up and down the road. Ultimo's gone full circle and is an upmarket place now, full of yuppies living in converted designer warehouses and renovated terrace houses, but back then it was real honest-to-goodness working class.

Early one morning, not long after the bloke impaled himself on the railings, I was trundling along with my four-wheeled billycart when I saw a drift of smoke coming from a street near the markets. 'By Crikey', I thought. 'It looks like the lolly factory's gone up in flames.' And so it had. I was standing around, watching the firemen mop up, when one of the big multi-paned glass doors burst open from the weight of the accumulated water. As the water spewed out, it dumped cartons and cartons of slightly wet lollies at my feet – musk sticks, clinkers, toffees, you name it. Even though the sweets had become wet, and were stuck together, I wasn't going to let this manna from heaven go to waste, so I packed the boxes into a six-foot high stack in my billycart, tied them down and took off. I was the most popular kid in Ultimo.

The fire that brought Billy instant popularity had broken out on the night of 13 September 1933 in a confectionery factory owned by Biddell Brothers, in Lackey Street, just alongside Paddy's Market. Although the fire brigade arrived within three minutes of the alarm being raised, the firemen were unable to save the top floor, which was destroyed entirely. However, by concentrating their hoses from every point, they were able to stop it spreading to the two lower floors and destroying the machinery. As the journalist covering the event reported, 'Considerable damage was done by water to sweets'.

I didn't like formal school lessons, especially spelling, but I had a thirst for knowledge and loved reading, which was given a big boost by an old lady who befriended me one Saturday arvo while I was minding produce for the barrow in a lane behind her house. After giving me some lemonade, and a slice of buttered – yes, buttered – Madeira cake, she handed me a magazine for boys, called *Triumph*, that had come all the way from England. On the cover was a picture of a dashing pilot in a biplane, chasing some crook. It had belonged to her son when he was a little boy, and I could hardly wait to read it. After that, she met me each Saturday, with a drink and something to eat, and a magazine from her son's collection. Best of all, at Christmas she presented me with a *Bumper Annual* for boys, which was chock-a-block full of all kinds of adventures.

The Jepsons' house had only one gas mantle in the kitchen, and no electricity, so at night I'd roll up the canvas blind screening the open upstairs verandah annexe where I slept, and read by the light of the nearby street lamp. Despite my love of reading, I was never overly fond of school and played truant whenever I could. Dad, when he was at home, didn't force me to go, so my formal education was very hit and miss. I'd much rather be out and about, helping Ma at her stall and earning a few bob here and there, than sitting cooped up in some overcrowded classroom.

I did go to school on and off, and tried out quite a few, including a posh – well, posh by Ultimo's standards – St Barnabas's C of E school on Broadway. Before that I'd spent a short time at St Benedict's, a Catholic school on the opposite side of the road. I don't know who paid the fees or moved me from the overcrowded

Ultimo Public to St Benedict's, but I'm pretty sure it must have been Aunty Ilma, and that Uncle Vince footed the bill. However, I also reckon my Nana Young got wind of it, because next thing I was out of there and enrolled with the C of E. I didn't last long there either. When Dad, who'd been away at the time, came back and found I was in a privately run church school, he took me out quick smart and re-enrolled me in the egalitarian Ultimo Public. I didn't mind one bit. It was far easier to nick off from the state school and, in any case, I didn't fit in at St B's with all those middle-class kids, especially since they had proper uniforms and wore shoes, and I didn't.

Although my Dad was not at all religious, I did go to Sunday school in Ultimo for a while. I can't remember what denomination it was but it was definitely not RC or C of E. An old bloke who ran the local coal yard during the week was the pastor, and his two unmarried daughters, aged about thirty and forty, organised the Sunday school. The big attraction was that each kid who turned up on Sunday was given a peppermint lolly. I don't think the ladies had much success with saving my soul, but the younger one certainly did a lot for my self-esteem, when she remarked that I had the most beautiful fingernails. Beautiful fingernails! What a boost to my ego, as a kid who rarely, if ever, received a compliment.

Then quite suddenly, my life changed forever. In 1934 my left-wing father went even more to the left and converted to a new ideology – Communism.

CHAPTER 2

FENDING FOR MYSELF

1934 – July 1941

Although he had always been a champion of the underdog, Big Bill was not accepted immediately into the Australian Communist Party. He started off by joining the Unemployed Single Men's Group, and then the Unemployed Workers Movement, or UWM, whose Glebe branch operated from a hall above a garage at 96 Glebe Point Road. However, his various arrests, although on petty criminal charges, were no secret, and the local party bosses, mindful that the communists were always under surveillance, did not want the law sniffing around. Being arrested for disturbing the peace at a demonstration to uphold the rights of the downtrodden was acceptable, but engaging in criminal acts, no matter how trivial, was not.

Before Big Bill, who was regarded as a bit 'wild', could become a fully-fledged member he had to prove himself worthy. So he gave up drinking, avoided contact with shady characters such as George Owen/Jepson and became a law-abiding citizen. Accepting that he was now a reformed character, the Party welcomed him with open arms.

My Dad's conversion to the ideals of Communism was immediate and absolute, a blinding light on the road to Damascus. Talk about an enthusiastic zealot. It was comrade this, and comrade that, and meetings that went on interminably into the night. The party's newspaper, *The Tribune*, was his bible and, as a loyal foot-soldier, he enthusiastically participated in its distribution, along with the local *Workers' Weekly*, by tramping for miles around the streets.

His heroes were Comrade Stalin and Comrade Lenin and he hated the right-wing Fascist movement with a passion. His ultra-left-wing views caused him to come home with a few black eyes when he got into punch-ups over political ideology with the right-wing New Guards, who loathed communists as much as he loathed them. My Dad was a real fanatic, a total convert to the cause. When the Italian Fascist dictator Mussolini invaded Abyssinia, I can remember waiting late at night in the freezing cold on a bridge overpass, expecting the cops to arrive at any moment, while he took an eternity daubing HANDS OFF ABYSSINIA in big letters on the side of the wall of the power station in Ultimo. The reason it took so long was because the wall, which was cement rendered and just right for anyone who wanted to make a political statement, was about five feet from the bridge. In order to leave his message, Dad had attached the paintbrush to a length of timber, so you can imagine how long the process took. As I huddled against the parapet, wishing I were at home, safely in bed, I wondered why it had to be Abyssinia, and not some place with a shorter name, like Libya.

When Abyssinia fell to the hands of those who wanted it, he mercifully left it to the League of Nations try and sort it all out and moved on to his next cause – Fascist fifth columnists – and his next slogan – THEY SHALL NOT PASS – emblazoned in even bigger letters, this time right across a road intersection near Wentworth Park dog track, just down the hill from our house. I had to wait by a telegraph pole while he did it, and it took him hours. It must have been good paint, though, because his message was visible for years.

Although I didn't like being party to Dad's political daubings, or having to go along to Communist Party meetings, I did look forward to the Happy Times Social Club dances held in the upstairs hall on Glebe Point Road on a Saturday night. The 'band' was an old bloke with a piano accordion who played for hours, providing music for such old favourites as the Pride of Erin and the Barn Dance.

At the end of 1936, when I turned eleven, I was old enough to go to Boys Brigade. Meetings, which were under the control of a World War I army captain, were held each Tuesday in a large building that had a well-equipped gym in the basement. The meetings were well organised and on special occasions, such as Easter and Christmas, we'd get treats and small gifts. The captain had no trouble getting kids to join Boysies or to attend the trade classes, which offered tuition in plumbing, carpentry, cabinet making and the like. A hundred or so boys turned up each week, not to improve their trade skills but to see the latest episode of *Tarzan of the Apes*, a nail-biting serial that was shown to the 'troops' provided they attended trade school first. No lesson, no serial. To really sweeten the deal, as we filed into the hall to see the show we were given a cake or some lollies to munch on.

Tuesdays couldn't come round fast enough, and as soon as I'd finished working at the fruit barrow I'd run all the way to Boysies, desperate to get my class out of the way and see how Tarzan was going to manage to escape from the jaws of death that week. If I'd been playing up, the worst punishment my dad could inflict was to bar me from Boysies by sending me to my room with instructions to stay there. Of course, I never did. As soon as he'd gone off for the evening to spend time with his mates, I'd grab my Boys Brigade uniform (a rather scruffy blue shirt), shinny down the drainpipe and tear off to the meeting, anxious I'd miss the next instalment of the serial.

On the night that the final exciting episode was to screen, I was late getting away from the markets for some reason and missed my class. I pleaded and begged, but it was no use. They wouldn't let me in. The best I could do was to listen to a second-hand account from my mates.

As a totally committed communist, my Dad no longer disappeared from my life for weeks or months at a time, but spent all his spare time taking up whatever cause needed taking up. He continued to look out for the needy, especially those who were facing eviction.

The lengths that Big Bill would go to in his efforts to help the homeless were legendary. Having moved a destitute woman and her brood to an empty house, he was taken aback somewhat when she complained that there was no bath. After thinking it over for a bit, Bill replied, 'We'll be back soon.' Marshalling his team, he raided a row of nearby empty terraces and returned to his 'client', who was presented not only with the much-longed-for bath, but also a stove.

Not only did Dad embrace, full on, the idea of sticking up for the poor, the oppressed, the downtrodden worker and the underdog in Australia, he expanded

Dole queue during the Depression

his horizon to overseas causes. In 1937, not long after we moved to Bulwarra Street, he got it into his head that Spain, which was engaged in a civil war, was in need of his services. Next thing he was off to England to recruit soldiers to join the English Battalion of the International Brigade and support the Spanish Republicans in their fight against General Franco and his fascist army. Despite pleas from our government for Australians not to become involved, fifty men made their way to ports and quietly slipped out of the country.

Neither Dad nor the local branch of the Communist Party had any money to pay for his fare, so he stowed away on a cargo ship, hiding in a coal bunker. His unauthorised presence was finally discovered by a couple of very surprised stokers but, instead of being thrown in the brig, he was treated like a hero and given a job onboard the ship when the crew learned he was off to Spain to fight in the Civil War. The story even made the papers. Imagine that! My dad, Big Bill Young, Freedom Fighter, the subject of a newspaper article.

He left me behind, along with his girlfriend Marie, who worked in the city as a secretary. At the time, I was rather annoyed that he was shooting through and thought he should've stayed home with me, instead of haring off to the other side of the world to fight in some flea-bitten war. By way of appeasement, before he left he bought me a brand-new suit and an overcoat, along with a shirt, socks and a pair of shoes. I was tickled pink. It was the first overcoat I had ever owned. I would have liked the suit to have long trousers, instead of short pants, but he said I was larrikin enough already without getting into long duds.

I wasn't in Sydney when his ship sailed. I was on another ship, on my way to Hobart with Nana Young, who said she would look after me even though she didn't approve of Dad going off to war, just like that, to fight for a foreign and, even worse, a Catholic country. My dad must have been worried about the kind of company I might keep without him to keep me in check, so he agreed that I should go south to Hobart, where he knew that Nana would keep me on the straight and narrow. Dad and Marie came to see us off, and the last I saw of him was a tiny figure, standing on the dock and getting smaller and smaller until he disappeared.

I wasn't just going to Tasmania, I was going to a whole new existence. Nana didn't stand for any nonsense. After a free-and-easy life with Dad and the Jepsons in Sydney, pretty much doing whatever I wanted, and hardly ever getting punished for anything, it was a big shock to my system, I can tell you. I now had to do as I was told, even to the extent of going to school. Nana enrolled me at New Town Public, a long, red-brick building on Forster Street, which was a bit of a hike from Nana's place and on the other side of the railway line. One of my teachers, Miss

Elliott, was okay, and there were actually a couple of highlights during the year I spent at the school, like learning to sing songs in harmony, and a fancy dress ball. I went dressed as a jockey, in cut-down racing silks belonging to my bigamist uncle, and won a prize.

Billy in his prize-winning jockey outfit

Uncle Cocky was also back in Hobart, working on the construction of the Royal Hobart Hospital. I missed my father very much, so when Nana was not around to purse her lips like a cat's bum in disapproval he would yarn to me, telling me stories of how my dad pulled cons on some of the richer types who came into the SP shop or the billiard parlour. According to Uncle Cocky, my dad was always up to something. He didn't criticise Dad's behaviour but he was careful about repeating stories of his scams in front of other family members, who thought them disgraceful. And there were quite a few disapproving relatives to watch out for: besides Uncle Cocky and myself, my Uncle Doug, aunts Ada and Else and cousin Irene all lived in Nana's house. I had the distinct feeling that my dad, like my shunned Catholic mum, was definitely on the outer as far as Nana and our more upright relations were concerned.

The extended and somewhat disapproving Young family now lived at 7 Hay Street (now known as Clarendon Street, as Hay Street was constantly being confused with nearby Haigh Street), not far from the rented home at 7 Tower Road where Billy was born. When the shift took place, Big Bill and Adora had moved into a house of their own, most likely to escape Nana's dominance. The family in Hobart must have been aware, from Ilma and Vince, that Big Bill had a criminal record in Sydney and had spent time in gaol. However, to their credit they continued to keep up the charade so that Billy was not forced to face reality.

Clarendon Street house.

But Uncle Cocky's company and stories did not make up for living in a house where everyone had to mind their P's and Q's all the time. I did as I was told, because I had to, and Nana's word was law. I begged her to allow me play footie, but she refused to let me go to training after school because I had chores to do each afternoon. That was Nana for you. Rules were Rules and No Exceptions. Consequently, when Marie came down for a visit over the Easter break in 1938, and suggested I go back with her to Sydney, I was only too happy to go.

Marie lived in Glebe, another inner suburb and not far from my old stamping grounds at Ultimo and Pyrmont. As she was busy working five days a week, the responsibility of looking after me was shared with two couples. Marie, being the daughter of a schoolmaster, was very keen on education and enrolled me at the Glebe Public School. But she was no Nana Young and I was soon skiving off again, spending my time down at the wool stores or mucking around on the log rafts in nearby Blackwattle Bay. But when I suddenly worked out that I hadn't been to school for three whole weeks, I got a bit rattled. Desperately needing an excuse for my prolonged absence, I paid a penny to an old bloke to write me a note, claiming that I had been sick for three weeks with the mumps.

Marie and I kept tabs on Dad, who wrote the occasional letter, through articles published in the *Workers' Weekly*, the journal of the Australian Communist Party. It didn't occur to me that he might not come back, and I reckon it didn't occur to Marie either. They were supposed to be married when he returned. But they weren't, because he didn't. Sometime after August 1938, just after going to the front, he and another bloke from Sydney went missing in action at a place called Ebro River, near Barcelona. A letter written by one of his mates had reported that my dad, who had been promoted to *Cabo* (corporal), and Bill Morcom, also from Sydney, were missing. No news had been received of them since they had gone 'over the top' into Fascist territory in an unsuccessful charge on a hill. Dad had last been seen getting water from a well. As time wore on, even the most optimistic of the local comrades gave up all hope of the pair turning up alive somewhere. After a few weeks passed with no sign of them, they were presumed to be dead.

In October, the Workers Weekly ran a tribute to my dad under the heading 'TWO COMMUNISTS DIE FOR DEMOCRACY. AUSTRALIA WILL NEVER FORGET'. So, just a few days before my thirteenth birthday, I had to face the fact that I was both motherless and fatherless.

Soldiers fighting at the battle of Ebro, where Billy's father was killed

In December, Big Bill Young again made the news, this time in London and Melbourne. However, there was no cause for rejoicing.

BACK FROM SPAIN

BIG WELCOME IN LONDON

Independent Cable Service

LONDON. Thursday.

Still wearing their uniforms and berets, four Australians and two New Zealanders reached London last night, with 303 British members of the International Brigade, who have been repatriated from Spain.

Thousands of cheering and singing people, who crammed every corner of Victoria station welcomed the men. Thousands more who had waited all the afternoon outside the station broke the police cordon time after time in scenes that have not been witnessed since the Great War.

Wildly cheering crowds blocked the streets and held up the traffic as the troops, with three bands, began to march to Stepney.

The wounded men were first, some of them hobbling, then came the standard-bearers with Republican flags mingling with Union Jacks, then the officers and men some in tattered uniforms and some in civilian clothes provided by the Spanish Government

All of the men from the Dominions took part in the heavy fighting on the Ebro front.

Franklyn said – 'We sometimes spent 15 days continuously in the front line without relief. They hit us with everything except the garden gates. There were sometimes between 60 and 100 bombers in the air and at the same time it would begin to rain trench-mortar shells.'

Both Wounded

'But it took Franco four months to regain what we took in a few days. We are all convinced that the Government will eventually win, although it is handicapped by lack or supplies. Both McNeill and I were wounded on the Ebro."

There are still three Australians, Lloyd Edmunds and Kevin Rebeocha, of Melbourne, and E Robinson of Sydney, in hospital near Barcelona. Two Australians Bill Morcom and Bill Young of Sydney were killed on the Ebro. There were originally 56 Australians in the International Brigade, some of whom are in prison in Spain but many were killed."

It was one of the comrades, Diana Gould (no relation to Wingy), who told me my dad had died. But she didn't say how or where. And neither did anyone else, although it was reported in the *Workers' Weekly*. It was not until I was 90 years old that I learned the truth from my co-author. My dad, after attacking Hill 481, was taken prisoner at Gardesa, where he was shot dead in cold blood by Italian Fascist officers.

Despite being a communist, Diana was a beautiful English lady aged about 25, who had the poshest voice and taught elocution at a private school. An expert horsewoman, she took me riding at a friend's place on the outskirts of Sydney, where she kept a couple of horses. She was married to Harry, who lectured at Sydney University, so I was staying with them at the time in their big house in St John's Road in the suburb of Glebe, where I still went to school.

Diana was a real firebrand who had almost been expelled from her upper crust school in England for daring to wear a Labour Party badge. Encouraged by her parents, she then progressed to handing out radical literature at London University.

Diana, who also had a great flair for drama and had appeared in a production of Murder in the Cathedral, *emigrated to Australia to take up a post as a speech training teacher. She arrived in Sydney at the height of the Depression, to be confronted for the first time in her life by real poverty. Moved by the plight of the poor, she joined the Communist Party and the Workers Education Society at Sydney University, where she met Llewellyn Henry Gould, a Jewish-Irishman always known as Harry. The pair, who had similar political ideologies, married in 1937.*

The local communists did not quite know what to make of Diana. She recalled, 'They looked me up and down and said "Oh my God, a bourgeois intellectual – let her go into the New Theatre League and keep her quiet there".'

She was far from quiet but enjoyed working with the League, which in July 1936 staged a big production of the acclaimed anti-Nazi play Till the Day I Die *at Sydney's Savoy Theatre. However, three weeks into the season the play was banned by the Chief Secretary, Mr Chaffey, following representations from the German Consul. In spite of the ban the show went on, only to be interrupted by the police, who removed people from the theatre, creating an uproar at the venue and in the press, fuelled by enraged citizens protesting about rights of freedom of speech. In defiance of the ban, and encouraged by the level of support from the public, the League continued to perform the play to 'private' audiences in its rooms in Pitt Street while the controversy raged on. Billy was taken to see a clandestine performance. The audience, which sat on hard stools, clapped and applauded, but Billy was bored witless. It was not until 1941 that the ban was lifted.*

Now Dad's death was officially official, I became a Ward of the Communist Party. He must have signed me over to them, before he left. My guardians were both bachelors. One was a bloke who wrote for *The Tribune* as 'J McP'; the other was Stan Moran, a rabid unionist who was big in the Waterside Workers Federation. Apart from being a communist he is best remembered for promoting the name 'Pig-Iron Bob' for politician Robert Menzies, whose government in the late 1930s was selling scrap iron to Japan, to be used for supposedly peaceful purposes.

J McP was Leslie John 'Jack' McPhillips, a larger-than-life trade unionist from the Iron Workers Federation, who joined the Communist Party in 1929. Jack, who died in 2004 at the age of 94, authored a number of articles and publications throughout his long life. Like Big Bill, he too was out of work during the Depression. Bill, Jack McPhillips and Stan Moran, who headed the very active and militant Glebe branch of the Unemployed Workers Movement, had worked together to provide relief and sustenance to the homeless and hungry.

Leslie John 'Jack' McPhillips.

Despite Moran's claim that the term 'Pig-Iron Bob' was his invention, it was actually coined by 'Ma' (Mrs) Gwendoline Croft in January 1939, during a rowdy protest against the export of scrap iron to Japan, which had invaded Manchuria and slaughtered hundreds of thousands of Chinese civilians in a purge that had shocked the world. In November the previous year, aware that iron being loaded onto the tramp-steamer Dalfram was being taken to Kobe, where the Japan Steel Works was manufacturing weapons to be used against the Chinese, wharf labourers at Port Kembla walked off the job and went on strike for nine weeks. While other wharfies had been protesting for some time over the export of iron to Japan, and had raised public awareness with the slogan 'No Scrap for the Jap', they had been too afraid to take militant action for fear of being forced, under the draconian Transport Workers' Act, to become licensed, which would take away their right to strike.

The Act was invoked against the recalcitrant Port Kembla workers, but as only one man became licensed there was no labour force available and the impasse continued. Menzies, who was Attorney-General at the time, and who went on to become Australia's longest-serving prime minister in the 1950s and 60s, was determined to put an end to the strike, which had attracted national interest. As the wharfies were striking for a principle, not in their own self-interest, they gained widespread support. On 11 January 1939, in an attempt to find a resolution to the Dalfram Dispute Menzies attended a meeting in Wollongong Town Hall, where he faced a hostile crowd, hurling abuse and demanding 'No Pig Iron for Japan'.

Menzies, a most imposing figure and a great orator, towered over Mrs Croft, but he was no match for the feisty 52-year-old woman, whose cry of 'Pig-Iron Bob' was heard loud and clear above the general hubbub. The name stuck, and was used to such effect by Moran in his anti-conservative government speeches in the 1940s and 1950s that most people, including Menzies himself, believed he had coined it.

The heroic action taken in Port Kembla by the wharf labourers put an end to exports of scrap iron to Japan, but Menzies remained Pig-Iron Bob for the rest of his life.

Angry mob demonstrating against Pig-Iron Bob

Stan also handed out propaganda leaflets and took part in a lot of demos, both of which were illegal activities, so he was often arrested and sent to gaol. An eloquent orator who held forth in Sydney's Domain, where he argued the benefits of communism, he was equally eloquent on the shop floor, arguing for the rights of workers.

Now I was an orphan, the Comrades rallied round. The Happy Times Social Club organised a Christmas party at the hall, loading me up with presents the like of which I'd never seen before – a watch from the District Committee, woodworking tools, clothes and chocolates from other well-wishers, and a summer holiday, donated by Harry and Diana, at the Eureka Youth Holiday Camp, near Blackheath swimming pool.

Not only was Diana definitely not your average Communist Party comrade, but she had made a name for herself a couple of months before when she held a one-woman anti-Nazi protest in Pitt Street, waving her arms about and shouting, 'Down with Hitler. We want peace.' When the police turned up to see what the fuss was about, she climbed on the bonnet of a car and yelled 'Here come Hitler's Storm Troopers'. This didn't go down too well with the cops, who arrested her for disturbing the peace.

She had to front up to court, where the magistrate found her guilty. Telling her 'You are certainly a most undesirable person to be teaching children', he bound her over to be on good behaviour for twelve months.

The holiday from Diana and her husband was a wonderful idea, but the best gift of all was a reconditioned two-wheeler bike. Whoever had done it up was an expert, and it looked as good as new. Stan and J McP tried to big-note themselves by making out they were responsible, but it was actually a present from the Western Sydney branch. I thanked everyone and said I wanted to be a good communist like my dad

I had a great time at the holiday camp, swimming, camping and hiking. The pool, which was enormous and had seen a few drownings since it was opened to the public in 1931, had started out life as a reservoir for steam trains. When the camp was over, I spent some time staying with Marie's parents out at Kingswood. They lived way out in the bush in a very basic house, made of timber slabs lined with wall-papered hessian, beaten-earth floors and a large open fireplace, built from huge river boulders and big enough to take an entire log. I loved to sit beside the fireplace on a cold windy night, listening to the hessian walls flapping in the draught blowing through the gaps in the slabs. There was no electricity and the water was siphoned from a nearby spring.

Marie's dad, Mr Barker, had been a schoolteacher so he made sure I went to school. However, politically he was a conservative, so when Marie visited there would be clashes of ideology, which made it hard for me because I was almost duty-bound to side with her, especially since my dad had died for the cause. Eventually, due to the friction, we agreed it was time for me to move on.

My next and final billet, organised by the Comrades, was at Corrimal, a coastal village south of Sydney, where I lived with Sam Blakeney and his wife. Sam was a retired miner who was very into lawn bowls and growing roses, and so was his wife. School, which was just down the road, wasn't too bad, mainly because the deputy head, Mr Leslie, who'd been a seaman in the Great War, injected a bit of interest into the lessons. Being a good teacher didn't stop him handing out a few cuts with his cane to the kids in his class, including me, but he certainly had plenty of stories to tell about the places he'd been to, and what he had seen.

For once in my life I actually enjoyed being in a classroom, and I didn't wag school – not once. I even gave a geography talk to the class, which earned me a book prize from Mr Leslie and a round of applause from the rest of the kids. It wasn't the first time I had been singled out for special praise. Just before going-home time, a few weeks before, Mr Leslie had asked us all what day it was. After exhausting all the special days we could think of – Empire Day, the King's birthday, Wattle Day – he announced that it was the first day that Keith Young had not received the cane – an achievement that definitely called for a round of applause.

The Blakeneys were nice enough people but I was a kid, they were retired, and helping out in the rose garden and carting buckets of horse manure, which they expected me to do, was not my thing. One day after a disagreement about something so trivial that I can't remember what it was, I got on my bike and took off to Canberra, barefooted and dressed only in shorts and a singlet. Despite the left pedal on my bike being broken, leaving just the central shaft, I made it up Macquarie Pass to the Southern Highlands town of Robertson, where I spent a freezing night trying to catch some sleep in a phone box.

On reaching Moss Vale I followed the Hume Highway to Goulburn, and then took the Federal Highway to Canberra. By this time the sun was blasting down and it was boiling hot. The sole of my left foot was so sore from pushing on the hard metal shaft that I resorted to using the tips of my toes as I pedalled along the road that clung to the shoreline of Lake George. I was labouring up the hill at the far end of the lake, using my big toe to turn the pedal, when a red sports car came round the corner on the wrong side of the road, forcing me to swerve onto the gravel shoulder. The bike skidded and came to a stop, with me underneath it.

The driver, after a cursory look and a couple of words, drove off, figuring that as I was able to pick myself up I was okay. I wasn't. I had broken the little toe on my *right* foot. Fortunately a bloke driving a ute came by, put my bike in the back and drove me to Canberra Hospital, where I received plenty of attention and sympathy for my injury. After an overnight stay, the police contacted the Blakeneys and arranged for me to return home by train.

Everyone was as nice as pie when I got back. I didn't get into any trouble at all. Mrs Blakeney was so sympathetic at the sight of my expertly bandaged foot that she made me a big bowl of warm bread and milk, sweetened with currants. I finished the school year but, as the Blakeneys could not afford to support me while I went to high school, it was agreed that I should take up an apprenticeship, as I had just turned fourteen. So after Christmas I left Corrimal, and school, for good, and headed back to Sydney.

Ma Jepson had died from pneumonia that year. As I wanted to prove I could look after myself, I rented an attic room in a 'residential' – a four-storeyed terrace at 133 Dowling Street, Woolloomooloo, not far from the docks. Next door, on the corner of Cathedral Street, was the Fitzroy Hotel, an old pub that had been there for years. 'The Loo', as they called it, was not the most law-abiding suburb in Sydney, so when I returned home after riding my bike, I lugged it up several flights of stairs to make sure no one nicked it.

My landlord, Mr Sandblom, who had communist sympathies, came from Finland. He lived in the basement of the terrace with his rather plain wife, who wore round glasses with lenses as thick as milk bottles, and their three little kids. He didn't say much, and she said even less. As laundry service was supplied to tenants for a small fee and, as Mr Sandblom didn't contract it out, his poor wife seemed to be always slaving over a copper, hauling sheets and pillowslips out of the boiling water with a wooden stick, before feeding them into a huge heavy mangle. It took a fair bit of muscle power to move the rollers so, more often than not, I was volunteered to turn the handle.

Still waters are said to run deep. Billy's landlord was Johan Jules Sandblom, born in the quaintly named town of Snappertuna, Finland, in 1895. He was a committed communist as was his 35-year-old de facto wife, Sylvia Lord, who originally came from Manchester in England and was a long-time card-carrying member of the Party. Johan had migrated in 1924 with his then wife, Elna (nee Ekholm), but she had divorced him in 1932 on the grounds of adultery with Sylvia, who had been brought out to Australia in 1927 under the Domestic Scheme.

On arrival in Australia, Johan, a former merchant seaman, had worked for Victorian Cabinet Works in Redfern as a cabinetmaker, but was now employed by the Perfectonala Company, which made gramophones in its factory in nearby Bourke

Street. Despite his communist beliefs, he had pronounced capitalistic tendencies and over the years had bought up various properties in the slum areas of East Sydney, which he had then converted into boarding houses or flats that he sub-let. By the time Billy became a tenant at 133 Dowling Street, Mr Sandblom owned no less than ten properties in the immediate or surrounding area.

However, it was Sylvia who, in Billy's eyes seemed to be a colourless housewife weighed down by a life of domestic drudgery and looking after three small children, who was the real dark horse. Later described as an 'old time communist' by the Australian Security and Intelligence Organisation (ASIO), which had her under surveillance, she had made the headlines in 1931 following 'wild scenes' and an 'all-in fight with hands and handbags' at an anti-communist meeting held at the Sydney Town Hall, which she and like-minded female comrades had sought to disrupt. More than half a dozen 'shrieking, gesticulating' women had been ejected from the meeting, after fierce struggles with the police. Three had been arrested. One of them was Sylvia, who had assaulted a policeman trying to arrest a comrade. After punching him on the cheek, she had fled down the steps leading to Druitt Street, but had been pursued and caught. Found guilty as charged at Central Police Court, she was ordered to enter into a twelve-month good behaviour bond which, if breached, would see her sent to gaol for a month.

Despite her arrest, she may have stayed under ASIO's radar had it not been for the fact that Johan (whom she eventually married in 1947) had come to the attention of the police and wartime security services in May 1940, after the Communist Party was declared illegal. Security police were now authorised to search the home of any person deemed to be a potential threat. The public also reported suspicious activities and individuals to the police.

Sybil's 'mug-shot', taken by ASIO

An unnaturalised 'alien', Sandblom had been reported for organising meetings of a number of aliens in a house owned by him. It was also reported that some kind of machinery had been installed in his property at 133 Dowling Street and that it operated in the wee small hours of the morning.

Interviewed by police, Sylvia, who was found to have in her possession a collection box for the Miners' Relief Fund, stated that she was a member of the East Sydney branch of the No Conscription League, and was also President of the Plunkett Street School Mothers' Club in Woolloomooloo. However, while she was a person of interest, it was Johan who was at that time the focus of attention. His own home at 21 Harmer Street was raided, on the grounds that it may have held material that constituted a 'war offence'. Although a quantity of Russian and Finnish literature found was not confiscated, he was now very much in the spotlight. The fact that, in 1941 he was re-classified as an enemy alien, kept him there. He was informed that he could no longer use or have in his possession any radio set without the permission of the Postmaster General.

The screws tightened even more in 1943 when he was issued with a Restriction Order, which required him to report to the police each Thursday at 8 am. Prior to this, as an 'ordinary' alien, it was just once a month, something with which he had evidently not bothered. He complied with the new order two or three times but then refused point blank to report again, an action which eventually resulted in his arrest in 1944 on the orders of the Security Service. He pleaded not guilty, but changed it to one of guilty, following the presentation of evidence to the court. His stubborn recalcitrance earned him a fine of 25 pounds, plus two pounds ten shillings in costs, in default of 55 days' imprisonment. In addition, he was ordered to lodge the sum of 50 pounds to comply with the Aliens Control Regulations, under which the restriction order was made.

Four months later, having won the battle and forced him to comply, the authorities removed the weekly restriction order. For the remainder of the war he was obliged to report only once a month, as required by the Aliens Control Regulations.

Johan died in 1951 at the age of 56. Sylvia, however, was regarded as a 'security risk' by ASIO and remained under surveillance for a further ten years.

I needed employment, so when my comrade guardians raved on to Mr Sandblom about a small cupboard I had made for the Blakeneys, he took me on as an apprentice. I was not a roaring success, and he was a hard taskmaster, but I was able to earn a few bob by doing odd painting and maintenance jobs at the various rental properties he owned. I was also delegated to clean up after departing tenants. Many of the rooms were rented out to alcoholics or to people with mental health problems, and their habits when it came to sanitation often left a great deal to be desired.

I also had the task of keeping up the wood supply to a boiler at a Finnish steam bath my boss had created in a shed at much larger premises he owned, further down Dowling Street. There was no way he would ever pay good money for firewood, so another of my jobs was to scrounge scrap timber, which I then hauled on a hand-cart to the shed. A less onerous task was to bundle up branches of gum-tips, well past their prime and bought cheaply from Paddy's Market, so that the customers, who paid a couple of pence a bunch, could whack their bodies with them as part of the cleansing process. Entry to the steam bath was a shilling per head, and there was no shortage of customers. Although Australians had not yet discovered the delights of a Finnish steam bath, there were plenty of 'foreigners' from Scandinavia and other European countries who lived in the nearby slum houses and who lined up eagerly, more than keen to part with their hard-earned cash.

As I took after my dad and was big for my years, I tried to join the navy during this period. Although I passed the medical, they discovered I was under age and I was busted. So I took a job with Houghton and Byrne, Pest Exterminators, whose head office was in Bridge Street, in the city. We tackled all kinds of pests, including rats and cockroaches, which infested houses and commercial buildings, including the many bakeries owned by Sergeant's Meat Pies. The area under the conveyor belts, strewn with bits that had fallen off the pastry, was a favourite haunt of the cockies, which hid among the machinery. We started work at about 2 am, when the night shift had finished. It took a while for the pellets and powder to work, so I made good use of the time by making myself massively big sundaes from the bulk ice-cream stored in the outside café section.

To eliminate rats in larger establishments such as factories, we sealed up the doors and windows and fired cyanide caps at them, using a special gun to turn it into gas. One of our regular clients was at Riverstone, outside Sydney, a meat works that had huge pickling vats for the corned beef and silverside. Above the vats was a network of rafters that the rats used as a highway. Crouching in the shadows, we waited for them to appear. Pow! One shot and the rats fell down, stone dead, into the pickling vats. It's funny, but ever since then I've never been keen on corned meat.

Fumigating an entire house or warehouse took three or four days. After sealing the windows and doors, bar one, we covered the building with canvas tarpaulins. When the inspector was satisfied no gas could leak out and kill the locals, we lined up pots of sulphuric acid and, on the inspector's signal, dropped cyanide pellets into the acid before running like hell for the exit door, which was then sealed behind us. The downside was that we had to post a guard, 24 hours a day, working in shifts, until it was safe to re-enter the building.

I also worked at the firm's big warehouse at Woolloomooloo, which had a large gas chamber for treating borers in furniture. We tackled everything from grand pianos to kitchen chairs to antique banqueting tables for the homes of toffs who lived in the posh eastern suburbs.

At about his time I discovered that Woolloomooloo also had a Police Boys Club, where I was allowed to sign in as a visitor. The coppers were very keen on physical activity, especially boxing, and it was here that I palled up with John Licciardo, an Italian kid about a year younger than me. He was a pretty good boxer, built like a junior Atlas. I was drawn to him, as he was a good athlete, agile and very skilled on the parallel bars. John's dad was a fisherman, which is why the family lived near Woolloomooloo. John was good company, but he had a bit of a chip on his shoulder because he was a Dago, which is what we called Italians, and because his father, who had applied for naturalisation and regarded himself as a loyal Australian, had been classified as an enemy alien and been interned. As there were five kids to support (three girls and two boys) and as his dad had been contributing to the food supply, John thought it was all very unfair.

We got on pretty well, so one day when John told me there was a job going at the Eastern Extension Cable Company, where he worked as a telegram delivery boy, I and my bike applied. We had no trouble getting the job as, with the war now on, delivery boys were in demand. The pay was good – thirty bob a week – and if you landed the night shift it was easy money, as fewer messages came in at night. The most exciting telegram I ever delivered was in May 1940, to the offices of the upper-class newspaper *The Sydney Morning Herald*, announcing that Winston Churchill had been elected Britain's new prime minister.

To be eligible, prospective employees at the Cable Company needed to young, fit and own a bike. In reality, any bike would do, as long as it was even slightly roadworthy. The company provided a weekly bicycle allowance and after a few weeks there was enough money in the kick for a newcomer to buy a new one.

As if riding a bike for a living was not enough physical exercise, John and I took off at every opportunity. We were both very fit, and on weekends we thought nothing of pedalling to Wollongong, more than 60 miles away, buying a pie for lunch and pedalling back. These excursions annoyed my guardian Stan Moran, who was always at me to spend my free time attending meetings at the Communist Party's Young Comrades' Youth Club.

John was also being hassled – by his brother Tony, who was four years older. With Mr Licciardo locked up in detention, his eldest son had assumed the role of head of the household. Mrs Licciardo, who was a meek kind of lady and spoke no English, allowed her eldest boy to lord it over his four siblings and to throw his weight around. John rebelled. Unable to put up with Tony's standover tactics any longer, he told me that as soon as he had saved up enough he intended to leave home and ride his bike round Australia.

It sounded a good idea to me, so we quit our jobs at the Cable Company, put our ages up and got a job at the Bradford Cotton Mills, which paid better. By mid-December we had enough money in the piggy bank and decided to take off at the Christmas break.

By this time I was even keener to join John on the big adventure as I had received a most unwelcome visit from my communist guardians Stan and J McP. They had come to my lodgings in Dowling Street and confiscated my bike because I had not been to any youth club meetings. It was no good appealing to Mr Sandblom for help, as he was on their side. Seventy-five years later, in 2015, I learned that he and Stan were far more connected than I imagined. Stan moved into 133 Dowling Street in 1940, after the party was outlawed, and was still there in 1941, when he was arrested for soliciting funds without permission in The Domain.

I needed to get my bike back. The big question was, where was it? Not far away was another property belonging to Mr Sandblom, where I knew bikes were stored in a shed. I figured that my guardians had most likely taken it there, with my landlord's connivance, to be held until such time as I toed the party line and attended some meetings. We raided the shed without any difficulty. My bike wasn't there, so I just took another one, which was in good nick and looked very like the one Mr Sandblom rode. With transport assured, we pedalled off towards Melbourne with our few possessions and a pound or so in cash to tide us over until we found some odd jobs.

We couldn't get lost. All we had to do was to follow the Princes Highway, keeping the ocean on the left hand side – and we already knew the way to Wollongong. We cycled through the Royal National Park and Corrimal, where the Blakeneys lived, and then on down to the far south coast, where cows were up to their middles in lush green grass. We took whatever jobs were on offer, in small villages and big towns, sleeping under bridges if it was raining, and under the stars when it wasn't. Eventually, after pedalling across the border into Victoria, through the great and lonely eucalypt forests of East Gippsland, and the tiny holiday place of Lakes Entrance, we reached the flat plains near Sale. From there it seemed just a hop, step and a jump to the Dandenong Ranges, just outside Melbourne.

On our arrival in the big smoke around the end of February, we spotted a board advertising for workers, propped against a wall of W H Wells & Company, in the northern suburb of Abbotsford. It was a metal pressing and stamping company, turning out brass buttons, buckles and the like for the army. By putting our ages up to seventeen we were able to apply for the late afternoon-night shift, which paid a slightly higher rate, and got the job.

We had employment but our dough had run out, and we had nowhere to stay. All the affordable lodging houses nearby wanted cash in advance, which we didn't have, so we headed over towards the markets. As we wandered along the aisles, we noticed a dumping area for waste and surplus produce, where someone had left a huge pile of grapes. Most were well past their prime but some looked okay. I noticed a woman aged about sixty, with rather unkempt hair and wearing a long shabby black dress and apron, sorting through them. Moving on, we continued to the far side of the market where we spotted a sign on a house in Victoria Street – Room to Rent. It was one in a row of fairly rundown terraces and the area was pretty rough, but we thought we'd give it a go. To our surprise, the grape lady owned the house. She said the tiny attic room was ours, if we wanted it, for five bob a week.

'We've got jobs at a factory', I said. 'We're a bit light on cash at the moment, so can you chalk up the rent until payday?' No dice. The area was full of fly-by-night types, and she wanted the money up front.

The room was too cheap and too well located to let it slip through our fingers so we persuaded her to hold it until we came back with the necessary lolly. We had nothing of value apart from our bikes, so we sold mine. The buyer said he would pay us a quid but when the moment came for him to part with the money he said that we looked a bit dodgy so he'd only pay us ten bob now and we would get the other half tomorrow, after he'd made enquiries. As we were both runaways, he had us by the short and curlies, so we handed over the bike, grabbed the ten-bob note, and scampered back to our new landlady.

The room was now ours – provided we paid two weeks in advance. A total of ten shillings. We were now penniless again. We had no money to buy any food, but our landlady took pity on us and offered us some – a bowl of grapes. We were so hungry we ate them, and for the next week we paid to regular visits to the market dump to see what we could scrounge in the way of tucker.

We enjoyed Melbourne, but we still had a long way to go on our ride around Australia. So, in mid-April, we decided it was time to move on. The problem was that once again I had no bike. In an effort to rectify the situation we scoured the city streets, without success. The Melbournites were an untrusting lot and every bike we saw was securely chained and padlocked to a lamp-post or fence. Finally, we spotted one outside a pub in Port Melbourne. It was a Panther model, pretty old, but it had a luggage rack. It was also unchained, and unattended, so we took it.

We were usually able to cover at least a hundred miles a day, so it took less than a day to cover the fifty miles to Geelong, on the western side of Port Phillip Bay. We kept on going, taking the scenic coastal road that led towards Lorne. In those days it was just a gravel country road with very few cars to be seen. With the war on, petrol was rationed and people only ventured as far as was necessary.

We were not very far out of Geelong when disaster struck. I was so busy admiring the scenery that I failed to notice a huge pothole and rode right into it. The bike came to a sudden stop and over the handlebars I went, severely skinning my knees and arms on the rough road surface. As I sat there, blood dripping steadily into the dirt, I almost burst into tears of self-pity. My misery deepened when I looked at the bike. The front wheel had collapsed and was now hopelessly buckled.

There was no way we could fix it so, holding the front of the bike clear of the ground with one hand, and with blood trickling from my various abrasions, I limped along the road towards a small town. We had not gone very far when we spotted a bike, clearly abandoned by its owner, lying in the grass beside a farm track leading through the bush to a house way up on a hill. As the bike was quite old, and did not have a luggage carrier, we decided not to make a total switch but to find somewhere away from the main road where we could swap over the front wheels.

Reaching the town with the three bikes, we took the second turn on the left and headed up a hill to a grassy paddock. Realising that the tyre on my wrecked wheel was in better condition than one of the tyres on John's bike, we decided to change them over. This took quite some time and we were halfway through our task when an old codger came along and asked what we were up to. 'We had an accident with our spare bike', we glibly lied, 'and we are just changing over the wheel.'

Leaving behind the cannibalised bike, the busted wheel and the discarded tyre, we headed off again before darkness fell. We had no further trouble as we pedalled past the Twelve Apostles the following day, before continuing on towards Warrnambool. The next day, as we neared Portland, about fifty miles from the South Australian border, we caught up to a large truck laden with pipes as it laboured up a hill. We grabbed hold of the tray to indulge in a free ride, which was fine until the truck started down the other side. It was a long downhill run and, as the truck picked up speed, the front wheel of my bike, which had not been tightened properly, started to wobble and jammed against the fork. Grabbing onto a pipe that extended beyond the tray I managed to lift the front wheel clear of the road with my knees as the truck gathered speed. It was doing about fifty miles an hour, and I was hanging onto the pipe like grim death. Fortunately at the bottom of the hill the road forked, left to Portland and right towards the South Australian border. As the truck slowed to make its turn to the left I let go and rolled into the grass.

With the wheel retightened, we pedalled towards the town of Heywood, eleven miles away, where we stopped to have the biggest chocolate milkshake I'd ever seen, made by a Chinese kid who was minding the shop for his father. Full to the brim, and burping from the bubbles, we had only gone a short distance when came to a hobo camp just outside town. It had started off as a forestry relief camp a few years before to provide employment for local men. Right alongside the camp was a huge rabbit warren, swarming with hundreds of fat little bunnies: a good reason to stop for a few days. The rabbits were delicious, but it was a bad move to stay there. The bike theft had been reported by the owner, we had been seen changing the wheels, had left ample proof of what we had done on the hillside and been noticed heading west. The local policeman did not need to be Sherlock Holmes to put two and two together, and the hobo camp was the first place to look for a couple of delinquent kids heading towards the border on bikes.

John, who had his own bike, immediately protested that he had done nothing wrong, but the copper took no notice. After slinging the bikes into the back of his old ute, he took us into town, where he lived on the job in a house attached to the station. We were too young to be put in cells but as the policeman's wife was very nervous about having potential felons in such close proximity to her family, he asked if we minded spending the night in the small lock up. It didn't worry us. The cells were clean with comfortable mattresses so, as we had no idea it was illegal, we agreed.

The next morning, adopting a fatherly approach, the policeman asked if we had done anything that we would like to talk about. He advised it was better to come clean now than later, because rest assured the truth would out. And so, being young and basically honest, I owned up to the fact that we had stolen two bikes. Three, if you counted the one in Sydney.

The policeman who caught up with Billy and John was Constable Gerhardt Friedrich Stehn, known as Fred. A former farmer from Natimuk, near Horsham in Victoria, Fred had quit the land in 1924 to join the police force. He was posted to Heywood in 1927 and had been there with his wife Emma ever since. Now aged 39, Fred was a committed family man with a son and three daughters. His standing in the community was such that when he died unexpectedly in 1954, at the age of only 52, he was given a police funeral with full honours.

The town of Heywood had a Court House, which convened as a Children's Court when required. As the two boys were clearly juveniles and their immediate welfare was of the most importance, their bikes were confiscated and they were escorted by bus to Melbourne, where they were taken into temporary care at Royal Park Depot, also known as the Boys' Receiving Depot.

Located at 900 Park Street, Parkville, and originally established in the 1870s, it was the state-run reception centre for children committed to state care, and a clearing house before they were boarded out, sent out to 'service' or, if the situation warranted it, to reformatory school.

Police records show that Billy and John were only there for a few days when Detective Lester Benjamin Burrows made the journey from Geelong to follow up on information passed to him by Constable Fred Stehn.

Arriving at Royal Park at 2 pm on 28 April, he told the pair that he wanted to talk to them about a Radford Star bicycle, stolen near Geelong on the 15th of that month. Billy immediately admitted to the theft, but once again John tried to protest his innocence by claiming that he didn't take the bike, as he had his own.

After having John admit that he was there, and that he knew full well what Billy was doing, Burrows also elicited from them the admission that they had not only stolen a Panther bike from Port Melbourne, but had also swapped the tyre from the damaged wheel and put it on John's bike. When asked if they had any explanation to offer as to why they had taken the bikes, they replied, quite truthfully, 'We were going to go round Australia'.

Their ambitious attempt to circumnavigate the country on two wheels came to an end at Geelong Children's Court on 5 May 1941. Giving his last address as 133 Dowling Street, East Sydney, Billy stated that he had been born in 1924, thereby making himself a year older. His court record held few personal details – just the name of his father and the fact that both parents, including his 'unknown' mother, were dead.

Detective Burrows, appearing for the Crown, produced in court the Radford Star bike, recovered from the field, and also the confiscated Panther. As the boys admitted that they had taken both bikes, the magistrate had no option but to find them guilty. He also directed that they be made Wards of the State.

The judge was kind enough, pointing out that we needed some direction in life before we found ourselves in serious trouble. To my disgust, during the proceedings I discovered that the theft of the bike from outside the Port Melbourne pub had never been reported. I reckon it was so decrepit the owner didn't bother. That's honesty for you. In my naivety I had confessed to a crime that, according to officialdom, had never happened. Moreover, we actually didn't steal the second bike – just the wheel, and we left the busted one in exchange.

Watching the proceedings from the public gallery was the owner of the second bike, a young boy, and his mother. I didn't feel any great guilt about the theft, because my need at the time was great, and he had just left the bike lying carelessly beside the road. However, I felt bad when I learned from the magistrate that we had pinched a little kid's bike. On seeing how small he was, I wondered how he had ever managed to ride it.

After the court hearing, John and Billy were transferred back to Royal Park where they were formally admitted as Wards of the State of Victoria. John was assigned number 67242 and Billy 67246. Believing that both boys were already State Wards in New South Wales, Mr Read, the Depot's superintendent, contacted the Child Welfare authorities in Sydney, seeking advice as to their 'disposal'. The NSW Director, Mr G D Martin, replied that as neither boy could be identified as a State Ward of New South Wales, he did not desire them to be returned to Sydney. Billy had no one to care for him, so he had to remain where he was but, as John's mother was keen to get him back home, arrangements were underway to escort him as far as Albury, where he would be handed over to NSW authorities.

I had no worries about staying at Royal Park. The accommodation section at the Boys' Home, as we called it, was brand new. It was wonderful. Good food and plenty of it, clean and modern bathroom facilities, with loads of hot water. Each room in our wing had only two beds, equipped with individual bedside tables and lamps – a far cry from the open verandah at Ultimo where I had read by the light of the street lamp. It was by far the best place I had ever lived in, and I could hardly believe my good luck. I got on well with the other kids and also the child welfare officers, one of whom had been a warder at Pentridge Gaol. They were there to make sure we behaved ourselves and, if we did, they didn't give us any grief. There was plenty to do to occupy our time, as facilities included a well-equipped school, which also offered occupational training in plumbing and woodwork. I was spoilt for choice.

Visitors were allowed each week. I didn't have any of course, but my room-mate did. He had severe scoliosis, like that bloke Richard the Third – the hunchback King. His doting mum, who had spoilt him rotten – so rotten he had gone off the rails – came every week to see him. He was an angelic looking kid, with a sweet cherubic face and a mass of long golden curls. It was hard to imagine that he had got himself into trouble, let alone end up in the Boys' Home. His mum overcompensated for his trauma by bringing loads of goodies each week, which he shared with me. I was as happy as a pig in mud, and felt as if I was set for life.

Like most institutions, there was a leader of the pack. I'll call him Jim because his real moniker has slipped my mind. He was a blond bloke, quite tall and about the same age as me. He was affable enough, but his deputy, a shortish (well, shorter than me), dark-haired cove, was a rather taciturn bugger. Many years later, as I didn't want anyone to know about my problems with the law, I let people believe that his name was Don and that he was the boy I'd run away with from Sydney.

Research undertaken in 2015, which also yielded a photograph, revealed that Jim's offsider was seventeen-year-old Phillip Patrick Barker. Prior to finding himself on the wrong side of the law, he had lived in the east Melbourne suburb of Abbotsford with his parents, James, a process worker, and Mary, known as Mollie.

One morning, after I'd been there for a few weeks, we were lined up for the day's job allocation when one of the officers – a kindly if somewhat fussy bloke – noticed that Jim was absent. He was not well. The officer was a bit put out by this news as Jim and Phil, who were in positions of trust, were scheduled to complete some tidying up work in the grounds outside the perimeter fence. Being a bit of a worrier, he wanted to stick to his timetable, so he told Phil to take me with him, which surprised me a bit as I hadn't been there very long.

Phil never said much at any time, so we spent the morning working in silence. However, after lunch he came over to me and said, 'I'm going to nick off, later this afternoon. So keep your flamin' mouth shut.'

Momentarily dumbfounded, I asked, 'But where will you go?

'I'm going to join the army.'

'You can't do that', I said. 'You're too young. You're only a kid, like me.'

'It's all right', he said, 'if you know where to go. There's a recruiting place in the city where age is overlooked as long as you are fit. A couple of my cobbers got in.'

'Gee! I'll be in that!'

I must have suffered a brain melt-down. It's the only reason I can think of why I would have considered for one second leaving such comfortable and congenial surroundings, which offered three square meals a day, and the chance to finish school and learn a trade. But consider it I did, and in that split second uttered the five words that would determine the course of the rest of my life.

It was certainly a life-changing moment for Billy. However, he would not fully appreciate how momentous an occasion it was until the advanced age of ninety that he looked back across three-quarters of a century of a long and eventful life to that day when, with the impetuosity of youth, he made that snap decision. The path he chose would take him from an aimless existence, governed by Rafferty's rules, to a life where discipline reigned and the bonds of mateship were integral to his very existence. Away from the influence of the petty criminal element, he would meet men, real men, who would guide him through the coming years, giving him a purpose in life, a set of decent values and an opportunity to appreciate and develop his life skills.

We didn't duck off straight away, as I had expected. Phil must have been planning to do a bunk for quite a while because he had it all figured out.

'We'll stay on the job for the rest of the arvo until just before it's time to knock off', he said. 'At around four o'clock we'll make our way across the road to those old buildings, where there's a clothing store. We need to ditch our uniforms and get some new duds. If we don't, we'll stick out like sore thumbs. The staff doesn't leave until six o'clock, so we'll hide in a shed at the back until they've gone.'

Pretending to get on with our work, we edged our way round to the other side of the main building. Jim must have been faking his illness, or had experienced a miraculous recovery, because he was in the common room on the ground floor, along with a couple of smaller kids. Spotting Phil, he waved him over. The windows were plate glass, so they shouted and mimed to each other. Phil must have invited Jim to come along with us because when Jim said, 'The door's locked', Phil grabbed a fire extinguisher and started to bash at the big padlock that secured the door on the outside.

He attacked it like a madman, making such a noise that a bunch of little kids ran into the room and started to yell and jump around in a frenzy of excitement. The racket they made alerted a staff member, who came in to see what the fuss was about. At that point I decided it was high time to depart and took off for the shed, with Phil at my heels. Obviously Jim came up with some plausible story to account for the little kids' excitement, because no alarm was raised.

As it was mid-winter it was already getting dark when we reached the safety of the shed but Phil wasn't taking any chances and waited until about 9 pm before he led the way to the big building. We didn't need to break in. He knew where the key was.

The store room was full of civilian clothing and essential toiletries, all neatly laid out on shelves behind a big counter, just like a shop, ready to be given to kids being moved on to a foster home or taking up employment. Stripping off our tell-tale monogrammed Boys' Home uniforms, we took two of the cheap pressed-cardboard suitcases stacked nearby and helped ourselves to underclothes, pyjamas, socks, shirts, trousers, a woollen jumper and a navy blue coat. To this we added soap and other basic toiletries. I also took a shaving kit, even though I was too young to shave.

With our kit ready, we settled down for the night on a pile of blankets, stored on a kind of raised platform. We had intended to leave for the recruiting office at around 5 am, while it was still pitch dark, but at about two o'clock we were rudely awakened by the light of a torch, shining full on our faces.

'Dear! Dear! Whatever are you two boys doing here?' came a voice from behind the blinding light. 'You've frightened the life out of the old lady who lives in the flat downstairs. She heard noises and has been worried stiff.'

It was the kind officer, the one who always fussed and who had given us the job outside the wire. Obviously disturbed that we were not in our own beds, and that we clearly intended to run away, he pleaded, 'Now, now, boys, be good lads. You don't want to run away and get into worse trouble. Why don't you just go back to your own rooms and climb into your own beds, before anyone finds out you are missing?'

Phil had no intention of doing any such thing and yelled, 'Come on. Let's go!' So we picked up our cases and fled towards the road running along the western boundary of the Home and which led the city. Oak Street, I think it was. This eventually led us on to Flemington Road which, had we stayed on it, would have taken us straight to the Town Hall. However, somehow we made a right-hand turn where we shouldn't, and that's how we found ourselves at Spencer Street Railway Station, just as the morning rush began, that cold July day.

And it is also how two delinquent youths, under age and on the run from the law, jumped on a tram to the city to join the Australian Imperial Force.

CHAPTER 3

YOU'LL BE SORRY

July – November 1941

Grabbing our papers from the counter of the recruiting office, we ran to the General Post Office, which stood just around the corner in all its Victorian majesty in Burke Street. By this time it was well and truly open for business and, more importantly, it had desks holding pens, ink and blotting paper, all free to use and at the ready. Phil said we had to be nineteen to enlist so we did the sums before signing each other's permission forms in the names of our guardians. Not having had any experience with bureaucrats, especially the military variety, I didn't realise that the army would want to know where I was living. Phil said to keep it simple. I could hardly say my last abode was the Boys' Home, so I wrote down 207 Victoria Street, Carlton, my old lodging house and the only address in Melbourne that I knew.

Phil gave his address as 18 Fairchild Street, Abbotsford, where his parents lived, and named his father James as next-of-kin, while Billy nominated a completely fictitious 'Aunt Martha Young'. Following his own advice to keep it simple, Phil stuck to his full name but Billy dropped the Keith completely. Their occupations were listed as press hand and labourer.

The lower age limit for enlistment in the AIF in 1939 was 20 years, but by 1941 it had been reduced to nineteen, and by 1943 would fall to eighteen. However, signed parental consent was required for anyone under the age of 21. Eighteen-year-old Phil, born in October 1922, wound his birth year back by two years, while Billy added a whopping four years to his real age. They both stuck to the correct day and month. With their falsified birth dates, Phil would turn 21 in October and Billy would be 20 in November.

Billy's enlistment form

The supply of willing recruits, at that time, just couldn't keep up with demand. The mass production line of human raw material was not only working overtime, it was roaring away at full pelt. The British Empire, which included us True Blue Colonials, was on the receiving end of the powerful German war machine. In North Africa they were getting stuck into us and handing out a father of a hiding, hence the urgent, continuous demand for fresh blood. At the recruiting office near the Town Hall they were taking just about anyone: old blokes from the Great War who put their ages down, young blokes who put their ages up. Anyone was welcome to apply for enlistment, especially those stupid enough to volunteer for the foot-slogging infantry. As far as army recruitment was concerned, we were real pushovers: cold, hungry, dumb 'Johnnies-on-the-spot', at the right place, at the right time, tongues hanging out for a bit of excitement. First-class gun fodder.

The alarming war situation, the pressing need for reinforcements and the desire to fill their particular quota went part way, at least, towards explaining the smile on the face of the lieutenant as he glanced from one form to the other.

'Hey', he said, to his two offsiders. 'Take a look at this lot then. Can you spot the similarities?' Nodding their heads, they chuckled and chortled over our literary efforts as they returned to their desks.

Willing recruits must have been in really short supply because, despite the obvious flaws in our paperwork, the lieutenant finally looked up, pointed to a door and said, 'Okay, you two, go through there and if you pass the medical, you're in.'

The door opened into a waiting room, where we waited and waited, outwaiting our earlier wait at the front door. We hadn't eaten since lunch at the Boys' Home the day before, and we were ravenous. Gurgling noises from our food-deprived stomachs, exacerbated by nervous apprehension, joined the digestive rumbles of other early arrivals, all similarly waiting. We tried to keep our minds off our hunger pangs by listening in to the older blokes discussing which branch of the army would be best to join. Most favoured infantry or artillery, but a few advised that if you wanted to keep away from the pointy end of the war, which I didn't, then a transport unit or some mechanical-type outfit was the way to go.

Now and again a forlorn-looking figure clad in khaki clomped across the room on hobnailed boots, looking neither right nor left as he passed though one doorway and out through another. Occasionally as he went by we heard a barely audible 'You'll be sorry' – a remark obviously directed at us, to digest, ponder on, think about.

His gloomy comments didn't put us off. Impatient with the length of time it was taking the bureaucracy to turn us into soldiers, how we longed to be in uniform, if only to parade about and mutter our own 'You'll be sorry'. Finally, after what seemed an eternity the long-awaited call came from a disembodied voice in the room across the way.

'Young. William Young.'

A tall, thin, bespectacled fellow in a long white coat peered at me through thick lenses and barked, 'Read the top line of the chart'. This was hardly a challenge, as the letters were big and bold, and the chart was almost large enough to lead a May Day procession. After checking that I had two eyes, as well as noting their colour, he rated my vision as 20/20 – an A-grade rating and well above the standard required to shoot anyone.

This was the first test I can ever remember passing and, moreover, it was with Distinction! However, I was pleased my name wasn't down for brain surgery with this bloke. Seventy years later I can still smell the whisky fumes that puffed out with every wheezy breath and permeated every pore of his well-pickled skin. With the eye test more than satisfactorily concluded, we moved on to Phase Two.

'Right lad, strip off, good good. Hop on the scales, good, good. Right now, umm, bend over – right over – good good. Turn around, face me, good good, breathe-in-out-in-out, mouth wide, say ah-h-h, good good.'

Then, to my alarm, he grabbed my balls, and weighing one against the other said 'Cough – again – good good, now sit down, cross your legs', and, with that, whack! He hit my knee with a hammer, and almost took a bow for the reaction it achieved.

With a final 'Good good – excellent excellent', I was allowed to get dressed and that was that. The ordeal was over. I'd passed with flying colours and been declared medically A1, fit to be a soldier in the King's army.

The medical examination to get into the army was a slapdash affair, unlike those conducted today if you are a veteran and trying to gain a service pension from a supposedly grateful government. Provided a potential recruit had two arms, two legs and one arsehole, which was inspected at disconcertingly close quarters, he was in, and it was a 'Well done. Good on yer mate. Have fun. Kill a Hun'.

In those grim days, when things looked crook on the war front and we were being hammered good and proper, almost anyone who turned up at the Town Hall recruitment centre was accepted with open arms. A pyramid full of Egyptian mummies could have passed that medical in 1941. Anyone knocked back as medically unfit must have been really bloody crook.

By the time the doc had finished with me it was way past time for morning tea, but there was one final stop in the Joining-the-Army Production Line. After receiving our army numbers – VX60083 for me and VX60084 for Phil, as he was behind me in the line – we were marched, for want of a better word, into a book-lined room with about eighteen others to participate in what we were informed was a Swearing of the Oath Ceremony.

After the usual 'let them wait a while for impression's sake' interval, in strode a giant of an officer. The sergeant, who had tried to march us in, let forth with a mighty 'TEN HUN', so loud and unexpected that we almost jumped out of our skins. The results were not good, not pleasing, and it was hinted that we had a lot to learn, as the officer gazed towards the ceiling. So we shuffled about, a few turning right, the others left. The rest stayed where they were.

Red in the face, the sergeant muttered that we were 'a bloody disgrace', saluted The Brass, did a double shuffle-cum-tap dance, came to attention and shouted 'All PRESENT AND CORRECT, SIR'. The giant roared back 'RIGHT SERGEANT. AT EASE MEN', while staring down at us from his great height.

This bloke was a sight to behold. He was army personified, from his bootlaces to the top of his peaked cap. Rows of gongs from the Boer and the Great War covered his chest, while his brown leather Sam Browne belt looked only just strong enough to support the cannon-like revolver at his waist. Holding a bible aloft, he growled that he was about to swear us in, as Soldiers of the Crown. Pausing, he concentrated his radar-like eyes on each of us in turn and said, 'Now hear this and listen good, while I explain to you lot some of the more important facts of ARMY LIFE, the ONLY life that will matter to any of you, from now on in.'

He then listed, in no uncertain terms, the many things for which we could be hung, drawn and quartered. His welcoming speech finally concluded, he looked sternly at me, Phil and one or two other young blokes and said, 'Some of you jokers look rather young, under-age even. Now you may think that you can fool the army and get away with it. Be warned. You will be the fool if you do, so now is the time to consider your crime. NOW is the time to fall out. After I've sworn you in it will be too late. Time will have run out. You will, without doubt, do TIME in GAOL.'

Throughout this tirade it seemed to us that he had grown at least another foot in height, as well as a couple of horns, and we had shrunk, midgets all. It was now that I understood the true meaning of the expression 'a breathless hush'.

Following his intimidating threat, a ripple of apprehension spread across our little band, followed by silence so absolute it amplified out of all proportion each breath we took. If someone made a sound, no matter how insignificant, it echoed round the room, inviting fierce frowns to be directed at the culprit, with devastating effect.

Eyes that had held steady and strong gradually weakened. No longer staring boldly straight ahead, they turned shifty and anxious. Throats, bone dry from the fear of betraying any sign of a guilty conscience, gulped and gagged, vibrating

Adam's apples that toggled between chins and collars.

Bodies, stiff with the strain of maintaining a relaxed and innocent front, broke under the pressure. Some began to twitch. Others were suddenly afflicted with bouts of nervous coughing. Suddenly, and to our complete surprise, out from the front line stepped a bloke, who, if someone had been running a book, we would have backed as being one of the elders of the bunch. He certainly looked the part in his snappy sports jacket, pork pie hat and black pump shoes, not to mention his confident, knowing air.

'Please sir', he sobbed, 'I'm only seventeen.' And with scarlet face and tear-brimmed eyes he scarpered, leaving us staring in startled surprise at his hastily retreating figure.

There were no other confessions. At long last it was over.

To get a feed we said 'My Oath
We will serve the King' – us both.
The officer said, 'Well done you chaps!'
While the corporal snarled, 'Yer stupid saps!'

Despite the pep talk and scrutiny from the senior officer, Phil had chosen the best booth in Melbourne to enlist. At Royal Park Depot the recruiting staff were far more diligent than those at the Town Hall. They not only rejected anyone who could not produce a birth certificate, but also took action against those who sought to put their ages up. On 30 May, The Argus *had reported:*

> The problem of boys overstating their ages for both the AIF and home defence units is creating considerable embarrassment at Royal Park Recruit Depot. Their splendid physique frequently enables them to enlist, but production of birth certificates between enlistment and embarkation brings their discharge. This causes serious waste and inconvenience to the Army. A warning was issued yesterday that action would be taken against youths who gave incorrect age.

The warning had no effect on some young hopefuls. On 30 August, a month after Billy enlisted, The Argus *reported:*

> He was only a boy. Anyone could see that – and the officers at the Royal Park Depot yesterday said so – to themselves – as a fresh-faced young Australian strode in and confidently tossed his enlistment papers on to the counter.
>
> They showed his age as 18, but the practised eye of an officer told him otherwise.
>
> I'm afraid', he said, 'that we'll have to see a copy of your birth certificate. You

can get it at the Government Statist's office, in the Titles Office building.'

The boy departed to return in a few minutes for further directions. Then realising that his bluff had failed, he confessed his correct age as 16.

'Go home, son. The Army can't do anything for you', said the officer, and after the boy had left, 'They're as game as Ned Kelly, but we can't take them'.

There was no warning this time in the newspaper about the folly of trying to enlist if under age. Instead, the article ended on a high and positive note, and one that was sure to stir other youths to test the system. The paper reported that the room was full of AIF recruits and returned soldiers, enlisting in garrison battalions, who 'admired the boy's' courage'.

We were in the army now, honest-to-goodness soldiers. Signed up on the dotted line, witnessed, signed, sealed and delivered. What a bargain we had negotiated! Three square meals and five bob a day, an extra bob for deferred pay, and another two bob a day if posted overseas, plus untold numbers of officers, sergeants, corporals and lance corporals to take care of every need. What more could one ask for?

We were trucked to Royal Park Barracks, which was next door to the Boys' Home, from which we had so recently absconded. Our reception, however, was not what we expected. From every side, blokes showing off in their brand-new uniforms bombarded us with a derisive 'You'll be sorry'. This catch-cry soon became reality with the arrival of far more menacing types with stripes of authority on their shoulders, yelling out all kinds of orders that served only to add to our confusion. To further dampen any enthusiasm, we discovered that the cookhouse was closed. The cupboard, like Mother Hubbard's, was bare. The cook had left, selfish bugger, without so much as a single thought for his newly signed-up, starving brothers-in-arms.

At long last, someone took pity on us and some grub arrived: two large white basins of left-over snags and mashed potatoes and a jug of gravy, salvaged from the Sergeants' Mess. Told to 'Hoe in', Phil and I did so, and with gusto. The rest of the mob, a bunch of soft city-slickers, turned up their noses at what they called 'Bloody army pig-swill'. As there were no other takers, we scoffed the lot. Our appetites were more than up to the task, to the amazement of the others, who stood around watching, open-mouthed.

'Army swill', they cried, and stepped aside.
But we two blokes gobbled the lot.
Which only goes to show, you know,
You're either hungry, or you're not.

That feed at Royal Park ranks high on my list of top ten memorable feasts. Many a time I have rehashed and savoured it, especially to my mates in the prison camps during the hungry years of captivity. But I am getting ahead of myself, and it is just as well that I had no idea of the lean years that were yet to come.

The first night was 'under canvas'. For someone who, apart from the little holiday at the Boys' Home, had been riding a bike around the countryside for weeks, it was bliss. We slept in pyjamas, between soft woollen blankets, on a palliasse filled with fresh straw. Cosy and warm, with a full stomach, I was certainly, and definitely, NOT sorry.

Here with a full tummy, beneath a tent,
A cup of tea, and you pay no rent.
Me, sorry?
No flamin' way.
Army life is heaven-sent.

Phil, who had taken heed of the discussions overheard at the recruiting office, decided he no longer wanted to be at the pointy end of the war and put his hand up for a transport job, after telling them he could drive a tractor. So we shook hands, said goodbye and I haven't seen or heard from him since.

Over the next week or so I wandered around the camp alone, absolutely skint and with nowhere to go. Then along came Pay Day. I'd never seen so much money. It was a Hip-Hip-Hooray kind of day. A Red-Letter-Day-of-Plenty.

The sergeant counted 35 shillings into my trembling hands. In a daze, I made my way to the canteen, whose windows I'd been gazing into longingly. I bought two ounces of Wild Woodbine Ready-cut Tobacco, some cigarette papers, a bag of boiled lollies and a *Phantom* comic book.

Alas, as I made my way back to my tent, I heard a siren's call, and was foolishly enticed to a game of swy, or two-up.

Come and play the army game of swy
Two-up's the call, two-up's the cry
Let's get set in the guts before we go
Come on mates, we need your dough.
The centre's set, get set on the side,
Come in spinner, see the pennies skied.

I want four bob in the guts to go.
Four bob in the guts, gets ya dough.
Four bob in the guts, is the cry.

Four bob in the guts in the middle sees them fly,
Sidies set on this game of swy.
Come in spinner and send them high.

Up and away, over crowded heads, way above the circle of eager players, spun two bright copper pennies. As every eye watched their progress, heads tilted back, the coins did a final upward spin and spiralled back down.

'Heads! Heads it is, you little bloody bewdy! We'll let it ride.'

'Eight bob' was now the cry.

Two-up

I did my dough, every last penny, and for the next fortnight I mooched aimlessly around, absolutely and totally stony broke. But I still had my smokes, my comic book and my bag of lollies, along with as much food as I could eat and pudding almost every day. Life was good, but not perfect. We had no uniforms. Without one, we were sneered at constantly by those who had, and had to pay full fare on the trams.

After a week or two of existing in a frustrating half-way house dressed in civvies – no longer a civilian, and not quite a soldier – we were at last fitted out with our army clobber. Hobnailed boots, woollen socks, woollen serge tunic, pants, slouch hat, mess gear and shaving tackle. All brand new and all khaki. We were now able to join the throng at the gates and yell 'You'll be sorry' to each new batch of recruits, and to shake our heads and remark 'Not a chance in hell of making soldiers out of that mob, Sarge', as the new men made the usual hash of forming up and numbering off.

We had not been issued with any weapons, so had to use wooden broomsticks to practise our bayonet charges. We were supposed to get ourselves all worked up as we charged the Hun, but it was hard to get enthusiastic about killing a straw-

Billy in his brand new uniform

filled sack with a wooden stick. Things became a great deal better when I became the proud owner of a gun – sorry, rifle. With it came the promise of some bullets, if and when I graduated to the lofty rank of a 'proper soldier'.

In order to achieve this, the army imposed hours and hours of 'bayonet practice': not on the training circuit but in the flamin' cookhouse, on tubs and tubs of flamin' potatoes. An army marches on its stomach, and I can confirm it does – a stomach full of spuds. I know, because later on I helped peel tons and tons of the rotten things. It was actually punishment for discharging my rifle without permission, during a night-time exercise – the highlight of our training – when we were supposed to be sneaking around, undetected, in search of our enemy.

We'd started off all right and, loaded down with dummy hand grenades and blanks in our rifles, it was almost for real. Silence, boldness and enterprise, we were told, were the keys to success in battle, along with our training. Following the leader, we'd counted the 1000 paces along a prescribed compass bearing, and then changed direction for another 800. It was all going along so well, a piece of cake, until I tripped over my own feet and dropped my rifle, which went off with a bang. Out popped a ball of fire which, in the pitch darkness, gave away our position to the enemy. They ambushed us from all sides, showering us with debris from their blanks and the double-bungers tossed by their bombardiers.

I'd always wanted to know if blanks really fired. I now knew that they did, and that I had wrecked the exercise. Lieutenant Tranter, who was not at all pleased, placed me under open arrest and confined me to camp to peel spuds. I also got to know every inch of ground inside the camp, from walking around on what the army called 'emu parades', bobbing up and down picking up every scrap of litter.

Eventually, and with great ceremony, we were given real ammunition for our rifles – two bullets, along with the order to look after 'em. We then went out to a paddock to see if they worked. They did, and it's about the only time I fired a rifle during training, other than in a small competition that was held.

With our two bullets fired, at long last there was movement in the camp. On 6 August we piled into the backs of canvas-covered trucks and were off, far into the hills and way beyond, to the Bacchus Marsh Training Camp. It was out there, miles from anywhere, in the freezing, hilly wilds, that we began our crash course in soldiering. Keen to make the grade, 'soldiering on' became the catch-cry of our draft. The countryside around Bacchus Marsh echoed with the sounds of our soldiering, and the hills with the rhythm of our marching boots – left, right, left, right. 'Not that right, Private Young, the other right!'

On we went, charging up hill and down dale, forming fours with right and left wheels, until the sergeant called a halt and we were allowed to go home. We had just about got this stuff down pat when they brought in a new set of regulations. Forming in fours was out. Forming in threes was in. Changing from fours to threes was destined to create a right cock-up. But then what wasn't? After all, it was the army.

Happy hour came with washing dishes
And carrying out our sergeant's wishes
Forming fours in close order drill
Marching to our corporal's shrill
Left right, left right, left those feet!
Miles to go and we're bloody near beat.

Day after day we soldiered on until we were drilled and skilled in the art of warfare; straining and training until, just five weeks later, we were deemed worthy enough to be posted to the 3rd Reinforcements of the 29th Infantry Battalion of the 27th Brigade of the 8th Australian Division, 2nd Australian Imperial Force, which was about to be sent 'somewhere overseas'. Rugged up in heavy thick winter uniforms, greatcoats, balaclavas, long johns, woolly socks, the lot, we were more than a match for anything the Eskimos faced. Trained to withstand the onslaught of Arctic blizzards, we were then sent to Singapore!

A work detail that included me was sent to Port Melbourne to help load the troopship *Marnix*, which sailed for Singapore with the bulk of the 2/29th. Shortly afterwards, the 3rd Reinforcements were given pre-embarkation leave. I was asked where I wanted to go when I picked up my leave pass and travel warrant, but I just said Melbourne, worried that if I went home to Tassie my Nana might dob and the army would find out my real age and kick me out. However, I didn't know anyone in Melbourne and after a few days got so lonely I thought I'd chance my luck and go and see the family in Hobart. I had just enough money left from my leave pay for a passage on the Bass Strait ferry *Tarooma*, but that was all.

Disembarking at Devonport, I jumped on the night train heading south and nicked into the toilet to evade the conductor. I shouldn't have bothered. With a line of impatient blokes queued up along the corridor, all dying for a pee and bashing on the door and demanding to know what the hell I was doing in there, I was discovered by the conductor, who laughed and told me not to worry. However, he warned me to hop off at Glenorchy, as the stationmaster at New Town was a bugger of a bloke. It wasn't far to walk, only a mile or so. As Nana's house backed onto the railway line, I walked along the tracks and hopped over the back fence, only to find the house in total darkness. Everyone was in bed, including Uncle Cocky who was sound asleep on the back verandah, snoring his head off. Although he was pleased to see me, he and wasn't all that thrilled to be woken up at 2 am.

Cocky was sure that Nana, who had frogmarched my under-age dad off the ship, would dob me in, but she surprised us all. Maybe she realised that she was to blame for Dad running away and taking up with a Catholic, and she didn't want me to run off as well. Nana called a family conference in the kitchen, from which I was excluded. I could hear the rumble of the conversation but try as I might I couldn't hear what was being said. Finally, after what seemed an age, they agreed that the army might be the making of me. My Uncle Dougie, who gave me the verdict, passed the hat around and he and his brothers provided enough money to get me back to Melbourne.

On returning to camp we were met by a very excited 'Pat' Green, a popular cove who, to his and our disappointment, had missed the cut for the 3rd Reinforcements. He could hardly wait to tell us that he would be coming with us, after all. Pat told us that some rat had deserted the ship, and that he was taking his place. He didn't have time for final leave, because he had to race off and get his vaccinations, but he was raring to go.

Pat's real name was William Claude Green. A timber worker from Swan Hill, in far western Victoria, he turned 29 on the day the 3rd Reinforcements sailed. He had enlisted three weeks before Billy. The bulk of the battalion, composed almost entirely of Victorians, had sailed with 27 Australian Brigade in early August 1941. Billy, William Green and the 3rd Reinforcements did not leave until 17 September.

One of those selected to sail with the reinforcements, but had deserted, was Billy's erstwhile companion, Phillip Patrick Barker, who did not succeed in his quest to join a transport company. Although they were at the same training camp, Billy did not see him again as Barker took leave without pay almost immediately after enlistment. When he returned to Albert Park Depot he was sent to 6 Training Battalion, but in a different squad from Billy, who was at a more advanced stage of training. Five weeks later Barker deserted, after learning that he had been posted to the 2/29th's 3rd Reinforcements and was to sail for Singapore in five days.

Phillip Barker on his first enlisment

He remained at large but, in early January 1942, and now supposedly 21 years old, he reversed his given names and re-enlisted as Patrick Phillip Barker, nominating his mother Molly his next of kin: same recruiting office, same birth date, same place of birth, but a new occupation – timber worker – and a brand new army number. Sixteen days later he again deserted. On 9 March, while on the run, he enlisted for a third time, possibly in an attempt to avoid payment of considerable and steadily mounting fines and inevitable punishment. For Enlistment 3 he reverted to his original occupation, press hand, but otherwise his personal details were as for Enlistment 2. This time, he was posted to a Pioneer Battalion. Evidently he liked it no better than the infantry, lasting just eighteen days before he once more went AWL. He was declared an illegal absentee and three days later, on 29 April, was arrested by the military police. When the army, which had given him another new number, realised who he was, he was fined yet again, and sent to Bendigo for a month's detention.

After his release he lasted almost two weeks before absenting himself again. Over the next few weeks he went AWL five times, before being declared an illegal absentee in early August. During this latter period he and two others were arrested for housebreaking and stealing. They appeared before Judge McIndoe for sentencing in the General Sessions Court on 3 September.

One of Barker's accomplices, who had joined the army under a false name, had a similarly undistinguished military career. As he was of age, the judge sent him to Pentridge Gaol. Barker, not yet 21, was dispatched to a Reformatory where he was detained at the governor's pleasure.

Barker was released in mid-1944. The army, however, backdated his discharge to 11 November 1942. His accomplice, who had been sentenced under his real name, had been located in the interim and identified by the military. He was escorted from gaol, under guard, to be formally discharged in June 1944. After having his papers stamped with 'Discharged on account of Misconduct or Discreditable Service', he was taken back to prison to finish his sentence.

Loaded up with all our gear, and with an excited Pat Green nursing a sore arm after his vaccinations, we took the train to Sydney. The long journey was uneventful apart from an accident when Ernest Chetkett, known as Checkie, who had joined up the same day as me, managed to break his hand when it collided with a pole while he was waving from the train window. He had to wait until we got to Sydney to receive proper medical attention. To my surprise, the train didn't terminate at Central Railway Station, but took a branch line all the way to the docks at Pyrmont, where we boarded the small Dutch vessel, SS *Sibajak*, to take us to Singapore.

The ship didn't go on its own, of course, especially not across the Indian Ocean where German raiders were knocking off merchant shipping. In our little four-ship convoy we also had *Aquitania*, a good-sized ocean liner; *Marnix*, which had returned from Singapore after delivering the rest of the 29th, and HMAS *Adelaide*, our naval escort. Somewhere off the south-western coast of Victoria, *Adelaide* handed us over to the pride of the Australian fleet, HMAS *Sydney*.

As we crossed the Great Australian Bight we ran into one of the wildest

SS *Sibajak*

storms our ship's captain had ever experienced. Nearly everyone was seasick. *Marnix* and *Aquitania* were undamaged, but almost all the crockery on our ship was smashed, and *Sydney* needed running repairs to a turret. When *Sibajak* and *Sydney* unexpectedly docked at Fremantle, nine days after leaving Sydney, we were fortunate enough to be given a day's leave while the crew got things straightened out and repaired. I hadn't been at all sick, and couldn't wait to get ashore, but Pat had to stay on board as he was still feeling crook.

He, and the poor blighters on *Aquitania* and *Marnix*, both anchored offshore, certainly missed out on a great welcome. With the officers and crew from *Sydney* leading, we marched along the streets, basking in the glow as hundreds of people clapped and cheered. The people of Fremantle were very hospitable and I was taken under the wing of a lovely couple, who had a son and a very pretty, fair-haired daughter about my age, whose name I forget, so I'll call her Beryl. We had a picnic in the park and then walked around town to see the sights, with Beryl holding my hand and her dad keeping an eye on both of us to make sure that's all it was. Her parents wanted to know all about me, so I told them about the family in Hobart, that my dad had died in the Spanish civil war, and about my heroic bike trip all the way from Sydney to the South Australian border, taking care to edit out the not-so-good bits. Of course, I didn't say anything about how I ended up in the Boys' Home, or that I had run away and joined the army and was way under age.

After saying goodbye to the family and to Beryl, who gave me her address and promised to write, I returned to the ship on a bit of a high. I thought I might be in love and the next morning woke up thinking about her. I was wondering if I would ever see her again when a mate told me to take a look out the porthole. I did, and saw that hundreds of coves, who had decided to extend their holiday, were squeezing out the portholes like rats deserting a ship. The tide had dropped, and the cabins were now below the wharf. By grabbing one of the barnacled, slime-covered piles, it was possible to clamber along the wharf substructure, out of sight of the topside guards. A couple of old blokes from the last war were on duty at the gate, but they just waved us through, telling us to take care we were back before the ship sailed.

I joined a mob of NSW blokes from 2/30 Battalion, who made a beeline for the nearest pub. I got out my bit of paper with Beryl's address, but the barmaid said it was way out in the sticks. I made an attempt to get there, but in the end gave up. It was all a bit hard – and there was also the matter of what her father might say if I just turned up. So I spent the remainder of the afternoon until the pubs shut at six, mooning over what might have been and getting progressively more under the weather, as the older fellas teased that they hoped I had behaved myself and not made my new-found love pregnant. Pregnant? I had hardly any experience with girls, just taken one to the flicks while living at Woolloomooloo, but even I knew you didn't make babies by holding hands!

We found a place near the docks to have a feed and were sitting there trying to sober up when someone yelled 'Hey! The ship's leaving!' We tore off to the docks, but it was too late. The vessel was out in the harbour, and there was no way we could sneak back on now. To make sure that everyone who had gone ashore without permission was caught, the captain had slipped the moorings and anchored about 800 yards out, leaving the miscreants stranded and with no option but to get in the launches thoughtfully provided by the provos for transfer back to the ship.

Given the terrible sea voyage we had endured, I thought it was only fair to have extra time to recover, but the army didn't. We all received a severe lecture for our supposedly 'unsoldierly-like behaviour', which I think showed initiative and was pretty typical of Aussie diggers. On top of that, for 'breaking ship' and being AWL for ten hours and thirty minutes, I was fined three pounds, which was the equivalent of twelve days' pay. I was lucky it wasn't more. A roll call had been held at noon, but I'd nicked off at about 9 am. Unlike some of the other overstayers, I didn't lose any seniority because, as a private, I didn't have any.

We were just out of Fremantle when Pat Green was carted off to the ship's hospital. He was not seasick after all. We were not told much, only that he had meningitis, and was very seriously ill.

Pat was suffering from a severe brain inflammation, but it was not meningitis, as Billy and his mates were told. He had post-vaccinal encephalitis, a complication from his smallpox vaccination. The odds of contracting encephalitis in this way are 1 in 110 000.

Symptoms, which include vomiting, appear from seven to twenty-one days after vaccination. In Pat's case, due to his last-minute posting to replace the deserter, this time frame put the ship in the Great Australian Bight, at the height of a storm, when he first became ill. Early diagnosis would not have helped. There is still no effective therapy for post-vaccinal encephalitis, and survival rate is only 50 per cent.

Two days later, we were west of Broome on 1 October when an officer came down to our berths and said Pat's mates had better come quick smart as he was fading fast. There was nothing that could be done to save him, and he died shortly afterwards. As we were in the middle of the ocean, we had to bury him at sea. The ship stopped its engines. The water was very calm and clear and the only sound was the slap of the water against the hull.

Pat's body had been sewn into a weighted canvas shroud, and we stood in silence as it slithered down a board held over the side of the railing, and slipped beneath the surface with barely a splash. The padre conducted the burial service using the C of E Book of Common Prayer. He said a special prayer about committing Pat's body to the deep, but as I leaned over the railing, watching it zig-zag into the depths I was not too sure how the next bits, 'in sure and certain hope of the resurrection', and that 'the sea would give up her dead' (when the time came), were supposed to work.

Ah, the resilience of youth! With the ceremony over, and poor Pat consigned to the depths, any fleeting thoughts we may have had in regard to our own mortality were pushed aside, to be replaced by the thrill of anticipation of what was to come. To amuse ourselves over the next few days, some blokes set up a gambling school in the ship's saloon. We all felt flush with funds because, just after we left Fremantle, the purser had converted our money into Singapore dollars, with each dollar worth about five shillings.

On the second night, I had a really good run of luck and won nearly twenty dollars playing heads-and-tails dice, which was beaut because I was three quid (about twelve dollars) in the red with my AWL fine. Feeling lucky, I joined a poker game and won a few hands. I was thinking of taking my winnings and running, while I was still ahead, when I was dealt three fours. I put in my stake of a dollar, discarded the other card, and bought two. One was the fourth four.

I and a couple of blokes from Queensland, who looked and played like cardsharps, raised the stakes until the pool reached $60. Two players folded, leaving just four of us. I hardly dared breathe. Because the stakes were getting so high, the game had attracted quite a crowd and the tension was terrific. I held firm, clutching my four fours to my chest. Then one of the card shark blokes lost his nerve, said 'I'll see yer', and lay down his cards.

My hand was better than his, and the next bloke's, and the next. My four fours beat them all! As the place erupted, I scooped up my winnings, all $117 (almost 30 quid), and called it a day. True to form, when I went shopping in the canteen I bought lollies, comics and proper, tailor-made cigarettes, which we 'roll-yer-owns' could rarely afford.

As we sailed further north and it became progressively warmer, we could hardly contain our excitement to be on the high seas, being sent 'overseas'. For most of my generation, going off to war was about our only chance of experiencing the adventure and the delights of foreign travel. And now, here I was, aged just fifteen, travelling the same road as those other great travellers – Bing Crosby, Bob Hope and Dorothy Lamour – The Road to Singapore.

The Road to Singapore, *released in 1940, was the first of a popular series of comedy films, starring comedians Bing Crosby, Bob Hope and pin-up girl, Dorothy Lamour. Often referred to as 'The Road Movies', they combined adventure, comedy, romance and music. The minimal plot line was secondary to the wise-cracking gags, said to have been ad-libbed by Hope and Crosby during filming. The highly successful* Road to Singapore *was followed by the* Roads to Zanzibar, Morocco, Utopia, Rio, Bali *and* Hong Kong.

As the ship threaded her way through the mass of small islands just off Singapore, boys from the fishing villages swam out to dive for the pennies we chucked overboard. We were puzzled why so many had bits of their limbs missing until we learned that sharks had bitten them off. With this rather interesting introduction to Singapore, we were looking forward to going ashore but, to our dismay, there was no time for any sightseeing. Our mob was no sooner on dry land than we found ourselves being trucked from Keppel Harbour and right across the island to the General Base Depot at Johor Bahru in Malaya, via the causeway that links Johor State with Singapore Island. The AIF training camp at JB, as we called Johor Bahru, was on the outskirts of Tampoi village. We were allowed to visit it during our free time, and to take our Kodak Box Brownie cameras to record the scenes for posterity. The most photographed feature in Tampoi by far was a soft-drink factory in an old, unpainted timber structure with a huge sign announcing that it housed the Fook Heng Cordial Company.

It wasn't the sign that put me right off any thought of sexual activity. Not that I'd ever had any. The closest I'd come to any kind of physical contact with a girl was holding hands with Beryl. The sex lectures by the medical officers were not about how to make babies, or even how to prevent making them. They assumed everyone knew about that. Their sex lectures were far more basic – how to avoid contracting venereal disease which, as far as I could make out, was so contagious you could catch it from a toilet seat. The MO's lectures were fairly graphic but it was picket duty at the brothels, which were filthy and rife with disease, that really made an impact. As if the smell and sight of the girls offering their wares amid the dirt and grime of Tampoi's back lanes was not bad enough, there were also lurid, live sex shows, which some of the patrons joined in. All pretty confronting to a naïve fifteen-year-old boy.

I may have been raised in a pretty tough part of Sydney, where petty theft and scams were common, but the people who lived there were actually quite prudish. If there were any brothels, I certainly didn't know about them. Poor as they were, the people in our neighbourhood believed that 'manners maketh man'. Kids were taught to mind their Ps and Qs, to treat women with courtesy and to respect their elders, even if we didn't agree with them. No man could swear in front of any female and get away with it, and we'd never think of calling anyone older than us by their first names. It was always Mr This and Mrs That or, if we knew them well, Uncle This and Aunty That. If you ever forgot your manners, you were liable to get a clip over the ear.

Well away from the tawdry fleshpots of Tampoi, I discovered a river and a beautiful little bay with a small timber jetty. It wasn't far from camp so, after a training session in what they termed the 'bull ring', we'd race off to the river, drape our clothes over the sign 'Swimming Forbidden by Order of Army Command', and dive in.

We were splashing about one day, having a great time, when one of the cockatoos yelled 'Provos!' No one wanted to mess with the military police, so we were out of the water like a shot. Grabbing our clothes, we ran across the lawns of a large garden. We were so busy trying to dress and to put as much distance between us and the law that we failed to notice, until it was too late, that we were surrounded by people with deformed limbs and horribly puckered skin. It wasn't until we reached the ornate iron gates on the way out that we saw the sign – Johor Bahru Leper Colony. We spent the next couple of weeks constantly examining our skin for the tiniest blemish or spot, convinced that leprosy was contagious, which it wasn't.

The unfortunate lepers were the first of many surprises. In those first few weeks we were allowed to spend some leave in Singapore, where I was constantly wide-eyed, mouth agape, amazed at the wonder of it all. Everything was so different, so exotically foreign. The people acted foreign, looked foreign, smelt foreign, and talked in foreign tongues. What a conglomeration of different races

– Malay, Chinese, Indian, Burmese, Siamese. What an assortment of movement and colour to gladden the eye. The only people I came across who weren't foreign were Europeans just like us – 'white men' descended from a mixture of Anglo-Saxon, Scottish, Irish and Welsh.

Back then Singapore was not the metropolis it is today. No matter where I looked there was something different to see: the great swathes of grass, cut by chocolate-skinned Indian workers wielding long-bladed scythes – unhurriedly and with rhythmic grace, like a kind of ballet in slow motion; rickshaws clattering past; monkeys chattering in the trees; Indian soldiers in immaculate turbans; coolies wearing nothing more than a G-string or loincloth; people with no shoes, and others with clumpy platform thongs made of wood. Along the streets were countless food vendors, selling all kinds of meat on skewers, bean soup, little packets containing sticky rice, and drinks dispensed from huge jars.

The drinks were a great disappointment – sickly sweet and lukewarm, as there was no form of refrigeration – so we wandered off to one of the amusement parks. We had expected it to be like Luna Park at home, but although there were rides there were also outdoor Chinese theatres and ballrooms where, for the price of a ticket, you could have a dance with a beautiful Asian or Eurasian girl. There was no hanky-panky allowed, however. Each of the girls, known as Taxi Dancers (probably because, like a taxi, they were hired) had a fierce-looking female chaperone, who made sure that the only physical activity undertaken was dancing, on the dance floor.

We thought we were onto something good when we came across an open-sided marquee, with low tables set for dining and nice plump cushions instead of seats. We had no sooner settled back, waiting for someone to take our orders, when a Pommy officer came by and said, 'I say, old chaps, I think you've got the wrong place. This is a private wedding.' Oh yikes!

Gee, if only things had continued in the same way as those first delightful months of discovery, what a nice comfortable war it would have been. The five bob a day that had evaporated so fast back home had three times the buying power locally and was a veritable fortune. We were like our rich Yankee cousins – big spenders in a poor man's economy. Cigarettes and beer, so vitally essential to life, were unbelievably cheap – one cent bought a packet of Flag brand cigarettes – while store-bought food and clothes, along with entertainment and transport, cost very little.

What a transition it was for me: an under-educated, under-disciplined orphan, but now over-awed and over there. To be on the receiving end of such bounty; to be actually paid the princely sum of five shillings every day, come what may, with Saturdays and Sundays thrown in for good measure, with full board and lodging and free transport to a battlefield of our nation's choice, was absolutely unbelievable.

I was growing up fast. On the first Tuesday in November, I turned sixteen. It was also Melbourne Cup Day. Checkie, my mate who had broken his hand waving out the train window, cleaned up in the sweep when Skipton won the Cup. Although I had bought presents to send home with what was left of my $117 poker win, I still had some left to join a game of two-up down by the main gate. We played sudden death, using three pennies, and I spun eleven heads in a row. If it had been payday, which was Wednesday, the betting would have been heavier and I'd have won a motza. Even so, with Checkie's cup winnings and my little windfall, we had plenty to celebrate my birthday.

We went into the village for a meal, and ended up getting full as farts. 'Lights out' found us staggering around in the dark – lost, outside the camp, out of bounds, and AWL. We woke the next morning in the guardhouse, wishing with heart and soul and roaring headaches that we hadn't woken up at all. The guards told us that, after we had roused half the camp trying to crawl under the perimeter wire, they had found us trying to walk down a line of slit trenches. This revelation went some way towards explaining the cuts and bruises, but did nothing for the hangover. We were then lectured on the stupidity of our actions, and to add insult to injury were each fined a fiver (five pounds, or three weeks' pay) plus seven days CB (confined to barracks).

I even managed to blot my copybook when stone-cold sober. For a visit scheduled by our Commanding Officer, Major General Gordon Bennett, I was assigned to the honour guard. The army likes snappy moves and in order to make 'present arms' even more snappy had devised a little trick of pulling the cartridge clip out a short distance so that, when your hand came round on the order of 'present arms', you hit the clip, which then popped back in and made a satisfying sound. Except mine didn't. When I brought my hand up, the clip fell out and rolled along the ground. The general, being an officer and a gentleman, pretended not to notice, but the sergeant major did. I got two more weeks' CB.

It's hard to believe, but I was actually sober when I tried my next stunt. I was in the tent, lying on my charpoy (a kind of Indian bed), when a mate came in and gave himself a tattoo, using a darning needle pushed through a cork, and a bottle of Indian ink. It looked like a good idea, so I thought I'd give it a go. Being right-handed, the easiest and least painful place to do it was my left forearm. I managed my regimental number, and was about to add 'AIF' when my thoughts turned to Beryl and I decided to do a portrait of a girl instead. The pain was too

Major General Bennett inspecting reinforcements from Billy's group

much, though, and I only managed the outline of the hair and forehead before I gave up. I've still got it, but as the skin on my arm is no longer smooth and tight as it was in my youth it's a bit hard now to tell what it is.

In no time at all we were acclimatised and familiarised as our bodies tanned, and expanded, under the tropical sun. However, with no sign yet of any action, and thousands of miles from the front line in Africa, where we hoped to be sent, it didn't take long for disenchantment to set in, despite having regular leave. Drilled and marched along miles of jungle paths and through countless rubber plantations (taking care not to damage any of Mr Dunlop's trees), we trained, toughened up and prepared. For what? To be ready to take our place, as proper fighting soldiers, with strategies in place, and movements planned to the last detail, in case the Japanese attacked – not that anyone actually expected they would dare to do such a thing.

We had been brainwashed by our superiors about the invincibility of our positions, about the strength of the Allied armies, the poor quality of our potential enemy, the inferiority of their eyesight and equipment, and the readiness of our forward lines in the northern part of Malaya. Any seaborne attack, we were assured, would be thwarted by the array of great naval guns on Singapore Island. Their long steel-grey barrels, disguised with camouflage nets, covered the shipping lanes to Singapore, daring any nation that might have the nerve or cheek to even think about attacking to just try it on and take the consequences. Singapore was not called invincible for nothing and the big guns stood at the ready, ready to reinforce the message.

The Japanese heeded the warning. Instead of trying to batter down the front door, they crept in by the back, down tar-sealed roads so thoughtfully constructed by the pre-war British administration through the otherwise impenetrable jungles and vast rubber plantations.

> *Steel fingers jutting, across the bay*
> *Grey barrels fixed, accurate lay,*
> *Awaiting an enemy, and, come what may.*
> *Alas! The enemy came, the other way.*

The Japanese cut their way through the Allied defence with an ease that made complete asses out of the politicians and generals who for years had based Singapore's defence on the assumption that any threat would come from the sea. Our generals were old soldiers from another, older war, filled with old ideas, old prejudices and ongoing rivalries, where jealousy reigned and ignorance ruled. They were Yesterday's men, overcome by, and unable to cope with, events of Today.

Fortress Singapore was certainly ready for any attack from the sea, as was the southern part of Malaya, whose eastern beaches had been heavily mined and wired by Australian troops. However, in the early morning of 8 December 1941, an hour or so before Pearl Harbor was attacked, a Japanese invasion fleet steamed to Kota Bharu in the far north-east of Malaya, where landing craft were guided inshore along a waterway near the Beach of Heavenly Passion, aided by the small lanterns of local fifth columnists.

Although the Indian troops stationed along this coastal strip, and at Malaya's other most forward defences, fought bravely and suffered huge losses, within a few hours there was virtually no air cover. What was available was no match for the enemy's vastly superior Zero fighters. Once ashore, the Japanese moved further inland, captured the airfields, and steamrolled their way down the Malay peninsula – 64 000 well-trained, battle-hardened soldiers.

They also had tanks. Scores of them.

Poor, neglected Malaya had none.

CHAPTER 4

WAR GAMES

8 December 1941 – 13 February 1942

The war came to me, and much faster than I expected, at Tampoi. I was on guard duty at the main gate of the camp, just at the back of the village and about four miles north of Johor Baru, when the planes came over. It was around midnight, and quite dark; so dark that the duty officer came out of his tent, holding up a hurricane lamp as if to help him see what was going on. He'd only just remarked that he didn't know we owned that many planes when the anti-aircraft gun positioned at our rear opened up. And that's how we realised that we were now at war with Japan. It was soon officially confirmed by Captain Lloyd, who emerged from his tent to announce the bleeding obvious: 'The balloon's gone up'. To celebrate this self-evident fact, we tied a bunch of inflated condoms to his tent pole, a gesture that he failed to appreciate.

Although Singapore had been bombed, targeting Chinatown and killing a number of civilians, we'd remained pretty relaxed at Tampoi. But the brass was no longer relaxed, and from that day on it was panic stations all round. So we rushed from here to there, and there to here, and then back to where we'd just bloody well come from. It didn't matter where we rushed as long as we were not caught standing still.

After a week or so of planes passing overhead, an occasional one-sided dogfight, and digging an interminable number of foxholes, a party of us was lined up for inspection by the CO. He must have liked what he saw, because we were given the nod and whisked off on a hush-hush mission to Segamat, about 120 miles to the north, on the border of Johor State. Our orders? To protect and defend a dam on the upper reaches of the nearby Muar River.

We did, of course, defend it most valiantly, and would've kept on defending it right to the end, if some Poms hadn't come and told us bloody colonials to 'push off quick' as we were in their territory and we had no right to be there. What a cheek, after tramping for days at a time along the edges of the dam, not knowing what kind of dangers lurked in the water. To make matters worse, I had contracted a very severe case of tinea, not just on my feet but all over my body. It was so severe that on returning to Tampoi I was admitted to 2/13 Australian General Hospital. And on New Year's Eve, too.

With all the action taking place in Malaya the hospital, originally established in St Patrick's School on Singapore Island, had moved closer to the front line and taken over a brand new mental asylum in Tampoi. The asylum wasn't quite finished, but the army had commandeered it before the mental patients had a chance to move in. Although I was hospitalised for more than a fortnight, and missed the New Year celebrations, it wasn't all bad news. Turning my bed into a makeshift table, I whiled away the nights and added to my finances by playing cards with other patients and, on one occasion, a visiting doc from 2/10 AGH, Captain John Oakeshott. Bespectacled and prematurely balding, in Civvy Street the doc had been a country GP in Lismore, New South Wales.

Captain John Oakeshott (Dr)

CHAPTER 4 War games

While Billy was in hospital at Tampoi, playing cards and awaiting discharge to the GBD for eventual posting to the battalion, the AIF went into action, far earlier than it had anticipated. For the past six weeks, and with ever-increasing confidence, the invading army had rampaged over hundreds of miles of northern and central Malaya, brushing all resistance aside. It was not until they engaged the Australian battalions of 8 Division, tasked with defending Johor State, that they encountered some real opposition. As the Japanese commander Lieutenant General Tsuji later remarked, 'the Australian 8th Division fought with bravery that we had not previously seen'.

The first to go into battle were troops of 2/30 Battalion, who pulled off a well-executed ambush at Gemas after blowing a bridge and trapping hundreds of bicycle-riding Japanese infantrymen in a road cutting. Although a large number of enemy soldiers were killed in the hail of cross-fire and grenade attacks, communication was lost with the supporting artillery when enemy troops, allowed to pass through the cutting before the trap was sprung, found and cut the signal wire linking the forward observer with the big guns, stationed far to the rear. Although the gunners were at the ready, waiting to blast the remainder of the enemy column to bits, no signal came, and the infantrymen were unable to carry out the final phase of their plan. Quickly regrouping, the Japanese recovered their momentum, and forced the defenders to hurriedly retreat.

A few days later our under-strength 2/29 Battalion (one company was deployed somewhere else) was dispatched to help take care of what was, according to British intelligence (an oxymoron if ever there was one), an enemy force of 200 that had landed near Muar. The Aussies very soon found themselves in deep trouble, dealing not with a ragtag force of 200 short-sighted Japs using antiquated equipment but with an entire Division of elite Imperial Guards, reinforced with tanks and heavy artillery. For four blood-drenched days, an uneven battle raged – 500 against an estimated 10 000.

The 2/29th was dug in at a rubber plantation about a mile from the Bakri Crossroads, awaiting the arrival of enemy troops, when a rumble was heard, followed by the unmistakeably mechanical creak of steel tank-tracks scrunching along the narrow bitumen road. Unaware that a perfect ambush had been set in a tree-lined cutting, the tanks blundered into the trap, where gunners from 4 Anti-tank Regiment reduced them to burning piles of scrap metal. Anyone who managed to flee the conflagration was cut down in murderous cross-fire from the infantrymen. But, although the ambush was brilliantly executed, with thirteen tanks destroyed, it was not enough.

The Japanese infantry pressed on, outflanking the 2/29th and setting up a roadblock ambush, which took the life of the commanding officer, Colonel Robertson. Vastly

Tank ambush, Bakri

outnumbered, what was left of the 2/29th, along with 2/19 Battalion sent to reinforce them, was forced into a desperate fighting retreat. Fending off attack after attack, and with the number of wounded mounting at an alarming rate, they finally reached the perceived safety of the village of Parit Sulong, only to find it in enemy hands and their line of retreat cut off.

In the face of unrelenting pressure, the troops fought bravely, striving valiantly to hold the enemy at bay while they waited for a show of concerted effort from Malaya Command. Alas, the anticipated relief never came. Almost encircled by a relentless foe, the beleaguered column had two options: surrender or try to slip past the blockade. Their commander, Colonel Charles Anderson, who would be awarded a Victoria Cross for gallantry, had no intention of surrendering. Slipping away in small groups, the able-bodied, supporting the wounded, made good their escape. The seriously wounded, some 100 Australians and 35 Indians, were left behind in trucks and ambulances, under the protection of a Red Cross flag. The Japanese murdered all but three of them.

The losses sustained by 2/19 and 2/29 Battalions were substantial, so much so that on 26 January both units took on hundreds of reinforcements. Some, like Billy, had been in Malaya for some months, anxiously waiting for such a moment; others had arrived just two days before.

After days of fighting, backpedalling from one impossible position to another and sustaining thousands of casualties while fighting a delaying action, the battered Allied army, which we 'reos' officially joined on 26 January, Australia Day, reached the narrow Straits of Johor. Pursued by a vastly superior enemy, the Allied forces had retreated down the entire length of Malaya and had now run out of room.

CHAPTER 4 War games

Reinforcements arrive

Now an official member of C Company, I was in a group sent to the Singapore docks to collect the reos for the 2/29th who had just arrived from Australia. I was eyeing off the new chums trudging down the gangplank when I recognised a very familiar face – Don Trewin, the lieutenant who had sentenced me to a week of spud peeling for wrecking his night exercise.

He recognised me at once. 'Good grief, Private Young, what are you doing here?'

'Saving Singapore from the Japs, sir.'

Saving Singapore – what a forlorn hope. A few days later, with the Japs hot on our heels, our only option was to abandon what was left of Malaya to the enemy, blow up the causeway and take up defensive positions on Singapore, which, according to British Prime Minister Winston Churchill, 'had to be held at all costs, and to the last man'.

If it'd been like the last war, we would have. We were very adept at digging trenches and were very well trained in the use of gas masks. We would have beaten the Japs hands down if they'd done the right thing and dug a trench right across Malaya and then tossed gas canisters at us. But they didn't. They'd moved into a new era while we were stuck in a World War I mindset. Mind you, although Malaya was a lost cause, we newcomers were confident we could do it. After all, the British had been in control of Singapore for more than a century, and in the 1930s a vast amount of time and money had been spent planning the construction of defences. The reality, however, apart from the recently completed and hideously expensive naval base, built to accommodate a non-existent Far

East Fleet, was that it was nothing but smoke and mirrors.

There were no fixed defences, at all. Nothing. Not even a strand of barbed wire. I still scratch my head over how it ever happened. Just before the war began, a highly qualified engineer, a brigadier no less, came out from England to assess the situation. He wrote a comprehensive report on the defensive position in Malaya and Singapore, pointing out all the shortcomings, of which there were many, and offering solutions to rectify the situation. It was a waste of time. No one wanted to know. According to the brass, defences were bad for civilian and military morale. The brigadier also outlined the way in which Singapore could be overrun by attacking Malaya's eastern seaboard, but the only people who took any notice of this were the Japs. Following his advice like a 'how to' manual, the blighters gained entry via the vulnerable, undefended back door.

The day before the Japs launched their attack on the island, the brigadier actually arranged for the delivery of five truckloads of barbed wire and other defensive equipment to our sector, only to have the entire consignment sent back to the British base on the immediate orders of their General Percival, the boss cocky.

On Singapore, that fingernail of land, there were supposedly 100 000 Allied troops expecting to put in train a well-rehearsed plan of defence. There wasn't one. Most of our reos, who had arrived so late in the day, had been in the army for scarcely a month. They had spent the first week being kitted out, the second at home on pre-embarkation leave and the next two at sea. They had received no training at all and many had never handled any kind of firearm before they reached the battlefield. Talk about raw recruits. Compared to them, we looked like Duntroon graduates.

I talked to some of the new blokes who, only a few short weeks before, had been fully paid-up civilians. They now found themselves thrown into the deep end, posted to our company as soon as they arrived to make up for our big losses at Muar. One had never fired a rifle, of any kind, at all, in his entire life, ever. Not even a pellet gun at rats raiding the feed in a chook-shed. He and quite a few others in the same boat were taken to the Bukit Timah Range so that our senior NCOs could show them how to load and fire their rifles. This was followed by a two-hour training course on how to be a front-line soldier, the most important lesson of which was not shoot at your own side.

But it was far too little, and far too late. The eighth day of February 1942 marked the beginning of the end. Late that night, after a day of almost non-stop artillery bombardment, which the old World War I fellas said was equal to anything they had experienced in France, the Imperial Japanese Army, using just 30 000 of its available 64 000 troops, stormed across Winston Churchill's 'splendid moat'.

Blowing a hole in the 1100-yard causeway had contributed nothing to assist in the defence of Singapore. Lieutenant General Percival, the senior Allied officer, against the advice of his more junior commanders, gave permission to blow up just 70 yards, close to the Johor Bahru shoreline. It was no impediment to the Japanese – they simply waded across the breach at low tide. Twenty-four hours later, thanks to the efficiency of their engineers, the gap was repaired, allowing their tanks and transport to cross unimpeded.

The hole in the causeway

The Australians, meantime, had been given the task of holding the north-western sector of the island. The 22 Brigade's three battalions, including the 2/19th, which had taken on hundreds of raw reinforcements following the mauling near Muar, were strung out along the north-west and west coast. Two of 27 Brigade's three battalions were further to east, on the other side of the Kranji River estuary, near the causeway, with the heavily reinforced 2/29th held in reserve.

The coastline along which the heavily outnumbered troops were thinly deployed – about one combatant for every 100 yards – consisted of mangrove swamps and mud flats, fragmented by numerous streams and rivers. Believing that any attack would come from the east, General Percival had positioned his freshest troops, the newly arrived British 18 Division, in that sector, despite warnings from General Wavell, and Australia's Major General Bennett, that the Japanese would focus on the north-west.

Percival made the wrong call. Late on the night of 8 February, thousands of Japanese troops swarmed across the Straits and into the north-western area in an assault so fierce and overwhelming that the overstretched Australian lines, once again, were forced to retreat as dawn broke.

American journalist Otto Frederick, in an article describing the events of that night wrote:

> Shortly before midnight on February 8 1942, under heavy bombardment, 13,000 Japanese surged across the straits on a fleet of collapsible plywood boats and landing craft. A battalion of 2,500 Australians fought them off all night, but by dawn the Japanese had their beach-head, and then the tanks started across ... when the Japanese had conquered half the island, British Staff officers could still be seen sipping drinks at Raffles, and civilians stood in line to see Katharine Hepburn in The Philadelphia Story.

The survivors from the night's onslaught regrouped at Bulim village, near Tengah airfield, where three companies of the 2/29th, including Billy's C Company, were hurriedly deployed to strengthen the line. Although C Company displayed 'resolute and courageous defence' to ward off enemy attacks, they were ordered to join the general withdrawal to a new position, south of the village.

> *The cause was lost at the causeway*
> *By planners too dumb to be true,*
> *Who placed all their eggs in one basket*
> *And left us Australians to stew.*

The thought has often crossed my mind that maybe, just maybe, we were the proverbial 'staked goat', placed there not so much to trap the tiger, but to appease it. Far too many troops were held back 'in reserve'. As it turned out, all they were reserved for was the capitulation ceremony.

Unpreparedness, I reckon, sums up the difference between the two armies. We, fighting for the British Empire, were a conglomeration of different nationalities – Indian, Australian, British, Malay, Chinese. Too few had skills. Too many were dills – the sweepings of the British Raj.

On paper, we seemed up to the task of defending Singapore, the supposedly impregnable fortress. Unfortunately, that's all it was – paper. Paper dolls. Paper tigers. Paper soldiers. Indeed, many of the young Indian troops we were relying on to cover our flanks took off like startled rabbits almost at the sound of the first shots.

One could hardly blame them. Rounded up by the thousands from the slums of overpopulated cities in India, these newly arrived troops, many still teenagers, had been shipped off to help defend the Empire with little, if any, training. A number would defect to the enemy, naively seduced by promises of a better life under Japanese rule.

Our opposition was an army of highly trained professionals, with years of combat experience. When a Jap went into battle, he carried his weapon, his ammo and a bag of dried fried rice, along with a few sweets. His survival depended on himself, and his training.

They were certainly well trained and were masters at using the terrain for their advantage, moving through 'impenetrable' jungle and tying themselves to trees to bump us off from above, a most effective method of fighting. I know, because one of them later tried it on me and if it hadn't been for Paddy O'Toole, I'd have been trading my 'dead meat ticket' (identity disc) for a harp. Paddy was a good soldier and a great mate, who bailed me out of difficult situations after I managed to get myself in hot water, which was most of the time.

We'd been held in reserve throughout the first proper day of the battle. I can remember looking across to where the Japs were, thinking about how ordinary it seemed, and that the same sun that was shining on us was shining on them. It was not until early on the morning of 10 February that our turn finally came. We'd been at stand-to, full battle readiness, at our position near Bulim village for hours. So long, in fact, that my hand had become part of my rifle, tension the glue. I had thought that the shelling would never stop, but when it did the blessed silence had been shattered by machine-gun fire, making it clear that the Japanese were not in retreat. The war was still hanging on, and our turn would not only come soon enough, but would undoubtedly become close up, and very personal.

Out in front, the black line of trees was developing a reddish haze, and it wasn't from the sunrise. Right behind them the heavy machine-guns began bip-bip-bipping, tearing away at the branches, cutting up the foliage. The waiting was definitely over now. It was a bit like waiting your turn at the dentist, only considerably worse. The exploding thuds of six-inch mortars, creeping closer and closer, drowned out the sound of the small-arms fire. I could actually feel the thump, thump, thump through the ground.

We fired a few rounds, mostly as testers, into the trees. We couldn't see the enemy, but we blazed away anyway, hoping to hit a few of them. It was still too dark to see anything, but we heard them right enough, and it was at about that time that we started to move out – backwards.

The attack that night had concentrated on the remaining two battalions of 27 Brigade which, although they were not overrun, were ordered to pull back to a new position three miles from the causeway, in the belief that the enemy, infiltrating the area in boats and landing craft, would outflank them and cut them off. The Japanese, who were about to retreat after suffering huge losses when the Australians flooded the Kranji River with petrol and set it alight, saw the movement to the rear and pressed home their attack.

Daylight arrived. Ducking and weaving, the Japs still had us under fire. The most frustrating part was not knowing exactly where they were – but at least trying to guess where they might be took my mind off worrying. However, the situation kept deteriorating, and all we could hope for was that we weren't popping off any of our own blokes. In that kind of a muddle, things happen quickly, all too quickly. There is no time to think what to do. There's no second chance.

Anything can happen, and it did. We ran into a real hornets' nest, with enemy fire coming at us from every direction. To top it off, an enemy mortar landed about a yard away. Fortunately it was a dud, but despite being pinned down we were mesmerised by the sight of it, just sitting there, its tail stuck in the air.

A fellow Tasmanian, George 'Tich' Bennetts of HQ Company, who was near some blokes with a mortar, was the first to cop it. The bullet passed through his body, entered his neck and lodged in his jaw. Miraculously, it didn't hit any vital organ. The boys had no sooner dragged him away when a bullet slammed into the tree that was supposed to be protecting me. It made a hole as big as a fist. The buggers were using hollow-nosed dum-dums. Two more shots and two more holes appeared, just inches above my head. A sniper had me pinned down from behind. I yelled and Paddy, turning round, saw that the firing was coming from behind us. 'One of the bastards is up a rubber tree', he shouted, 'and if he doesn't blow yer bloody head off with the next shot, with a bit of luck, I'll spot him and get him.' Well the Jap didn't, and Paddy did. One shot and the sniper was dead as a doornail, dangling from the tree by his sling.

Paddy was typical of the blokes looking out for me. They called me Billy the Kid, not because I was an expert with a gun but because, aged only sixteen and a bit, I really was just a kid. Lance-Corporal Bob Shipsides was in charge of our section. A born leader, he was a tremendous fella, and a great friend and cobber to us all. He seemed ancient to me, and looked out for me with paternalistic care.

Lance-corporal Bob Shipsides

O'Toole, who was thought to be Irish and actively promoted this belief, was actually born in Launceston, Tasmania, in 1919. Baptised Leonard John, he was known as Paddy, and was universally described as 'mad'. Bob (Robert Andrew) Shipsides not only seemed ancient to Billy –by army enlistment standards he was. He was born in 1900, in the small town of Dimboola in the Wimmera region of western Victoria. Too young to join the army in the Great War and, with the cut-off age for World War II set at 39, Bob had put his age back a whopping thirteen years to enlist. Now aged 41, not the 29 he claimed to be, he was old enough to be Billy's father.

Billy's mates Paddy O'Toole (left rear) and Harry Longley (front right)

John Holden, a bushie from Rochester in Victoria who went by the name of Dave and was five years older than me, was our Lewis gunner. Being the gunner he had the exciting part. I was his offsider, which meant that it was my job to carry all the ammunition and feed it into the gun, and also to try to keep snipers at bay. A quiet bloke, Dave was blessed with that dry laconic humour that sets country people apart.

We spent that night in a swamp, unsure of where we were. The mozzies were ferocious, and so were the leeches, but at least we were protected from tank attack. I hauled myself out of the muck and propped myself against a tree, too tired to worry about the Japs. I let Paddy and Bob take care of that. As they had both survived the Muar battle, I reckoned they knew what they were talking about. I didn't give a bugger.

The next morning, after a fitful rest, a passing intelligence officer gave orders for two men to go up a hill to find out where the Japs were and what they were doing. Dave volunteered us for the job, but I wasn't at all keen after my close shave with the sniper the previous day and said I didn't want to go. A stern reminder from Bob Shipsides that it was an order, plus a bit of plain old-fashioned blackmail on my part that resulted in the loan of his much-coveted Tommy gun, saw me scampering off like Al Capone, after Dave and up the hill. Taking cover on the brow, we could see that the Japs were bracketing the slope below with mortar bombs as they slowly advanced towards our position. After watching for a few minutes, Dave turned to me and said, with all the nonchalance of someone leaving a movie at intermission, 'Come on Billy. We've seen enough. We can always come back later and catch the rest of the show.'

We returned to deliver the news to the intelligence officer, only to discover that he'd scarpered and the rest of the platoon had moved on, apart from Paddy and Bob and a couple of other blokes who gave us a ticking off about the length of time we had been away. After handing back the Tommy gun, I picked up my rifle and the almost empty ammo tin and trudged off. We soon caught up with the others, who were dug in at a rubber plantation. This was a great possie. It had a terrific field of fire and, with plenty of cover from the spreading branches of the rubber trees, we were well hidden from the prying eyes of the Zero fighter pilots searching for any sign of life below. Lying in wait, and well prepared, we were itching to have a go at a group of Japs who had moved forward after the mortar barrage and were now massing at the edge of a jungle outcrop. Dave and I lined up the Lewis machine-gun, ready for action. Over on our left flank the others waited in the same state of high alert.

We never had the chance to deal with the sitting ducks we held in our sights. At the eleventh hour, orders came to retreat. It came as no surprise. 'Retreat' and 'fall back' (army-speak for retreat) were two orders with which we were very familiar. We'd had so much practice we had become experts: 'Retreats and Defeats – A Speciality'. It was so frustrating. As soon as we had dug ourselves into a place of concealment, and created any kind of advantage, we would be ordered to 'withdraw', also army-speak for retreat. You could bet your pay-packet on it, odds-on, every time. We 'fell back' so often that finally we had no back to defend.

We'd asked that intelligence officer, 'How come, sir, every time we get set up in a good position, we are ordered to fall back?', and he'd replied, 'It's for strategic reasons.' Strategic reasons! Strewth! We finished up with more strategic reasons on that one little island than we could possibly afford. So, once again, it was dig a hole, set up the gun and wait. Wait for what? To be told to fall back.

This time, after receiving the order to withdraw, we were instructed to follow the trunk road and railway line leading south to Singapore city and to stay close to the rubber trees and patches of jungle. It was while we were carrying out this order that the opposition caught us out in the open. We were now the sitting ducks. There is no cover in a rice padi and the Japs, who had us under observation from a hot air balloon, immediately relayed the information to their mates. They peppered us with machine-gun fire, assaulted us with mortar bombs and, as an added touch, a Zero zeroed in. We ran like rabbits and by some miracle reached some rubber trees without anyone being hit. Although were spread out in a line, about six feet apart, every one of the bullets went between us, not in us.

Luck had run out, however, for Captain William Bruce 'Bull' Bowring, Billy's company commander. An accountant before the war, he had covered himself in glory during the Muar battle by leading two bayonet charges and advancing to within 100 yards of enemy tanks, which he then attacked with an anti-tank rifle – actions that earned him a Military Cross. He was the only company commander at Muar to survive from the 2/29th, which took on nineteen new officers, mostly reinforcements. As Bowring ran for cover from the Zero on 11 February, he was stitched up by a machine-gun and hit four times – in both calves, his back and his neck. He was evacuated to hospital, patched up, and became a prisoner of war, later surviving the terrible deprivations experienced by F Force on the Burma-Thai Railway.

Digging in hurriedly, Dave and I squeezed into our little hole and as far into the ground as the gun and ammo, which took up more than their fair share of space, would allow. A few minutes later we heard the crump of artillery, and shells started whistling over our heads. The Zero pilot, having failed to finish us off, had radioed our position. I hugged the ground in our rabbit scrape as if my life depended on it, which it did. Suddenly Wham! A shell landed right slap-bang in the middle of the fork of the tree we were sheltering under, killing two blokes to our rear in a deadly spray of shrapnel.

The effect of the explosion was tremendous, almost a physical assault in itself, the noise smashing into our eardrums and the concussion pushing us further into the dirt. Decapitated, our tree, or what was left of it, smouldered – its trunk splintered, like a discarded cigar butt from Thor, the God of Thunder.

Smell of cordite. Smoke from the explosion. Pulverised treetop. A proper cocktail of war, swirling around and above us, in slow motion. After the roar came silence, following by the sound of distant ringing. It was some time before

I realised that the tinkling sound was much closer than I thought – in my ears. They kept on ringing, like an unanswered telephone call.

I also became aware of pain in the region of my right thigh. Gingerly I pushed my hand towards the spot. When I withdrew it, it was covered in blood. Not just any blood. My blood. I was sure I'd lost my leg, like Les, the old fella from the First War who had lived with us in Ma Jepson's house in Ultimo. Fortunately, the injury proved to be much smaller than the sickening image conjured up in my vivid imagination. I'd been hit by a sliver of shrapnel, about an inch long and a quarter of an inch wide. It was only a flesh wound. What a relief! My leg (amazingly) wasn't hanging off, so I would not be condemned to stomp around on a peg-leg like Les for the rest of my life.

An unsympathetic Paddy O'Toole, who had come to my side in response to my panicked cries that the Japs had taken off my leg, slapped on a field dressing and remarked, 'You're lucky, Billy. It missed middle stump. In any case, it was a no-ball, so I wouldn't have given you out.'

By this time it was late afternoon. The remainder of our platoon had moved on, leaving Bob, Paddy, Dave and me to follow. Our orders, considerably delayed by the close encounter with the exploding shell, were to fall back to Bukit Timah, a village more or less in the centre of the island, where we expected to pick up supplies of food and ammunition. We had eaten the last of our iron rations hours ago and the ammo in the bag I was lugging around was so low that, unless we restocked, we would have to resort to throwing rocks. I had just one hand grenade, half a clip for my rifle but no bullets at all for the Lewis gun. I said to Dave, 'Why don't we throw the bloody thing away? We've got no ammo for it', but he said the gun was his responsibility and we had to keep on carrying it.

Constantly harassed by enemy gunfire, we kept on the move but even with Paddy helping me it was a slow process. Long before we reached our destination, night fell: a most apt expression because, in the tropics, that is exactly what happens. The speed at which the daylight vanishes takes all those used to a lingering twilight by surprise. As the sun drops out of sight a heavy black curtain descends, as fast as a lift when its cable is cut – and the inky blackness soon gives way to a wondrous sight.

Stars punching holes of light
Through the velvet of the night
Creating for the rising moon
Sparkling chains, silver festoon.

But this was not a night for star-gazing. Little did our little band realise, as we stumbled on, that we were moving slowly but surely towards disaster, stalked by a malevolent shadow that was not only about to cover, but to overwhelm us.

We were almost into Bukit Timah when we saw, by the eerie red glow cast by burning buildings, that the Japs had beaten us to it. They had taken over the village and captured the supply base. As we drew closer, a palm-thatched hut burst into flame, illuminating a group of enemy soldiers. 'Japs! Get off the road!' warned Bob. Lady Luck was with us this time, however. The Japs not only failed to see us, they had not yet realised that they had us surrounded, giving us enough time to dive into a deep monsoon drain beside the road.

The drain was about ten feet wide and six feet deep, and when it rained it filled quickly with a torrent of water. Fortunately, the weather had been dry so the drain was empty, apart from a trickle flowing down the shallow culvert in the centre. We huddled there, pressed against the slippery curved concrete, certain that the Jap troops would notice our shadows. They had better things to look at than a monsoon drain, though, because at that moment a flare shot skywards, bathing the entire area in blinding light. What a magic lantern sideshow of war it revealed. We were surrounded by half the Jap army, or so it seemed. Tanks, trucks, foot soldiers in two long columns, and troops on push-bikes, all projected in silhouette onto the walls of the drain, a flickering, ever-changing procession of grotesque black shapes, rolling past in a cinemascope of black and white, with red overtones.

We crouched, hearts racing, pressed against the concrete, listening, waiting, wondering, sweating. Our luck held. Not once, during what felt like hours – but in reality was about the three or four minutes it took for the brilliance of the flare to fade – did any of the enemy have the urge, from either curiosity or the call of nature, to wander over and inspect the drain.

The column had finally passed by and silence descended, along with the welcoming cloak of darkness, when we heard another, very disturbing sound. A grating, discordant, metallic sound. More tanks! Or so Paddy said. For once in his life he was wrong. The source of the racket turned out to be push-bikes, pedalled along by hundreds and hundreds of Jap soldiers. As most of the rubber tyres had given up the ghost, the cyclists had replaced them with lengths of green bamboo fastened with wire and were riding along as if they hadn't a care in the world. We later learned that they had pedalled all the way from northern Malaya. We had been invaded by Japs on bicycles!

The Japanese, who brought thousands of bicycles with them from Japan, estimated that, had they used more conventional forms of transport, Malaya would have taken twelve months to conquer. Unlike motorised transport, bikes were not complex mechanically, did not require fuel, did not become bogged in soggy ground, could be picked up and carried across a makeshift bridge or around any obstacle, and could easily be replaced by commandeering bikes belonging to the locals. Not even the inconvenience of flat tyres stopped their remorseless advance, once it was realised that the bicycles ran perfectly well on the rims – an aspect that had an unexpected bonus when the metallic sound on a hard road surface tricked a British commander into ordering his troops to retreat in the face of what he believed to be a tank attack.

While all this was going on we were joined by some Indian sepoys, who said that their British officers had abandoned them. They had only just made themselves comfortable in the drain alongside us when three blokes from our battalion suddenly appeared. Paddy heard them coming and fortunately recognised them before firing his Bren, which would not only have wiped them out but also given away our hiding place. Motioning to them to be quiet, Paddy whispered 'Jeeze, this place is like bloody Flinders Street Station.'

The newcomers were Sergeant Brian Dobson and Private Doug Cameron. They were lugging a Lewis gun and half-dragging along an officer from our battalion, Lieutenant Butt. The boys had found him on his own, wandering around in a disoriented state.

Doug Cameron came from Colac in rural Victoria and 'could fight like a threshing machine'. His enthusiasm was matched by that of Brian Dobson, whose real name was Brian Vance and who had been accepted for officer training at the prestigious Duntroon Military College in Canberra. On finding the pace a little too slow for his sedate for his liking, he had shot through and enlisted in the AIF as Brian Dobson. His war service had been unexpectedly enlivened a few days before on the Bukit Timah Rifle Range when Billy, encouraged by Paddy to show off his skill, took a potshot at a jam tin, incurring Dobson's wrath – he'd been standing only a few inches away.

Lieutenant Arthur Butt, aged 30, from Melbourne, hailed originally from Northam in Western Australia. He had been cut off in the fighting when A Company had become detached from the remainder of the battalion at Bukit Padjang, four miles to the north of Bukit Timah. Dobson and Cameron had found him wandering, alone and disoriented, suffering from severe shell-shock.

The lieutenant, who was obviously very traumatised, tried to climb out of the drain. Bob ordered me to keep him still, shut him up and calm him down. Me, a kid of sixteen, telling an officer what to do! Shaking and crying, he kept on repeating 'It's not right. It's not right'. All I could do was push him to the floor of the drain, pat him on the back like a small child in need of comfort and reassure him with a 'Shhh. Shhh, sir. It'll be okay sir. You'll be all right. You'll be all right'.

There was soon more Japanese activity, this time in the form of a staff car that pulled up along the roadway diagonally from our position. Its passenger must have been a personage of some note, because troops were buzzing round it like flies. Next, a motorbike dispatch rider showed up to have a pow-wow with the chief. Their strange-sounding, unintelligible chatter unnerved the lieutenant, who became even more agitated, necessitating some soothing words from Bob to quieten him down. As soon as the car and motorbike departed, Bob decided it was time for us to move, but before we had a chance to get organised Lieutenant Butt took off, up and out of the drain and onto the road.

Shouting incoherently, he stumbled in the dark towards the Japanese sentries. A flare rocketed skywards, bathing him in incandescent light. A machine-gun rattled and that was it.

Billy and his companions were the only Allied witnesses to the death of Lieutenant Butt, whose body was never recovered. His date of death is still presumed officially to be 10 February 1942, the day prior to his actual death and the date on which he was last seen at Bukit Panjang. He is commemorated on the Memorial Wall at Kranji War Cemetery, on Column 129.

There was no hope of retrieving the lieutenant's body and when the same flare also revealed more enemy troops, coming along the road in single file, we flattened ourselves once more against the side of the drain. After a whispered conference between Paddy and Bob, word was passed around to dismantle the Lewis guns, take our boots off, tie them to our belts and creep away.

Dougie Cameron and Sergeant Dobson were dismantling their gun, which they had inherited after the original gunners were killed, when all hell broke loose. The weapon still had a bullet up the spout. When Dobson pressed the trigger to release the butt to access the body-locking pin, in the black confines of the drain the resulting explosion sounded more like an artillery shell than a .303. The bullet ripped through Dougie's hand, ricocheted off the concrete wall and lodged in the shoulder of one of the Indian soldiers.

The effect was immediate, with Dougie getting religious and telling God all about it and the Indian screaming to his God in his own lingo. 'Run like buggery!' yelled Bob. We needed no second order. Grabbing hold of Dougie on one side, and supporting the wounded Indian on the other, up and over the drain I went before another flare could light up the sky. Hearts racing and blood pumping we fled into the night, eerie red smoke flickering behind us, away from what was left of the burning village. Many a time we had passed through the village on our way to enjoy a spot of leave in town. It had taken a pounding in a few short days of unending misery, and now we were in real danger of being destroyed along with it.

There's nothing like great expectations to spur you on, especially when it's the prospect of a bullet in the back or being sliced to bits by a bracket of high-explosive shells. The difference between life and death is certainly a powerful incentive and, in our race for that far-off tree line, I forgot about my wounded thigh and discovered just how fast I could run. We finally reached the shelter of the trees, all of us, and not before time. Right at that point a flare went up, revealing what seemed to be half the Jap army running around firing, but fortunately not in our direction.

My feet were a total mess and, to make matters worse, I discovered I had lost my boots during the scramble out of the drain. There was no way I was going back to find them, so I had to walk the rest of the way in my socks, trying to find our lines and trying not to step on sharp objects. It was a futile exercise. The rough ground, combined with the tinea that had left my skin soft and raw, soon cut my feet to shreds.

After a night spent dodging Japs, we reached the Bukit Timah Racecourse, one of our designated fallback positions. The rising sun revealed a sorry sight. The entire island, it seemed, was ablaze, with billows of thick dark smoke covering the sky, enveloping the trees, the ground and every living creature with a layer of black, oily sludge. The news was not good. Our forces were being hard hit on all fronts. Unless some kind of miracle occurred, the end must surely be nigh.

After being admonished for 'insolence' by an immaculately turned-out British officer, who emerged from his tent at the racecourse to ask an incredulous Paddy where the 'Jappies' were, we trudged on along Bukit Timah Road, passing through a devastated landscape littered with wrecked military equipment. Ahead, we saw one of our Bren-gun carriers, going hell for leather with a Jap Zero pumping bullets at it. The carrier fired back, but as the plane zoomed overhead it dropped a bomb. The carrier swerved furiously and landed upside down in the monsoon drain. I took a potshot at the plane, but unlike my previous good effort with the tin can, I missed. I knew it was futile, because by the time I had it in my sights it was gone.

As we passed by the wreck, a couple of medics taking care of the survivors told us that there was a regimental aid post in a nearby rubber plantation, where Dougie and I became official casualties of war. After receiving emergency treatment for his shattered hand, Dougie was led away to an ambulance. I had on-the-spot first aid to extract the shrapnel, which I kept as a souvenir, from my thigh. Although this injury was minor, my feet were severely lacerated and I was given the option of being stretchered to an ambulance a short distance away, or walking to another, parked nearby. The thought of not having to go another step was very inviting but I figured that others were in far worse shape than me, and said I'd go to hospital with Dougie and the other 'walking wounded'.

My little bitter taste of battle over, I rode away from the aid post in the luxury of an ambulance, with bandaged thigh and feet, munching on an army biscuit and not giving two hoots if I never passed that way again. Never, ever. I'd lost my watch, so I asked someone the time. It was 1300 hours, on Thursday 12 February. Destination – 13 Australian Army General Hospital.

Billy's decision to join the walking wounded that fateful day almost undoubtedly saved his life. He'd been given the choice of two ambulances: 'If you can walk, then get yourself into the ambulance on the left'. He'd hobbled over to it and lived. The walking wounded went to Katong, a beachside village on the outskirts of Singapore where 2/13 AGH, previously at Tampoi, had been re-established at St Patrick's College. The stretcher cases were taken to the Alexandra Military Hospital where, two days later, on the afternoon of 14 February, enemy troops entered the grounds, in spite of a white flag held in surrender. Supposedly enraged that some Indian soldiers had set up a machine-gun inside the grounds of the hospital, a site traditionally off-limits for engaging in warfare, the rampaging Japanese killed not only the doctors and nurses, but also patients undergoing surgery on the operating table. They then entered the wards, herding about 200 patients and staff into a nearby building. A few managed to escape but the others were bayoneted to death the following morning.

CHAPTER 5

RELUCTANT GUESTS OF THE EMPEROR

13 February – 7 July 1942

Our meat wagon, chock-a-block with battle casualties, took off at high speed towards the eastern end of the island, with instructions from a Bren-gun carrier driver not to stop for anyone. However, there was only one road leading to St Pat's College, and the entire area was in disarray. The fortress and local volunteer troops assigned to this sector were all over the road, desperate to reach the final perimeter before the Japanese, advancing towards Changi from Ubin Island, caught up with them. As we stopped to avoid running some of the pedestrians down, two of our shell-shocked blokes, who'd been quivering like jelly in a corner, leapt from the ambulance. Despite my painful, bandaged feet I was the most able bodied of the rest of us, so I had the task of hobbling after them and persuading them to get back in.

Billy arrived at St Pat's late that afternoon. The perimeter for the final defence of Singapore had been drawn, and the hospital was outside it. This meant, in effect, that all those unable to leave would be abandoned to the mercy of the enemy troops now advancing along the east coast.

Billy was awaiting medical attention and looking forward to the tender ministrations of the army nurses when a lovely blonde nursing sister came into the ward with the news that she and her colleagues were being evacuated. Thirty army nurses had sailed for Java the previous day on Empire Star *and now the remaining 27 sisters were on their way. The sisters had protested about the evacuation orders, but their superiors were resolute.*

Many of the nursing staff taken prisoner in Hong Kong had been raped, and Malaya Command was not taking any chances. With tears streaming down her face, Billy's visitor said her goodbyes and kissed him on the cheek.

With death or capture inevitable, any convalescent fit enough (Billy would not be among them) was given permission to attempt escape. Some managed to obtain boats from the beach and reached Sumatra, where they were put on an escape route established by SOE Far East – an offshoot of the British Secret Intelligence Service, also known as MI6. The more fortunate were picked up by merchant or naval vessels from Padang, on Sumatra's west coast, and taken to India, Ceylon or Australia. Many others, however, perished en route, fell prey to Japanese submarines and surface craft, or were taken into captivity when the Dutch East Indies fell to the Japanese. Others released from the hospital headed east, for nearby Bintan Island in the Riau Archipelago, where they were captured and executed.

The 27 sisters from St Pat's were transported to the Singapore docks where they, and 38 nursing staff from 2/10 AGH and 2/4 Casualty Clearing Station, were squeezed onto the already overcrowded steamship Vyner Brooke. *Anchored just offshore while a convoy was assembled, the vessel left Singapore waters the following morning, Friday the 13th, only to be sunk by enemy aircraft off Bangka Island, near Sumatra. The survivors who made it ashore were subsequently captured. One group of 33 were marched into the sea off Radji Beach and machine-gunned. The 2/13 AGH's Sister Vivian Bulwinkel, who was shot through the hip but feigned death, was the sole survivor.*

The day after we waved the tearful nurses goodbye, the Japs came along and overran the place. It was quite an experience. Without warning, at 1300 hours on Friday 13 February, they came trotting through the ward, leaving one of their squad propped beside the entrance. Despite my faith in number thirteen, things did not look so good now, especially since an hour or so earlier we'd watched from the window as the advancing troops killed five of our soldiers guarding the gate – *after* taking them prisoner.

When all was quiet, the doctors had ventured outside to examine the carnage and discovered a sixth man, Private Bill Cooke, a bloke from Queensland, lying at the bottom of the heap. He was still alive – just. Apparently the swinging sword meant to decapitate him had hit a rock. The blade had deflected and his life was now hanging by a thread, literally. The doctors were able to sew him back together, and put him in the ward with the rest of us, with strict instructions to keep the scar covered lest the Japanese see it and realise he had survived an attempted beheading.

Having witnessed murder most foul, and helpless to resist, we regarded our unwelcome visitors with a certain degree of apprehension. However, apart from pilfering cigarette lighters, watches and money, none of which I had on me, they were content to let the medical staff tend to our wounds, and left us alone.

Nevertheless, they were taking no chances and had left the sentry outside the door. This was our first experience of being placed under guard and of being prisoners of war, so it was with a mixture of fear and nervous tension that we watched him slowly turn around, spit on the floor and then glare balefully at each of us in turn.

Oh, Crikey! What a shock to the system to see him face on. I'd seen some gruesome cartoons in the local papers depicting the enemy but this bloke, whose already ugly countenance was hideously disfigured by a pronounced harelip, did not look like the sort of fellow you'd care to come across in a dark lane.

He stood glaring at us, a box-on-legs, his bowed shins protesting the weight they carried. All in all, he made a highly believable enemy, and one so easy to dislike, with the harelip splitting his face into a permanent snarl to expose a mouthful of black, protruding teeth. I wondered if there were many more like him.

It was at about this point I realised I'd had enough of war. When I first joined up and proudly donned my uniform, I'd been so idealistic, but the glamour of fighting for the King had begun to wear off when the first bullet had zapped past my head. Someone out there was actually trying to kill me! The fact that I was hellbent on doing the same thing did not alter the fact that the enemy was shooting at me, and wanted me, Billy Young, dead. Well, I was lucky to be still alive, but I wondered for how long.

With slitted eyes darting left and right, the sentry started to count us, using his rifle as a pointer while he checked out each of our beds. Finally satisfied with the count, he slowly lowered the rifle and stood at ease, allowing us to start breathing again. Little did I realise that this was the start of three-and-a-half years of being counted, Japanese style. They were obsessed with the business of counting. *Ichi, ni, san, shi*. Time and time again, making sure it was right. If at any time the count didn't tally, there was bound to be trouble.

When the Japs first entered the ward,
I knew our world was turning sour
When Quasimodo started counting us
Confirming we were in his power.

As it turned out, despite his alarming appearance the sentry proved to be a well-trained and well-disciplined soldier whose main concern was to be a good guard, and to count us at regular intervals. This was also true of the rest of his squad, unlike their counterparts who'd turned on the bloodbath at the Alexandra Hospital. It was not until I learned of the massacre there that I fully appreciated the truth of the saying, 'You go one way and you live, you go another way and you die; choosing which way to go, that's the tricky part – the rest is easy'. I have no problem, not any more, with number thirteen. As a matter of fact, it's now my favourite number.

By the night of 15 February, the entire island was forced into a shameful capitulation by our generals. One thing's for sure, none of the troops ever envisaged, or sought, such a surrender. Time was the essence of the contract. The 8th Divvie had fought on regardless, and were still fighting when they were told to lay down their arms. It was over. We had been surrendered. Late in the afternoon General Percival had gone to a meeting with the Japanese commander, General Yamashita, at the Ford Motor Factory at Bukit Timah, and unprotestingly signed away our lives on the dotted line. Fifteen thousand Aussies handed over, just like, that, along with tens of thousands of Brits and Indians.

Some of the thousands of Allied troops taken prisoner when Singapore fell

Unconditionally surrendered. End of story. What else is there left to say? The results speak for themselves. Overall it was a one hundred per cent, right old ball's-up. The Top Brass, boosted by the arrogance of past and glorious victories against the enemies of the King, turned out to be nothing but a bunch of overweight punch-drunks. The enemy, on the other hand, were trimmed down lightweights – fast, well trained and well equipped. Cocky, full of fight and packed to the brim with confidence. A jab or two at the flabby body of unpreparedness. An uppercut fair on the point of a glass chin of over-developed conceit, followed by a thump in the ribs of ingrown prejudices. Bang! It was all over, bar the shouting, which the victorious Jap troops did in full voice – 'Banzai! Banzai! Banzai!' – adding to our humiliation.

What a difference losing Singapore made. What a comedown. Such a blow. Such a bleeding shame. What a loss to our pride, pomp and prejudice. One moment we had been mighty Lord Jims, Cocks of the Walk, White Supremos, Kings of the Castles. Then crash, wham. We were skittled for six. Roosters one day, feather dusters the next. And all this, in just one short week.

Our armies had been preened and groomed. Led like prize thoroughbreds at the Melbourne Cup. Paraded for all to admire, but when it came time for the ribbons to be handed out, we were left standing in the stalls.

What a difference from days of yore
When as Pukka Sahibs we'd held the floor.
No longer pukka. Sahibs no more.
We'd been pukka-ed and sahibed out the door.

For millions of people in that part of the world, it was as if a veil had been lifted, and our nakedness revealed; it was not so much that the mighty had fallen, but, that we white fellas had come unstuck. The trifecta of Empire – White, Might, Right – lay exposed to the elements, bringing about the end of dominance by skin colour.

Who'd have thought that what had happened could have happened to us? Even when I was being driven away in the ambulance, I had still thought that we would hold on. But we didn't, we bloody didn't. I certainly had no idea that surrender was on the cards, even though 2/13 AGH was surrendered before anyone else. What was the use of getting wounded, just to be taken prisoner? It wasn't fair. On the other hand, I did get some letters after my name – Bill Young, POW.

It was another week or so before we were loaded onto trucks and taken to the central holding area for prisoners of war on the south-eastern corner of the island, a vast area known simply as Changi. This whole section, which included three separate barracks (Selarang, Kitchener and Roberts) built to accommodate the pre-war British garrison, and a fourth called the India Lines, was in the process of being fenced off – not by the Japs but by our own men, using tons of the precious barbed wire that General Percival, the Pommy officer in charge of defending Singapore, had withheld from us as defences were bad for morale! The very wire that may have made such a difference to our defence against the Japs was now being used by them to keep us in line.

When the fence was eventually completed, it didn't stop us from getting out to forage for food, or even to escape. Because of the terrain, there were gaps all over the place, and if there wasn't a gap handy it didn't take long to make one. The guards were few and far between and I had no trouble wiggling under the wire to go on foraging trips into nearby coconut groves and to small farms, where the Chinese were always happy to trade or to even give us free handouts.

Some blokes who got out didn't come back. Some reached Malaya where they joined the Chinese guerrillas, but many were recaptured or shot. One bloke who came to grief was my mate Herb Cruikshank, who slipped away one night about a fortnight after we arrived. Word had it that he had been shot while trying the swim the Straits of Johor, although others said he had drowned. We got news of failed attempts from escapees who had been recaptured and brought back to Changi. They were corralled in the tennis courts, guarded by Sikhs who had been in the Indian Army under the British, but had now switched sides. The Sikh guards were big blokes, even without their turbans, and were more intimidating than the Japs. But not all defected to the enemy. Some remained loyal and quite a few were used as bayonet practice for their trouble.

We AIF blokes were imprisoned in Selarang Barracks, previously occupied by a battalion of Gordon Highlanders. The barracks and associated grounds covered a huge area, with six main three-storeyed blocks around the parade ground, and dozens of bungalows and married quarters dotted about the place. Our six infantry battalions were each assigned one of the three-storey buildings. It was a tight squeeze, so some of the fellas made makeshift accommodation on the flat roofs.

Selarang Barracks before the war

CHAPTER 5 Reluctant guests of the Emperor

The Pommies, and the hospital, were in Roberts Barracks, about a mile away. To visit anyone in hospital, we had to go in a group, accompanied by a guard. Most people think we were in the gaol itself, but that was not until much, much later.

No prisoners of war occupied Changi Gaol until May 1944, when the civilian internees, imprisoned there since February 1942, were moved to a camp at Syme Road. The relatively few Australians not sent out on overseas or local work parties, and who were still occupying Selarang in 1944, were moved to the gaol, where atap-roofed huts were later erected outside the high grey walls to extend the accommodation. As the depleted parties returned from working on the Burma-Thai Railway, they too were housed in the gaol precincts. The gaol itself served as a dormitory, with the main door left open to allow access to the outer areas, encircled with barbed wire. The congestion inside the gaol itself was so great during peak periods that senior officers asked if a second exit could be created by knocking a hole in the opposite wall. The Japanese, it is said, refused on the grounds that, if they did this, the British would be very angry.

The cordoned-off area of the Changi peninsula, of which Selarang Barracks was just a part, was a conglomeration of concrete barracks, atap huts and the handsome black-and-white bungalows assigned to married officers. A place of temporary confinement for many, and a permanent home for those fortunate enough to stay, Changi was to witness a constant coming and going of work parties. Many thousands of men left, and few returned.

Selarang Camp, as we called it, was part gaol, part asylum: a place where a defeated army was trying to come to grips with the cold hard facts of imprisonment. Our war was over, but the melody lingered on; a cracked record of a war that was being played over and over again. For some it was all a tragic mistake, and the Yanks would soon take care of it. Scores of armchair critics spent hours analysing the situation, pointing out just where things had gone wrong. Perhaps if we'd turned right, instead of left, they would argue. We young blokes, however, were worried about far more important questions – such as was the next feed was coming from.

While we understood that we were captives, we did not entertain any thought of being prisoners for any length of time and, although rations were not the best, never imagined that conditions in the coming years would sink as low as they did. Instead, we seesawed between optimism and pessimism. The youngsters sided with those who predicted that the Yanks would be landing at Penang, and soon – a mantra that was constantly recycled. The old blokes were on the side of those who chorused 'You'll never get off the island'. Those who conjured up visions of rescue and liberation were indulging in dreams in keeping with the back lot of a film studio, with the director putting an end to the current action by calling 'Cut', followed by a new scene that saw the Yanks come sailing in with a fanfare of trumpets, DA-DA-DA, and a long roll of drums, dum-dum-de-dum, allowing life to return to normal.

The reality, of course, was that we were in an overcrowded prison camp, with all kinds of problems to be sorted out and rules and regulations to be laid down and, even worse, enforced. One thing however had not changed, not one little bit. Despite everyone being a prisoner of war, officers were still being very officerish, strutting around importantly just as they had in peacetime, swagger sticks at the ready, batmen on hand to attend to their every need, and always quick to tell the rank and file that whatever new rule they had just dreamed up was 'absolutely essential for the good of the camp and terribly necessary, chaps, for the morale of the troops'. Well, maybe it was. Who was I, a mere private, to argue?

One senior officer we didn't want to cross was the 2/30th's Lieutenant Colonel Galleghan (known as Black Jack, but never to his face), a stern disciplinarian of the spit-and-polish kind. No one was safe from him in Changi, not even the Japanese. He treated them as if they were part of his command and had no qualms about stopping a Japanese patrol for inspection, and giving them a flea in the ear if they didn't measure up.

I always found it a bit weird to be soldiering with a bloke who was also a personal servant to some officer or other. So I made a vow that, if ever I became King, I'd bring in a law forbidding all batmen. If officers must have servants, then let them employ civilians! I also made a promise to myself to ban separate officers' messes in time of war. There were far too many trappings for my liking, leftovers from the Middle Ages, not to mention hand-me-down privileges and perks that interfered with the successful running of a decent modern war. Even as the Japs were storming across the Straits of Johor, one of our blokes, sent to report to a Pommy officer on our right flank, had found him sitting in the officers' mess tent, eating his breakfast from a table covered in a starched white cloth and set with the regimental silver.

Another bugbear, and a good example of being wise after the event, was the compulsory attendance by other ranks at the many lectures delivered by our intelligence officers. Now, there's a contradiction in terms. Brainwashing in those early POW days was considered to be absolutely necessary. The Chinese call it correct thinking; our superiors called it morale boosting. These officers were the same blokes, the very same experts, who had only just recently been filling us with stories about how easy it was to beat the Japs. 'A piece of cake', they had said.

'They can't fight their way out of a paper bag, and can't even shoot straight as they are blind as bats. As for their equipment, what a joke. It is made in Japan!'

Now we were told that the baddies had won in the face of everything and that we had been magnificent in defeat. Generally the lecturer would give six or seven reasons for Singapore's fall. One, two and three highlighted the fact that the island's big guns were fixed and all pointed the wrong way, out to sea and that we would have annihilated the blighters if they had come the way any decent white bloke would have come.

It is a complete fallacy that Singapore was lost because 'the guns were all pointing the wrong way' or that this even contributed to its fall. While the vast array of naval guns had an impressive field of fire to protect any seaward approach to Singapore, almost all could be, and were, turned 180 degrees to fire on the enemy massed on the far side of the causeway connecting Singapore Island to Malaya. The 'trouble' was that the ammunition provided was armour piercing, designed to penetrate the hulls of warships before exploding, not high explosive for use against personnel. Apart from one shell, which happened to land on the Johor Bahru Railway Station, damaging a section of the roof from its sheer size and weight, the armour-piercing ammunition, which could have been used to devastating effect against an invading navy, fell harmlessly onto the soft, rain-soaked soil of Malaya.

Reasons four, five and six were related to our lack of air cover and the fact that the Japanese had better and faster planes. All this, they said, 'Put us in such an impossible position and, in any case, we also had to think of the civilians, chaps'. And so we did. However, no one dared ask why so many of the civilians had been allowed to stay until it was too late. As for excuse number seven, that the Japs had very unsportingly cut off the island's water supply, piped in from Malaya – hadn't they noticed it rained nearly every bloody day? In any case, the Japs hadn't cut the water supply – we had, when we blew that useless hole in the causeway.

The lectures were designed to make us feel better and, I suppose, for those who needed propping up, in a way they did. The capitulation was a kick in the guts, which left us feeling lost, bewildered, humiliated. One day we are invincible, the next we are part of the worst military disaster in the history of the British Empire. We needed to believe in the propaganda, to clutch at every straw of hope offered.

Distant flashes of lightning, rolling crashes of thunder that heralded the approach of a storm, must be the gunfire of an Allied army as it pounded away at the retreating enemy. Oh yes, we agreed, a definite sign that relief troops were on their way, they had to be. We were still too close to those last days of fighting to harbour any doubts. We needed to be further away from the reality of defeat, and now was not the time for asking why, for raising doubts, or to wonder how it all came about.

Our camp, meanwhile, was developing a character of its own – as would be expected, with thousands of POWs of all sorts, sizes, shapes and ranks living cheek by jowl in an enclosed area, large as it was. It evolved into more of a large village than a POW camp, complete with its own council, bureaucracy and town planning committee. One section of the grounds was put aside for a veggie garden and to raise chooks. A library with several thousand books was established, as well as a university, which ran such well-conducted courses that some blokes actually attained the same level of study as at a university at home. In addition there was a first-class concert party, which boasted professional entertainers and a swag of musical instruments, including a piano that some enterprising blokes scrounged, and carried in, from one of the nearby abandoned homes.

For those who weren't into the arts or study there was always sport. We had a beaut cricket team, captained by Ben Bennett, who had been the Australian wicketkeeper with Bradman's team, before the war. The Rugby types also formed a team and played against the Poms but, as the English didn't know the first thing about Aussie Rules, those of us who did just played among ourselves. We did have a star player on one team – Captain Vern Rae, who had played for the North Hobart Football Club. He was so football mad he had taken his football to war, and somehow had managed to hang on to it.

As a self-governing community, Changi enforced its own rules and regulations. The Japs were allowed in only occasionally, so it was only on working parties outside the wire that we had any real contact with them. To their way of thinking, anything that fell to the conquering army was theirs, to be used and abused. As victors, they laid claim to everything that came their way, no matter what – civilian belongings, military spoils, animals, private homes and vehicles, and masses of warehouses, known as godowns, stuffed full of commodities ranging from rubber and machinery to food. These all had to be transported to the docks for shipment to Japan. No prizes for guessing who was earmarked to do this work.

Our capitulation had placed an immense and, dare I say it, unexpected workforce in the hands of the Japanese. Changi Camp was the holding camp for this huge pool of slave labour and it was from here that the future labour needs of the Japanese Empire were supplied. Building a railway in Thailand or an airfield in Borneo, slaving down a coal mine or working in heavy industry in Japan: it didn't matter what the nature of the work was and no thought was ever given to the difficulties that might be encountered. Nor did our captors ever evaluate the risk to life and limb. Prisoners of war, like beasts of burden, were of no consideration whatsoever.

Almost immediately, prisoners were sent out of the camp to work on various tasks. One project, not far from the fence line, was the clearing of the ground for an airfield whose frail beginnings were to evolve into the famous aerodrome known simply as Changi Airport. POWs also worked on building many of the roads that have since become vital links in the commercial life of the modern island. Slaves of the Eastern Sun King, they hacked away, creating roads through virgin jungle with the sweat of their brows and a few picks and hoes.

They worked in the teeming monsoonal rain, and in the malaria-infested swamps. Others, sent to camps in Burma and Thailand, fell victim to that cruellest of pestilences, cholera, together with the debilitating effects of slow starvation. The survivors were forced to work on, regardless. Railways were built, roads were constructed along mountain ranges, airfields were hacked out of the jungles.

Contrary to popular belief, the safest place for any POW to be was inside the Changi compound, which was run like a normal military camp. Your troubles began when you left it. Wherever it happened to be, that was it. Borneo, Burma, Thailand, Japan – the odds of returning in one piece were fixed and there was no escaping destiny. Every second man who left Changi became part of a lottery, where life was the prize to be won and death was the price of the ticket. Once the moving finger stopped, and pointed, that was that. There was no knowing if you would ever return, and many were to die building a vainglorious empire.

The moving finger points
And, having pointed,
You hope to God it wasn't you
The bastards had anointed.

However, for the first few months the work parties were stationed in and around Singapore. I wasn't in Changi Camp for any length of time, but in between jobs it became a home base. To determine who would do what, we drew lots. Some went with one group, others went elsewhere. Our labour was in great demand to clean up the mess left by the fighting, with a continuous stream of repair gangs moving backwards and forwards, all around the island.

I was among the hundred or so chosen to go on one of the first working parties. On asking the sarge why I had been so lucky, he replied, 'Listen kid, it's because you're a model soldier.' I was preening myself when he spoilt it by adding 'The real soldiers get to stay in camp'. As they say, ask a silly question.

We marched out so innocently that day, happy to be out and about, like a bunch of schoolkids on an excursion. The Jap guards also seemed happy enough, and we began to think that maybe they were human beings like us, after all. A few days labouring on the wharves and loading the rice trains soon dispelled this notion. Hardly a day passed without our being unwilling witnesses to some piece of cold and calculated bloody-mindedness. It was a chilling insight into the psychological make-up of our captors and a sobering understanding that we were part of something that was returning us to a Dark Age.

The day-to-day cruelty manifested itself with such dramatic intensity and brutality that it took our breath away. But when whatever nastiness they had inflicted was over, the perpetrators would show us photos of their wives and children. This Jekyll-and-Hyde type of behaviour took some getting used to. So did walking past lines of severed heads. This vivid demonstration of a medieval indifference to the value of life was chillingly effective, even though the sight of chopped-off heads was hard to believe. Real human heads, with neatly parted hair, spiked onto bamboo stakes and put on show all around the city, while everything else around them was so everyday, so innocent. Their bloody message seared itself into my memory, like a red-hot branding iron on a young heifer, leaving a scar that will never be erased or forgotten. After a while we got used to it, but we still didn't quite believe it. It's a bit like seeing a sign that reads 'wet paint'. You understand the sign, but you still have the compulsion to verify it for yourself.

Three heads, strung along the road
Three heads, standing there on show
Three heads, a warning to the people
Beware, the Samurai swordsman's blow.

Newly initiated, we were also struck by the surrealist quality of the scene, but later would come to accept that the staked heads were part of the landscape, and that life must go on, no matter what. For the local population, severed heads spiked onto blood-drenched poles, displayed on tables or tied to lamp posts were part and parcel of everyday life, because that was how things were. Before the war was to finish, many civilians would die in much the same way, but the living would go about their business, no matter how gruesome the street decorations became.

While the roadside 'billboards' were hideously confronting, we naively believed that this must surely be the limit of our captors' inhumanity. It wasn't. Not by a long shot.

One day, on rice-loading detail, we were perched on top of a stack of bagged rice, idly watching a Jap sentry check papers and direct traffic while we ate our lunch when, from the far side of an idling truck, a rickshaw appeared. The Chinese coolie,

CHAPTER 5 Reluctant guests of the Emperor

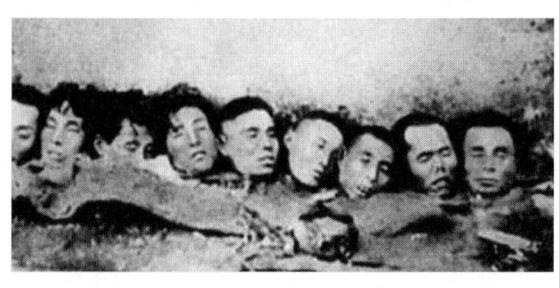

The heads of Chinese civilians murdered by occupying troops in Singapore

oblivious to any danger and obviously not noticing the sentry, passed through the checkpoint on the blind side of the truck. With a cry of '*Kora!*' (Hey!), the guard rushed forward, rifle butt swinging. The first blow, delivered fair and square to the coolie's face, felled him, stone dead, but the sentry didn't let up. Like a madman he then attacked the rickshaw, smashing it to bits. In what seemed a matter of seconds, the rickshaw lay in pieces on the roadside, a crumpled mess, while beside it sprawled the broken body of an inoffensive Chinese workman: a fellow human being, who had been destroyed, cut down, right before our eyes; killed, not in the frenzied bloodletting of battle, nor while committing some wanton criminal act. He had been slaughtered simply to demonstrate who the masters were, an act so devastating in its message, so cruelly simple, and so simply cruel.

Shouldering his rifle, the sentry returned to the truck, finished inspecting the papers and waved the driver on, as if nothing had happened. The poor inoffensive coolie lay dead and forgotten in the burning sun. His remains were still there when we left the wharf at the end of the day's work.

A few days later I came down with a high fever and was carted back to Selarang, but it was not to be for any length of time. No sooner was I back on my feet than blow me down, my number came up, again, along with almost the whole of C Company, including Captain 'Bull' Bowring, who had been discharged from hospital after making a remarkable recovery from his wounds and was supposed to keep us in line.

This project was something new, at least according to the Japanese, who proudly announced that this was the first time that we would be working under something called the Far Eastern Co-Prosperity Sphere, or words to that effect. It was some kind of beautification and construction work and it sounded all right.

Our new base camp, under the command of Black Jack, was at Thomson

Road, a leafy thoroughfare lined with lovely big houses. As hundreds of POWs were earmarked for the project, we made the journey on foot; a march that was made more than bearable when the guards decided we should have a two-hour lunch break at Lavender Road, in the heart of Singapore's red light district. There was no chance for anyone to take advantage of what the girls had to offer, but we certainly scored well in the food and hospitality stakes when they came out to give us presents of food and even money.

Our billets in Thomson Road, once part of a well-to-do, middle-class suburb, were the former residences of some of the island's leading citizens, who had either escaped from Singapore in time or were now banged up in Changi Gaol. Just a few short months before, the occupants would not have been seen dead in the company of lowly colonial soldiers, let alone have invited them into their private domains. So it was with a certain amount of satisfaction that we moved into these posh empty houses and made ourselves right at home. This was my first experience at living in such a magnificent piece of real estate, even though it had been looted and stripped. My imagination refitted the rooms so that I could see just how nice a lifestyle it must have been. No wonder so many of the owners had waited until it was too late to leave.

A typical house used to accommodate POW working parties

Our task was to build couple of roads through a patch of jungle at Bukit Timah, not far from where we had huddled in that monsoon drain with the Indian sepoys. The roads were to create an access to a memorial which, according to one of our blokes, commemorated 'the great sense of compassion, and love of humanity, possessed by, the ordinary Japanese soldiers, in so many kinds of ways'. If only.

CHAPTER 5 Reluctant guests of the Emperor 109

Billy's working party was part of a much larger force, numbering in the thousands, sent to the Bukit Timah area. Here two ambitious projects were in full swing. The first of these, on a heavily forested hill overlooking the McCritchie Reservoir, was a large Shinto temple, consisting of several open-sided, colonnaded buildings roofed in traditional style with material specially brought in from Japan. The approach to this complex, named Shonan Jinjya after an old Japanese shrine built in Singapore before the war, was via an ornamental bridge spanning an arm of the reservoir and a flight of granite-hewn steps.

Billy's party was working on the other, equally ambitious undertaking at Bukit Batok, behind the Ford Motor factory where the surrender documents were signed. Bukit Batok is Malay for 'Coughing Hill', a name coined in the early 1930s when the entrEpreneurial Mr J Hindhede obtained the rights to quarry granite on nearby Bukit Timah. The short, explosive sounds of the dynamite used in his quarry gave rise to the rather unusual name.

Bukit Timah, or Tin Hill, has never been mined for tin. The name goes back to 1909, when T C Loveridge found a tiny pocket of tin ore, amounting to four pikuls – a traditional Asian unit of weight that equates to a shoulder load (as much as a man can carry on a shoulder pole, deemed to be about 135 pounds or 60 kilograms). The Crown was entitled to its due, so the bureaucratic Mr Farrer, the Collector of Land Revenue, solemnly collected the royalty payable for the four pikuls on behalf of His Britannic Majesty King Edward VII.

The Japanese had earmarked Bukit Batok for the Shonan Chureto War Memorial, a slender 60-foot wooden obelisk to commemorate their war dead. As roads and footways, as well as the bridge, had to be constructed to access both the temple at Bukit Timah and the obelisk site, the labour force required was considerable.

When it was discovered that the memorial was actually to honour the Japanese war dead, some blokes deliberately misbehaved so that they would be sent back to Changi as punishment.

And it was punishment because, while conditions at Selarang Barracks were quite good, life there was strictly controlled by the Australian administration. Initially, working parties sent out from the camp to labour for the Japanese had been selected from the ranks of the less well disciplined. With camp discipline a major problem, quite a number of the 'volunteers' placed on drafts for outside work were high-spirited youngsters such as Billy or those who had demonstrated a rather cavalier attitude towards camp rules and regulations. Working on the premise that a stretch on the outside, working under Japanese control, might encourage better behaviour in future, the working parties had been seen as a heaven-sent opportunity to get rid of the rebels.

However, while accommodation outside Changi was not the best and the guards in control of working parties could be unpredictable, the POWs soon discovered that the possibilities for scrounging (the polite word for acquiring goods that did not belong to you) were endless.

When the workers began to send scrounged medical supplies, food and tobacco back to the main camp, it didn't take long for the word to spread that life was better outside Selarang than in it – a revelation that forced camp administration to rethink the criteria for the selection process.

With the benefits of being outside now realised, there was no shortage of eager volunteers for the next or subsequent drafts. The demand increased even more when a medical officer, sent out to check on conditions, reported that in addition to a meat ration of four ounces (about 115 grams) a day, prisoners on outside working parties were actually paid – 25 cents a day for sergeants, 15 for other NCOs and 10 for privates. By May, with the Japanese finding plenty of outlets for labour and the prisoners only too happy to provide it, there were more POWs outside the Changi area than in it. To maintain disciplinary control in the outside parties, the punishment for bad behaviour was reversed – toe the line or go back to Changi.

Early each morning we'd leave home from Thomson Road for the 'office', with tools in tow. Armed with pick and axe and changkul (garden hoe), we'd march to the work site, where hundreds of us were split into various groups, graded according to experience. When it came time to tackle the thickest part of the jungle, we were fortunate to have plenty of expert bushmen. Their know-how, together with their amazing ability with the axe, gave us a vital edge in filling our daily work quota, come what may. Their judgment was so good that they were able to time the speed of work to finish within the narrowest of margins, satisfying both the Japs and looking after our wellbeing. Too slow, there was trouble. Too fast, the Japs loaded us with more work. It was a marvellous demonstration of how to think ahead in order to work slowly at the fastest rate.

It was while we were working at one of more isolated spots that I made an unexpected and unforgettable discovery. We were marching along when the guard called out 'Resto', giving us a five-minute pit-stop. When I went off into the bush for a pee I came across a dramatic tableau that graphically demonstrated the tragic, grim, wasteful stupidity of war.

In a quiet little clearing were the remains of a dead soldier, his body lying on an army groundsheet, his head resting on a haversack. His arms were folded across his chest, and clutched in his skeletal hands was the British Army *Red Book*, opened at the page marked 'Burial Services'.

CHAPTER 5 Reluctant guests of the Emperor

The trees 'stood-to' in silent grief
The flowering shrubs a living wreath.
They'd laid him on his army mac
His head upon his haversack.
With folded arms across his chest,
A brave young soldier's final rest.

The scene couldn't have been more clearly described if it had been carved in stone. It had happened in the heat of the battle and, with time running out, his companions had done all they could for him. He lay there waiting, his bleached bones white against the remnants of his rotted uniform. Given a little more time, nature would have quietly and gently reclaimed him completely. It was such a beautiful setting, of trees and flowering shrubs, of twittering birds and open sky. What a pity we could not leave him undisturbed, at rest and in peace; no longer afraid, having fought and lost his final battle.

However, even in captivity, correct procedures had to be observed. So we carried him from his personal Eden, and lowered his mortal remains into a hole dug into the bank on the side of the jungle road.

For the remainder of my time at Thomson Road, going to and from the day's toil, I would salute my young, unknown English soldier, lying in his new grave, his rusting steel helmet marking the lonely mound of earth.

There in a lonely grave he lays.
There, in the layered dust,
Of yesterdays.

Work on roadway leading to the shrine continued seven days a week. Not far from where we were hacking away at a rather difficult section, running through a stand of large trees, were some buildings housing the Catholic Order of the Little Sisters of the Poor. One Sunday morning, the sisters somehow got the Japs to agree to allow the 'Micks' to attend mass. Despite some ribbing from their less pious co-workers, my mate Harry Longley, along with three or four brave souls, made the effort and went off to church. On his return Harry described, in mouth-watering detail, the huge feast of banana and pineapple fritters that had been forced upon them after the service, as 'extra blessings that come the way of true believers'. We poor sinners were now green with envy, and ripe for conversion.

It so happened that on the very next Sunday we were still working at the same location. To say that the sisters were overwhelmed by the tremendous numbers converting to the Catholic faith would be something of an understatement. Alas, this was not destined to be our road to Damascus. The Jap sergeant in charge of our working party, obviously a heathen, nipped this fantastic spiritual opportunity in the bud.

Up until this time, the guards assigned to our work parties and sub-camps were fighting soldiers, drawn from the conquering army until such time as occupation troops arrived. We woke up one morning to find there was not a guard to be seen. At first, the rumour mill reported that the Yanks had landed, but it turned out that, with the changeover of personnel, there had been a huge administrative mix-up. Our regular guards had marched off, but had not been replaced.

With no one around to make us do any work, Harry Longley suggested that we visit a nearby Chinese cemetery, in the hope that mourners had left some edible offerings for the spirits of their dearly departed. We were out of luck. The only offerings were made of paper. However, we did find a stretcher abandoned beside a large pit, and were about to take possession of it when a heavily laden truck came crawling up the slope. Standing on top of the load were two workmen, with what appeared to be big clothes-pegs clipped on their noses. It was then that the stench hit us. The truck was full of decomposing bodies.

There were at least forty dead men, women and children, all hideously mixed together like a scene from Dante's Inferno. Picking up the stretcher, the workmen began carrying the corpses to the pit, watched by a bored-looking driver and an equally bored young Eurasian medical officer. The reason for their disinterest became apparent when the MO told us that these mass burials occurred three or four times a day. The dead were not, as we had first thought, massacre victims but casualties of war, killed by illness, hunger, injury and disease. Each day their bodies were dragged out on the street for collection, in the same way that those who had died from the Black Death during the Middle Ages were piled into anonymous heaps and taken on carts for burial in mass graves. Scrapping any thought of sticking around to appropriate the stretcher, we quickly headed back to camp.

As we approached Thomson Road village, we ran smack-bang into a group of Jap soldiers leaving an open-sided Chinese coffee shop. Unable to do anything other than put on a bold front, we marched on past in true military style, counting time, left right, left right. As we drew level, Harry barked, 'Eyes right' and, as one, we threw them the smartest salutes we could muster – salutes I am certain our drill sergeant would not have thought possible. The Nips quickly came to attention and saluted back. From then on, whenever we met any Japs we saluted them. They always returned the compliment, evidently assuming that we were part of a large contingent of European civilians, yet to be interned as they were working on essential services.

The replacement guards for our camp did not materialise for a few days so, along with hundreds of POWs, we took full advantage of the situation and enjoyed the hospitality of Singapore. Of course Black Jack, who did everything by the book, ordered us to remain in camp but, as he had no means of enforcing the order, we took no notice.

The Chinese, who hated the Japs, were certainly not going to dob, and went out of their way to help whenever they could. Of all the kindness and generosity we encountered during this unforgettable period, the most memorable was the unexpected meeting with a young boy. Harry and I, and another mate, Joey Crome, were making our way through a patchwork of small market gardens when the boy, beckoning to us to follow him, led the way to his family's humble home – a small atap house on the side of a hill. Inviting us to go inside and help ourselves to the food that was on the table, he explained that he could not stay as the risk to his family, should the Japanese come by, was too great.

We enjoyed a wonderful meal that day, a feast fit for a king. The Chinese are great cooks, and the food, which included bowls of succulent little prawns, was delicious. It was humbling to realise that these people, who were so poor, could jeopardise their lives to help utter strangers. The only evidence we could leave to show our appreciation was the empty bowls; our only thanks for their kindness a brief, discreet wave to the distant, coolie-hatted figures toiling away on the hillside.

Our stint of freedom came to an end when the new guards, who finally arrived and discovered what was going on, posted sentries around the camp perimeter. Harry and I were on our way back, after finishing our little holiday on a high note, and it was only due to good timing that we were not caught in the net.

We had spent a good part of the day gorging ourselves at a huge feast provided by a wealthy Chinese businessmen, a grandfatherly type who had many children and grandchildren. A good Catholic, the same as Harry, he was a director of Hume Pipes, an Australian-based company. The factory was at Bukit Timah but he lived in a huge terrace house in town, along with his numerous family members. The old rumour that the Yanks had landed at Penang was doing the rounds yet again, so when he saw us in town, and on the loose, he figured it must be true and waved us over.

Some of the other blokes had gone off to Lavender Street to visit the girls but, as brothel creeping was not on our list of things to do in Singapore, Harry and I settled for the generous hospitality of the Chinese grandpa and his family. Having been royally entertained, and with our stomachs close to bursting, we were making our way back to Thomson Road when we spotted a big contingent of guards running at the double towards our billets, and in the nick of time scampered over the single wire marking the camp boundary. Others were not as lucky. Anyone caught on the wrong side of the wire, including Bob Shipsides, was confined to a tennis court by the Sikh guards and forced to remain there, in the open, for several days until Black Jack considered they'd been punished enough and demanded that the Japs set them free. As Black Jack also took a dim view of any NCO being involved, on his release Bob was busted back to private and sent to Changi.

It wasn't long after this that I had a very personal run-in with Black Jack. No one had bothered to tell me that the boss was on the prowl, visiting our part of the camp, so I was completely unprepared for our meeting.

I guess he was, too.

I came running around the corner of a house, and crashed straight into him. He went down with a thump, head-over-turkey. As soon as I saw all the 'Red Tabs' (soldier-speak for senior staff officers, identified by red tabs on their lapels) following along in his wake, I took off – fast – ignoring Black Jack's enraged bellows of 'Stop, soldier', and the intimidating sight of his big black-headed Malacca cane waving threateningly in my direction. Spurred on by sheer fright, I managed to make a successful retreat, my identity never detected.

Shortly afterwards we began working our way through an area of Bukit Batok which only a few short months before had been a battlefield. The story of what had occurred lay woven in a tapestry of leaves and broken branches, of shell and shot, and of human remains. Lying near the overgrown traces of a foot track was an army stretcher with the skeletal body of an Australian soldier. Bleached finger bones, dug deep into the earth as he'd tried to drag himself clear of bullet or bayonet thrust, told the story of his vain attempt to escape from a merciless enemy. In front and behind the stretcher lay all that was left of his two stretcher-bearers, their Red Cross armbands torn and faded.

Over by a stand of trees was further evidence of the fierceness of the fighting, a last-ditch stand marked only by a scattering of bones, remnants of uniforms and broken weapons rusting away among the grass. The clamour of war had long since departed. The shouting, the agony, the sighs of departing life had been replaced by peace and serenity as the bush reclaimed its own. The birds, the animals, the insects, had all returned. Here, among the regrowth of shell-torn trees and scrub, we paused and searched among the scattered scraps of clothing and bits of bone, picking through the leavings of the battle. We, who were here only by chance, read the story of the bones, and having collected what we could of them, dug a hole, buried them, and bowed our heads. There was no need for words.

Billy did not remain at Thomson Road Camp long enough to see the completion of the obelisk project, which also incorporated a small, far less obtrusive wooden cross to commemorate the Allied dead. Although the prisoners were taken aback by the decision to allow them to erect their own memorial, they were unaware that the reasons for doing so were not as altruistic as they appeared. While Lieutenant Nekemoto, the Japanese officer in charge of the construction work, had given the idea his enthusiastic support, his commanding officer had only given his approval when its propaganda value, to be captured on Japanese newsreels, was pointed out. Although some Australians were not at all keen on building monuments to honour the enemy war dead, others, who had placed termites beneath the foundations, were not troubled in the slightest. Their confidence, it seems, was misplaced. While quite a large number of the voracious timber-eating insects had been successfully relocated, it appears that the termite queen, the colony's sole egg layer, did not survive the move. Shortly after the war ended, the obelisk and cross, along with the shrine on the adjoining hill, were destroyed.

Bukit Batok Memorial opening

My time at Thomson Road came to an abrupt end when I fell victim to a touch of dysentery and was sent back to Selarang. Like the prodigal son, I had returned. However, I discovered that one of the penalties of youth, when you find yourself among a bunch of old POWs, is that there is no fatted calf. We young blokes were deemed to be fit and well, even when we were sick, because we always looked fitter than the old blokes, who were not sick.

The doc ordered me to cough, looked down my throat, and that was that. 'Corporal! Mark him as fit and well.' It was now official. I was fit enough to be harnessed by thick ropes to a Changi Trailer, a truck chassis used to haul heavy and cumbersome items; well enough to become part of a transport team carting things from the depot to here, there and everywhere. Whether delivering wood to the cookhouse, rubbish to the tip or supplies to a corner of the vast Selarang

Camp, I liked to imagine that we were eighteenth-century sailors hoisting great canvas sails to the mainmast, or Egyptian slaves hauling huge loads of stones to build the pyramids, all to the rhythmic chant of 'Hi-he heave-ho, hi-he heave-ho'.

With the day's work done, on odd occasions we went under the wire at night to forage for extra grub and to keep ourselves up to date with what was going on in the outside world. On one occasion, three or four of us had enjoyed a fairly successful few hours' scrounging and were returning to camp, loaded down with coconuts, when we struck trouble. Not from the Japs, who were outside the wire, but from our own flaming mob, inside the wire. The brass, who disapproved of anyone going outside the camp without authorisation, must have decided on a sudden crackdown; the camp's military police were everywhere, and we had to dump our cargo to escape their clutches. Stone the crows. You wouldn't read about it. If our MPs had been as diligent when we were fighting the Japs, we might not then have been in the absurd situation of being chased by them, inside a POW camp! I have often wondered who among the posse that night got to enjoy the fruits of our labours.

As a still-growing lad and eternally hungry, I took a keen interest in any enterprise that involved food. One day I was sitting behind our building, enjoying a game of poker with a few of the blokes when Keith 'Shearer' Gillett, a big bloke who had worked as a shearers' cook, looked up from his cards and asked if we had any contributions for the Changi Surprise Stew he was thinking of making. We scratched around, and between us managed to provide some salt, a good-sized yam, a heart of palm (also known as rich man's cabbage because the entire palm tree had to be chopped down to get it), plus a few leftover bits and pieces, thus ensuring that each of us had a share in the nosh. Keith placed our offerings into a 5-gallon kerosene tin before revealing his own 'special' contribution – Bongo, the prized pet monkey belonging to our battalion cook, Two-Ton Tony. There was no doubt about the monkey's identity. His name was clearly engraved on the tab on his collar.

Being now accomplices before the fact, we hurriedly beheaded and skinned the poor little blighter, tossed him into the stew and returned to our card game. After a while, Keith said to me, 'Go take a look at how the stew is going, kid', so I did. What a shock! When I lifted the lid, floating on top of the thick bubbling mess was what looked exactly like the decapitated head of a tiny child. Hearing my cry of horror, Keith took a look. 'Shit!' Grabbing a parang (jungle knife), he hacked into Bongo, saying 'Just give it a few more minutes. She'll be right'. And it was. Bongo tasted real beaut. The only downside, which came close to ruining our feast, was the plaintive voice of our poor cook as he called in vain for his little pet.

We felt rather bad about it at the time, but this was rather early into our captivity, when we were still burdened with a conscience of sorts.

Sitting around with the fellows, plotting and scheming, working out ways of outwitting the officers in charge, having a joke, a bit of a giggle, and a laugh, were the best part of being back 'home'. Friendships are like steel, toughened in the fires of adversity – the greater the adversity, the stronger the bond. Once hammered on the anvil of tribulation they are rustproof and no matter how long the friendship lies unused, when you come to pick it up again you know that you hold a trustworthy blade. I was always glad to be back with the battalion.

Unfortunately, my joy was to be short-lived.

CHAPTER 6

TO SANDAKAN

7 July – November 1942

Of all the activities held in Changi, the big event of the 1942 theatre season was the production and presentation of *Outward Bound*, a 1920's play (later made into a film featuring Leslie Howard). The plot centres entirely on a group of passengers who meet in the lounge of an ocean liner at sea, but have no idea of why they are there, or of their destination. Nevertheless, all are in high spirits, completely ignorant of the fact that they are on their final voyage. Everyone is actually dead. The ship is a Ghost Ship, and the passengers are departing spirits.

On 7 July 1942, shortly after seeing this play, some fifteen hundred of us were assigned to a group called B Force, packed onto trucks and driven to the Singapore docks, where we were loaded onto a ship. Well, some of us were packed onto trucks – the old blokes and the sick. Young fellas like me had to walk most of the way.

As we drew closer to the bridge spanning the Singapore River and the wharf area, a gruesome sight left us in no doubt that the Japs still meant business. Displayed on tables and spiked on poles were the freshly decapitated heads of Chinese civilians who must have really upset their new masters.

A further short walk brought us dockside, the same dockside where, just a few months before, I had disembarked with such high hopes and expectations. Like the characters in the play, who'd had no idea of their situation or destination, we were now Outward Bound and our ship was, to all intents and purposes, a Ghost Ship. The countdown had started. For almost everyone who went on board that day, it would be his final voyage.

Throughout 1942 and 1943, the Japanese transferred large numbers of POWs from Changi to new camps overseas, where it was claimed there were plenty of rations and medical care and only light work to be done, if any. To make life agreeable in their new homes, prisoners were encouraged to take whatever they could, including large musical instruments. No one had any idea of the hardships and misery that lay ahead.

The first group to move out was A Force, which departed in May 1942 for Burma where, after airfield construction, they would be put to work building the notorious Burma-Thai railway. The next group, of which Billy was part, was B Force, earmarked for Borneo. In order to reach the quota of 2000 men requested, the Japanese claimed that the new camp would be a Convalescent Camp, suitable for 'old men' (anyone over 35) and all those who were recovering from illness or battle wounds.

To look after the sick, a disproportionate number of ambulance men and medical orderlies were added to the draft. Also included was a large number of officers who, as they were not required to do any work at Changi, were regarded as 'useless mouths'; the so-called 'troublemakers' who had been sent out on working parties but had been returned to Changi as punishment for flouting rules; and some annoyingly high-spirited youngsters. Billy, who fitted into the two latter categories, was guaranteed a place on the list. Also with him were Privates Harry Longley, Joey Crome, Crome's mate Walter 'Henry' Ford, Keith 'Shearer' Gillett, Sid Outram and his best mate James Donohue, and Billy's mentor, Bob Shipsides, who had not regained his corporal's stripes. When departure day arrived, B Force totalled only 1496 men of the 2000 required. As they soon discovered, the voyage would be no picnic.

Crammed in like cattle, packed down in the holds, stacked shoulder to shoulder, we sweltered in the bowels of *Yubi Maru*, a filthy, dirty rust-bucket previously used as a coal carrier. To add insult to injury, it was actually one of the outdated cargo ships that Pig-Iron Bob had sold to the Japs. I didn't know the actual name for some time, as I'd only bothered to remember the *Maru* bit. After getting a few raised eyebrows every time I referred to 'that bastard of a ship, the *Maru*', someone eventually enlightened me. 'Every bloody Jap ship is called *Maru*, Billy. The trick is to remember which bloody *Maru* it is.' Even then, the know-alls got it wrong. They called it *Ubi Maru* – ubi is Malay for 'potato'. It took me another 55 years to discover from my co-author that the correct name was *Yubi* (or *Yubai*) *Maru*. Yubi is a boy's name in Japanese that means gracious or elegant.

Talk about a misnomer! Apart from being barely seaworthy, it was so crowded that only those less than four feet in height could find enough space to lie down. So it was a case of 'knees up Mother Brown', sitting one behind the other with the bloke in front using your knees as a backrest. To move at all was almost impossible, but not to move was so painful that it became impossible not to move.

It was bad enough where we were in the stern, but it was worse for the poor coots in the other two holds, which had been divided into two floors to fit in extra cargo, making the space available for the POWs even smaller.

Rumour was rife. We were going to Siam, or Burma. No we bloody weren't, we were off to Java, or maybe it was to Japan. Not one of the guesses was right. It turned out that we were sailing to Sandakan.

'Sandakan, where in the hell is Sandakan?'

'In bloody Borneo!'

'Borneo! Whereabouts in Borneo?'

'Shut up Billy, you'll soon find out.'

The one thing we did find out, and quick smart, was not only that breathing was difficult, but the air quality was downright disgusting. With the thick layer of coal dust, and hundreds of sweating bodies crammed together, the smoggy atmosphere below deck was beyond belief. We sat at anchor in the harbour, waiting for hours in that semi-dark hothouse of a hold, breathing more or less by numbers; gasping every mouthful we could possibly salvage from the meagre trickle of humid air drifting down from the open hatch.

We all cheered with relief when the ship finally gathered steam and, with a last hurrah from the smokestack, sailed out and away from the stifling confines of the harbour. After a while the Japs got around to rigging a tubular canvas vent, and we luxuriated in the cool, clean airflow; one hundred per cent pure sea air. As if it were cold beer flowing from a tap, we drank greedily, in great gulps.

The buggers soon made up for this show of consideration for our wellbeing by lowering into the hold tin drums filled with rice into which sulphide of lime, used to control pests, had been mixed. This horrible, pebble-like grit turned the cooked rice a nasty greenish yellow colour; it stank of sulphur as well, which made it a most appropriate gruel for a hellship. It also gave everyone the 'runs'. Until that time, I had thought that the expression 'to shit through the eye of a needle without splashing the sides' was nothing but an exaggerated impossibility. Not anymore.

Dysentery, the posh medical term for 'the runs', is a coot of a thing at any time, but on board *Yubi Maru* it was torture. Apart from the awful griping pains, it placed an impossible stress on the makeshift toilet system hastily provided by the Nippon Shipping Service for our 'convenience'.

On the section of the deck allocated to our hold was a 'four-pooper' – a timbered toilet platform with an atap roof, split into four semi-partitions and extending precariously over the water. Desperate to make use of our four-man dunny, the 400 men in our stern hold strong enough to climb the narrow iron ladder were forced to wait in line. However, many were too sick to move, or simply couldn't wait and, in consequence, the rungs and railings of the ladder, as well as the hold, became a miasmic cesspool. The fortunate blokes who made it to the top in time perched on the plank – four white bums hanging out above the sea, holding on grimly to the rails, doing their best to coincide their 'disposals' with the surge and roll of the waves, and at the same time trying not to fall through the hole.

Yubi Maru toilet facilities

We spent eleven days on that rundown old tub, which rocked and rolled and at times seemed to be sailing backwards. Constantly at odds with the elements, *Yubi Maru* swayed across the equator and then the South China Sea before taking a left turn, up the west coast of Borneo. Conditions for the passengers seesawed from one day to the next – having the shits and being shat upon, being scorched by the heat or steamed by the humidity.

By the time we arrived off the oil town of Miri, in northern Sarawak, we had managed to rig a system of 'locks', where the stronger positioned themselves on the ladder to assist the weaker to climb to the deck. Actually using the facilities was a secondary aim; getting them topside, where they could breathe in some clean sweet air, was far more important.

We anchored off Miri in the stifling heat for three interminable days. On the first night Joey Crome and I found a little niche between the dunny and a storage box, from where we assessed our chances of swimming to the not-too-distant shore. The lights of Miri beamed enticingly – so bright and just over there – close enough, it seemed, to reach out and touch them. Freedom beckoned and, with the advantage of a pitch-black, moonless night, we decided to give it a go. Hunched in our little hideaway, we were trying to gee each other up with a series of muttered 'whad-da-ya-thinks'; 'it's just a bit of a paddle'; 'yeh, piece of cake'; 'you go first'; 'naw, you go first', when the galley door opened and a Jap cook threw a bucket of swill overboard.

Holy mackerel! No sooner had it hit the surface than all hell broke loose. In less than a flash the dark waters became a battlefield, ablaze with tracer-like streaks of fluorescence – bullets of light, firing through and across the blackness beneath the ship. Hundreds, thousands of fish, were fighting for their supper. Then, up from the depths like the beam of a searchlight, a flaring glow of fluorescence was upon them. With one mighty swish and a swirl, a large shark gatecrashed the party, causing a multitude of fiery streaks to zap, criss-crossing the bay as the small fry fled the scene in frenzied retreat.

We couldn't help but shiver at the thought of almost being part of the meal, possibly the main course. As we silently reassessed the situation the waters settled back into an innocent black silence. With one final look at the now far-too-distant, no-longer-inviting lights of Miri, we made our way back down the ladder. The stinking hold from which we had been so keen to escape seemed so much more friendly now, and we settled down to sleep.

After leaving Miri and its perilous waters behind, there was talk of taking over the ship, using a silver revolver and half a dozen bullets that Shearer Gillett had scrounged in Singapore. He had dismantled the gun to smuggle it on board, giving Bob Shipsides one half and keeping the other, and distributing the bullets among the blokes. I had mine hanging on a cord around my neck, like a souvenir. However, when Mo Davis, gazing out to sea while peeing from the topside facilities, saw the conning tower of a Jap sub that was shadowing us, we immediately scotched this half-baked idea.

Eighteen-year-old Eric Davis, of 2/20 Battalion, was also an under-age recruit. Known universally as 'Mo' because of his well-clipped, dapper moustache, he had left home at the age of thirteen. After working at various jobs in outback New South Wales he had signed on as a boiler man to the troopship Queen Mary, *before volunteering for the AIF.*

Mo had good powers of observation. While the ship was anchored at Miri he had noticed light from a naked bulb shining through the floorboards as he crouched in the double-decker for'ard hold, knees tucked under his chin and eyes lowered. With the help of two other teenaged prisoners, Keith Botterill and Sid Outram, he prised up the boards to see what was below. To their delight they discovered they were sitting on cases of meat and vegetables, plundered from the godowns in Singapore and now destined for Japan.

Eric 'Mo' Davis   Keith Botterill

It was fortunate Mo had discovered the cache for, although the Japanese guards returned from their shore leave loaded down with pineapples, not one sliver reached the POWs. Billy, unfortunately, was not able to partake of Mo's unexpected feast, being stricken with a bout of dysentery at the time.

Still heading north, we skirted the island of Labuan and the port of Jesselton, the towering summit of Mount Kinabalu, south-east Asia's highest peak, clearly visible above the cloudline. At the most northerly tip of Borneo we turned eastward and passed the 'other tip', then followed the coastline south. On reaching an island with great towering red cliffs, which I later learned was Berhala Island, the ship headed west to enter a large harbour, where we tied up against an old, clapped-out timber wharf. Exhausted, filthy and stinking to high heaven, we had finally arrived and, thankfully, all in one piece.

Sandakan, with its beautiful harbour, its lovely colonial bungalows on the foreshore, and the escarpment behind covered in green lush foliage, looked like a tropical paradise, but this benign, welcoming appearance was to prove cruelly deceptive. After having our legs and feet sprayed with phenyl toilet disinfectant, supposedly to kill any dysentery germs lurking there, we were allowed to disembark.

A short distance away was a town green, or padang, where we were counted. *Ichi, ni, san, shi* – one, two, three, four – which some of the wags had turned into 'itchy knees can't see'. Supervising all this counting business, watched by a crowd of interested locals, was a tall, slender, good-looking Jap officer whom we learned was Lieutenant Hoshijima Sushumi, the camp commandant. Unlike the peasantish guards, he had a definite air of culture about him, civilised even.

Our mob, along with everyone in the stern hold, was marched back to the ship for the night. It wasn't until later that we learned that all those in the double-decker holds were to stay ashore, as the Japs wanted to unload the cargo from below. So I wasn't among the hundreds of fortunate blokes who, after the usual revolting rice dinner, walked up a nearby hill to spend the night at a big stone C of E church that overlooked the town. The officers, being officers, had separate accommodation in the timber, colonial-style boarding school next door. The next morning, when we all joined up again on the padang, one of the NCOs told me he had seen a dead Chinese man who must really have upset the Japs. He had been suspended upside down from a tree by a wire passed through his Achilles tendons.

Breakfast was a mug of lukewarm, stewed tea and the same rotten-tasting limed rice, now stone cold – leftovers from the day before. However, hope springs eternal and so, totally ignorant of what was to come, we set off up the winding road to march the eight miles to our new camp, singing 'Waltzing Matilda' – not because we particularly wanted to sing, but as an act of pure defiance. It was a bit of a hike but despite being tired and worn from the sea voyage I couldn't help but take an interest in this new country.

Reaching the top of the escarpment, the way then wound through lushly tropical greenery, past coconut and rubber plantations and skirting dense patches of jungle festooned with a multitude of diverse and brightly coloured flowers. But for all its natural beauty it was a Judas Road: a road that led through village and field to a camp of death, where self-proclaimed Knights of Bushido and Japanese officers, while condoning mindless acts of cruelty, boasted of principles and ethics and of upholding the honour of their Emperor.

The frontrunners reached Mile 8 at around lunchtime. The camp itself was down a dirt side-track, well off the main road, which ended in the grounds of the large agricultural Government Experimental Farm. Crossing a small stream, we turned right at a small power plant and followed a road that swept in a semi-circle to bring us to the top of a hill, and the camp entrance. Palm, kapok, cinnamon, coffee and coconut trees surrounded a cleared area that sloped towards a small swamp. In the far distance, at the edge of the rainforest, were a couple of small villages.

The Eight Mile Camp, as it was known, had been constructed by the British before the outbreak of war to house personnel to build, and then defend, a proposed airstrip. The airfield site had been surveyed and the large trees removed when hostilities put an end to the project. The wooden barracks buildings were used, instead, to intern enemy aliens. However, the Japanese inmates had been in occupation for only six weeks or so when the tables were turned and Sandakan surrendered to the Japanese. After hurriedly erecting additional huts, the occupying enemy force had a ready-made camp in which to imprison their POW labour force.

The Big Tree

POW huts near the swamp

Dominating the site was a very large, extremely tall tree, some 200 feet in height. Dubbed 'The Big Tree' by the prisoners, it was a mengaris, a South-East Asian species favoured by honeybees as the first branch is always a long way from the ground, making it difficult for the native sun-bears to climb. Estimated to be hundreds of years old, the Big Tree had a hollow trunk and was in poor shape from repeated lightning strikes.

The camp certainly looked good from the distance, with rows of palm-leaf huts spilling down the side of a hill, framed by shrubs and bushes in various shades of green and the dark entanglement of the encroaching forest. A veritable Garden of Eden, after eleven days at sea.

Close up, it was another story. The buildings had lain empty for months, and were filthy and in a poor state of repair. They had been attacked not only by the elements but also by local scavengers. Despite the overall dilapidated state of the camp, the section to the right and left of the entrance gate had the look of British Colonial spit-and-polish. A number of timber-walled huts, each split into four separate rooms and designated for officers, NCOs, hospital, cookhouse and cookhouse staff, spread out across the crest of the hill. Running at right angles all the way down to the swamp were 24 far less sturdy huts, built on stilts – four rows with five huts and one with four. All were constructed entirely of atap. Each hut was partitioned into three rooms some fourteen feet square, with a four-foot wide verandah running along the entire front and sets of wooden stairs to provide access.

Atap, when properly dried and shrunk, makes a surprisingly efficient all-weather shelter. However, as the huts for the ORs had been put up in something of a hurry, the atap had not been cured and already had significant gaps in it before the local scavengers had set to work. The hut my mates and I found ourselves in, right down the end of a row on the edge of the swamp, was one of the worst – some bugger had pinched half the roof.

The old fellows reckoned we were a cheeky lot of young scamps and, as we were way down at the far end of the camp, they called us the Dead End Kids; I don't know about the 'dead end' part of it but we were, after all, definitely just kids, and for us life was a game, a bit of a giggle. Officers and sergeants, with their focus on discipline, were just a few of the hurdles to jump on the obstacle race that we had to run.

Our room was on the far right of the hut. It had two raised timber and bamboo platforms either side of a central aisle where we slept, eight men on each side, making 48 men to each three-roomed hut.

I was so buggered after the march from Sandakan that I went to sleep almost instantly, only to be awakened at some ungodly hour to find we were being battered by a terrific storm. With water cascading down inside the hut, and out, coupled with the intense lightning and thunder, we had Buckley's chance of getting back to sleep.

It was that storm and its consequences that cement our arrival at the Sandakan camp well and truly in my memory. How the rain teemed during those first few days. It was as if our huts were built under a celestial tap. In their poor state, the atap roof and walls of our new abode offered little protection, leaking whenever it rained and growing mould the like of which we had never seen. It seemed to me that 'Hughie', as Australians called The Bloke Upstairs, was enjoying himself by showing us mere mortals who was boss. The storms he threw at us, flicking thick cords of lightning that knifed across the landscape while whip-cracking rolls of thunder reverberated over, above and through the huts, seemed out of this world. The walls shook, and our eardrums rattled. The bang, crash, wallop of them scared the life out of the unwary, like a paper bag being burst beside an unsuspecting earhole. In the tropics, there is no room for tardiness. Heat and damp = mould. It's a potent mixture, so fixing the roof was now our top priority. Everything I know about the making and fixing of atap stems from the experience.

When the rain stopped, the sun came out; blazing away, frying everything in its path and spraying the air with steam. Then the rain returned – and so it went on, a fight between sun and rain. Sizzle and drizzle. A constant drip, drip, drip. Then the sun reappeared, shining fiercely on the lines of huts, and moisture steamed from the forests, the rubber and coconut plantations, the swamps, the rivers and the lakes. The clouds built up, and round it all went again.

We were cut off from most of the swamp by two lines of barbed-wire fencing, rolls of concertina barbed wire whirled between them, half-submerged in the mire. Where the land rose clear of water, this arrangement gave way to six-foot-high cyclone wire fences, topped with half a dozen strands of barbed wire. A path circled the perimeter fence as far as the swamp, where a curved wooden walkway spanned the water and gave access to two rarely used timber observation towers. There was only one gate. Perched on spindly stumps just outside the gate and overlooking the huts were a guardhouse, guards' quarters and Hoshijima's office. The atap-covered Central Command Post, with its machine-gun mounted on an open-sided platform, was a constant reminder of our position in all things Japanese.

Electricity for lighting and to pump water to the camp came from the power plant we had passed on our way into the camp proper. It consisted of a boiler and a steam-powered engine connected to an alternator, all bolted to concrete slabs inside a couple of sheds. Split wood was stacked along the sides of the boilerhouse to feed the fire, while raw copper wires, looped from tree to tree, carried the power up the hill to the huts. A single light globe, dangling from the roof of each partition, was our only source of illumination.

Electric lights were also ranged around the perimeter. These burned all night, but electricity to the huts was cut at 9 pm, controlled by the main switch in the guardhouse. The water supply, pumped from a nearby river to a big orange storage tank beside the boiler, was sterilised by excess steam before being pumped up the hill to concrete tanks behind the guardhouse. From here, the water was gravity fed to the cookhouse and showers, or Asian-style tubs called tongs, under the huts.

Conditions in the camp were a nightmare, exacerbated by food shortages, a wreck of a cookhouse, leaking roofs, and latrines so overflowing with sewage from the previous inhabitants that they could only be described as 'shithouses'. Trying to settle in was hard enough without these added aggravations. Our only option was to grit our teeth, tighten our belts, and dream of the Land Down Under.

We set to work immediately, repairing leaking roofs, making badly needed improvements to the cookhouse, and fixing the latrines. But a couple of days after our arrival I and my mates, along with the other youngest and fittest, were singled out for other work. We didn't know exactly what was in store, but we formed up bright and early at the base of the Big Tree in a cleared area that formed a kind of parade ground.

After distributing changkuls and small wicker baskets, the guard commander climbed onto a wooden crate and announced, 'Will be you honour to make road for Nippon. Ah so! *Kora!* (Hoy! Pay attention!) Mens all work good, plenty food, Nippon good you.'

The day was all downhill from there. No sooner were we out through the gate than a king-sized storm hit. There was no question of turning back. Orders were orders, and that was that. Even so, it took a monumental effort not to brave the wrath of the guards and turn tail for the comparative safety of the camp. Pelted by driving rain, blitzed by lightning, our hearing shattered by the deafening thunderbolts, we churned along through a sea of mud and swirling water, navigating our way by clinging blindly to the bloke ahead.

Parts of the trail resembled rivers, which we now stirred into a quagmire, a strength-sapping tug-of-war. Feet sucked out of the mire were so thickly covered in mud that no one realised when boots had been left behind.

Trees lay on the ground, victims of lightning strikes, making it that much more difficult for those tasked with clearing the track. Other trees that had weathered so many storms stood silent and forlorn like wounded war casualties, their limbs shattered and trunks split. And if all that wasn't enough, we also had to contend with a multitude of things that bit and scratched, sucked and gouged, bled and stung. The snakes, funnily enough, weren't too much of a worry, being far too busy looking out for their own skins to bother with ours. The worst by far were the horrible, blood-sucking leeches.

> *Of all of Borneo's creatures*
> *Worst of all were the leeches*
> *The snakes, we could abide,*
> *And from large animals hide.*
> *But those sucking leeches!*
> *Gawd! How we 'ate yers!*

After what seemed forever we arrived at the work site, which was nothing but a bloody great sea of mud. Nearby stood a marker showing a record rainfall. I don't remember the amount, but it was in the order of hundreds of inches. The Jap sergeant, using a combination of fractured English and much arm waving, told us we had reached the site of a yet-to-be-constructed airfield.

The landscape didn't look like airfield country to me. Hills and gullies were covered with rubber trees and stunted shrubs, tall coconut trees and strips of secondary jungle, all struggling for a fair share of space: an undulating indiscriminate mix, rolling on to the far horizon, a steaming hothouse of life and death, of eating and being eaten. I reckoned it would take years, even with heavy machinery, to turn it into anything remotely resembling an airport.

As the sun came out, the Jap sergeant scrapped the plan to build a road. Instead, we would begin work by flattening some of the land for airport facilities. Standing on a rise and pointing with a pick handle, the sergeant issued instructions.

'Hill here go in valley there. All mens get changkul and basket. *Ichi* metre *ichi* man dig (One metre, one man dig). When finish all mens go back to camp.'

Wet and hungry, bothered and bewildered, we set to work, hoeing away at the white glue-like mud, which stuck tenaciously to everything except what it was supposed to stick to. Coaxing recalcitrant lumps of goo onto the flat woven-cane baskets was only half the battle. The loads then had to be lifted onto our heads and transported, with much slithering and sliding, into a hollow where, like demented slapstick comedians, we somehow got the mud to let go, only to watch it swirl away in the floodwaters.

Finally, even the Japs realised it was an utterly useless exercise and called it a day. Heads down, as thunder roared and lighting flared, we started back into the wind and rain, pushing our way homewards into the fast-approaching night. No prison camp would ever again look so inviting. After demolishing a bowl of gluggy rice stew we collapsed onto our allotted two-by-six-foot bed spaces and fell into a blessed sleep.

A few days later, giving no further thought to the airfield the Japs said they were going to construct, we were still fixing up the camp, trying to organise supplies of food and deal with shortages of almost everything, when Hoshijima ordered us all to assemble beneath the Big Tree. Climbing onto a platform he gave us a motivational talk, through Ozawa, his interpreter, on the wonderful advantages of being part of the Japs' co-prosperity sphere.

Why Hoshijima used an interpreter, a weedy little bloke we dubbed Jimmy Pike after a famous Australian jockey, I dunno. Probably just to show off, because he spoke English perfectly well. After winding up his propaganda spiel, he announced that Japan would be victorious, even if it took 100 years. We thought that was that, but then he told us an airfield was to be built, and we were going to build it

Lieutenant Boundy, one of our engineers, went out to inspect the site. On his return, word circulated that yes, the Japs intended to construct an airfield on a site already surveyed by the British, but we should not concern ourselves over being involved in a military project because it would take at least ten years to finish, by which time the war would be over.

Days passed. Nothing happened. We kept on with our camp improvements, and digging drains and building bridges along the access track, all of which lasted only as long as the next downpour, necessitating another long detour back to camp. At times the drains were so awash with fast-flowing water that our guards allowed us to ride the rapids on the way to work. I sometimes caught sight of gangs of Javanese coolies or locals toiling away in the distance, but despite Hoshijima's pronouncement, no real work was being done on the airfield by any of us.

The camp, however, was far from idle. We also had to carry out general repairs, collect supplies from Sandakan, chop wood for the boiler and take part in the general clean up. The entire area was overrun with rats and large snakes, which dropped without warning from the trees while searching for food – mainly rats and other small animals. Thousands of rats lived in and around the swamp. They ate anything, except snakes, which ate them. Prior to our arrival, the rats had provided a warm dry home for millions of lice. The lice now abandoned the rats to take up residence with us.

As the lice and the snakes depended on the rats, we figured that if we could get rid of the rats we could wipe out all three. There were no cyanide guns here, so we held rat-catching competitions. The contests were taken very seriously. Immediately after dinner we'd arm ourselves with boots or any other suitable missile and take up our positions. Sitting silently in the dark with ammo at the ready, we would wait for the tell-tale rustling sounds in the atap. Switching on the light, we'd then let fly. Total chaos erupted with boots flying, rats squeaking and tumbling, and the attackers laughing as they dodged the dead or frightened rodents.

It didn't take long for the surviving rats to call it a day and retreat into the scrub. Any snakes not killed and eaten – they were good tucker – also gave up and slithered away into the rainforest and swamps. The lice, unfortunately, were much more persevering, and stayed with us to the bitter end, by which time those who'd engaged so energetically in the rat competitions realised how extravagant they had been in their premature eradication of such a potentially good food source.

In the first year or so, there was plenty of food, with the rice ration set at 770 grams per man per day. This was way beyond what any European could possibly eat, or want to eat, so the excess was hoarded. After a few months the prisoners were able to trade their excess rice ration for fruit and vegetables from local stalls set up near the airstrip. Meat, however, was always in short supply.

There was plenty of rice

Among the young blokes, escape and food were always the main topics of conversation. Whenever we ate, we talked escape; whenever we were hungry, we planned escape. Food and escape equalled each other. They were interlocked – the staples in the diet of our imagination. Dreaming of escape is an occupational therapy for those who are locked up, and freedom takes on a dimension of its own, forever beckoning. However, like an incandescent light that attracts the moths, those who flit too close will suffer burns.

We had only just settled into our first week at Sandakan when five blokes from

CHAPTER 6 To Sandakan

my battalion took to the bush from my own battalion, including Norm Morris, who had sailed with me and the 3rd Reinforcements to Singapore. Shortly afterwards, another six, all from the Australian Army Service Corps, also escaped.

These blokes were willing to take a chance. They rode life's course with flair and daring, giving it their best shot. They'd bucked the odds, but these early escapes worried our officers as much as they did the Japs. One of our blokes overheard Hoshijima ranting and raging about them to Captain Cook, our Australian camp administrator. When Hoshijima did his block, everyone within a hundred yards knew about it. It was reported that Hoshi was making all sorts of threats about what he would do if there were any more 'incidents'; he took the escapes as a personal insult. His ranting did have some effect, as it wasn't long before our own officers, in the interests of their own survival, began a 'no escape' campaign, sending word down the line that escapes were forbidden: the Japs were threatening them with severe repercussions.

Well, as far as repercussions were concerned, they couldn't have been any worse than what the bludgers handed out towards the end of the war. In any case, if Hoshi did give the officers a bit of a serve, it didn't hurt them much, because we'd have heard about it. A couple of the men in our hut were officers' batmen, so there wasn't that much that went on 'Up the Hill' without us knowing about it. We were pretty well informed and, despite the edict from above, kept our own council whenever escapes were being planned.

The warnings were real enough, as were the possibilities of group punishment if the escapees were caught. The Japs had a far more direct way of dealing with escapes than the Germans ever had. Perhaps this is why I have never heard of any officers' escape committees in Jap camps, apart from four officers who later escaped from a temporary camp on Berhala Island while en route to Sandakan.

It seemed to us ordinary blokes that B Force kicked off on the wrong foot. Right from the start we were top-heavy with officers and trying to dodge 150 of them as well as hundreds of NCOs (which was anyone with a stripe) was quite a business. We had far too many chiefs for the number of Indians. It was an unwieldy and an almost unworkable force, with a large number of other ranks who were either too old or too sick, even before we left Changi. B Force was very lopsided, especially since we were journeying to an unknown place. Whoever picked the team made a mockery of the meaning of teamwork, the lack of which led to some of the blackest events in our entire military history.

We were told that the reason for having so many lame ducks in our force (most of the officers, the older soldiers, and the sick) was that the Japs had given a glowing account of the conditions to be expected in Sandakan: a holiday camp, with no work. Our brass fell for it, hook, line and sinker, adding anyone whose behaviour was poor, including the more criminally inclined, the intractables and teenaged soldiers full of high spirits. In other words, get rid of any useless mouths and anyone who might cause a problem.

The camp was so overburdened with brass that it was almost impossible to move without bumping into pips and crowns. In addition, there were 312 corporals and sergeants. A bloke had to have eyes in the back of his head. If we'd had to stop and salute every time we met an officer, it wouldn't have left much for work. We were overworked, underfed and overled.

As far as prison camps went, this was probably the first time that large numbers of ORs and officers had been housed together. It was certainly the first camp where the captors insisted on treating all prisoners as equals, irrespective of rank. We were all supposed to be slaves, and therefore to be treated equally – equal rations, issued on the basis of no work, no food.

At Changi the brass had thought differently and whenever possible they had behaved differently. They managed to hold greater sway, standing up to the Japanese administration about rations and working conditions for the men. The internal administration at Changi therefore experienced far less interference from the Japs than those in outside work camps.

In Sandakan the emphasis was on deference to rank, not towards the Japanese but to our own officers, who were not required to work, at least not in the beginning. Later on they were forced to supply a squad of about fifty of the most junior lieutenants, who worked for a short period when there was an all-out effort to finish stage 1 of the airstrip. The batmen reported that the composition of this party led to a lot of argument Up the Hill over who was more senior to whom.

Education wasn't anywhere near the level it is today, and we still had remnants of class superiority. So the officers, despite being prisoners, just the same as us, were still pulling rank and claiming whatever privileges they could manage. There was a line that we ORs were expected to toe and the expectation that we would blindly obey inevitably resulted in a breakdown of relationships between officers and the men. As a consequence, general intelligence gathered by the airfield workers about the local area was not passed on to our superiors.

The Dead End Kids probably knew more about the countryside around Sandakan than anyone else in the camp. We roamed for miles, gathering information about the people and the kampongs; learning who could be trusted, and where food could be found. Along the edges of the rainforests were many areas where sweet potatoes, yams and tapioca flourished in the wild. As the camp was sitting slap-bang in the middle of the agricultural Experimental Farm,

CHAPTER 6 To Sandakan

there was also an abundance of coffee, cinnamon, coconuts and various kinds of tropical fruit.

I have a sunny memory of our first big excursion outside the wire, which turned out to be a particularly adventurous day. We headed over towards the river, near the spot where the camp drew its water supply, following a track that went through part of the rainforest. Harry Longley, in the lead, suddenly yelled, 'Cripes, come and have a look at this. It's a bloody great gorilla'. Sure enough, when we came around the corner, beside the track stood this huge, hair-covered beast, giving a tremendous yawn. His mouth was so big that he seemed to be all jaws and teeth. He also seemed to be all arms, and what long arms they were, reaching out here, there and everywhere, like a great hairy windmill. His huge hands seemed to be full of fingers, tugging and pulling and scratching. It was a bit like one of the serials I had watched at Boysies, and I half expected Tarzan to come swinging by on a vine, giving his war cry and looking for Jane.

Although this massive creature didn't seem to be worried about us, we stayed alert, ready to run at the first sign of an attack. Of course it wasn't a gorilla, as we found out when we returned to camp to excitedly recount the story of our narrow escape. In those days there were thousands of orang utans in Borneo. Like the one we met, they were gentle enough, and friendly, providing you let them be and stayed out of their way, which we did.

The Japanese took a different view. They used these magnificent 'men of the forest' for target practice.

It wasn't all that far from where we encountered the orang utan that we came across what we thought would be an ideal hideout if we managed to escape – a rocky outcrop close to the river, out of the way of prying eyes, and perfect for storing our bits and pieces. We had managed to get a collection of useful escape items, including a couple of long-bladed parangs and a few army water bottles. But creating a food store was a problem. The climate, the insects, the mould, were our greatest enemies. Everything that didn't rust went mouldy, or rotted away altogether. What we wouldn't have given for a few strong containers, some jugs or pots – anything that could hold food or water.

As we later discovered, while we had dithered and dallied, worrying about the food situation and a dozen other potential problems, just over the river from our hideout were Norm Morris and his mates, our five battalion cobbers, living the life of Riley as they formulated plans to sail home. If only we'd known, we lamented, perhaps with our combined efforts we could all have made it. On the other hand, we might also all have died in the attempt.

The tropics, at least the jungle part of it, are not kind to strangers. It's not a bit like the jungle in the Tarzan movies. He never seemed to have any of the problems we had, like lack of food, being eaten alive by mosquitoes and leeches, and having to be on the watch constantly for other nasty creatures.

About two weeks after the blokes escaped, and just as we thought Sandakan might not be such a bad place after all, Lieutenant Hoshijima was promoted to captain. To celebrate, he called a parade to show us exactly who was boss. Climbing onto his platform, and again using Jimmy Pike to interpret, he announced:

'You have been brought here to Sandakan to have the honour to build for the Imperial Japanese Forces an aerodrome. For this you will be paid ten cents a day. You will work. You will build this aerodrome if it takes three years.

'I tell you, I have the power of life and death over you. You will build this aerodrome if you stay here until your bones rot under the Borneo sun.'

Work began a few days later. Hoshijima meant what he said. And he certainly was not going to allow us Lieutenant Boundy's estimate of ten years to build it. To make sure we put in maximum effort, he appointed a gang of bashers, armed with wooden sticks, whose sole aim was to ensure that an airfield was built in the shortest time possible.

While one mob headed for the site, another was set to work creating a road network able to take vehicular traffic. The Dead Enders drew the short straw. We arrived at the airfield where a short-statured buck-toothed lieutenant pointed out the dimensions of the strip and announced that we would work from dawn until dusk, six days a week, until it was completed.

Each of those six days was very long and very hard. Hacking away at scrubby undergrowth in the boiling hot sun was back-breaking. Although we had a ten-minute break each hour, and a fifteen-minute smoko mid-morning, it seemed like forever until lunchtime – the usual rice, stewed greens and weak tea. The rice was terrible, as the cooks had not yet worked out how to cook 44-gallon drums of the stuff without turning it into a gluggy mess. The afternoon was even longer than the morning. When I lined up at six o'clock to return my changkul, I looked around to see how much progress had been made. Hardly any. I thought that maybe Lieutenant Boundy would prove Hoshijima wrong, and the airstrip *would* take ten years to build.

We settled down to a steady grind of monotonous work: clearing the land, digging away at the hills, filling in the valleys, attempting to satisfy the requirements of our taskmasters: the ever-present engineer guards, always at the ready to inflict punishment for the slightest thing. We worked through the tremendous monsoonal downpours, in whirling winds, in energy-sapping humidity and days of unrelenting sunshine, when the light bounced off the white coral-like surface of the runway. The threat of blindness was so great that we made slit eye-shields from two pieces of wood, fastened to our heads with strips of cloth or string.

One day ran into the next, with nothing to break the monotony and no respite in sight until, a week or so after we'd started on the airstrip, I was woken from a sound sleep with a kick to the ribs to find the whole camp in turmoil. Dawn hadn't yet put in an appearance and it was still black as ink outside. Confused by the uproar, the men wandered around rubbing sleep from their eyes while guards ran hither and thither, yelling and screaming and adding to the general chaos. It was as if the sky had fallen in or there had been a collision of worlds.

Our hut stumbled up the hill like a mob of sheep being driven to the top paddock, with the Japs carrying on like a pack of blue heelers, snapping away at our heels, prodding and jabbing with their rifles and bayonets. Eventually they herded us into some sort of order as dawn broke, pushing away the night and allowing us to see just what was going on.

And what was going on soon became evident.

We were hemmed in by fully armed Jap troops. Not our regular camp guards, but as mean a bunch as you could get. They may have been just pawns, but they sure had us in check. We eyed each other off – us wondering, and them knowing. They held all the high cards: a fearsome machine-gun, poking its snout from the platform; dozens of soldiers, armed with rifles and fixed bayonets; and a posse of Jap officers with bloody great swords. These blokes didn't just have a winning hand. They had a stacked deck. I remember thinking, 'My goodness, Billy, could we be about to have some sort of a massacre?' For more than a few moments, it sure looked like it.

Bob Shipsides gathered our little band together and led us over to a spot near the officers' huts, where he warned, 'Take care and stick together, and watch out for these little bastards. Something's up, so no matter what happens, make sure we all stay together.'

A sudden scream of '*Ki-wo-tsuki!*' (Attention!) drew a momentary curtain of silence across the parade ground, setting the scene for the arrival, like a feudal prince, of Hoshijima, accompanied by a retinue of officers.

Somewhat surprisingly, it was not Hoshijima but our own commanding officer, Colonel Walsh, who climbed onto the box that served as a dais. I can see him now, as he quietly stood there, looking around the assembly before he began to speak. 'Men, Lieutenant Hoshijima has asked me to read to you this document.'

He then paused, holding a paper aloft, before reading from it, in a loud voice, 'If I or any of my companions try to escape I wish them to be shot'.

Looking up, the colonel continued, 'The Japanese are demanding that we sign a similar document, on oath.'

At this point, he straightened and, with his jaw jutting out, proclaimed in a defiant voice, 'I for one will not sign such a document'. To emphasise his words, he threw the paper, with a most dramatic flourish, at the feet of the Jap officers.

Holy mackerel. The worlds had collided.

We were all momentarily stunned. I know I was, and I could see from the looks of disbelief on faces of our own officers that they were too. The colonel had surprised all of us, simply because it was so out of character. Walshy was a quiet, almost ineffectual sort of fellow, the last person I imagined would make a stand like that. I'm sure most of the blokes thought he'd gone completely bonkers. As for the Japs, this was a turn of events that they had least expected. Disbelief and anger showed clearly on their faces.

The reaction came fast and furious, guards running in from every which way, kicking out at all and sundry. They grabbed Walshy and dragged him outside the gate where a firing squad was formed up, their rifles aimed as they prepared to fire. The next few minutes were hairy indeed. Shouts of '*Kora!*' and '*Bakayaro!*' (Moron!) mingled with the clicking of rifle bolts, clearly and terrifyingly vivid. It was one of those situations that you hear about but can't imagine will ever happened to you. But here we were, right in the middle of it: guards with their fixed bayonets; a thumping great machine-gun; Japanese officers shouting face to face at our officers; and we ordinary blokes shuffling about, bewildered and apprehensive, ready to make a break for it when the shooting started.

Shippy had sized up the situation much earlier than most. With the hostility of the guards becoming more evident, he warned, 'I think this could be it, fellas, so be ready to run, and make sure that everyone keeps together'.

By this time the Japs had us encircled completely, and it looked as if the moment of truth had arrived, when a cry of '*Ki-wo-tsuki!*' brought us back from the brink, and to attention. We had a last-minute reprieve. A compromise had been reached.

Colonel Walsh climbed back onto the box to speak to us again: 'Men, our captors have threatened to drag the sick out, and leave them in the open, if we do not sign this reworded paper. I will quote from it: "If I escape I know I will be shot to death" – and men, I have made it clear to Captain Hoshijima that I will sign it, but only under protest, and so I ask all of you to sign it under that same protest.'

So we all signed that paper, which was big deal for the Japs, but not for us.

As far as I was concerned, the only good thing to come out of that day was in the calm, collected way that Colonel Walsh handled the Japs. It showed to me, a youngster, how a good officer went about performing his duty.

Lieutenant Colonel Alf Walsh, Billy's hero

Billy was unaware that Colonel Walsh did not enjoy the support of his officers or indeed, many of the men, especially those of his own unit, 2/10 Field Regiment. Shortly before the Japanese had invaded Malaya, the 2/10th's charismatic and very popular commanding officer, Lieutenant Colonel Gordon Kirwood, who had raised the wholly Queensland-based unit and welded it into a fiercely loyal outfit, was relieved of his command after he had fallen out of a taxi in an inebriated state following an indiscreet 'assignation'. The gunners, seething with bitterness and indignation over his removal, had not been placated in the slightest to find his successor was the recently promoted Lieutenant Colonel Alf Walsh who, apart from not being a Queenslander, was a 'staff wallah' – a member of the much-derided Staff Corps, deemed to be long on textbook tactics but short on practical experience. His appointment as commanding officer of B Force was also not popular, but this seems to have more to do with the infantry's traditional dislike of non-infantry than anything else.

Walsh, behind the eight-ball from the start and considered weak by many of the B Force officers, had no hope of forging any kind of working relationship, let alone a close one, with the men under his command. Perceived as a bit of a dud, he retreated into his shell and kept a low profile, a decision that did nothing to enhance his image

Apart from his being rather short and a bit on the chubby side, both qualities that tended to make him appear somewhat unprepossessing, word had circulated that Walsh was not popular with his own men and not really up to it under pressure. While this assessment, though subjective, appears to have had some foundation, the colonel's lack of popularity was not entirely of his own making.

Why he was selected over other more senior officers to lead B Force is not clear. It is possible that Brigadier Callaghan, previously Commander of Artillery and Walsh's immediate superior, may have considered that, as Walsh was a competent enough administrator, he was suited to oversee a convalescent camp rather than a working one.

Despite Walsh's perceived shortcomings, his defiant stand made a deep impression on Billy. Ironically, it was this defiance that resulted in his being sent to Kuching, and out of Hoshijima's hair.

Similar 'no escape' documents presented in other camps were also signed, also under duress, and also after a show of resistance. Thousands of Allied soldiers still in Singapore's Changi camps, the vast majority of whom were British, were herded onto the parade ground of Selarang Barracks, where they held out for four days in the boiling sun, without proper sanitation and little water, until the execution of two Australian escapees and the suffering of the ill forced the commanding officer to capitulate. Like the prisoners at Sandakan, the Changi inmates not only signed under duress, but also signed as popular cartoon characters, politicians and folk heroes.

The Japs thought they had won, which was good, because they have a deeply ingrained feeling for what is generally referred to as 'face', something that they must never 'lose', at all costs. The business of 'saving face' is powerful, and an important part of the Japanese psyche.

This was also true of the guards down at the airfield. They were a ruthless lot, so lacking in compassion and with imaginations so stunted that they failed to detect the hatred around them. Ignorant, lacking understanding and unable to think for themselves, they were the product of a thousand years of feudalism. Inflicting pain bolstered the feelings of inferiority of these one-time serfs, now victims of their own officers who, as products of Japanese society's topmost strata, the Samurai and the Knights of Bushido, used their absolute powers, absolutely. The authority of the officer class was boundless; their swords were weapons, a phallic symbol of their supposed manliness, and used at the slightest provocation.

Of all the Jap officers Hoshijima intrigued me most – an excellent example of a conflict of interests. Compared with the other officers, he impressed me as being capable of honourable intent. Unfortunately, his intentions conflicted with his traditional upbringing and military training. He certainly stood out: over six feet tall, a well-educated engineer who spoke several languages reasonably well and, at least while I was there, appeared to get on quite well with some of our senior officers.

At the other end of the scale was the officer responsible for ensuring that the labour force at the airstrip carried out the necessary work. This was Second Lieutenant Moritaki – a cunning bastard and the biggest mongrel of them all. I suspect that he had worked his way up through the ranks, and I can imagine him trampling over anyone who got in his way. Lieutenant Colonel Suga, the boss cocky, was another a victim of the system; an in-between man, a sly bugger who promised the world but delivered nothing. He was stranded between two cultures, a soldier who had fought on our side during World War I, and had then spent some time in America before becoming a headmaster. He found himself on the opposite side in the next war; a war that propelled him to field rank, only to have him topple from his perch into the pits of oblivion as a POW camp administrator.

These were the men, together with their superiors, who would be responsible for the deaths of thousands of POWs and countless civilians. This mixture of ignorance, irresponsible pigheadedness, brutality and pride allowed them to override any twinges of conscience. Lacking in the essential human feelings of justice and mercy, they sought revenge for their own inadequacies, taking it out on all who were subjugated to their regime by treating us as slaves.

In about October, just before Walshy was packed off to Kuching where he could no longer annoy Hoshijima, we received our first visit from the chief gaoler of Borneo, (the then) Major Suga. He'd come to inspect the work. Assembling hurriedly around the Big Tree, we couldn't help but wonder about the identity of the much-bemedalled field officer waiting impatiently nearby. A rather tubby little fellow, he was dressed in a baggy uniform consisting of a safari jacket and drill trousers tucked into brown leather riding boots. Perched on his head was his signature tropical pith helmet. An oversized pigskin holster hung from his belt, along with a sword that was far too long for him and threatened to trip him at every stride.

More than fifty years later this outfit, displayed in a glass case, formed part of a POW exhibition at the Australian War Memorial. Even though I was standing at least a hundred yards away, I knew instantly that the clothes had once belonged to Suga. The years rolled back and I could see him so clearly, standing on a box, declaring: 'I am Major "Sugar". S - U - G - A. I am the Commandants of all the prison camps of All the Borneos. Japanese government be very good peoples, and treat you peoples very well, so you must have impatience, while we get inconveniences for you.'

This garbled mangling of our mother tongue had sent ripples of laughter along the ranks, much to the annoyance of Major Suga, who so prided himself on his grasp of English that he refused to use the services of Jimmy Pike. In his rage at our discourtesy, Suga roared, 'That – is – FACT!' Unfortunately for him his pronunciation was not quite right, turning 'fact' into a very crude word that really broke up the ranks.

It took more than a little effort on the part of Jimmy Pike to pacify Suga, who was clearly insulted by our laughter. However, he finally accepted Jimmy's explanation and resumed his speech, promising on the word of a Samurai that if we worked hard on the airfield, we would be treated fairly. Warming to his theme, he concluded his pep talk with 'All Japanese officers – Samurai, all Japanese soldiers – honourable Bushido. You work hard, finish airfield, you be fine.'

We left the parade ground, our confidence in the future buoyed by the assurances delivered by the commandant of all the prison camps of All the Borneos. We were not to know what an amazing piece of hypocrisy he had just dished out, as if butter wouldn't melt in his mouth. Suga's promises, we would discover, were a bob a dozen, as cheap and as brittle as a handful of uncooked spaghetti. Who would suspect that such duplicity would be so ingrained in a man who spoke so glowingly of honour and nobility of mind?

And so it was with renewed hope that we went off to finish the airfield, and it was with that same hope that we continued until the job was completed, for, in spite of terrible working conditions, we had the word of Suga – S - U - G - A – a Japanese man of honour.

CHAPTER 7

CAMP LIFE

September 1942 – February 1943

We had a respite from our monotonous rice diet at about the same time as Suga's visit took place, when a ship en route to Japan called in at Sandakan. On board were the cremated remains of four Japanese sailors killed after their midget submarines had attacked shipping in Sydney Harbour in May that year. Returning the ashes of the war dead to their homeland was important to the Japanese, and the Australian government scored quite a few points by offering to do this. Sadly, such honours would not be accorded to ten of our men, beheaded in 1945 after raiding ships in Singapore Harbour.

The ashes of the Japanese sailors were taken to Japan by Kawai Tatsuo, the Japanese Minister to Australia, who had been interned when war broke out. The urns containing the cremated remains were handed originally to the Swiss Consul in Canberra, with the expectation that they would be returned to Japan after the war. However, in mid-1942 the Japanese government agreed to the release of Allied civilians interned in Japan in exchange for the 800 Japanese nationals held in Australia. In August, Kawai Tatsuo and the Japanese internees boarded Kamakura Maru in Melbourne. The ship was bound for Lourenço Marques (now Maputo in Mozambique), in what was then the neutral colony of Portuguese East Africa. There they met the Allied vessel City of Canterbury, carrying the Allied internees from Japan. After transferring to Kamakura Maru, Kawai Tatsuo continued his journey to Japan, stopping off at Singapore and Sandakan.

During the voyage, the ashes of the sailors were treated as if they were living heroes.

From Melbourne to Lourenço Marques, they were kept in an altar in Kawai's first-class cabin. Once on board the Japanese ship, they took pride of place in one of the first-class lounges, which was declared a shrine. The progress of the voyage was followed closely by Japanese media, which broadcast on national radio an account of the arrival of the ashes at Yokohama on 9 October.

Our gaolers showed their appreciation of our nation's generous gesture by declaring a special holiday, as well as providing the camp with a whole dugong, otherwise known as a sea cow. What a feast we had that day! The cooks, who had finally mastered the knack of cooking large amounts of food in their giant woks, produced a magnificently flavoured stew. I never knew that dugong, which tastes like red meat, was so delicious. It's little wonder they are now an endangered species.

There was a suspicion that the banquet might be in part a bribe, for the feast had scarcely been digested when the Japs really stepped up the pace at the airfield. The demands of 'all mens work more' increased dramatically. In hindsight, perhaps our victory in the Coral Sea had something more to do with it, because they began swinging their sticks and pick handles at us with even greater vigour. All along the airfield, the shouts of '*Kora!*' rang out, followed by the sounds of some poor fellow being struck with a length of timber.

The original quota of 'ichi man, ichi metre' was escalated time and again as we hacked away into the sides of the hills with picks and shovels and carted away tons and tons of overburden, balancing our little baskets on top of our heads. In those first few months we must have carted enough dirt to fill in Sydney Harbour. Plodding along, line after line. Backwards and forwards, day in, day out.

Quotas were the only things that mattered to the guards. The blighters constantly checked and rechecked, measured and re-measured our progress throughout the day. If you were up with your quota – fine, good, *joto* (excellent). If you were unlucky and struck a bad patch – bloody hell! And if any gang was perceived to be slacking, it was one out, all out: group punishment.

The favoured method was Flying Practice. With cries of 'Bad mens no hard workie, *Nippon binta no*' (Nippon beat you), the guards forced us to form up in four or five lines in the centre of the airfield. There we would stand, arms outstretched, sometimes for hours, while the engineer guards patrolled the ranks slowly, pick handles or heavy wooden sword sticks at the ready, waiting for tired arms to sag. When they did, Whack! A hearty crack across the back for each offence.

Back at the camp, the proud boast would be, 'Hey! What do you know! I made sergeant today at flying practice', with the three black and blue stripes across the bragger's back proving the promotion. Many were the hard-gained sergeant's stripes won out there at the 'drome. We ORs often wondered if the Flying Practice system should be instituted to promote our own battalion sergeants; a fairer and more telling method perhaps, but an idea that I doubt was ever voiced to any of our NCOs!

Flying practice

The guards responsible for our misery were mainly newcomers from Formosa (now Taiwan), which had been occupied by Japan for decades. After years of being bullied and lorded over, they now had someone they could bully without restraint, making up for their feelings of inferiority by dreaming up all kinds of inducements to work – called 'encouragement'. We classified them universally as bludgers, with some of the bludgers qualifying as bloody rotten bludgers, and so on up the scale until they reached the status of bloody rotten dirty bludgers. The one thing they had in common was competing with one another to see who could dish out the most effective punishment. It didn't matter much to us where they came from, or what their Japanese names were, because we soon gave them new ones: BH, for Boofhead, The Big Black Bastard, Masturbation, The Black Panther and so on.

The guard I loathed the most was the one who fancied himself as a ladies' man and dressed in an assortment of clothing best described as 'Eastern Western'. I called him The Dude. He seemed to have an unlimited supply of Johnson's Baby Powder, which he used to dust under his arms, and also carried a tube of toothpaste around with him as mouthwash. We figured these toiletries must have been part of his war booty.

However, his real pride lay in his 'ability' to sing the first line of the song 'Lady of Spain I Adore You', after which he would tell those unfortunate enough to be anywhere near, 'That is English song'. To which they would show their appreciation by nodding and agreeing, 'Yes by golly, it is English song', before adding 'Until you came along, and bloody well spoilt it'. My mate Keith Botterill called him Ramona, after another of his favourite tunes that we were forced to endure.

The recital over, The Dude/Ramona would squeeze out an inch of toothpaste and gargle his precious throat before sauntering off to see which gang he could promote to the Flying Practice Squad, thereby ensuring that his show ended with a hit.

Another major tormentor was The Big Black Bastard. His three stars on a yellow stripe, denoting his rank as sergeant, gave him a hell of a lot more authority than our sergeants. He was a swine; a real pig, the pits, and he loved nothing better than getting stuck into us serfs with his pick handle. Despite this, The Black Bastard once provided us with a most enjoyable spectacle.

It started with a buzzing bee or, more correctly, a hundred buzzing bees. We hadn't been long on the job that day, looking as if we were busy, heads down, butts up, picking away at the edge of a clump of trees when without warning The Black Bastard came rushing out from some scrub. Snorting and roaring, he was just looking for trouble, and he found it. Like an animal rushing in for the kill, he bellowed '*Kora, Kora!* Faster, faster! All mens working, must be faster. *Kora! Bakayaro!* All mens *shigoto takusan* (work much),' swinging his pick handle above his head to give emphasis to his words. In his frenzied excitement, may the gods be forever praised, he swung it a mite too high and his backstroke dislodged a wild bees' nest from a branch a few inches above his head.

It was sheer poetry in motion, a ballet of such sweet comeuppance, as The Black Bastard leapt, stepped, somersaulted and pirouetted, trying to escape the angry bees as they chased and stung. Oh! That such talent could not be applauded. To be unable to cheer and clap, or to ask for an encore, was agony itself. All we could do was lean back on our shovels, and marvel. It was better than *Swan Lake*. Such artistry, never to be forgotten. Those who had witnessed the performance dined out on it for weeks.

By now the runway stretched on for hundreds and hundreds of yards – a long, dazzling white blaze, ripping through the landscape, straight as an arrow towards the far horizon. To hasten the proceedings, railway skips were brought in and several narrow-gauge lines were laid from the hillside diggings to the fill sites, some of which were more than 40 feet deep; in fact whole trees were left to be buried where they stood. Like the Changi Trailers, the skips were propelled by manpower. From the top of the hill the construction area looked like an infestation of giant ants, scurrying with their loads across the ant bed of an airfield.

Working on the airfield

There was one satisfying outcome of the Japanese policy of filling in the valleys and not bothering to remove the trees. The Japs also neglected to provide for drainage, declaring it was not necessary. With the onset of the monsoon rains, however, strange things began to occur. The ground developed the shakes, and the skips started jumping off the rails. Work began falling behind schedule and the Japs became very worried – the situation was serious and heads would surely roll.

They couldn't blame us, not this time, as our engineer types had warned them about the lack of drainage. Vast amounts of water lay trapped above and below the ground. With nowhere for the water to go, the surface began to shake, like a gigantic jelly.

With Suga due for an inspection visit in November, it was obvious that something needed to be done, but what? The Jap engineers were facing a massive loss of face. We also managed to look seriously concerned, offering such comforting words as 'Goodness gracious me, skips shouldn't do things like that!'

It was then that our masters came up with a masterstroke of lateral thinking, a monumental piece of reasoning. Rather than go to all the trouble of digging trenches and laying drains, thereby delaying the completion of the runway, why not squeeze the excess water out using a steamroller. Like a lot of great ideas, they probably wondered why no one had thought of it before.

They commandeered a giant old-fashioned steamroller, awesome in its hugeness. As it came chuffing along, puffing out streams of smoke and steam, we couldn't help wondering which museum it had come from. It puffed right up to the edge of the fill and then, to our delight, it went a little further. The great ornate wheels started to sink and the whole thing slid gracefully into the mire, forcing the Aussie driver, and his Jap minder, to jump for their lives. Taking our cue from the scowls of our overlords, as dutiful slaves we looked suitably downcast, at the same time giving three silent cheers for Borneo's steamrolling *Titanic*.

Several attempts were made at salvage, almost consigning two trucks to the same grave. It was a black day for the Japs, who lost much face along with the roller. With Plan A in tatters, the Japs sent for an excavator owned by the Public Works Department. We viewed it with some alarm. It looked so efficient, with its articulated arm and bucket, that it seemed the drains would be dug in no time. Determined to delay the opening of the airstrip as long as possible, the Australian driver appointed to operate the machine declared it had a minor mechanical defect and had to be taken to the power plant for repairs. As soon as it arrived, Sergeant Stevens, who was working at the engine house, fixed it for good – by pouring sand into the sump, ensuring that the excavator never worked again. His sabotage was a bit of a two-edged sword. The excavator was dead but the drains still had to be dug. The Japs moved to Plan C.

So we dug box drains by hand, which we then had to line with timber. Unfortunately, we did too good a job. The flood subsided, and the airstrip dried out. I often wonder if anyone ever dug up that roller. If not, developers extending the runway facilities at a future date are going to be in for one heck of a surprise.

With the drainage under control, attention turned elsewhere. Down at the end of the runway nearest the camp was a gigantic tree, standing tall and proud. Once it had been a monarch, with jungle all around, but now it stood alone, towering over the landscape and with branches thickly spread threatening to wipe out any plane trying to land. The Japs decided it had to go, and our

The excavator, which never worked again, is one of the few remaining relics at the Sandakan Camp

gang was detailed for the demolition.

We were digging trenches around the base of the trunk to expose the roots when a truck pulled up and several Japs got out and ordered us off the job, yelling 'Nippon fix'. We watched on in alarm as they proceeded to pack bundles of old and very leaky gelignite into the holes we had already dug. Sweating gelignite! Taking off at some speed, we retreated a safe distance as the Japs unwound the fuse, knelt beside their truck and pressed the plunger.

The explosion was certainly impressive, a Big Bang almost large enough to create another universe. Up and out went great clouds of rocks, dirt and pulverised tree roots; such an astonishing amount of stuff that it stopped the rest of the workforce in its tracks. We stood awestruck as the tree rose from the middle of this maelstrom, like a monstrous rocket about to go into orbit.

Whoosh! It soared ever upwards, until gravity called time out and, like a modern-day rocket failure, it disintegrated. Huge lumps of tree, rocks, roots and earth scattered in all directions. For one horrible moment it looked as if the truck, under which the Japs had frantically scrambled, would be saved, but the gods in their infinite wisdom thought otherwise and sent a couple of nice large pieces crashing across the cabin, badly denting it.

The hole the blast left was enormous. We stood around its rim, like visitors to the Grand Canyon, gazing down in wonder. It took us an extra day to clean up the mess and to find enough fill to fill it. Some of the blokes reckoned it was a flamin' pity to fill in hole like that. It would have made a fantastic tourist attraction: the biggest man-made lake in All the Borneos.

Not long after the Big Bang we had our first taste of capitalism, Nipponese style, when Suga, arrived for his scheduled inspection of stage 1 of the airfield. We were lined up, ready to go to work when, with a great deal of oriental fanfare, he announced that our host, His Royal Omniscience, the Emperor of All the Japans, as well as All the Borneos, had seen fit to award us unworthy lot a pay increase. Not only that, His Royal Holiness, again in all his munificence, was to allow a Best Workers' Competition to be held. The sheer magnanimity of this announcement brought lumps to our collective throats – to think that recognition of our worth had come at last, and from so way on high!

Double rates of 20 cents a day (tax included) was now to be paid in full, each month, in pretty Japanese play-money – so with a week's wages I could buy a banana or two, or perhaps even a piece of coconut. Of course, there was a catch. Where were we to spend it, and who were we to buy from? So far the Japs hadn't let any of the locals come anywhere near us, let alone allow us to buy anything they might have to sell. There was a canteen at the camp, but it was for officers only, who were receiving between $10 and $15 a month and had plenty of money. They also had time to shop, as only a few were required to be at the airstrip each day.

According to Captain Jim Millner, only one officer was sent to the airstrip with each group of men, to act in a supervisory capacity. Apart from a couple of weeks when a party of junior lieutenants was formed to speed up construction, and one day when the entire camp was sent out to work, including the sick, no officer was engaged in manual labour at the airstrip. Colonel Walsh had fiercely resisted any attempt to have officers work, and it was not until after he was transferred to the main POW camp at Kuching in October that the party of junior lieutenants was forced out to work.

Although we didn't have a canteen, and we didn't have real money, we were able to gamble with the funny money. Two-up, crown-and-anchor and cards were the most popular games of chance. Other than gambling, along with the occasional chance to buy something from the locals at the airstrip, money was of no value. There was no incentive for saving any of it, a sad state of affairs for us newly made capitalists.

The awards for Suga's innovative Best Workers' Competition were given out just before the lunch break, when a guard selected a winner from among the various work gangs. The lucky prizewinner would be given a *presento*, a wooden coffee-token, and off he'd go to collect his well-earned prize: a mug of coffee, made from bitter, burnt grains, with no milk or sugar.

On the first of the presento occasions I managed, with the aid of a certain degree of animal cunning, to be rewarded, by drenching my shirt with water so that the judge could see the evidence of my hard labour: my honest-to-goodness sweat. It worked, and I was selected as the best worker in my group. With joy in my heart and clutching my prized wooden token, I went off to collect my well-earned reward.

The blasted coffee hut was way down the far end of the runway; a good fifteen minutes' walk there and back, in the burning noonday sun. To my disgust, the stuff tasted like shit and, to add insult to injured taste buds, when I got back to my gang work had started and I'd missed out on my bowl of rice.

> *Good workers, so it was spoken,*
> *Get awarded a prized coffee token.*
> *If this you believed,*
> *Then later you grieved.*
> *Coffee! Ya gotta be joken!*

Suga and Hoshijima seemed to be playing a game of good cop, bad cop. We'd only just received news of our pay rise when Hoshi introduced a new form of punishment – a small cage perched on stilts which the guards called Esau. Unfortunately, Joey and I were among the first to sample its cramped accommodation.

The POWs were unfamiliar with the Japanese language. Esau appears to be a bastardised version of aisu (ice) and probably equates to the English term 'cooler', meaning prison or cell.

During a rare rest day, Joey and I attached ourselves to a gang that collected and carried the dunny cans from the latrines to the far side of the swamp, the main dumping area for sewage. This was a regular chore assigned to a permanent gang.

Over the previous few weeks we'd watched the workers carrying out this task. It looked a rather relaxed procedure. The dunny gang moved back and forth and, as the guard on the gate didn't appear to count them or to take very much notice of their comings and goings, we more or less 'volunteered' our services.

We put a bamboo pole through the handle of a can, hoisted it to our shoulders, and joined the rear of the line, which then trooped through the gate and out along the track to the swamp, where we slipped away from the legitimate workers. After washing out our can, we filled it with an assortment of coffee beans, coconuts, a few yams and a chook that had managed to fly into it and break its neck.

Shouldering our load, we rejoined the gang on its next return trip, more than happy with the result of our day's labour. We were just inside the gate, home and hosed we thought, when the guards jumped us. Luck is like the curate's egg, good in parts, but mostly bad. Of all the rotten things to happen! Needing the usual less-than-conscientious guard, we'd struck a day when a new and vigilant guard was on the gate, and he had counted us.

The platform on which the machine-gun guarding the camp gate was positioned was accessed by a flight of about six wooden steps. And standing fair and square on the top step was The Big Black Bastard himself: the prima ballerina who had lost so much face when he had danced to the *Flight of the Bumble Bee*. What a bloody bad stroke of luck. Of all the guards in Borneo, it had to be him. He was a big bloke, like a sumo wrestler, and now here we were once again, face to face. But this time, we were the ones about to lose it. We knew it, and he knew it.

He was fit to bust as he shouted '*Koi!*' (Come!), so we koied two steps up, leaving him two steps higher. 'What's in the can?' he asked. 'Can?' we said. 'What can?' One of the guards then kicked the offending can over. Out rolled the coconuts, the yams and the piece de resistance, the suicidal chook.

That's about all I remember. Apparently, while I was looking with feigned surprise at all the goodies that had materialised from goodness knows where, the sergeant hit me with a real haymaker. Some of the blokes watching the goings-on told me later of how I'd sailed out from the top steps, much like a kite, and fluttered to the ground.

In the meantime poor Joey, seeing what had happened to me, automatically and instinctively ducked the swinging fist that was coming his way. Now that kind of evasive action is definitely a no-no if you're dealing with Jap guards; more particularly so if one of them happens to be a sergeant. Through half-closed eyes I took in the scene and, since there was really nothing constructive I could do, slipped back into the comfort zone of unconsciousness. Later, a couple of buckets of water were thrown over me to aid my recovery. Joey and I spent the rest of the night standing in front of the guardhouse, before enjoying two days in the cage. Such were the wages of sin, of crime – and punishment.

Released from Esau, it was back to the 'drome where, after Colonel Suga's visit in early November, the Japs had pulled out all stops as they wanted the work completed in a month. There was no let up and definitely no time off this year for

Esau, the punishment cage

the rank and file on the normally hallowed first Tuesday in November. Melbourne Cup Day came and went like any other – slaving away on the strip – although we did hear later that Up the Hill, in the officers' lines, there had been some kind of Cup Day bash. Whatever it was, invitations to attend were not issued to our part of the camp. The news certainly didn't reach the ears of either of our resident bookies, Gunboat Simpson and Keith Gillett, or they would have been running book on the outcome, for sure. The most exciting happening that week was my seventeenth birthday. It fell on the Wednesday (the day after Cup Day) and since it was a date of great importance Bob Shipsides was determined it should not pass unnoticed.

The rumours about a Melbourne Cup event held Up the Hill were correct. Flush with funds from their recent monthly payday, the officers held a Cup Race, complete with an improvised trophy fashioned from an empty bully-beef tin secured with nails to a wooden stem set into a roughly-hewn, octagonal wooden base. Two galvanised handles secured the 'cup' to its plinth. Engraved on a piece of metal, attached to the tin with rivets, were the words 'Melbourne Cup 1942'.

The race was run between the officers' huts, where a straight track, divided into thirty squares, had been set up for each 'horse'. For the barrier draw, each of the ten entrants, wearing a coloured top of some kind in place of jockey's silks, selected a playing card from a deck. Once the bets were laid, the race caller drew cards to determine how many squares each 'horse' could advance. The first to cross the finish line won the Cup. To add atmosphere to the occasion, some of the officers decorated their slouch hats for a Best Hat Parade.

In October 1943, when the officers were transferred to Kuching, the Cup went with them. For the race that November they constructed a circular track. The winner on this occasion, and possibly also the previous year, was Lieutenant Bill Peck, of 4 Anti-tank Regiment. It is also thought that a third race was conducted in 1944.

Despite claims made in the media in 2015 that the Melbourne Cup held at Sandakan had been conducted to 'raise morale' in the camp, it was strictly an officers' only affair. Not one of the six survivors, including Bill Moxham, who was mad about horse racing, or any of those sent to Outram Road Gaol, has ever mentioned it, or referred to it. Other than vague reports from the officers' batmen that something had taken place, the details were unknown to Billy. The only record that any race was run is in the catalogue of the Australian War Memorial where the cup, retrieved in 1945 from the officers' quarters in Kuching by an Army History Unit, forms part of the Memorial's collection.

The officers' "Melbourne Cup"

The workers didn't get an invitation to the officers' Cup Race but we were all invited by the Japs to attend the official opening of the airstrip in early December 'to improve our morale'. To improve it even more, sporting events were to be held the following day, with Hoshijima handing out prizes of chickens, fruit and other goodies confiscated from local farmers.

The opening almost rivalled a Royal Coronation, with huge arches of flowers and a rent-a-crowd of locals, all supplied with Japanese flags that they were instructed to wave on cue. We were told to make ourselves look presentable, which was a big ask, as our clothes were tattered and raggedy, our boots pretty much non-existent and, as razorblades were scarce, our beards long and unkempt.

Still looking very down at heel, we marched out to the airstrip where we lined up alongside some very well-turned-out spectators – Chinese and Malay coolies, dressed from top to toe in brand-new Australian army shorts and shirts. Hoshijima, looking every inch the commandant, arrived in the big black Buick that he had appropriated, along with a palatial house belonging to a senior civil servant.

To our disappointment, the light bomber ferrying the general invited to open the airfield made a perfect touchdown. Like all VIPs invited to open things, he had plenty to say – and all of it in Japanese. Nevertheless, the rent-a-crowd did their bit by clapping and waving their flags at the appropriate places. When it was all over, we marched back to camp while the general and his fawning entourage disappeared into a tent for refreshments.

If the grand opening was a bit of a fizzer, the sports day was a big hit. The definite highlight was a footy marking competition, organised by Vern Ray, the Hobart Aussie Rules footballer who still had his football. The Japs watched all the races and contests with special interest, taking note of the miraculous improvement in the health and fitness of a number of those previously classified as unfit to work.

We'd now been at Sandakan for the best part of five months. During that time, we had worked hard at improving the conditions inside the camp. Thanks to the scrounging abilities of the work parties, all kinds of small comforts designed to make life a little easier had begun to appear in and around the huts. Since most of the occupants had lists of things that needed doing, or fixing, a never-ending array of bits and pieces was smuggled into the camp. How these tasks were accomplished, and the lengths to which the smugglers went, was amazing.

We were blessed with an abundance of innovative people, whose talents were used to overcome many of the camp's shortcomings and hardships. I'm sure that this adaptability can be traced back, in no small part, to our Australian heritage: the initial remoteness of the strange Great South Land, together with the lonely exile that faced our early pioneers and the rough and tumble of the convict era. Added to this was a shortage of many everyday things that made improvisation essential.

Our prison camp was like the early days of the colony. We were treated as convicts, conditions were tough, and the acute shortages made scrounging and adaptation a way of life. The things that would suddenly pop up in the middle of our godforsaken hole defied the laws of probability. That prisoners overcame scarcity and adversity to make the camp habitable convinces me that, given just the slightest chance, the bulk of them would have survived.

I have never ceased to wonder at the things that were made, and at the things they were made from: gadgets, and thingummybobs, whatchamacallits and doodahs, along with thingummyjigs. A part would go missing from a Jap truck while the driver sat in the front seat. Smuggled past a guard it became the centrepiece for an electric fan, hung within the leafy fronds of the ceiling and designed to pop up into the atap, if necessary. If something were needed, there was always someone in the camp who would find a way to get it.

Each hut had its own unique inventions. The materials used to make them and the ingenious tasks they performed were testimony to many hidden talents: talents that were used with wonderful effect for an Arts and Crafts display organised to coincide with the opening of our brand new Hospital Ward and Chapel.

With stage 1 of the airstrip complete, permission was granted to build a hospital ward, with one end screened off to create a chapel. This was welcome news as the original hospital, built by the British, had fallen prey to scavenging locals and was a total wreck, stripped of its doors and windows, along with anything else remotely useful. The brick wall of the cookhouse had suffered a similar fate and was partially demolished, leaving the chimney in ruins. However, the remainder of the building was sound, and as the only food the kitchen staff had to cook was rice, and a few veggies, the loss of the chimney was of no consequence.

Now that Hoshijima had given the green light to construct a new hospital, a team of enthusiastic tradesmen was soon hard at it, using timber cut straight from the trees. Unlike the other huts, which had a simple gabled roof, the hospital had a hip roof, with four sloping sides. When the end-product was unveiled for inspection everyone, including the Japs, agreed that it was a masterpiece of ingenuity. The carpentry and cabinet making, indeed the entire construction, were a real labour of love. Not a scrap of steel was used, or nails, or metal hinges or catches. Everything was glued, wood on wood. Only the piers were masonry, using bricks salvaged from the cookhouse wall, held together with mortar concocted from seashells ground into a fine powder and pulverised recycled cement. I might be considered biased, having helped to make the mortar and carry some of the bricks and timber, but we were so proud of it. To celebrate the grand opening, it was decided to hold an arts and crafts show, displaying the exhibits in the new chapel.

What an occasion it was! The show, which we regarded as a gala affair, was a sellout, and no wonder. The range of the exhibits and the types of craftsmanship were truly astonishing. Their quantity and quality were equally amazing. The hall was filled with carvings, paintings, drawings and models of all kinds. What a heck of a surprise we had when we first walked in. We toured around the benches, gaping at the carvings and at the many other articles, made from so many different materials, and at the walls, covered with colourful paintings.

The quality and the quantity of the items on display bowled everyone over, and I am sure that a fair few would have held their own at an international expo. It was miraculous that such artistic pieces had been produced in a POW camp; that our men had made these beautiful things, and under such trying circumstances. It was this aspect that surprised us Dead End Kids the most. We youngsters hadn't stopped still long enough to appreciate the talent that surrounded us, day in, day out. In the arrogance of our youth we had sat dreaming and speculating about what was going on outside the camp, blinded to what was going on inside. Who'd have thought that these old blokes were capable of making such things? By jingoes! And where did they find the time to do it?

The winner's sash went to a man who, despite being crippled with leg ulcers, had carved from a solid five-foot-long teak log the most beautiful birdcage. The cage itself was about twelve inches across and about eighteen inches high, but the most amazing part was that the carving was all in one continuous piece: the cage with its wire-like sides; the Oriental-style roof with its little rounded tiles; and the bird perched on the swing, together with a long chain – each of its links separate, like a real chain, and yet still part of the whole. I still find it hard to believe. We Kids pondered long and hard on just how it was done. We examined it again and again, but failed to find any hidden joins, or anything else, to explain how its creator had produced such a complicated and delicate carving.

Out of curiosity, a few of the off-duty guards came in for a look-see. They were so impressed that they asked for the show to be held over for another day. Captain Hoshijima, basking in our reflected glory, took the opportunity to invite a few of his friends from the town, and also the governor. The visitors were so impressed that the camp scored another dugong for supper.

The commandant was so taken by the superior quality of the building itself that, when barracks were built for the guards some months later, our beautiful hospital was jacked up from its foundations, placed on rollers and relocated in the Japanese compound to serve as an administrative building. Sadly, all that is left of the actual art and craft show is a small wooden carving of an Australian digger, dressed in tropical kit and tin hat, with his rifle in 'reversed arms' position. Along with a few drawings, a watercolour painting and odd badges, buckles and buttons, this exquisitely crafted artwork was one of the very few items to survive the war. The fixers, the procurers, the creative artists and the inventors who devised that most wonderful display were not destined to return home to tell their stories or exhibit their works of art.

Over the years, whenever I have mentioned to officers who were transferred to Kuching the construction of the hospital and chapel and the monumental exhibition that is impressed so vividly in my mind, all I have received are blank looks. Almost all have no recollection whatsoever of the new hut, or of the arts

The carving of the soldier

and crafts. The few who did recall something were so vague about it that I even started to doubt my own memory. Fortunately my co-author Lynette came to the rescue. She unearthed not only the name of the man (an ex-officer) who had supervised the work, but also the fact that he had a diary; a memoir in which he had recorded the use of bricks for the piers, and even how the mortar had been made.

At about the same time as we built the hospital, Hoshijima gave us permission to construct a timber platform to serve as a stage and double as a boxing arena. It was erected in a grassy hollow beyond the officers' huts. Over the coming months we held several concerts and singalongs and, to the obvious enjoyment of almost everyone including the guards, exhibition boxing and wrestling matches.

Bob Davidson, a staff sergeant in my battalion whose brother was a well-known dance-band leader, formed a choir that was to become the backbone of the camp singalongs and theatrical nights.

Bob Davidson's brother, Jim, a talented musician, was the leader of the highly successful ABC Dance Band, which performed over the national network in all Australian states. In 1936 the band, along with its trumpeter Jim Gussey, vocalist Alice Smith and trombonist George Trevare, became the most popular dance band in the country, touring with such well-known entertainers as Tex Morton, Bob Dyer and Gladys Moncrieff.

In 1941, after being appointed an honorary lieutenant in the AIF, Jim and his orchestra performed in variety shows for troops based in the Middle East and South-west Pacific. By 1943, he was in charge of all the AIF's concert parties.

Much to my surprise, a couple of us young fellows were roped in to join the choir group – a decision that sent the other occupants of the Dead Enders' hut into a state of shock. Joey Crome, Henry Forde and myself supplied the voices, and MP Brown the music. I also recall that it was MP who persuaded us to join. What inducement he used I have forgotten. However, I do remember our choirmaster talking about the importance of our being able to harmonise, and Joey piping up with 'Har-mony does it take to harmonise, Staff Sergeant?' which we thought was a great joke – but you really had to be there.

Walter 'Henry' Ford

Anyway, about a dozen or so of us started singing as a group and the fact that I now remember our participation with fondness gives some indication of how enjoyable it was. This was due entirely to our choirmaster Bob Davidson, a really good bloke who put every effort into teaching us how to sing, as well as giving us an appreciation for music. We'd perform under a canopy of moon and stars that reminded me of the domed celestial ceiling of the beautiful Capitol Theatre, back in Sydney.

The star piece of our small repertoire began with the line 'What a day was yesterday, for yesterday gave me you'. It is a lovely song, and those poignant words, especially when sung in harmony, brought us together in a way that nothing else could. If ever a song was made for a time and place, this was that song. On those beautiful, balmy, tropical evenings, when the music wafted its way down the hill and into the huts, the magic of our voices filled the air. The words of 'Yesterday' floated across the campsite, enticing others to join in, to become one voice, one song – and, for at least one little moment, our thoughts returned to yesterday, to our homes and families back in Australia.

It's funny how memory darts about. Like a spotlight on the back of a truck it goes bumping along a track, lighting up some little thing or other, but leaving the mountains dark in the shadows. The man who sang bass in our choir was a big Englishman who, except for those few moments of song, I hardly ever knew. His name was Huckle. I can still see his big form in silhouette, and hear his deep bass voice creating a backboard for the rest of us.

Conditions improved in the last weeks of 1942. The workload lessened considerably, the rice ration increased and, for the last six weeks or so, the Japs had allowed us to trade with locals at the airstrip. So, with one thing and another, it made waiting out the war a much more attractive proposition. The wise heads advised us to stay put. 'Ride the storm out' became the motto of the day.

'Bear up chaps, keep your heads down, hope the guards will lay off with their sticks and give us a fair go' was our rationale as the old year came to a close, prompting hope that the new year would have better goods on its shelves. The future was bound to be kinder. Best to settle down to work and wait the arrival of our victorious armies.

With this in mind, and Christmas rapidly approaching, we made preparations for the festivities: brewing batches of coconut toddy and laying down a supply of plug tobacco, using various secret recipes. Ours was a very special mixture.

Method: Onto a layer of partly dried paw-paw leaves sprinkle a mixture of used tea leaves, coffee dregs, Javanese rope tobacco and a smear of molasses. Add another layer of paw-paw leaves and continue layering until the ingredients are all used. Compress the layers with any heavy object to hand. Leave it to mature for a week or two until the layers are reduced to a thickness of about one inch. Pare some of the now hardened and cured mixture into a corn-cob pipe and light up. If you can smoke it, you are definitely a man.

To brew the toddy was far less complicated. We simply tapped into a green coconut shell, added some molasses and whatever else came to hand to encourage fermentation, plugged the hole and buried it, making sure that careful note was taken of exactly where it was buried. I'm afraid I wasn't a very successful brewer, as my coconuts kept on blowing up underground. In any case, it was dreadful stuff to drink, and not worth the effort. Just a mouthful was enough to zap you from top to bottom, and you'd go around feeling as if your head had blown up.

The cooks made a Christmas pudding out of rice and a special secret ingredient called 'don't ask'. With a splash of toddy over it, it wasn't all that bad and, apart from the total lack of threepences and sixpences, the final product made it seem a bit like home – if we used some imagination. We also gave and received presents: small things like corn-cob pipes, plugs of home-made tobacco, second-hand books. Gunboat Simpson started a game of two-up, and that night we had a special game of blackjack. Most of us did whatever dough we had. Gunboat didn't lose, of course, as he worked on a percentage basis.

A concert was held to celebrate the arrival of 1943 and to help welcome in the New Year Hoshijima invited the governor as his guest. We'd seen him before, at the arts and crafts show. A queer old chap, he looked like the original Old Man of the Orient, with a wrinkled face and long, grey, stringy beard. He was wearing shorts and a uniform jacket, with medals and ribbons, but the total effect was quite bizarre as he had also donned a pair of long johns that hung down to his ankles, just above the wooden clogs on his feet. We thought he may have been part of some comic act, but he wasn't. He was for real.

Hoshijima's guest was Tanuke Kumabe, the eccentric Japanese Governor of British North Borneo's East Coast Residency, whose habit of appearing in public wearing all his campaign medals, baggy shorts and old-fashioned suspenders around his calves to keep his socks up had made him a well-known local identity.

The choir sang a few songs – among them 'Yesterday' and 'The Silvery Moon', two of the most popular songs from our repertoire. The whole camp sang along. Everyone sang non-stop, right up until 'Auld Lang Syne', hoping that 1943 would be an improvement on the 1942 model.

It wasn't.

We were soon back working on stage 2 of the drome, the guards were as bad as ever, throwing their weight about and strutting about like peacocks. Nevertheless, our load was lightened whenever we took advantage of their conceit, for their vanity knew no bounds. The war to date had done them proud, and their propaganda machine played to their sense of superiority. As they swaggered past, lording it over us as usual, we brought our main defence system – humour – into play. Laughter was the grease that kept the wheels of our life turning – and there was always laughter of some kind going on in our hut.

The names of some of the Dead Enders have become hazy with age, although their faces remain clear. It's me that's become wrinkled and with a bit of luck we'll all fade together.

I do recall the names of some of them and several of the older blokes with ease. Among the sixteen bods in my room were Hilton (Terry) Riseley, Joey Crome, Jimmy Finn, Harry Longley, John (Snowy) Bryant, Walter (Henry) Ford, Trevor (Dobbo) Dobson, Myles Peace (MP or Jimmy) Brown, Keith (Shearer) Gillett, Bob (Shippy) Shipsides, Sid Outram and James (Punchy) Donohue.

Harry Longley

James 'Punchy' Donohue

Trevor 'Dobbo' Dobson

We also had a bloke named George Plunkett, who was a champion tennis player. He'd narrowly escaped death near Bukit Timah, when the Japs had lined up a whole bunch of blokes they'd captured and used them for bayonet and sword practice. George had thirteen bayonet wounds in his back, and a deep sword cut to his neck. With the help of a Chinese family, he and two others had survived and had been smuggled into Selarang Barracks when they were well enough to move. George was a really good sport, who didn't mind showing off his wounds so that I could count them.

Another familiar face was Bill Cooke, the other bloke the Japs had failed to behead at St Pat's College, the only survivor of the group attacked outside the gate. Aged 34, and with a mass of close-cropped dark curly hair, he was the second oldest in our immediate group, Bob Shipsides being the oldest by far. As Bill spelled his name the posh way, with an 'e', we called him Cookee. Before the war he had worked in the haberdashery section of a large store in Brisbane – Overell's, I think it was. Back then, staff had to be immaculately groomed, wellspoken and possess a congenial personality suited to actually serving the customers. Cookee, who loved his job, ticked all three boxes.

Nicknames, which were common at the time and often replaced the person's real name, had many derivations, some of them obscure. Some were simply shortened (or lengthened) versions of given names or surnames, while others reflected a place of origin or the physical appearance of the individual or, perversely, the exact opposite. Those who hailed from Tasmania were dubbed Tassie; tall fellows Lofty; small men Shorty or Titch; those with glasses Four-eyes or Specs; men of Aboriginal or Islander background Darkie and anyone with kinky hair Curly. Baldy spoke for itself, while those with very fair hair were known universally as Snowy or Blondie. On the other hand red-headed people could be called Carrots or Bluey (the opposite of red) and large men Tiny, while those with a reserved nature were often known as Rowdy, because they were not.

We also had our fair share of people we named Curly, and Shorty, although there was only one Boxhead. Poor fellow, we put a dead snake in his hammock one night. It was a dreadful thing to do: he didn't like snakes. We had a Lofty or two, and a couple of politically incorrect Darkies, and there must have been at least six Blueys. One, Bluey Anderson, who was in our hut, slept in the centre room with several other 2/30th men, including a bloke named Annear and another called Cross. I didn't know it at the time, but Bluey Anderson's real name was Bowe. He had joined the army under his correct name but when he was discharged he had adopted his mother's maiden name, Anderson, to get back in.

CHAPTER 7 Camp life

The blokes I was with were a great mob. With the day's toil behind us, and having eaten all there was to eat, we'd sit outside the hut. On these balmy nights, with the moon sailing across, so quiet and so big, against a backdrop of millions of twinkling stars, MP playing his mouth organ, and Dobbo accompanying himself with a drum he'd made from a box, would sing 'The Ringle Rangle Ram', a song that was a favourite of the Dobson family. It was also our favourite, all twenty verses of it, some of them quite bawdy, and each finishing with the refrain:

Hi Ringle Rangle.
Hi Ringle Ray,
It was the finest ram sir,
That ever was fed on hay.

But no matter how good our singing was, the boxing and wrestling matches were the frontrunners in the entertainment popularity stakes. Nothing in the way of any other entertainment stood a chance of competing with those lads. They carried too much punch, and always won with a knockout.

We seemed to have the best glovemen in the Eighth Division with us at Sandakan and so, in the biff-and-rip business of boxing and wrestling, we were the heavyweight champions in that part of the world. Every fight night, the announcer would jump into the middle of the ring and, shouting above the cheers of the fans to make himself heard, would read out the card, proclaiming the merits of each and every one of the night's contestants. Then, to the roar of all assembled, the gladiators would stand to be acclaimed by the ringing cheers of the multitude, especially their individual supporters.

Down our end of the camp we were overburdened with pugilistic talent, so much so that we Kids had to be careful to whom we gave cheek. Our primary claim to fame rested on the broad shoulders of Jimmy Darlington, an original member of 2/18 Battalion, and far and away the best fighter any of us had ever seen: a strong and agile man, not much given to talk, but when he spoke, we'd better listen. Big, and proud of his Aboriginal lineage, Jimmy was a tremendous athlete. Back in Singapore, before the Japs turned up, he'd taken part in an exhibition fight with the American champion, the Alabama Kid. Being an exhibition fight, there was no winner, but we were all in no doubt that Jimmy had 'won'.

Next in our talented line-up were Gunboat Simpson and Gunboat Smith. Both were big and tough, and also very rough. Gunboat Smith, whose nickname came from a distinctive gunboat tattoo, was more of a wrestler and was in the same hut as Mo Davis and Keith Botterill.

On one occasion he was pitted against a guard who was also the local Jap sumo champion. This particular match was a lesson in tact: how much we dared to cheer

Henry 'Gunboat' Simpson

our bloke and how much to boo his opponent. The contest was diplomatically judged as an honourable draw, to the satisfaction of all in attendance, including most of the off-duty guards and their officers.

Gunboat Simpson, also known as The Gunna, was a former provincial heavyweight champion, a rip-snorter of a fellow. I'd sure hate to pick a fight with The Gunna, who had the shortest of tempers and was inclined to go off his rocker and come out swinging if he heard a bell, any bell, ringing.

He had a shield featuring an American flag tattooed across his shoulder, along with its guarding eagle. When he wiggled his shoulder muscles the flag would appear to wave and the wings of the eagle to bristle. This party trick was his main talent, apart from fighting: his nose, but more especially his ears, bore witness to many hard-hitting bouts.

John Henry Simpson, universally known as Gunboat, was born in Stockton, England, in 1912. A man of strapping proportions, and powerfully built, from 1932 to 1937 he had featured in regularly fights in Shepparton, Victoria, where he lived for a time, and at the Fitzroy and Melbourne Stadiums.

In 1932 he held the title of Heavyweight Champion of the Goulburn Valley, but lost his crown the following year in a fight with Bobbie Birch. Determined to regain the title, 'the rugged gunboat fighter', as the press described him, continued to take on all comers. He had never suffered the indignity of being knocked out until January 1935, when he was defeated in the eighth round of a bout with New Zealander Bill Pascoe. The battering was so severe that Gunboat was forced back through the ropes, suffering concussion severe enough to see him admitted to Mooroopna Hospital. The referee stopped the fight, and awarded it to Pascoe on a technical knockout. Gunboat issued a challenge in the press for a return bout, winner take all, but to no avail.

CHAPTER 7 Camp life

When Tiger Fitzpatrick, who defeated Gunboat on points in a subsequent fight, went on to defeat the Goulburn Valley heavyweight title-holder, Bobbie Birch, Tiger was declared to be the best heavyweight fighter in Shepparton.

After that, Gunboat moved to Geelong and changed tactics. On 29 June 1935, the press reported:

> There was a side-splitting comedy fight between Gunboat Simpson and Jim Starr over four rounds. Gunboat, a tall, lathy, tattooed athlete, proved himself a real humourist. He swung blows from all imaginable angles and grimaced, postured, and gave an exhibition of ring antics that sent the onlookers into shrieks of laughter. Starr won on points.

Two weeks later, in a fight against Tom Ford, a hard-hitting left-hander, Gunboat provided 'the highlight of the night' in a 'farcical, fistic comedy'. The reporter went on:

> The antics, posturing and grimaces of Simpson had the audience in shrieks of laughter, and nothing half so comical has ever before been seen at the stadium. Simpson adopted every possible stance, and made fierce faces at his rival that caused even the ring official to roar with laughter. The referee appreciated the joke by declaring the six-round comedy a draw.

In July and September, after being defeated on points in two matches, Gunboat won the next on a technical knockout. It was to be his last serious fight. He married a girl named Lily and moved to Albury, where Gunboat became a part-time military policeman with the militia.

In May 1941 he was working as a labourer when he enlisted in the AIF at Royal Park Barracks, Melbourne, the nearest recruiting depot to Albury.

Gunboat's pugilistic tendencies, and his notoriously short fuse, landed him in trouble during training when, while undergoing hospital treatment for VD, he punched a fellow patient, giving him a bloody nose and abrasions. This escapade earned the aggressor fourteen days' detention, but no demotion in rank, and two months later he was promoted from Lance Corporal to Acting Corporal. He sailed for Malaya with 2/29 Battalion's reinforcements on 26 January 1942, arriving just in time to join the final battle for Singapore.

We also had Big Keith Gillett – The Shearer – he of the pet monkey stew. Keith was a roommate, and with him around there was never a dull moment. He was such a funny bloke, and the tales about his shearing days were certainly entertaining. Perhaps he didn't know too much about the science of boxing, but what he could do, and do really well, was go right in there and fight. He may not have won many bouts, but by the same token the other bloke wouldn't be too sure that he had won either.

Keith told us that while we were in Malaya he was one of the very few enlisted men to obtain permission from the Army to marry a local girl. He carried her picture with him everywhere. She was Eurasian and very, very pretty. She was expecting a baby, but what became of her I've not been able to discover.

There is no record on The Shearer's service papers to indicate that he was given permission to marry anyone, nor was there any change to his next-of-kin, nominated as his mother Rita. He was, however, in serious trouble in October 1941, when he escaped from fourteen days' detention after going absent without leave. Apprehended, he was given another 28 days. He escaped again, this time also destroying government property. The sentence for this string of misdemeanours, imposed by a court martial, was subsequently reviewed and suspended, on the grounds that the accused had 'acted under stress caused by unsympathetic consideration of his problems' – an act of mitigation endorsed by none other than the AIF's most senior officer in Malaya, Major General H Gordon Bennett. The court also observed that Private Gillett 'had the makings of a good soldier'.

From what Billy remembers, Keith was 'always up to mischief, so full of schemes and dreams, so chock full of the spirit of life, and ever willing to have a go', and it seems likely that The Shearer fell in love and did marry a local girl, probably according to traditional rites and definitely without official permission. Perhaps those who sat in judgment learned of this and, in what appears to be an uncharacteristic act of compassion, made the necessary allowances.

Coming down from the heavyweights, we had the smaller blokes, including my mate Jimmy Finn from the 30th Battalion. He was a very clever and effective featherweight, top-notch, a first-rate bloke who would be in anything that was going, no matter who or what. He backpedalled to no man. There were quite a few big blokes around who had found, to their sorrow, the power than came with a poke on the jaw from Jimmy. He had a punch that hit like a mule, as another of my roommates, Sid Outram, discovered when he received a gentle 'demonstration tap' on the jaw.

Snowy Bryant, also from our hut, was among the lightweight contenders; a quiet gentle man, the sort who looked a pushover and seemed to be out of place in a boxing ring. However, you would only get to kick sand in his face once.

There were many others around the camp who fancied themselves as fighters and wrestlers and entered any contest at the drop of a hat. There were always plenty of fighters to fill the bill on an occasional day off, or when we held a

Boxer 'Snowy' Bryant

specially arranged exhibition night fight under an electric light that shone from a pole near the corner of the ring.

The most memorable fight started out as a grudge match – one of those stupid arguments that had started quietly enough but, before you could count to ten, developed into the most hyped-up fight ever to be held in the camp, if not in All the Borneos. By common agreement the argument was deferred to a proper time and place, and it wasn't long before it was billed as the Fight of Fights.

Keith Gillett upped the ante when he decided to take over the management and training for Snowy Bryant, the bloke our hut had tipped to win. Keith, who reckoned Snowy was a dead cert, also set himself up as the leading bookmaker. Excitement reigned supreme, and I was reminded of the nights when I'd sold fight programs down at the big tin shed that served as the Sydney Stadium at Rushcutters Bay.

The anticipation of the fans reached fever pitch when Gunboat Simpson took over as manager-trainer of Snowy's opponent, Punchy Donohue, thus making a fair dinkum contest of it. With the challenge made and accepted, the boys, their managers and handlers went into strict training. A punching bag took over the free space under our hut and a skipping rope was supplied by one of the sponsors. All was in order to ensure that our bloke stayed on top and kept sharp with his punches. We were all so sure, so cocky, that he'd be more than a match when the time came to face his opposition.

A trophy and a purse with real money in it were produced and, to the cry of 'Money up, or shut up', bets were placed, and loyalties tested. With the training well underway and the betting books filling, excitement continued to mount, and by the time the bout drew near blood was really stirring in the veins of the two factions. Expectancy jostled with anticipation, right up to the night of the fight, which was a sellout, a record crowd. Even the guards who weren't on duty came down to see the show. Fame was there for the taking and, sensing this, the crowd overflowed the grassy banks surrounding the top side of the ring long before the preliminaries were half over. Although Punchy and Snowy were roommates, both part of our tightly knit band, our hut had backed Snowy to the hilt. Keith, as the bookmaker, was set to win a fortune and fully expected to be able to retire for life.

What a top performance our cove put up for the first two rounds of the three-round bout. He danced rings around his opponent, a jab here and a dab there – all good stuff, money in the bank. He continued on his merry way right up until halfway through the last round, when Punchy threw in an uppercut that seemed to come from off the floor. Bang! It landed on the point of Snowy's chin, and down for the count he went.

The Big Fight

At that point, Keith went missing. Not having nearly enough money to cover his bets, he was forced underground, and he stayed there waiting for the heat to cool down before offering to pay his creditors just one cent in the dollar. As the only alternative was for him to declare himself bankrupt, the payout figure was 'agreed on'. Being over six feet tall, Keith was able to explain these kinds of arrangements and get away with it. The taller and stronger you are, the easier it becomes to make people see reason, or so it seems to me.

The measly payout did not deter the punters from joining the games of pontoon (blackjack) that Gunboat Simpson ran in a cunningly concealed space excavated beneath his hut and draped in ground sheets to form a cave. It was the most coveted game in the camp, and was by invitation only. A bare copper wire, scavenged from the main supply, ran from the partition above, providing just enough current to light the single bulb that dangled over the square mat on the dirt floor. As gambling was forbidden by camp administration it was always a risky business, but playing pontoon was particularly hazardous at The Gunna's 'Casino Royale'.

To minimise the risk, there were two important rules to remember. First, to gain entry punters needed to have a stake of least ten cents, which they had to show The Gunna, who trusted no one, before he'd let anyone pass. The second was to make sure all winning bets were collected before the lights went out. This was tricky, because there was no warning and Gunna could never recollect any unpaid winning bets, not after the lights went out. On the other hand, if a punter owed money, no matter how dark it was, he had to pay up. One of the advantages of being a heavyweight champion is that you can develop a very selective memory.

To get around Rule 1, since we were nearly always broke, three or four of us pooled our resources. When we had a large enough stake to satisfy Gunna, the first bloke would crawl through the tunnel entrance, show the colour of our money, then pass it to the next member of the syndicate through a hole we had made in the groundsheet wall. This procedure went on until we were all safely inside.

We must have made a fine study of concentration, 'deciding' whose betting card to use, at the same time making sure Gunna didn't wake up to our scam. He was a big bad-tempered bugger; enough to frighten the life out of any of us little blokes. He was intimidating even in the full light of day, with his flat broken nose, long thin cords of lips, and heavy black eyebrows that extended past his temples to a pair of cauliflower ears. His strongly shaped head was typical of an old-time prizefighter, puckered and scored by the scars of many fights.

The game finished when the lights went out, and that's when Rule 2 became a bit tricky: trying to make sure that we collected our winnings before the electricity went off. Any transaction not completed, tough luck. There was no avenue of appeal. With the night's entertainment over, we would meekly crawl out along the tunnel, one after another, and whisper 'Goodnight, Gunna'. 'Goodnight fellas', would come the gruff response. 'See youse.'

Gunboat Simpson's Casino
'Twas the biggest game about
You had to have ten cents to get in
You needed nothing at all to get out.

Fortunately, for the peace of mind of the camp, we did have a few older and wiser heads among us. B Force seemed to be divided between blokes who were called either Kid or Pop. Anyone over 25 we kids considered ancient. Some fellas, the real oldies, had been in the First World War. We reckoned that a couple of blokes, well over 50, must have served in the Boer War. Ancient or not, they managed to keep an eye on us youngsters.

At night, Bob Shipsides and some of the other old jokers played chess, a game that could go on for weeks, and Gunna and Boxhead might come over for a game or two of poker. We played for huge stakes, sometimes hundreds of dollars. Not real money of course. We used IOUs, and if we'd had the funds to honour them we could have started our own stock exchange.

Others played cards or sang, and when the singing finished we'd talk about the feeds we'd cook up when we were free. How our mouths watered! It seemed as if, at one time or another, we'd all been great chefs. The extravagance of our favourite recipes was beyond belief: great big juicy, tender steaks; succulent turkey; eggs and bacon with mushrooms and onions; apple pie and cream, plus wonderfully exotic concoctions conjured from our imaginations.

On dark nights when the moon was down, or when the clouds lay low and thick, we went on scrounging trips to nearby kampongs, slipping out under the wire, and then wading quietly through the shallow swamp waters. Coconuts were out there for the taking, providing you could climb well enough. There is quite an art to climbing the tall thin trunks of the coconut palms, at the same time watching out for the things that bite in the night. Believe me, 50 feet up is not a good place to bump into a squad of soldier ants.

With the camp situated smack-bang in the centre of the agricultural farm, there was a fair chance of coming back with some treats – coffee for instance, from the bushes over by the cinnamon trees. The smell of roasted (burnt) coffee beans floating around the huts is a special memory. The grounds also added flavour to our tobacco mixtures.

Sometimes, if we were lucky, a chook might accidentally fly into our tucker bag, but the biggest prize in the culinary department was a big fresh patch of tapioca. It had to be fairly fresh, as the roots ferment if left too long in the ground. Many a time I felt like crying when I pulled up a large plant only to find the roots all squashy and sour. Fresh tapioca roots, sliced, make the best chips. An alternative use was gravy, made from burnt tapioca flour, which sure put life into the rice. We'd first dry the roots, then grind them with a rock or a lump of iron to a powdery pulp. This would be burnt over the fire for a minute or two, before adding a splash of water and a pinch of salt (if available), and swamping the rice with it.

The side of our hut shielded our private cooking area from the prying eyes of the guards. It was here that we lit our little fires, and cooked such culinary delights as finely sliced snake on burnt rice biscuit, served with palm cabbage. Another delicacy, more of a side dish really, was lightly toasted swamp snails. However, we had to make sure we washed them well, and avoided getting too much ash in the shell, otherwise the delicate flavours were ruined.

Most of these dishes went well with Palm Tree Cabbage Soup, or baked Wild Yam Surprise – little extras that improved the monotonous camp rations. Many and strange were the exotic recipes that we tried out in secret behind the hut. But no matter how good or exotic the recipe, or how capable the cook, tapioca chips remained the favourite: yummy to eat and almost impossible to ruin.

But the best food that came our way, and by pure chance, was the Wandering Billy Goat. From the moment that billy goat came into the camp, it was pure vaudeville, destined to become part of camp folk lore. Indeed, it is the one single event of our imprisonment that those who returned home could not only remember, but agree upon in regard to details.

A small herd of goats had been keeping the grass down outside the camp perimeter when the billy somehow managed to wriggle under the wire near the parade ground, on the far side of the huts and out of sight of the guardhouse. Never had the men gathered as quickly, or had plans been made so fervently, as in the anticipation of goat stew. From the huts around or bordering the parade ground the goat hunters assembled. Fires were made, knives were sharpened and pots were filled with simmering water.

The hunt was on, and it was every man for himself. All kinds of goat-enticing lures were devised, but it was a frustrating day. The goat had a mind of his own, and refused to cooperate. Off he'd go towards an eager group, then he'd turn our way, only to change direction yet again. Oh the agony of it! The taste of stewed goat was on everyone's tongue; a banquet in the making. Our mob had figured it out, right down to the size of the pot, but some other rotten lucky buggers managed to grab the prize. They killed, skinned, cooked and ate it, all in one go.

Being the only billy in the herd, it wasn't long before his absence was noted, and the alarm raised. Guards came running, and searched every hut. They looked high and low, drew a blank and searched again. The result was always the same. But when Gunboat Simpson held his next pontoon game, there on the dirt floor, spread out in a blaze of glory, was a goat skin, looking as good as sable.

The grass around the guardhouse stirred,
kept in control by a local herd.
Perchance one bright and sunny day,

a foolish Billy Goat did stray.
He wandered into Camp, our way,
and soon became The Gunna's 'O'lay!'

The camp got away with it that time, but my constant obsession with food almost was my undoing.

Joey Crome, along with me and Punchy Donohue, who had taken part in one fight too many, were doing a bit of scrounging in the farmland outside the wire when we were spotted by the Japs, who decided to do a spot of hunting – with us as the quarry. As the bullets whistled past, far too close for comfort, we took off. When we stopped for a breather we realised we were one man short – Punchy had disappeared.

We waited around for a while, as this was Punchy's first time out with us. Then, assuming that he would make his own way back, we went off to continue with our foraging: coconuts, tapioca roots and whatever else we could find. After filling our bags, and with night about to fall, we headed back to camp.

It turned out to be one of the longest, most heart-stopping journeys ever. It seemed that the entire Imperial Japanese Army was out searching for us, and the nearer we came to camp, the more this became apparent. We engaged in some very fancy footwork to dodge the Japs, a task made easier by the noise the searchers were making. We were also helped by the blackness of the night, which was so thick that it sucked up the light of their torches. We managed to make it back to the edge of the swamp undetected, only to discover that the wooden ramp that formed part of the perimeter path, and where the Japs rarely ventured, was now covered with the blighters.

The only way back into the camp was through the swamp and I don't think either of us thought we would make it. After slipping through the water, we would have to pass under the ramp where the Japs had congregated, and then crawl through the swamp to the other side.

Like swamp creatures ourselves, we slithered into the mire and edged towards the ramp an inch at a time through the black murky water while leeches clung to our exposed skin, and God knows what else passed us by. Our haversacks, draped with swamp weeds and held afloat by the coconuts within, earned their keep by camouflaging our painstaking progress.

Like a pair of swamp rats we slipped through the muck, with hardly a ripple on the surface. Steady as she goes, we passed under the wooden ramp, where the Japs were perched on the planks, their legs dangling just above our heads. Others had stayed on dry land chatting away, the glow of cigarettes and the sound of their voices inadvertently marking the boundary of the swamp. They were so sure of themselves, enjoying the night, having a yarn and a puff as they anticipated the sport that was to come.

As we always used the swamp to get in and out of the camp on our foraging expeditions, we had placed a thin rope under the water to send and receive signals. It ran from the foot of an outside fencepost, through the barbed-wire entanglements to our lookout on the inside. It also served as a guide, but that night its main purpose was the sending and receiving of signals. Two tugs on the line meant Japs were patrolling inside, too close for comfort. One tug gave the all-clear. Our nerves were stretched to the limit. The last hundred feet took an eternity.

Amazingly, we made it back into camp, and in one piece. Happy! We were so bloody happy, and very relieved. Then one of our officers came down to deliver some news that pole-axed us. He was a lieutenant. A young, fair-headed bloke, who said he was our hut officer. This was news to us because we'd never laid eyes on him before, and this proved to be his first and only visit.

'The Japs are holding your mate captive', he said, 'and they will execute him unless you two blokes go straight on up and surrender.' What a nice surprise. Instead of a victory celebration, we were to go to the Jap office and capitulate.

Crikey! What blow that was, and after such a seemingly successful night, to have it end with a kick in the guts. Home and hosed, and now we were back in the shit. There was nothing left for it, so we walked up that hill in the dark. Alone. The messenger officer supposedly looking after our hut had buzzed off. I can now understand why the ancient Greeks killed the messenger, if they didn't like the message. At least it gave them some satisfaction. We were two disheartened and apprehensive young tearaways, totally abandoned by the officers whose job was to look after us. Triumph and our superiors had deserted us.

Three Japs, dark shapes, were waiting in the shadows of the big tree, looking as unfriendly as could be. Three narks in the dark – Jimmy Pike the interpreter, The Black Bastard (the camp sergeant) and his equally evil corporal. Behind them stood our erstwhile companion, with his hands tied behind his back and looking very much the worse for wear.

As Joey and I braced ourselves, ready for the worst, we somehow remembered an important military principle: *Always carry out correct army procedures, whenever you are in trouble.* Knowing full well that we were in heaps of strife, we drew ourselves to attention, and saluted smartly. Addressing Jimmy Pike, Joey said in the politest voice possible 'We believe you are looking for us, Sir'.

All we got was silence. Things sure looked crook. Not good at all. Three pairs of cold, angry eyes glared down at us, enough to give anyone the shivers, and we expected no mercy whatsoever. The Jockey broke the silence, asking, 'You men got out of camp, even though my guards are there to stop you?' We wondered, for a moment, if he really expected an answer. He didn't, because he continued, 'You then got back into this camp even though I had trebled the guard, so as to stop you?', and I immediately thought, 'Shitty shit! This is it! The little bugger's really mad at us, and we're gonna cop it for sure!'

It was then that the 'face' thing reared its wonderful, beautiful head. The Jockey simply said, 'You may go now.'

And that was that. Off we went. No argument.

Jimmy Pike then waded into the sergeant with his sword – still in its scabbard. The sergeant did the same to the corporal, and so it went, right on down the line. Joey and I became instant converts to this idea of 'face', which surely had saved us both. It was commonplace to administer beatings in such a way – and the heavy sword and scabbard could do a lot of damage.

We didn't need much imagination to figure out what would have happened to us, if they'd caught us on the outside. We could well have copped it good and proper. A few months after our escapade, the Japs shot and killed two of our blokes, caught outside the wire while trying to escape.

The two escapees, shot without trial in May 1943, were signallers Howard Harvey, aged 21, from Townsville and a 32-year-old Thursday Islander, Theodore 'Mac' MacKay. Wanted by the military police for going AWL under his real name, he had re-enlisted as Daniel MacKenzie.

CHAPTER 8

ON BORROWED TIME

19 February – early April 1943

Optimism still waved in the breeze of Yuletide, and the just-celebrated New Year, but seven weeks later all traces of the festive season was about to depart, along with the bit about goodwill to all mankind.

Out at the airfield our rice, and whatever else went with it, was cooked in temporary kitchens in the cut-down 44-gallon drums. At mealtimes a representative of each work gang collected the rations from the cookhouse and returned the empty buckets to be washed and packed away, ready for the next meal. One day, in the third week of February, we brought our buckets back to be washed. While we were stacking them away, one of the guards came over, took one, filled it with water and proceeded to wash his dirty clothing. Our cook, a popular old bloke, tried to remonstrate with him: the bucket was for food, not for washing filthy clothes. The answer was a hefty slap on the face. When the cook fell over, the guard started kicking him.

Jimmy Darlington, our part-Aboriginal prizefighter and a good friend of the cook, jumped to his aid. The Jap took a swing at Jimmy who, naturally enough, ducked under the punch, and with the instinct of a born fighter came in with a counter-punch. Bang – the Jap went flying, out cold with a smashed jaw.

Well! We'd never realised, until then, just how many Japs there were out on that airfield. They came swarming like flies to a dung-heap, rifle butts and cudgels swinging. In a frenzy of revenge, some concentrated on Jimmy while others held us at bay with their rifles. The attackers grabbed Jimmy until he fell to the ground under the sheer weight of numbers. Then they hit him with everything they had. The savagery was unbelievable, like a pack of hungry wolves bringing down a bison.

Finally, when he was spent and broken, lying bloodied on the ground, his attackers set about building a platform of split firewood, with the jagged edges uppermost. Dragging him to his feet, they forced him to kneel on the sharp, splintery ridges, then wedged two sharp lengths of timber between his knees and then his arms, which were forced back behind his shoulders. Other guards began tying him up with lengths of thin wet cord, so that it was impossible for him to move in any direction. Before long the wet cords began to dry in the scorching sun, causing them to shrink and to cut deep into his wrists and legs. As the ropes tightened, the bonds cut deeper and deeper, cutting off Jimmy's circulation. We didn't have to be medical experts to know that once that happened, it would be the end of Jimmy.

Jimmy Darlington's punishment

A diversion needed to be, had to be, created. Some of the Dead End Kids, who'd also been returning buckets, were nearby. So we created a minor riot, making as much ruckus as possible to divert attention away from Jimmy. It worked. The guards were distracted long enough for one of our regular first-aid men to dart across from behind one of the skips and cut the bindings around Jimmy's hands and feet. This action, without a doubt, saved Jimmy's life. Unfortunately, we were unable to hold the Japs' attention long enough to enable the good Samaritan to get away. Jimmy's tormentors spotted him and, realising what he had done, grabbed him and gave him a severe hiding.

I only wished I could recall the name of that first-aid sergeant. I remember only that we called him Mac, that he belonged to 2/10 Field Ambulance, and that he worked as our first-aid man at the airfield. This job took him all over the place and since he'd witnessed many of the various punishments handed out, he'd have known only too well what his own fate would be if the Japs spotted him cutting Jimmy loose. In spite of this, he'd carried out his duty, and we were mighty proud of him. I have always thought of him as a hero, so I'll take this opportunity to mention him in my dispatches.

Billy's unsung hero was Sergeant William Joseph McDonagh, aged 37, who came from Queensland. He had already courted danger by supplying test tubes and chemicals to help construct a camp radio. When the radio was discovered in July 1943, he was arrested, tried and sent to Singapore for further punishment. He survived the war.

His good work, fortunately, was not in vain. When the Japs retied Jimmy, they were not as thorough and by then the ropes had dried out. However, the deep ugly scars around his wrists and arms were to stay with him for the rest of his life.

Later in the day, the guards tossed Jimmy into the back of a truck and drove off to camp. After spending all night in the cage, crying out with pain, he was taken to Kempeitai headquarters in Sandakan. Little did I know that I was destined to meet him again, and very soon.

Joey Crome had learned a lesson from our dunny-brigade escapade, and from our near-disastrous outing with Punchy, but I must have had a very short memory. Then again, perhaps it was nothing more than the daredevil resilience of youth, because the very day after Jimmy Darlington was so hideously tortured I tested my luck for the third and last time.

The difficulty with trying to explain the inexplicable is that today's attitudes and lifestyles are so different from those of seventy years ago. Adding a prisoner-of-war camp to the mix makes it even more unbelievable. It is like listening to the adventures of Robin Hood narrated by an American: the story doesn't fit the accent. In twenty-first century Australia we are too well fed to understand hunger; we are too well protected to understand real fear. Out on the airfield, fear, hunger and pain were constant, and real.

No one was ever safe from these scourges. We had heard the moans coming from the cage where Jimmy lay, powerless to help him in any way. We had seen so much hate and brutality that when the Japs came in the truck and carted Jimmy away, we had no idea it was merely a harbinger of things to come. Although the shadows of that day's happenings hung heavy over the camp, youngsters like me did not appreciate that clouds were gathering just over the treeline.

Growing boys are always hungry, and I was no exception. It was probably a combination of incessant hunger pains, and the belief that I was invincible, that seduced me into thinking that escape might be possible. After all, I'd had plenty of practice wagging school. The trouble was, I had carried it to the limit, which was way too far. I thought that by cutting out the kids' stuff, and giving the fundamentals, the so-called Three Rs, a miss, I could still get by. Forget English, I could already read, and stuff the grammar. Maths, no worries, I carried my own abacus – ten fingers and ten toes. Writing, however, was a worry. Like Clancy's shearing mate, in Banjo Paterson's poem, my scrawl could best be described as 'a thumb nail dipped in tar'.

Thank goodness for today's keyboards and computers. For people like me, a good spellchecker is better than the proverbial sliced bread. What I didn't appreciate was the necessity of having things drummed into my brain while it was still supple enough to retain most of the things considered essential by normal society: that is, the bits and pieces that make communication easier, and allow us to understand each other better.

If intelligence is the horse, education would have to be the jockey. And if that is so, then my horse was without a proper rider. So three cheers for the dictionary and the thesaurus! They act as rails, keeping my horse on the track, and all I need to do is hang in there.

When one of my old friends, Jimmy Collins, also a prisoner of war, urged me to record my war experiences I'm sure neither of us had any idea of just what it would entail. However, I've discovered that it is a hell of a lot easier to read a book than to write one, especially as all my material comes from the hard drive I call a brain. So, in order to protect the source, I got myself a computer, with a brain of its own, but I've found both hard drives to be equally unreliable. The electronic memory can crash, and just as often, as the human memory. Fortunately, the long-term memory, in my own ROM, has been well and truly etched into the silicon of my brain cells. I can still feel the original burns: of being bitten by a snake, and witnessing the brutal bashing of Jimmy Darlington, a combination of seemingly unrelated events that would save my life. It was a perfect example of good luck, bad luck, good luck, but it does need explaining.

Keith Gillett, Jimmy Finn and I were returning to camp from one of our nocturnal scrounging trips when I trod on what I took to be a sharp stick. I cursed up hill and down dale. 'Bloody hell!' I yelled. 'That's the trouble with these flamin' undeveloped countries. There're no street lamps to see where you are going.'

I hadn't seen what I'd stepped on, but it hurt like blazes. I hobbled along as best I could, trying to keep up with Keith and Jimmy, but by the time we reached camp my leg was giving me hell – so much so, I hit the cot.

Apparently the stick had turned into a snake. It can happen. It's in the Bible. It obviously wasn't one of those harmless snakes that the blokes had gone on about, because during the night my ankle blew up like a balloon. Oh the pain! Just looking at it hurt. It felt so hot I reckon I could have cooked a baked dinner on it.

One of our doctors came down and on taking a look shook his head and tut-tutted. Through a haze of fever, I heard him say, 'If he's not dead by the morning he'll live'. Well I wasn't, and I did.

The funny thing was that, although the pain nearly killed me for the first day or so, it disappeared. The swelling didn't, though, and my leg remained black and blue. It looked very impressive. The Japs certainly thought so.

Before work each morning, the guards held a sick parade, which was more about getting the sick off to work than anything else. The chance of being passed for light duties was pretty much zilch, unless you had something glaringly obvious, like a compound fracture, or a foot hanging off or an eye gouged out. Even then, you needed a lot of luck: sickness alone didn't get you a sickie.

The parade was just another Jap ploy to get the workforce out the gate. It was certainly not there to pander to any person foolish enough to think that he was actually sick – the Jap medic saw to that. You might be riddled with cancer, dying from heart disease, about to drop dead with cardiac beriberi or eaten alive with hookworm, but if the little Jap moron couldn't actually see a visible symptom, you'd fail the test. If it wasn't there to see, it didn't exist. You were fit and well, as sound as a bell. The Jap medico said so.

You no sick, he cried.
You bad man, you lied.
You go to work.

So he did,
and died.

Even Blind Freddy could see that I was crook. My leg was still the size of an elephant's so, using the Jap doctor's infallible reasoning, I was sick. I'd hobble each morning to sick parade with the aid of a forked-stick crutch, and get marked down for light duties. Easy as pie. Free for another day.

Jimmy Brown, who had turned up for the same sick parade sporting a couple of ugly ulcers, was also given a leave pass from work. I had found out that Jimmy's given names were Myles Peace, but the only person game enough to call him that was his mother. His initials, MP, which he shared with the much-derided red caps, or Military Police, caused some amusement, but it was better moniker than his real one. So he answered to MP and also to Jimmy or Brownie. As we were overloaded with Jims, Jimmy was ditched in favour of MP.

So there we both were, with all the time in the world – well, enough time to make preparations for the big day – D Day, Departure Day. After that it would be A Day, Australia Day. And then, Happy Happy Day. The brave music of the distant drum was loud and clear but Jimmy was tone deaf when it came to planning escapes. I put it down to his old age, and he was old.

By Billy's standards, MP Brown was old. Born in the northern NSW country town of Woodenbong on Armistice Day 1918, he had recently celebrated his twenty-fourth birthday. When MP was quite small, the family moved to northern Queensland where by the age of fifteen he had become an accomplished violinist. However, any chance of continuing as a professional musician was lost when, at the age of eighteen, while working for the Cairns Harbour Board, he lost the tips of two fingers after they were crushed in a winch. Married and with a small daughter at the time of his enlistment, MP was employed as a plymill worker at Yungaburra, on the Atherton Tableland. Despite his defective fingers, which he always tried to conceal by slightly clenching his hand, MP was passed medically fit by the recruiting officer in Cairns and was posted to 2/26 Battalion. Apart from an incident in his youth when he had borrowed a motorcycle without the permission of the owner, resulting in civil court action, MP had studiously avoided trouble. In keeping with his second name, which Billy thought for many years was Pearce, Myles Peace Brown avoided conflict, confrontation and anything that might possibly cause a ruction.

Myles Peace 'MP' Brown

Nothing I tried would shift him, and I tried everything I could think of, drawing on my vast knowledge of escapes. I argued, but my reasoning fell on deaf ears. I just couldn't get him to see how easy it would be. I badgered him about using his God-given talents, but MP couldn't or just wouldn't see. It was so frustrating. I even had a map, so we wouldn't be travelling blind. A few inches across Borneo, and then ten inches down was Australia. All we had to do was travel across a few hundred miles of unexplored jungle country, sail across a few little oceans, pass through the lines of three or four Jap armies and then, down there by that coffee stain, turn right, and we'd be home in Australia, easy as pie.

It was all there on the map, plain for all to see, but all MP could do was laugh.

MP was a real clever bloke, who could do almost anything once he put his mind to it. He was a terrific musician and could play any instrument he could lay his hands on. He had a very good ear and was also a very good linguist. He only had to listen to a foreign language and within no time, it seemed, could speak it like a native. To me it was nothing short of fantastic, as I have difficulty speaking comprehensible English. Once he heard a tune he could play it, and I guess it was the same with languages.

He spoke Malay like a native – handy if we had to talk to local villagers – and also Spanish – handy if we were swept towards the nearby Philippines. He also had a fair smattering of Jap – handy if they mistook us for one of them. His Dutch – handy for the Dutch East Indies – was limited to an extensive vocabulary of swear words, but the Japs wouldn't know any difference.

'Not to use talent like that is a wicked waste', I'd rant. 'A wicked, wicked waste.' My impassioned pleas were futile. MP took absolutely no notice.

So finally, when my foot went back to normal, we both went back to work at the airfield with nothing resolved. I didn't give up, though, and was still trying to urge him to plan an escape when we witnessed the horror of Jimmy Darlington's bashing. In spite of what we had seen, or perhaps because of it, I kept up the pressure and, twenty-four hours later, during the lunch break on 20 February, MP caved in and relented.

MP hadn't ever liked the idea of going outside the wire, and he had never taken part in any of our excursions. Quite the opposite. He was always telling us not to go, and warning how dangerous it was. So I must just have worn him down.

On that particular day we were working close to a track that led to a nearby kampong. I'd been there months before, unaware that it was where Mr Chun, a local man of some note, lived. Mr Chun was well acquainted with Dr Jim Taylor, an Australian who had lived in Borneo for years and, as I later discovered, was a kingpin in the local underground movement. Taylor, who helped smuggled money and drugs into the camp, was still at the local hospital, working under Japanese supervision. When Mr Chun had visited the Taylor family in the NSW country town of Yass, sometime in the late 1930s, who should befriend him but Harry Longley's Mum and Dad.

The Dead Enders had discussed with Harry the possibilities of trying to find Mr Chun and ask for help, but no one had been game enough to try it. Until now. The opportunity was too good to miss. The stars were in alignment. The track leading to the village was right beside us. So, I made a final pitch to change MP's mind. I told him that Harry Longley had an outside contact, a Chinese bloke, who could supply good quality rice; that I needed him as an interpreter; and that we'd never get a better opportunity to escape. To my surprise, the normally super-cautious MP nodded his head.

So, before he could change his mind, we skived off down the track to the village, only to discover that Mr Chun had gone off somewhere. After waiting around for as long as we could we left empty handed, apart from a couple of yams and a bit of tapioca we managed to scrounge. We got back to the edge of the airfield just in time to see the whole work force being lined up and counted. Obviously, our departure had been noticed. Perhaps a guard had spotted us leaving, or one of the villagers MP spoke to may have reported us, to cash in on the standing reward of $25 for information leading to the arrest of any POW found outside the wire.

Sitting in the thick scrub at the edge of the field we watched the show, listening as each gang was numbered off in Japanese. There seemed to be twice as many guards as usual, and they were all yelling and cursing, their shouts of '*Kora! Kora! Bakayaro!*' ringing out. The air was charged with high-voltage apprehension, and we were creating the sparks.

Our fears were very real, with images of the broken body of our friend all too vivid in our minds, as was the realisation that we could end up the same way if we were silly enough to give ourselves up. For the moment the Japs were way over there and we were here, safely out of the way, well hidden by the bushes.

Foreknowledge is a double-edged sword. It can lead to all sorts of problems, and it can also be of the greatest advantage. In the present circumstance, the punishment meted out to Jimmy became the deciding factor in our attempt at escape.

Our hideout was on the far side of the camp, some five miles from where we were crouching. With no option other than going back across the airfield and having the bejesus kicked out of us, we headed off, gathering a few more yams and tapioca roots along the way, and thinking that things could have been a lot worse.

We almost made it. We got to within about a mile of the hideout when the bounty hunters jumped us. There must have been six or so of the local native constabulary, together with three Jap NCOs and half a dozen little Formosan privates, whom I'd never seen before. They weren't from the camp, so they must have been part of the local occupation force. The posse had seen us coming along the track and waited in ambush. We'd been a bit too cocky, thinking we were home and hosed, but we didn't stand a chance.

The noise of the local police yelling like banshees was the first indication that we were busted. Treed by a pack of baying natives, we were then set upon by the Japs, shouting and yelling – a hunting party coming in for the kill, hitting out with their rifle butts and sword sticks. The locals also weighed in with their rattan canes. We were only too willing to surrender, but they weren't ready to talk terms.

In the end, their rage expended, they trussed us up. With ropes around our necks and some four or five feet of slack between us, we were propelled forward, urged along by boots, fists and sticks, to where a truck was waiting. Standing beside it was none other than the Biggest Shithead in All the Borneos: The Beast himself, Second Lieutenant Moritake.

Hatred oozed from every pore of his yellow skin. He was the last bloke in the world you'd ever want to be involved with, especially in a situation like this; a mongrel of the first order – hateful, rotten to the core, and a bastard to boot. He was always around whenever punishment was being handed out, and now, surprise, surprise, here he was again – waiting, watching, and ready to enjoy every bloody minute.

He got his kicks from having people kicked around. It gave him a real high. Whenever punishment was in the wind, he was there. He had a nose for it, and his men knew this and acted accordingly. Pleasing their master kept him off their backs, and these bow-legged little monsters didn't need much urging.

Waiting for the onslaught

Anticipation always ignited Moritake's perverted pleasure. We waited for the pressure to build and his anger to erupt. When it did, it was not a violent eruption – all fire and noise and over in a flash. It oozed out, like slow-moving lava. You could almost smell the sulphur.

A flick of his fingers signalled his troops, and we were thrown into the back of the truck and driven into the storm zone. The ropes around our necks made manoeuvring difficult and all we could do was try to brace ourselves across the floor. Some of the little Formosans 'helped' by sitting on top of us as we bounced along. The truck stopped beside the boiler and generator sheds. The lava was about to flow.

Moritake, nodding his head in satisfaction, took up a position above us on the bank: a conductor and his orchestra, with a sword-stick as baton and a loyal band awaiting the signal to begin. What an ensemble of villains – six Formosans and three Japanese: two corporals, one sergeant and Second Lieutenant Moritake. We were the kettledrums, waiting to be beaten.

But not yet. The Formosans chose their instruments from the stack of split firewood that we had helped cut and carry a day or two before. Moritake, who did things by the book, reminded them that they were allowed to hit each prisoner once only, so they took their time in selecting their respective pieces before taking a few practice swings, accompanied by numerous grunts. Eventually, satisfied with their choices, they lined up ready for the opening bars and, at the maestro's signal, we faced the music.

The strength of the human body, and the resilience of the life within it, are amazing. Jimmy Darlington was a big strong fellow. As for me and MP – well. It is still hard to believe that we survived. The bloody little bludgers came at us in turn, swinging with gusto. Every hit sent us sprawling on top of each other, the rope around our necks making doubly sure that we fell. If we failed to immediately get to our feet, the NCOs rushed over to kick us up.

The trees reverberated with '*Kora! Kora!*' and '*Bakayaro!*' as the members of the orchestra swung away with might and main. Thank goodness they were only small in stature, and their hands not large enough to grasp the splintery wood firmly. If we'd been hit that many times by one of the basher guards we'd have been dead at the first blow. When they were done, it was the turn of the NCOs. There was no limit on how many hits they were allowed with their sword sticks, and in the course of this beating my arm was broken. By the time they laid in with their boots we were all but oblivious to the pain and their insane shouts.

I was still lucid enough to notice a messenger, who'd seemed to arrive out of the blue, talking earnestly to Moritake. I had no idea what was being said, and MP was beyond acting as an interpreter. The message delivered, the guards dragged us up the hill to the camp, dangling on the ropes like puppets, jerking and flopping about, choking and spluttering, fighting to stay alive. I don't know how we managed to go the distance, but we did. Those last few yards were an eternity. What a relief when the puppeteers let the ropes drop and we fell like a pair of broken dolls, discarded and sprawled on the dusty track in front of the guard hut. Damaged, dented, cut about but, somehow or other, still alive and breathing.

Moritake called an end to the performance with a final flurry of kicks and headed on up to the guardhouse, imagining no doubt the cheers of 'Banzai! Banzai!' from his ancestors in hell, proud that an Honourable Japanese Bushido had just demonstrated how brave he was.

We never saw him again. That product of a thousand years of Bushido would die within a few days of the war's end – diseased, disgraced, lying on the floor of a native hut; unmourned, unloved, and certainly unmissed.

The boiler where we were almost beaten to death still stands at Sandakan. I stood before it fifty years later, and thought about all that it had witnessed: the mechanical digger, parked nearby, that Sergeant Stevens had sabotaged by putting sand in the sump; my mate Mo Davis, who had worked in the boiler house, stoking the fire to keep the boiler going.

The boiler's dry, the fire's out,
The years have laid the ghosts about,
With only now and then a sigh,
A whisper from the past – of Why?

We were still lying in the middle of the road near the gate when the working parties returned. I remember Bob Shipsides pouring some water down my throat, saying over and over again, 'The dirty rotten bloody bludgers'. But the guards came rushing over, bellowing 'Kora!' as they smashed him away with their sticks.

I was never to see Shippy again. Such a good bloke, one of the best. I wouldn't have traded Bob Shipsides for twenty bloody generals.

It is amazing how much punishment the human body can take, and still survive. I was bruised and battered all over, my left arm was broken, a few ribs seemed to be out of kilter and one of my ankles wasn't ankling. MP was still out to it, and from what I could see of him I'd got the better of the fight.

MP Brown, master linguist and fine musician, who had on so many nights entertained us on his harmonica, was an absolute mess. His hands were swollen and black, while his legs, never one of his strong points, were now not much more than bloodied pulp, with flesh peeled off and his shinbone clearly visible.

The boiler, another relic that survived the war

He never really recovered from that punishment, and the few remaining years of his life were to be full of pain and suffering.

One of the blows had torn his eyebrows so that they now hung across his eyes. This later led to a story that our eyes had been gouged out.

Many years later survivor Keith Botterill was amazed to learn that Billy was alive, as he and Warrant Officer Sticpewich had reported to War Crimes investigators that Billy and MP had been killed, and that MP Brown (misidentified as someone named White) had his eyes gouged out.

As I lay in the dark outside the open-sided guardhouse, pretending to be still unconscious, I saw Moritake in conference with Hoshijima. A short time later, on Hoshijima's orders, I was dragged to his office – MP was still unconscious. The commandant had just got off the phone and was sitting behind the desk with an open bottle of saki and an empty glass. He had obviously been drinking. For a moment, I thought that perhaps we were not on speaking terms, as he just sat and stared. Then, suddenly, he exploded into life with a vengeance, showering me with a confetti of Malay, English, Jap and God knows what else.

Standing on my one good leg, I tried to support myself by holding onto the desk with my one good hand. Still dizzy from the walloping, I did my best to give him my undivided attention, trying my hardest to look as if I understood.

The Commandant's office, just outside the gate, where Billy was flattened by Hoshijima

In the end I gave up trying. With the room swaying and him carrying on like a bloody lunatic, his words coming at me like bullets from a machine-gun, I couldn't possibly catch his gist. At that speed, and with his voice going up and down the scales in a discord of Jap, English and Malay, how could anyone? He was so mad with rage that he was frothing at the mouth, as if he'd been infected with rabies; his eyes were bulging as he struggled for self-control.

It was then that he began to call me names – '*Kora* Bastard, *Kora* Bakayaro, *Kora* bad bad mans, *Kora* coward' – reeling them off as if he were reading from a list, and jabbing his finger into my face with each new expression, forcing me to keep bobbing to protect my eyes. Standing up was enough of an effort, and in the end I thought, 'Oh bugger him'.

My good leg then got the wobbles, so I held on grimly to the desk with my good hand and let the words of this shining example of Japanese Bullshito wash over me.

My last memory is of a face distorted with rage, his prized wooden-holstered Italian revolver flapping at his side as he screamed, 'Kora, you bad man, you no honour, you coward prisoner. Japanese no prisoner becomes. Japanese always hara kiri.'

With that he lashed out at me with the leather ribbons on his sword. He was so beside himself that he even raised his beloved revolver but, fortunately for both it and me, he had second thoughts. In the end he came at me swinging with his fists. Although it wasn't the time or the place for any demented sense of humour, my last conscious thought was that if the silly bugger hits me like that with his knuckles, he'll do himself an injury.

What actually happened was that Hoshijima caught me with a haymaker, fair on the chin, and I sailed on out through the door, out like a light and onto the ground.

Hoshijima's act of bravado did him more harm than good. At his trial in 1946, Warrant Officer Sticpewich, who had been watching from his technical party workshop, some distance outside the wire, had seen Hoshijima 'knuckling' Billy's face and had reported that the commandant had gouged the prisoner's eyes out.

I came to just as MP, who was still unconscious, and I were being tossed onto the back of a truck. It must have been after 9 pm, because the lights in the huts near the gate were out. I had my last glimpse of the camp through my swollen slits of eyes, lying on my back: a star-blazed sky, a silver crescent moon, and the shadowy outline of the Big Tree. How many hundreds of years had that tree stood there on that hill? Three, maybe four? That aged sentinel of the rainforests, the last of the great Kings of Trees, had yet to witness many dark deeds; so many of our men would die within the shadows of its gargantuan trunk. Its branches waved in farewell until the bend in the road near the Jap cookhouse erased it from view, severing the last tie with my friends and comrades.

In 1947, Sticpewich returned to Sandakan to assist in the search for POW remains. For reasons known only to himself, he set fire to the base of the Big Tree. The hollow trunk acted like a flue and the tree was burnt out to a height of about 20 feet above the ground. In 1999, when Billy and I visited the site, all that was left was a termite mound whose voracious inhabitants were still feeding on the remnants of the massive underground root system.

The ride into Sandakan was a nightmare. After a great deal of bouncing and bumping, rolling from side to side at the total mercy of a manic driver, the truck

Lynette and Billy at the overgrown POW camp site, standing on the flattened termite mound, all that was left of the Big Tree in 1999

finally came to a stop. We had arrived at wherever it was and by that time, wherever it was, was good enough for me.

Their destination was the Kempeitai's torture house on Leila Road, set into the side of the hill to the west of the town near the timber mill and overlooking the harbour. Pre-war the building had been the palatial home of the manager of the Bacau and Kenya Extract Company, which extracted tannin from mangrove bark for use in the tanning industry.

In total darkness we were unloaded and dragged to small wooden cage-like cells or boxes, about the same size and shape as a large packing case. MP was still out to it, so they tossed him into the nearest one like a bag of potatoes. I fell into mine only too willingly. Sick, sore and exhausted, crushed by the uncertainty of tomorrow, I lay curled up in a corner waiting for pain to pounce; afraid to move for fear of waking resting aches. Low moaning coming from the darkness nearby told me I was not alone. I finally reached out, and it was a face. Whose face? I was too buggered to find out.

Daylight brought recognition: it was none other than Jimmy Darlington, who had been in this cage for the past two days. He was a complete wreck: lying in his own mess, his wounds uncared for, and absolutely helpless.

Life is a funny, in a queer sort of way. Only a day or so earlier I'd been feeling so sorry for what had happened to Darlo and now, here we were, sharing the same sweatbox. His appalling condition helped to take my mind off my own predicament. He was in a dreadful state, coiled in the corner with hardly a sign of movement; his wrists and ankles, where the cords had cut so deep, were angry with proud flesh and muck; his eyes were just slits in a swollen mass of black and blue, and his hair was completely matted with blood. His whole body was so bruised and caked with dried blood that his skin resembled the mud of a drought-ridden billabong. Even so, the strength of the man shone through when, after a while, a bloodshot eye peered out at me between swollen lids, and a muffled sound came through his puffed lips, 'G'day Youngie. What the bloody hell are you doing here?' Jimmy hadn't a clue what day it was, or how long he'd been there, or why. He was too weak to move around. Even talking was an effort.

The box-like cells had heavy 4 x 2 inch timber bars enclosing the front and two sides. The two cages that we occupied were about five feet square by four feet high, just enough room for two men to either sit up, or lie down. There was plenty of ventilation, but no toilet, so it was a good thing we didn't have much diarrhoea to contend with. The spaces between the bars provided an uninterrupted view of grassy bank leading to the backyard of a timber-clad building, where a flight of weathered timber stairs led up to an innocent-looking doorway. This led to the rooms used for interrogations. I wasn't to know just how familiar those steps would become, and how often MP and I were to climb them with fear and loathing. On the first occasion, we walked up unaided. After that we could only manage to crawl on our hands and knees.

MP was in the box next door, separated only by the wooden bars. For the first two days he was in such a bad way that it took all his strength just to lie still. Eventually, with a great deal of determination he managed to crawl towards us, close enough to celebrate a reunion. We were lying there, heads touching, our bodies filthy and aching, when room service rudely interrupted our tete-a-tete – in the form of a little, old, bow-legged Jap yardman, who hosed down our dung hole along with the occupants. He obviously enjoyed his work, giggling as he targeted our faces and more tender parts. I sometimes hear the same sort of inane laughter at popular tourist spots in Sydney, coming from neatly dressed, harmless-looking

Waiting for the call to climb the steps

little men, who bow to each other, ever so politely. The memory trigger is powerful, so powerful that I sometimes stop and ask myself 'Where are their hoses?'

Although Jimmy and MP were still as weak as kittens, they could move around a little and we were able to talk to one another. Jimmy was our main worry. The moving around hadn't done his arms any good and he kept drifting between reality and dreamtime. Mealtimes were erratic and sometimes the food didn't arrive at all, but when it did I'd force as much as I could down his throat. They were a desperate few days, and for a while I thought that both my mates were on the skids.

Not long after our enforced water-blasting, a Jap medic finally attended to us. It was a painful process, but he did wonders. Crawling out of the cage and standing upright took a bit of doing, especially for the other two, but if it were not for the medic I really don't think they'd have made it. He was kind and dedicated, treating our various injuries with such thoroughness that when his task was completed we looked like 'patients' for a First Aid Disaster Demonstration.

There was no plaster of Paris to set my broken arm, but the medic didn't need any. He improvised with a piece of giant bamboo, split in half to create a cradle. After making sure that the interior was smooth, he encased my arm in it and bound it in place before applying a khaki sling. My ankle was also firmly strapped and my ear carefully bandaged. By the time he had finished with us we were covered from head to foot with bandages and slings, while masses of cotton wool, soaked with the bright red antiseptic acriflavine, covered our multiple cuts and bruises. Covering our wounds was a real morale booster. Proof of how much better the other two felt was confirmed when our bowls of rice were delivered. They ate every morsel, which was a bit of a pity as I'd become used to eating their leavings.

Over the next few weeks Darlo continued to be our main concern. Jeeze, he was in a mess. His hands were such a horrible black colour, with no life in them – and the smell – Strewth! We were not sure if it was him, or us, or both, or the dreaded gangrene. Luckily, it turned out to be a mixture of him and us.

Not long afterwards, the interrogations began. Day after day we would be taken out of our cages, with MP and I taking turns at going first up the timber steps of the wooden building and into a small back room. Here we were forced to kneel in front of a desk while the same shortsighted little Jap asked us the same string of questions, over and over again, like a broken record. Every day for eight days the same questions were put to us by this seemingly mild-mannered Clark Kent lookalike, dressed in civilian clothes. His appearance was deceptive, however. He was a rotten little villain who delighted in using the carrot-and-stick treatment: nice as pie one minute, highly intimidating the next. The room, which was bare except for a table and chair, looked innocuous enough, but it was all a facade. It was a 100 per cent Kempeitai House of Terror. The interrogator – ordinary-looking, small, bland face, thick glasses – was a monster. A guard with a rifle stood behind whoever was being questioned, ready to strike when signalled. Recognising the signals became a sick sort of a game between us, but our tormentors cheated and kept changing them.

Because of my crook ankle, I wasn't too keen on the kneeling bit, so I'd try to ease the weight off it slowly, little by little. Then Bang!! *^++* BLOODY HELL!!! The bastard standing behind me would crack down hard on my shoulders. Surprise amplifies pain out of all proportions and, after a few surprises I let the ankle look after itself. Pain is like Vegemite: too much, and the effect is spoilt.

Sitting behind his little table, the interrogator was like a venomous reptile, ready to catch us off guard and strike out at our faces with a knotted rope, swung in time with the questions. My eyes would follow it as I tried to keep my mind on the question. Fortunately, I didn't lose concentration and survived the ordeal with both eyes undamaged. The rest of my face, however, took something of a beating.

The questions had us tossed as neither of us had a clue what the heck they were talking about or, for that matter, what they wanted us to say. Machine-guns? What did they mean by machine-guns? Submarines? What bloody submarines? The reason we didn't break down and give away state secrets wasn't because we were being brave; it was simply because we didn't have the foggiest idea of what they were on about.

Perhaps the most unsettling aspect of the question and answer sessions was the uncertainty of their timing. They came at any old hour, for one or the other of us, and up the wooden stairs we'd go for another little chat, another session of questions and answers, another game of truth or consequence.

'What did you do with all the guns? Who did you give them to? What were their names? Which and where were the villages?'

Guns? Kampongs? For heaven's sake! And with each question the knotted rope kept swinging. Round and round. Never mind the questions, just watch that rope. On and on it went, in a deadly sequence. Questions. Rope. Rifle butt. We hadn't the vaguest idea what he was talking about. Predictably, he didn't believe us.

The interrogations stopped just as suddenly as they had started. They'd given us a rare old time of it, and for what? We didn't know, or believe, that they were finished, and spent the rest of our time there waiting with nerve-wracking apprehension.

The Kempeitai believed we had somehow got ourselves mixed up in some kind of underground organisation, hence all that business of knotted ropes, stupid questions, ankle bashing and rifle clubbing. It wasn't until we got down to Kuching for our trial that the penny dropped. Also on trial were five Chinese civilians charged with espionage, and guns were mentioned.

The only undercover activities involving submarines that were taking place near Sandakan at that time (February 1943) were in the southern Philippines, where a liberation army of local guerrillas, backed by the United States, was harassing the Japanese with the help of arms, ammunition and supplies sent in by American submarines. Eight POWs who escaped from Berhala Island, en route to Sandakan in June 1943, joined this liberation army. The Mile 8 Camp underground, headed by Australian Captain Lionel Matthews, who was also in communication with the US-backed forces, was not uncovered by the Kempeitai until July 1943, when the civilian conspirators in Sandakan were betrayed.

One positive aspect of the cloak-and-dagger business was that it most likely saved us from being shot on the spot, back at the camp. Moritake had been beside himself with rage that night. I reckon the Kempeitai's intervention, based on the notion that we were possibly involved with the Chinese, may have stayed his hand. Was that what the message delivered to Moritake was about? Was that the reason for the guardhouse conference, and why Hoshijima was on the phone? Whatever the reason, we were spared, so I'm not complaining about that, but it was A Close Run Thing. Between Captain Hoshijima and Second Lieutenant Moritake, our heads could easily have been parted from our shoulders.

The Kempeitai philosophy was an odd mixture – a cross between flamboyant Western ideologies and medieval fatalism, with a dash of Eastern mythology tossed in. The power of the Kempeitai was absolute. Such power is almost impossible to deal with. To be above the judge is power beyond belief. They could, as indeed they did, pull prisoners from the cells and chop their heads off. That's power, with a capital P.

Power play is why they let us lie there for several days in those cages, then cleaned us up and interrogated us. It wasn't because we were masochistic hardballs who could endure the pain that they eventually gave up. We knew absolutely nothing, about anything. And knowing nothing, we could not tell them anything. If I could've, I would've. I'd have turned in my nearest and dearest, just to keep the mongrels off my back. Eventually, when our ignorance finally became obvious, it became a toss-up whether they executed us in Sandakan, or sent us to HQ at Kuching to face a military trial.

Once our fate was decided, there was little that we could do – just sit in our little boxes and wait it out. My sling proved to be a bonus; we turned it into a chessboard, with the aid of some cotton wool soaked in acriflavine to mark out the squares. Whatever was to hand – buttons, stones, slivers of wood – became our chessmen, one set coloured red, the other left plain. If any of the guards came along it was just a matter of slipping on the sling, and the set was hidden. When the guards were away, the pawns did play, and over the months we had many a hard-fought battle.

The days muddled along, but we were never free of thoughts of 'the return of the interrogator'. Then, about three weeks later, quite out of the blue, it was all over. Some guards came in a truck, shackled us, and drove us to the government wharf, where we were shoved aboard a small coastal steamer. It was as simple as that. Goodbye Sandakan, and hullo Kuching.

There were no streamers fluttering from ship to shore or bands blaring to mark our departure; just a few Japs, mostly guards, and the interrogator. MP told me that the main difference between that little creep and a crocodile was that the crocodile had feelings. MP farewelled him in Dutch. You haven't really been sworn at until you get it from a Dutchman, and MP knew all their choicest words.

We were just about to sail when we heard the unmistakable sounds of Australian voices. To our astonishment, over the rails came Norm Morris and his mates, The Five who had escaped from the camp months before. Propellers churning away, stirring up the mud, the steamer now pushed away from the black-timbered wharf. Our guards almost immediately became more relaxed. As it is for soldiers the whole world over, when the brass goes away, life becomes more of a holiday. With the guards taking time out, we were able sit back and take everything in without any fear of a crack across the back with a rifle butt.

With the crew busy with the essential duties of clearing harbour, and our guards enjoying their freedom from officialdom, we were able to pick up the reins of friendship with Norm and his mates and forge a bond that would prove stronger than the steel that physically bound us. The Five were handcuffed together, so it was interesting from a professional point of view to see how well they handled the mundane things, like eating, and going to the toilet – a case of one in, all in. While the crew were busy negotiating the bay, we took the chance to swap stories. We had a lot of catching up, some seven months' worth.

The Five told us that when they escaped their intentions had been to either sail down to Australia or, failing that, to attempt to join up with the guerrilla forces fighting the Japs in the Philippines. While trying to figure out how to do this, they managed to avoid recapture for an adventurous six months by living in and around the jungle's edge before making contact with a local group led by a well-known Chinese named Tec Sing. These brave and generous people gave the escapees every assistance, keeping them supplied with food and obtaining an ocean-going boat to make good their final escape. The only proviso was that each of the POWs sign a promissory note, asking for the Australian Government to repay an agreed sum to cover costs, when and if the time came.

Unfortunately, the escape attempt failed. The Chinese junk had a mind of its own and they finished up on a mudbank. A passing Jap patrol boat spotted the castaways and, as they said to me, 'That was that'. At least they'd given it a go, and gee whiz, what a run they'd had! I often think of The Five, comparing them with the bungee-jumping, thrill-seeking Rambos of today. These blokes, without any fuss or bother, collected a fistful of adventures: months of roaming around in the jungle, battling to sail a Chinese junk across an unknown sea, withstanding weeks of captivity and Kempeitai interrogations.

When Norm Morris, Alan Minty, Bruce McWilliams, Fred New and Bill Fairy were arrested on 27 January 1943, they were in a shocking state, suffering from beriberi, malaria and assorted skin complaints. They were so ill that they were incarcerated in Sandakan Civil Hospital where two doctors, and members of the local underground, Englishman Val Stookes and Australian Jim Taylor, were working on the orders of the Japanese. With the assistance of a warder, and other medical staff connected to the local underground, nourishing food and money was smuggled into them. The money sent in by Taylor was concealed in a bandage protecting McWilliams' injured foot.

The second escape attempt, made about the same time as Norm's group had left, was also unsuccessful. All involved were recaptured and sent to Kuching for trial. This did not stop other hopefuls and in May 1943, after Billy left for Kuching, Sergeant Walter Wallace escaped from the Sandakan camp with two companions. After some days spent wandering in the jungle, the group split up. Wallace eluded the search parties but the other two men were betrayed and shot. Unable to return to the safety of the camp, Wallace was smuggled to Berhala Island, at the entrance to Sandakan Harbour. There he joined four Australian officers and three ORs who had escaped from the newly arrived E Force. This group, some 500 strong, was being temporarily housed at the old Quarantine Station on the island until transfer to Sandakan by barge, up a nearby river. The eight men, with the help of local people, managed to reach the southern Philippines, where they joined the American-backed guerrilla forces.

At least The Five had managed to roam free for seven months without being detected, but the great pity was that they were unable to pass on their local knowledge. This vital intelligence, gained from wandering hill and dale, skirting the fringes of jungles, living among far-flung kampongs and making contact with many of the leaders of the local people, was lost.

After the war, the Australian Government honoured the promissory note presented to them for payment for the boat and supplies. They did so without question, even though it had been signed in the names of Ned Kelly, Jimmy Pike, Darby Munro, Shirley Temple and Bob Menzies. The story was reported in the Hobart paper, along with a photograph of the note.

By the time our boat had cleared the harbour, we realised the need for unity to face and overcome whatever the bastards had in store for us. The pact made, we settled down to enjoy the magnificence of our forthcoming Tropical Ocean Voyage. It was like a dream. After weeks of being locked up in a box, beaten and starved, here I was on the high seas, surrounded by open space, plenty of it, and good friends to share it with. Those ugly days were behind us, and we didn't much care what lay ahead. Nothing much could surprise any of us now. We had come through, and with companions like these, nothing else really mattered.

> *To be alone in Paradise*
> *is to be alone in Hell.*
> *Pity him in Paradise,*
> *with no one there to tell.*

Looking back along the trail of churning wake, a ribbon of lace on a cloth of emerald sea pointing back to where blue-hazed clouds covered the land where we had been, reminded me of those Fitzgerald Travelogues which we had watched so avidly at the local flicks. I could even hear Mr Fitzgerald's inimitable voice describing the scene: 'With the sun sinking low into a bubble bath of blue-rinsed sea, we say a fond farewell to Sandakan, the timber town of British North Borneo. Farewell, farewell, farewell'.

The only thing wrong was the time of day; we were on the east coast and the sun was still doing its job. However, scenery-wise it really was a top spot for a Fitzgerald film location. Indulging in some very wishful thinking I fantasised a bit more, imagining dawn and the day of liberation. 'A lazy sun stretches up from between silken sheets of ocean blue and azure sky and, with blood-red hands, he claims the day. But what's this I see? A great grey Yankee battleship, steaming up over the far horizon, with its guns blazing.'

Well, that's what dreams are made of, and being a dream, it just wasn't so; at least not then. My imaginary film still had a couple more years in production before it would be screened.

But it was spectacularly beautiful. Nature was so generous with its colours, painting a trail from island to island, running riot with exquisite scenery; enough to cause a chain reaction, enough to glut the market with explosive beauty. I realised an important lesson on that voyage. The world is abounding in abundance. We are limited only by our own capacity to enjoy and respect the things around us.

The vessel, so we were told, was *Treasure*, the private steam yacht of none other than the White Rajah of Sarawak, Robert Brooke. Well, well! Fancy that! Here we were, thinking that we were underprivileged, and all the time we were on his yacht. Even so, like us, it was in need of a good scrub. I bet it didn't look like that when His Excellency owned it.

A chain running through leg shackles anchoring us to the rail also linked us to each other. If anyone wanted to use the toilet, which was like an Australian dunny bolted to the deck, we all had to be unshackled and then re-shackled. It was a nuisance, for us and the Japs, who were keen fishermen and had brought their rods along. They saw the logic of our argument that there was no need to keep us chained up while we were at sea so once we were clear of the harbour they set us free, allowing them to concentrate on their fishing. They warned us that if there were any funny business they'd throw us overboard. We all nodded our heads in agreement and MP thanked them in his very best Dutch.

While the Japs fished, we relaxed on the stern deck, lounging around as if we were real tourists, watching the white foam spinning out from beneath the keel. Overhead, the sun coloured-in the clouds. Below, on the shimmering sea, dozens of flying fish skimmed from wave tip to wave tip, desperate in their endeavours to escape a hungry predator lurking beneath the surface. The sea had taken on the appearance of a padded quilt, with colours ranging from pale yellows, through the greens and on to the deepest blues, while here and there an embroidery of golden sand and green foliage gave promise of islands in the sun.

A sudden vibration from the engines as they went into reverse, followed by a gentle nudge against a long timber jetty, brought us to our first port of call: the island of Banggi, off the north-western tip of Borneo. Like holiday makers, we took a lively interest in everything around us. Who'd have thought, amid the turmoil of war, that such a beautiful, peaceful place could exist?

It seemed that the entire population of the island had come down to the jetty for the occasion, standing around with opened mouths, as curious about us as we were about them. Supplies were coming and going, and the whole of the wharf area was alive with activity. Our guards, after giving us the usual stern warnings, put us back in chains and hurried off to enjoy themselves in the village.

Although we were shackled again, there was plenty of entertainment. The local children were playing around, laughing and screaming, some of them swimming and showing off in much the same way as I had skylarked with my friends on Bondi Beach not that long ago. The kids brought us fresh green coconuts with channels cut into their tops to make it easier to drink the refreshing contents. We sat with our feet dangling over the side, savouring the taste along with the moment, talking and laughing and practising our Malay. But the time went too quickly. Our partying came to an end with the return of our guards and, with a final '*Terima kasih. Bunga bagus*' (Thank you very much), we waved farewell. Slowly our little island merged to be one with the haze of the horizon, as it is now in my memory. Back then, it had sparkled like a jewel.

Our ultimate destination, we learned, was a prison in Kuching, the capital city of Sarawak, the territory long ceded by the Sultan of Brunei to Clive Brookes, an ancestor of the peacetime owner of our little boat, now on one of its regular island-hopping circuits for the Japs.

Because of the rugged and uncertain nature of the coastline we tied up each night in one port or another. We woke each morning in anticipation of what the day might bring.

Our next major stop was Jesselton. It is now renamed Kota Kinabalu and is the capital city of Sabah, but it still graces a very beautiful and spectacular part of the coastline, set before a backdrop of high mountain ranges covered with tropical rainforest. The star of the ranges is the famous Mount Kinabalu. We didn't have much time to admire the view. On our arrival, we were bundled onto a truck and transported to the local prison, constructed by the British. It was built right on a swamp and was an absolute hellhole.

Although we were bone tired, and hungry, we got nothing; no food and definitely no rest, as the eight of us were crammed into a tiny cell filled with millions of the thirstiest mosquitoes in All the Borneos. They were the most ferocious mozzies we had ever encountered, and we became their personal blood bank. I can't remember how long we stayed there, three days maybe, but when we left there weren't any fond farewells from any of us.

Victoria Gaol was south of Jesselton at Batu Tiga (Mile 3) and had been built to accommodate 40 native prisoners. From October 1942 it had housed more than 700 British POWs working on the nearby airfield, now Kota Kinabalu International Airport. There had been so many deaths from malaria that the following April the survivors were transferred to Sandakan, while Billy was languishing in Kempeitai custody. Conditions at the filthy, mosquito-infested gaol were horrendous, as Billy so rightly recalled.

It was a relief to be back on board the ex-Rajah's ex-yacht as we chugged south, away from the shadows of the towering Mount Kinabalu. The guards now trolled for fish, and it is no exaggeration to say that catching them was simply a matter of wetting the line. The fish were so plentiful that as soon as the line hit the water a huge fish attached itself to the end of it. We urged the guards on, making all sorts of admiring noises and singing their praises, salivating at the prospect of a feed of fresh fish – a tail, a head, anything would do. We hungered for a taste of fish, and we stayed hungered. All we got was the same old bowl of rice and tinned fish balls, which were an unappetising brownish colour and appeared to be well past their use-by date.

Our next port of call turned out to be Labuan Island. Just a few square miles in size, it lies in Brunei Bay, just off the west coast of Borneo. I reckon that on a clear day, if you could jump high enough, from Labuan you could catch a glimpse of the peak of Mount Kinabalu.

We berthed for the night beside the wharf at Victoria, the island's only, but very charming, colonial town. By war's end it was no longer charming. In fact, it didn't exist. By the time our side had finished its bombardment all that was left standing, albeit in ruins, was the town's only landmark – the Queen Victoria Jubilee Clock. Like Jesselton, Victoria was completely rebuilt after the war, and in the process lost all of its former beauty and grace.

As usual, as soon as the boat tied up the crew buzzed off for a night on the tiles. The guards, handcuffing us to a steel cable on the wharf, went off to join them, leaving us to enjoy a few short hours of respite. Although chained to the cable, we felt as free as the breeze and could easily have sat out the war there.

At sunset we were treated to a symphony of clouds, land and sea. In an orchestrated display of colour, a multitude of changing hues danced from the heavens on the surface of the bay, so faithfully duplicated it was hard to tell which way was up. It was like watching a magical copying machine in action. Silenced by this kaleidoscopic entanglement, as the battle lines of encroaching night merged with the retreating day, we sat watching, motionless and utterly spellbound.

Across the wharf, from within a shed whose sides lay half-opened to the breeze, wafted the soft, gentle sounds of femininity, a caress of song and laughter. A group of young Malay girls were enjoying the cooling waters at their tong (bath tub). We watched, tantalised, teased by the suggestion of graceful movement within the shadows of their colourful sarongs, until the dusk faded and night blocked our view. Left with the faint echo of their voices we wrapped ourselves, cocoon-like, in our private thoughts and longings, as countless pinpoints of twinkling starlight greeted the moon as it rose from behind the far-off hills.

Bathed in its silvery glow, and lulled by the sound of the sea's gentle swell, we settled down to sleep, yawning whispers of goodnight with the certain knowledge that this was a night to remember, and one that would, in all probability, not be experienced again for many a long month.

I had never experienced a regular home environment, and certainly nothing even approaching what people take for granted today. I had never experienced the feeling of belonging to a proper family, or the warm comfort of a family home. Life for me had always been a game of chance; a matter of heads or tails. Yet it was here, on that faraway island, while chained to a cable on an old timber wharf, that I had my first yearning for home. I discovered I was longing for Australia, a homeland that I had taken for granted, but now that I was using it as a yardstick it stacked up well.

I hadn't realised before that those who live in a land free from tyranny do not value their freedom until it is taken away. How I missed Australia, with its wide, open spaces; the way it shapes our character; its rugged individuality with its ethos for giving, and receiving, a fair go. I went to sleep, pleased with the day, but especially that I was among friends, Australians, my people.

CHAPTER 9

OUT OF THE FRYING PAN...

Mid-April – 23 August 1943

By definition, the word 'police' means restriction and, at any given time, police can be a pain in the neck, for someone or other. For ordinary soldiers, military police were always a pain in the arse, but it was the Jap Kempeitai who really gave policing a bad name. They were a curse on the universe, engendering fear and hatred; killers, through and through. And when we arrived at Kuching, the City of Cats, they were at the wharf to meet us.

Apart from a bit of bowing and scraping from Treasure's guards, the handover ceremony was brief: a few *Koras*, *Bakayaros* and *Binta nos* (Hoy, morons, arseholes! Hit you!) as we numbered off. *Ichi, ni, san, shi, go, roku, shichi, hachi* – eight of us, enough to keep the new keepers happy. From the bowing and scraping, and MP's limited Japanese, we deduced that we were now in the hands of the Japanese military police. We only had time to notice the dock, and some shop-houses fronting onto a river, before they shoved us into the back of a covered truck and drove off.

Our destination, the Kuching Military Prison, was a real dump of a place that looked as if it had once been a warehouse of sorts. It wasn't much, just two floors, each 40 feet wide by about 80 feet long. Two lines of timber poles, about twelve feet apart, seemed to hold the place together and a secure area had been created by running heavy-gauge cyclone wire around the perimeters of the poles. Timber partitions, erected between each pair of poles, divided the floor area into ten or so cages. My first impression was of a huge aviary. Inside the cages, on long platforms, sat lines of prisoners, legs crossed, hands on their knees, chins up, and staring straight ahead. Perched like rows of roosting chooks. These days, whenever I see a hen-house I am reminded of my time in Kuching.

They put us gaolbirds in the first cage, on the top floor. It was the Star Chamber, taking up the entire space within the front four columns and facing the arched passageway that led into the guardroom. The front and both sides were covered with cyclone wire, and there was a small locked gate in the front. The back wall was built of solid timber, as was the three-foot-high platform that ran the full width of the cage. This dais was to be our home for the next five months, sitting on it throughout the daylight hours in two lines of four. The first few weeks were the longest, as we were not used to sitting for hours at a time, cross-legged, hands on knees, backs straight, eyes front.

To make matters worse, there were bedbugs. Bloody, horrible, blood-seeking bedbugs. Millions of them. Every crack and crevice in the whole flamin' building was full of them. At night they rushed out in open formation, literally thirsting for battle and forcing us into futile and unwinnable action, squish-squashing our way through the night. Our shorts and shirts, including my blue-striped pyjama-jacket shirt and my kit-bag duds, became spattered with red splotches but no matter how hard we fought the bugs would continue to attack with kamikaze zeal, never letting up until morning's light brought peace, and a day's respite to re-think our battle strategy.

Bleary-eyed, we'd show our wounds to the guards, pleading with them for some of their bug killer, which was distilled locally by the truck-load. At last they relented and gave us a pump-action spray. Armageddon time. How sweet revenge is, providing one is the avenger and not the avenged. The first spraying produced four heaped shovelsful of dead bodies. We kept on spraying, day after day, until that blessed time when we were no longer bugged, and managed to get some sleep.

> *Like autumn leaves upon the floor they fell,*
> *Heaped shovelsful by the door as well.*
> *With so many bugs lying there all dead*
> *It bespoke of peaceful nights ahead,*
> *To dive into clean depths of sleep*
> *Knowing full well that we would sweep*
> *Eight hours from off our gaol time sheet.*
> *Oh fantastic. Oh sublime*
> *We're dreaming in the boss's time.*

CHAPTER 9 Out of the frying pan ...

For occasional exercise, the guard would escort us down the fire escape to the back of the building to a grass-covered yard encircled by a high barbed-wire fence. On the other side of the wire was a lean-to Chinese cookhouse, which was quite large and evidently catered for more than just our small gaol. Ignoring the wire, we walked around in a circle on the little grassy patch, savouring the feel of the sun on our backs and the grass under our toes, and marvelling at the sight of trees, with real birds. Compared to the cage it was a Garden of Eden, and sure beat sitting upright all day.

If the guards were in a good mood they'd turn on the hose, and we'd take a shower and wash our clothes, along with the bandages that we'd been wearing since Sandakan. My arm was fine by this time, so I could have ditched the sling long before, but we needed the chessboard, even if it had become so ragged that it could have fallen apart at any moment and disgorged the chess pieces, which would have taken some explaining.

Oh the tussles we enjoyed playing chess. But it was a risky business and we'd often come close to getting caught. Once, when was I supposed to be keeping nit, the guard came hurrying along the passageway so fast that he took me by surprise and we just made it to our regular positions in time. He had passed me on his first patrol that day with my arm in the sling, but now, on the second, Alan Minty had the broken arm. The guard looked suspiciously at us for a moment, then shrugged and went off to bother other prisoners.

When the time finally came for the chessboard's last battle, with regret we put it out of its misery. The warriors were paid off, disbanded – dropped one by one into the grass of the exercise yard. Torn and faded, the battlefield was dispatched with full military honours into the rubbish bin. A sad and sorry ending. My sling was slung, our kings and queens uncrowned, the armies trodden underfoot. They had helped us through some tough times but, like old soldiers, they had just faded away.

In all the times I was a guest of the Kempeitai I was subjected to countless searches, and Kuching was no different. Every time we entered our cells we were searched. The routine was always the same: line up and bend over so they could look up the Khyber Pass; pick up our clothes and shake them while jumping up and down on the spot with arms outstretched, stopping only when the guard yelled out '*Yame!*' (Halt). We'd then scoot into our cage with whatever we had managed to scrounge – oddly, although the searches were thorough, the guards never looked in our hands. Never ever.

No matter what it was, if it fitted into your fist, it was yours. If the guard dropped a cigarette butt, or we spotted a piece of wire or a fishbone, into the hand it would go. It's surprising what can fit into a clenched fist. After each search we were marched to our cells, hands properly clenched in true military style, with our thumbs pointing straight down, holding in our curled palms our untold treasures. Once inside, the loot was carefully hidden in case of a further search. Cigarette butts were highly prized. They are marvellous things to chew and with care I could make a butt last and last. But a small stub of pencil was my best find. I managed to keep it with me right until the end.

We'd got rid of the bedbugs, but we were still bugged by two-legged pests. Whenever a guard first came on duty, he'd patrol around and around the cages, seeking out evil-doers: anyone not sitting in the required manner, or talking. The guards would stop at nothing in their efforts to catch us out, especially white blokes. All this sneaking around was unnerving but fortunately the heavy surveillance lasted only while officers were around. As soon as they left, the guard scampered off to the guardroom for a quiet sit-down and a smoke, allowing the prisoners in the rear to relax until those in front signalled to warn of his return.

The Chinese and Malay prisoners in the back stalls were happy with this arrangement but we eight, aligned in the front row with the passageway leading to the guardroom, had no protection from the prying eyes of the guard, who could sit inside his cubicle, have his smoke and still keep an eye on us through the glass. So we decided to play the watching game. We watched, and watched. Our eyes followed the guard, tracking his every move. No matter what he did, we watched. When he ate, we watched with open mouths. When he smoked, we 'inhaled' his tobacco smoke, adding a few smoker's coughs for effect. When he talked to someone, we all turned our heads to listen. When he put his head down for a rest, his efforts were in vain. Even with his eyes closed he knew we were watching. He couldn't even fart without us knowing.

The war of nerves paid off. Workmen came along with a light, free-standing timber privacy screen, which they placed about four feet in front of the front cages, blocking our view of the guardroom. But it turned out that our brilliant plan was not so brilliant after all. Unless we could hear the guard's footsteps as he crept along behind the screen, we had no idea he was there until he pounced. What we needed was an early-warning system.

Normie Morris noticed a tiny gap of light shining between two of the screen's vertical boards, where the thickness was irregular. He scrounged a small piece of wire from the exercise yard to enlarge the gap to alert us to the guard's presence, because he would block out the light. Our chance came a day or so later when we were let out for some exercise. After checking that the guardroom was empty, we dutifully followed the guard towards the stairs, where one of the blokes fell over to create a diversion. As MP yabbered excitedly in broken Japanese and we clustered around the accident victim, oohing and aahing, the guard was distracted long enough for Normie, at the tail of the column, to enlarge the crack into a hole just big enough to reveal a change in the light when someone moved along the passage.

To ensure we weren't rumbled we drew up a roster, taking it in turn to keep watching the light-hole while the others enjoyed a siesta. What a joy it was to see a guard come tiptoeing along and jump out from behind the screen, hoping to catch us out, only to find models of straight-backed, cross-legged propriety. The sense of satisfaction this gave us never diminished, and the Japs never tumbled to the trick. It also never occurred to them to switch off the guardroom light before leaving on their rounds, although even if they had, we'd still know they were on their way because the light was out.

We also managed to outwit the guards by tapping into a supply of food from the cookhouse, separated from the exercise yard only by the barbed-wire fence. On one of our visits to the yard we noticed a bucket of cold rice close to the spot where the Chinese cooks banged their woks against the fence, causing the wire to become loose. While a couple of blokes distracted the guard, the rest of us quickly grabbed a handful of rice as we passed by. Before we returned to the cages, Bruce McWilliams was able to drop into the bucket a small amount of money from the stash still concealed in his leg bandage.

After that there was always a bucket by the fence, filled with rice along with some rice husks, which tasted horrible but contained essential vitamins. Bruce even managed to make contact with the cook, and exchanged what was left of his secret bank account for some Javanese tobacco, dried palm-leaf cigarette papers and matches. The roll-yer-own fags were wonderful, as was the look of consternation on the faces of the guards when they came on their rounds to find the cages stinking of tobacco smoke. Time and again they pounced round the screen, trying to catch us out, only to find us all sitting cross-legged, hands on knees, backs straight.

One day, the guards arrived with a group of twelve or so Dyaks. What a sorry sight it was to see these proud warriors of the jungle, shackled together in irons, being led towards the cells at the back. Modern-day civilisation had passed them by and in the present oppressive regime there was no room for innocent primitives. From their arrival until the time we left, we witnessed their descent into hell. Week after week we watched these magnificent men, with their tattooed bodies and masses of long black hair, being escorted to the exercise yard. Week after week we heard the guards yelling out orders in Japanese, then kicking and beating them for not understanding. Exactly why they were in gaol we never knew, but we did realise what a shock to the system any imprisonment, at all, must be. They were men of the jungle. Born free. Kings of their environment.

Dyak warriors

To be locked up in such an alien world, to be deprived of freedom, was beyond their comprehension. For these people of the rainforest it must have been terrifying. They were the warriors of their tribe and I wondered who was left in their communities to protect the women and children. As time passed, despair stripped this group of jungle dwellers of everything. Belittled by ignorant peasants, these noble people, who had tamed and lived with the jungle for thousands of years, lost the will to live. At night we'd hear their pitiful cries.

Like the Dyaks, life in the cage was also reshaping us. Escape no longer occupied or even entered our minds. To be back in a POW camp was now the pinnacle of desire, for we were incapable of further contemplation and escape to Australia had become an impossible dream. Like grapes left hanging on the vine until they are shrivelled and hardened by drought, we too were slowly fossilising.

Then, about mid-August, after months of waiting and with absolutely no warning, the eight of us were herded into a truck and driven away, to be measured on the weighted scales of Japanese military justice. The venue was the main hall of the Catholic convent, which had been partitioned to create a court room. At the front, on a raised platform and just below a large leadlight window, sat the presiding officer, with an officer either side of him. Other officers were ranged on a lower platform, while down at floor level the court scribes sat on straight-backed chairs.

The Catholic convent where the trial was held

It was our trial, but we had no idea what was going on. Apart from the final few minutes, the entire proceedings were conducted in Japanese, leaving the accused to ponder the ins and outs of what was going on in a linguistic darkness. Talk about a kangaroo court! We only knew what had actually happened when the judges withdrew to consider their verdict.

The verdict had already been decided. Under the Japanese system, the mere fact that the accused were brought to trial meant that they were guilty. The purpose of a formal hearing was to present the evidence, not counter it in any way. There was no defence counsel and the accused were not invited or allowed to say anything in their defence. Once the prosecution had presented its case, the judges retired to consider the sentence to be handed down before the accused were formally pronounced guilty.

When the judges filed back in, proceedings resumed. We were now on centre stage, right in the spotlight. From bit players we had become the stars in this pageantry of Eastern law. Our cast of eight had increased to thirteen with the addition of five local civilians: thirteen players in a criminal trial, waiting a curtain call. We certainly looked the part – a scruffy mob handcuffed together, dirty and neglected, villains all. We had no idea who the locals were, what they had done, or why they were with us, but they looked even more villainous than we did: bloodstained and battered with their hair in tangled masses, clad in torn and tattered black cotton suits. Although we had had no speaking parts, no stars of stage had ever waited as anxiously as we did for the critics' final words.

No cries of encore.
No shouts of more.
The play was over,
The critic's a whore.

Japanese military court procedures hovered somewhere between high drama, and comic opera, not unlike Gilbert and Sullivan's *The Mikado*, featuring the Lord High Executioner. The trial made a mockery of justice, but the Japanese took it all very seriously indeed. Due process was followed, to the letter. Their main concern, as it in most of their dealings, was with the matter of face. The huge piles of papers that went backwards and forwards and up and down, the sucking in of breath, the snapping head-bows and the ah-sos were all part of face-saving procedures.

After another conference and a further shuffling of papers, the findings of the court were delivered to all those in court who understood Japanese. We had no idea what was being said, but we knew it was bad news. The Japanese use language as an auditory assault weapon and the prosecutor was no exception. He sounded like a cross between a bad case of laryngitis and someone who'd had their balls cut off – a high-pitched dissertation like a boy with his voice breaking, interspersed with trilling and trolling, rumbling and bumbling. On finishing his summation, or whatever it was, he bowed all round to the court, and gave way to the interpreter.

We were standing in a row, each one handcuffed to the next. The five locals and MP were on my right. On my left I was cuffed to Alan Minty. Then came the other four in his group. Jimmy Darlington, who was on the far end, was not restrained, evidently because of his injuries. The proceedings had been long and boring, but we were now coming to the understanding bit, the part that hit home. It was no longer a comic opera but High Drama Time, as the sentences were read out in clear English.

The verdict

The five civilians, found guilty of espionage, were all sentenced to death. Death! To be executed!

I felt MP's shocked reaction, a jolt that was transmitted all down the line to Jimmy Darlington. Like a black and white cartoon, words can give only an outline of the drama of what was taking place at that moment. There is no way to convey the depth of feeling, no inkling of the thoughts and fears that occupied the hearts and minds of the eight people standing in the dock, waiting to hear whether they were to live, or die.

I learned that day that the prospect of death makes all other options acceptable. Suddenly part of a presentiment of death, we all had an interest. But it was not the fear of death: it was the fact of it. Anyone not previously paying attention was certainly taking notice now.

The voice of the interpreter continued: 'Myles Peace Brown. You have been found guilty of escaping from a Japanese prison camp, and your sentence is' (we waited, tensed) 'to serve eight years' hard labour.'

Oh happy days! What a nice man!

Our end of the line relaxed, such was the relief and the desire for life when death was so close and beckoning. Then my name was called, and I tightened up; surely he couldn't turn nasty again. 'Eight years' hard labour. But because of your youth, the court in its mercy has decided to reduce your sentence to four years.'

Oh yes indeed, he was a very nice man. I relaxed. Life was sweet.

Alan Minty, six years. Fairy, McWilliams and Morris, five. Fred New, because of his old age, had his reduced to four. James Darlington, for daring to hit a Japanese guard, received six months. All sentences were with hard labour, with no allowance for the time we had already spent languishing in the various prisons.

The civilians received the news of their sentence with remarkable calm, managing to show very little emotion. We, who had been so much more leniently dealt with, could not help but be impressed by their brave exit from the stage of life. They are unable to come back and take their bow, so I will step up, and clap and cheer for them, right now.

I now believe that they had been mixed up with one of the underground groups that had been secretly at work undermining the Japanese – which is why MP and I were asked so many questions about guns and submarines. I reckon this is why we were all in court together. They seem to have been involved in the same kind of underground activity as our Captain Matthews and his men.

A few months after Billy stood in the dock at Kuching, charged with trying to escape, Lionel Matthews, along with a number of other Australians and a large group of members of the Sandakan underground movement, were tried in the same courtroom presided over by the same chief judge, Lieutenant Colonel Egami Sobei. Matthews and eight local people, found guilty of subversion, were executed by firing squad. The others were sentenced to various terms of imprisonment. Matthews was awarded a posthumous George Cross for Gallantry, the non-combatant equivalent of a Victoria Cross. The locals who died with him received nothing.

The behaviour of the Japanese was often hard to fathom. After the war I heard that, just before he was tied to the post and shot by a firing squad, Captain Matthews was given mail from his family.

Forty-two years after our day in court, while walking up Spring Street in Melbourne on my way to a reunion, an Asian chap asked me for directions. He was headed for the same place, so I invited him to come along with me. From this chance meeting in a city of three million souls I learnt that he was Johnny Funk, a member of the Sandakan underground and brother of one of the eight local men who'd been tried and executed with Captain Matthews. While awaiting trial, John had been imprisoned in the same Kuching gaol as me.

When I returned to Kuching many moons later and visited the area where the gaol had been, I came across a small memorial stone with the names of the five locals who had been executed. The inscription stated simply that they had died while in the Japanese prison – an epitaph very much at odds with the much more elaborate and better-known Memorial of Heroes, commemorating the sacrifice of Matthews and his eight companions. I find it sad that the five brave local men, all of whom had been sentenced to death for fighting the Japanese, are not given the honour accorded to the other eight. Those five young men, like the others, were also heroes.

As soon as our sentences were handed down, we were bundled into a truck and

The horse box

taken into town for transfer a proper Kempeitai gaol. We were off-loaded at a wharf, where we were placed in a horse box, complete with straw and horse manure on the floor. Mo Davis, who had been transferred from Sandakan to Kuching by our camp administration a few weeks after MP and I were nabbed, happened to be working on the Kuching wharf that day. Years later, he told me that the Jap guards had made his working party face the other way when our truck came into view. They weren't allowed to turn around until we were locked up in the box.

At first we thought the box made a pretty good cell, but that changed as soon as they closed the door. Within minutes it became an airless, steaming, stinking hot-box, pitch black inside.

Records compiled from various sources in late 1945, in preparation for war crimes trials, indicate that Billy, MP and Jimmy Darlington were tried in June and Morris's group a month later. However, Billy is certain that they were all tried together, and that the date was dictated by the departure of the ship. Any further delay would have meant a lengthy wait in Kuching, until such time as suitable transport was available to take them to Singapore and a high security gaol. With the records of the Kuching court proceedings compiled from a number of informants, it appears that there has been some confusion about the actual date. All eight were tried, and transferred, together.

Towards evening we felt the box lifting. It spun like a top, and then tilted, backwards and forwards, hurling us in all directions. After what seemed an eternity, the spinning stopped and the box was lowered in fits and starts until the last three or four feet, when it dropped suddenly to the floor. We all went sprawling, ending up in a tangled heap of arms and legs, straw and horse dung. After calling out to each other to check whether we were all still in one piece, we decided it would be best to stay put until we could see, to avoid falling over each other.

The throb of big engines under our feet and the hum of voices, clearly audible through the walls of the box, aroused our curiosity. We were in some kind of boat and on the move, obviously negotiating the Kuching River, but we were left in the dark, literally, until the top section of the door was opened. When our eyes became adjusted to the light, our eyeballs almost popped. We were in the hold of a troop ship. Around us on all four sides, like a theatre-in-the-square, were four tiers of sleeping platforms, filled with hundreds of Jap soldiers, packed like sardines and with their faces all turned towards us. Some were in uniform, others wore only lap-laps; some were sleeping, while others were sitting around, talking and arguing.

As we weren't on the friendliest of terms with our fellow passengers, we stayed in our little box for the duration of the voyage, welcoming the sanctuary that the half-closed door provided from the attentions of some of the more belligerent types. Although our fellow travellers left much to be desired, the abundance of food was the highlight of the trip.

The ship stopped for a day or so at the river mouth, why I don't know, but possibly to avoid a submarine threat in the South China Sea. There wasn't a great deal of swell, but the constant rocking of the vessel, and the lack of fresh air, did not agree with many of the Japs. The smell of cooking from the nearby makeshift kitchen did not help anyone who was feeling queasy, and quite a few of our first-class passengers were seasick. We didn't care two hoots, as it meant plenty of scraps for us, especially as some of the troops were seasick the whole way. What a binge we had. Rice, stew, fish pieces. We piled it all into a large basin, gave it a stir, and then gorged to our hearts' content. We even managed to put on a bit of weight.

After about three days, the throb of the engines slowed, and then stopped. Shortly afterwards our stable door was shut, the troops disembarked and, after a considerable wait, our 'cabin' was on the move again. The box bucked and swayed before landing with a thump on what we assumed must be terra firma. We had arrived. But where?

We had arrived, for we were there.
We had arrived, we knew not where.
Here we were, for what it's worth.
Here we were, some place on earth.

Borneo, and all that it had held, was now a thing of the past. Kaput. Finished. We were about to begin the first page of a whole new chapter.

The date was Monday 23 August 1943. The place – Keppel Harbour, Singapore.

CHAPTER 10

...AND INTO THE FIRE

23 August 1943 – early 1944

Outram Road Gaol, a brooding, menacing conglomeration of old buildings, set behind high stone walls, was a only a short ride from Singapore's harbour and dominated the lower section of the road that bore its name. Within an hour of docking we were pushed into the back of a canvas-covered army truck, positioned so close to the horse box that we had only to step from one to the other. After just a few minutes' drive, the back flap was raised and we were shoved into the dazzling rays of the midday sun. Like owls caught in the glare of a car's headlights, we stumbled about as we tried to blink some sort of focus back into our eyes.

Like Tasmania's infamous convict gaol at Port Arthur, Outram Road was a nineteenth-century penal institution built in the best colonial tradition. Its history stretched back to the days when Britain reigned with absolute power over the people of Singapore. For those not prepared to toe the British line, the grim old clink on the hill waited patiently: to restrain, retrain or drain the ungrateful blighters who dared to bite the white hand that fleeced them.

A gaol was an important part of the trilogy of the Empire Builders – along with a pub and a church – and Singapore's was a monument to Imperial British Justice. A corrector of ways and a bender of wills, it had served the system faithfully through the great and glorious days of colonialism. If imprisonment didn't pull recalcitrant locals into line, then the liberal use of the rattan cane, and the gallows standing like a terminus at the end of the journey, helped them get the message.

Time, as is its wont, had caught up with this land-anchored old hulk of a prison, wearing away at its very foundations until, vandalised by the wear and tear of outmoded ideas, assaulted by the oncoming era of reform and scandalised by cries of outraged nationalists, it had been condemned as unfit for human habitation.

A Modern Model Prison had replaced it at the Changi end of the island; with a remarkable sense of timing, this was completed in time for the Japs to turn it into an internment camp for British civilians. Far from being demolished, the old outmoded gaol on Outram Road was recycled for use as a military prison run by the Kempeitai, a task made easier by the fact that the departing British had left all the keys to the cells neatly hung on the wall of the superintendent's office.

Outram Road Gaol. Billy's cell block is on the right

Outram Road Prison, known as Her Majesty's Service Criminal Gaol, was built in 1882 at the foot of a landmark known as Pearl's Hill to supplement the nearby civil gaol, Pearl's Hill Prison. From 1936, following the construction of the new gaol at Changi, the British administration used Outram Road as a remand centre, and to incarcerate criminals found guilty of lesser crimes, along with opium addicts undergoing rehabilitation. The entrance was via a circular drive that also gave access to a school and police station situated across the road from the main gate. There were four main

CHAPTER 10 ... and into the fire   215

Main cell blocks and exercise yard. Billy was in the block on the left

cell blocks, A, B, C and D, with the two military wings divided from the civil section by an internal wall. When the prison was demolished in 1970 it was replaced by a housing estate which, in turn, was demolished in 2000.

Upgraded by the fortunes of war, the 60-year-old penitentiary was revitalised in 1942 by the change of ownership. Reincarnated, the cell-infested mishmash of high-wall-encased buildings became a sorting house for all kinds of humanity, who'd had the misfortune of being deemed a hindrance to the conqueror's plans for Japan's Far Eastern Co-Prosperity Sphere. And who better to do the sorting than the Kempeitai, with their thousand years of service to the overlords of perhaps the world's most suppressive feudal system.

Outram Road Gaol was a place of fear. It was designed to be feared, and was enough of a threat that the threat was enough. As well as serving as a huge holding pen for Japanese military personnel and POWs who had breached military regulations, it housed countless local civilians considered in need of corrective training.

Archaeologists are able to tell us a great deal about the past by simply digging among the fossilised remains of the last millions of years. They have collected an amazing amount of knowledge on almost everything, except how the ancients thought, and why they acted as they did. To find this out, students of ancient history need to be able to locate, and decipher, written records. No records – no information. The Japanese, who knew this, destroyed almost all their records.

However, they did not destroy the most vital evidence of all – the memories of the survivors.

One inmate who lived to tell the tale and record his experiences was the Australian doctor, Jim Taylor, who had played such a vital part in the Sandakan underground organisation until he was arrested and sent to Kuching for trial. Like us, he was sentenced to imprisonment in Outram Road although, as a civilian, he was not assigned to our section. He arrived in late 1944 and, being a medico, carefully recorded the conditions and estimated the number of deaths that occurred from disease, suicide and execution.

The exact number of civilian victims will never be known, as the Japanese tried their best to cover up their atrocities by destroying any incriminating evidence, along with the prisoners in their care. These poor souls have passed into the realms of the unknown, their presence erased from history, their individual names lost in the mists of time. However, the fact at these hundreds of people once existed is a constant reminder of man's inhumanity to man.

> *What grim stories those walls could tell.*
> *Such sad memories they'd bring as well.*
> *For beneath the weight of all those years*
> *There lie buried crimes and ghostly tears.*

Until we actually arrived at Outram Road Gaol we had never heard of the place. Didn't know it existed. When we saw the name over the gate, we thought that, as Singapore was a civilised country, it would be more of a POW camp than a gaol. Our captors soon put us right on that score.

As we were herded from the truck towards the massive, dark-green, iron-studded gates, set into huge white walls topped with broken glass, I heard someone yell out from the road, 'Keep your heads up, cobbers'. Years later one of our fellows, assigned to a POW working party at the nearby Outram Road School, told me he had seen us being taken into the gaol and had called out in encouragement, which only goes to show that there is always someone around to say 'G'day', no matter what.

Our Kuching guards, charged with the responsibility of delivering us to the gaol, were trying to outdo the Singapore lot, shouting at us and at whoever had called out. Once we had numbered off, the prison guards took over and, just to show their Kuching counterparts how it was done, made us number off once again, kicking and bashing us into line. We got the message and stood in a straight row, backs erect, chins in. Satisfied, the reception committee marched us through the door.

CHAPTER 10 ... and into the fire

Into gaol

We entered another world, a world where every moment was guarded, where every action was observed, where every regulation was interpreted according to the whim of the guards and was therefore open to arbitrary punishment. On top of this, every command was delivered in Japanese, with the expectation that it would be carried out immediately, and to the letter. If we didn't understand, or guess right, it was too bad.

After stripping off and being forced to jump up and down to make sure we had nothing hidden in any crevice, we all received a pair of greenish khaki shorts and a shirt with a number printed on the pocket. Mine was 515 (*gohyaku ju go*). I retained the number, the shirt and my shorts for the period of my imprisonment, by which time they were well and truly faded, and jaded. I also retained my small pencil stub, which I held in my hand as we did our physical jerks. Dressed in our (newish) green prison garb, and coming to attention at our guard's yell of '*Ki-wo-tsuki*', followed by '*Mae-sumei*', we marched off.

So far so good. It couldn't last, and it didn't.

He let forth with a string of commands: '*Yame! Gon-tia suro-mo. KORA! Bakayaro! GON-TIA SURO-MO! Kora, kora!*' This really had us flummoxed, and all we could do was prop in our tracks on the command of '*Yame*', and wonder what he was on about. We found out soon enough as he repeated the commands, at the same time bashing away at our heads with a great bunch of heavy iron keys.

'*Gon-tia suro-mo*'. '*BAKAYARO!*' '*Kora! Wakaru? Gon-tia suro-mo. KORA! BAKAYARO!*'

'OK, OK', we said. 'We've got half of it – *suro-mo* (idiot) – right? But what the hell does *gon-tia* mean?'

'*Hanasu nai no, BAKAYARO! Wakaru?*' (No talking, moron! Understand?)

We got to understand good and bloody fast. I remember this Japanese lesson whenever I pass a tourist shop with the sign '*Kora! Watashi wackaru* English' (I understand English).

In that first hundred yards inside the gaol, we managed to work out about half of their military commands. No ifs or buts, no time to try and understand. You got it right, or else.

We passed through the entrance to what appeared to be the larger of the two cellblocks in our section. Three long horizontal rows of iron-barred windows, like rows of medals on a general's chest, confirmed the gaol's status as a high-security prison. Within the building's greyish walls was a void about twenty feet wide, stretching from floor to rooftop, and lined with cells on either side. It cut a swathe all the way to the other end of the building, which was just discernible in the gloom of late afternoon. The light from a few naked bulbs, set high in the ceiling, hinted at the size of the block, and of the hundreds of cells, indicated by serried rows of narrow black doors pockmarking the walls, with an iron and timber staircase giving access to the upper walkways.

Streaked with sweaty, water-marked grime from the hot-house humidity, the layers of limewash on the walls were like growth rings on a tree, confirming the antiquity of the place. The stinking spoor left by hundreds of toilet slop-buckets suggested the presence of a large number of prisoners – a deduction seemingly refuted by the silent hush that hung over every cell. As we soon learned, there were hundreds of prisoners, friend and foe alike. The walls hid them from view, and the rules of silence completed the deception.

Each of us was then locked in his own dank space, closed off from the outside and from each other by a black, iron-banded door supported by three massive and ornate iron hinges set into in a thick stone wall. At its base was a perforated steel-plate ventilator about two feet wide, with a spyhole about a foot above that. As the cells were accessed from the ramp-like central corridor by two or three steps (depending on the degree of the slope) the guard could look through the spyhole from his side without climbing the steps. Above the spyhole, about halfway up the door, was a newly cut slot, large enough to pass through an Asian-style rice bowl. To make sure there was no chance of escape, the door was secured by a huge iron bolt, locked in place by turning a heavy, eight-inch-long iron key in a massive padlock. I was assigned cell 72, on the left-hand side of the block. If nothing else, the Japs were consistent – the cells were allotted in the same order that we had received our sentences at Kuching. MP was next to me on one side with Normie's mates spread along the other, and then Jimmy.

The cells were monastic in the extreme. The only furnishings were three bed-boards, a wooden block for a pillow and a filthy cotton blanket, which all had to be stacked along the wall during the day. Slots in the floor and the far wall, both recently cemented in, showed that there had once been some kind of support for the bed-boards, which were now laid flat on the concrete. There were also two small ventilators in the far wall, but as they were only to provide air to the wall cavity, they didn't lead to the outside and had been partially blocked off. Over in the corner near the door was a barrel-like benki bucket – a staved wooden toilet tub – with a removable inner wooden ring for sitting on, and a wooden lid to cover the contents. These were collected, emptied and washed out each day by the 'benki tobans', prisoners assigned to toilet duty.

The guards used a whistle to let us know when we could put the boards in place and lie down. Another whistle told us when we could rise. Fortunately the whistle gave out somewhere along the way and the order for sleeping became more relaxed. In the latter part of the war, when sitting for hours on the concrete floor became unbearable, I took to sitting in the corner on the toilet tub, my back against the wall, my legs outstretched. Whenever the guard approached I made the appropriate noises. Thinking I was suffering from yet another bout of diarrhoea, he'd continue on. Time out on the toilet bucket was always one of life's little luxuries.

Cell 72 I remember clearly, simply because it was the first of many I inhabited in Outram Road. As a rule we changed cells every month or so, as part of the search and destroy policy for any contraband and to deter escapes. Escape was not a possibility for us, but there was at least one attempt by much fitter Japanese prisoners, who used an electric cable running down a wall to attempt a getaway.

We had no contact with the Japanese inmates, who occupied the second floor of our block, but we could certainly hear them. Twice a day, in the early morning and again at dusk, like a town hall clock chiming at the beginning and end of each day, we would hear them call out their numbers as they marched from, or to, the little cloisters above our heads. Where were these phantoms in the upper cells going to, what were they coming from? Ghosts who walked, lived and died alone, in their caves upstairs.

Everything we did, we did by numbers. We went to the toilet by numbers, we ate, drank and slept by numbers, and were given our orders by numbers. '*Gohyaku ju go! Kochie koi!*' (Number 515! Come this way!) '*Gohyaku ju go! Modotte koi!*' (Number 515! Come back!) Wherever and whenever we were moved to a new cell, the tag with our name, number and sentence came along too, to be hung on the new cell door, a constant reminder of who we were and why we were there. And if Number 515 heard '*Gohyaku ju go! Kora! Bito no, bakayaru! Hanasu nai no! Kora! Binta no!*', he knew it meant trouble.

The only difference between one cell and another was the graffiti and the number and size of the cracks criss-crossing the walls through the multiple layers of limewash, so thick and soft it resembled putty. Otherwise, each was identical to its neighbour. Stretch my fingers out, and I'd touch both side walls; step four paces from the door, and I'd bump into the far wall where, high above and abutting the ceiling, was a small barred opening, almost hidden in the thickness of the outer wall, and impossible to reach. It allowed a little daylight, and some air, to filter through, but a steel awning effectively shut out any hope of seeing the sky, or anything else that may have been out there.

Centred in the concrete ceiling, high above my head, was an electric light bulb with a conical metal shade, whose output was far brighter than any daylight that struggled through the window. It shone throughout the night: night after long weary night, except during air raids towards the end of the war, when the Japs switched off all the lights. The best thing about those little breaks from constant surveillance was that we were able to move around in the dark, knowing that the guards couldn't see us, even when we stuck our tongues out at them.

The years had combined with the extreme tropical climate to play havoc with the gaol buildings: great long cracks, eaten out with mould, crazed the walls; the ceilings dripped with the humidity; the floors and steps were scored and worn by the countless feet of six decades' worth of inmates; and holes and crannies were everywhere, providing ideal havens for every kind of insect imaginable. Rising damp had long since risen to its highest point – the roof timbers. Three storeys above the ground, mould flourished. Dry rot and mould, mildew and rising damp. If it had not been for the sheer bulk of the place it would have been long gone, eaten away by the ravages of time.

For the first few months, an Australian army lieutenant named Penrod Dean delivered my bowl of rice and a small bowl of water three times a day. I'd come across him before, out near the causeway when we were defending Singapore Island. He had set up a machine-gun with some of the 2/4 Machine-gun blokes, only to disappear as quickly as he'd arrived. He and Lance Corporal John McGregor had been sentenced to two years' gaol in May 1942 for escaping from Changi and were the first Australians to be imprisoned in Outram Road.

Some of the blokes didn't like Dean much. I heard later that he had tried to do a runner before the surrender, and that the reason he had tried to escape was because the men from his unit were making his life unbearable in the Changi camp. Others resented him because he was in such good condition, which was one of the benefits of being in charge of the food delivery, I guess. Whatever he'd done or not done, he had played his cards right with the Japs and was now in a position of trust, with two Indian offsiders to carry the rice bowls on a long timber tray.

The sounds of the tray thumping on the ground at each stop, and the clanging and scraping of the bowls, was sweet music to our ears. Once we'd eaten the rice, tea would be served – weak tepid stuff that they *said* was tea. To get it, we'd hold our bowls up to the slot and hope, by cupping our hands above the rims to prevent an overflow, that some of the liquid, delivered via a spout from a kind of watering can, would actually make it into the bowl.

Food was an obsession. The body needs constant stoking and eats fuel like a steam engine, otherwise it runs out of puff. Having said that, as long as the heart keeps beating, the lungs continue breathing and the blood keeps on circulating, it's amazing just how long a person can last. I was growing up, literally, and because of this I became the most conscientious slot-watcher in the clink. We called the food Neville Chamberlain: an appeasement that never satisfied.

Hunger is the most debilitating, demeaning and dehumanising condition. It is torture of the mind. One lousy, miserable grain of rice falling onto a dirty, grimy, slimy floor becomes, within seconds, the size of a football, tantalising and teasing, until it is the most desirable thing under the sun. All the tenets of civilised behaviour go by the board in the attempt to reclaim it. The alternative is to risk spending the rest of the day regretting such wastefulness.

In places like Outram Road there is also no such thing as 'the whole man'. Bits, such as your dick, become a thing of the past, not even as a plaything. We had no problem with autoerotic feelings or, indeed, any other sexual desire.

> *If Marilyn Munroe*
> *appeared in the nude*
> *No one would have done*
> *anything rude*
> *Unless she was mug enough*
> *to be carrying food.*

Like the tattoos on my arm, the months spent in solitary are scars that fade a little with time, but will always be there: frustrating weary days and long sleepless nights, running on and on, one into another. Time was like a millstone, grinding the seconds off the minutes, and the minutes from the hours, wearing away at the days, and then the weeks, and eventually the months

On several occasions Pen Dean was able put his face up to the food slot to tell me a few things: such as what was causing the pimple-like rash, fast covering my body, that left me sleepless with the incessant scratching as I tore my skin to ribbons. I had scabies. The entire place was infested with a microscopic mite (*Sarcoptes scabiei*) that burrows into the upper layer of skin, where it takes up residence and lays its eggs. All of us were being eaten alive by these bloody little parasites. They set up a fierce itch impossible to ignore, and the scratching in turn created weeping areas of skin that scabbed over. During my time as a prisoner, I suffered from a multitude of nasty complaints, including malaria, dengue fever, dysentery, pellagra, beriberi and scurvy but, without a doubt scabies was by far the worst. Locked up, there was no way of protecting myself from the mites and their insatiable appetites, as they ate and burrowed away at my living flesh.

We were under constant surveillance, bound by strict rules. There was nothing the guards liked better than to sneak along the corridor in an effort to catch us out. They rarely succeeded. After being constantly foiled they took to removing their footwear, believing that the distinctive slap-slap of the thongs they wore indoors was giving the game away. The success rate was no better. They failed to realise that, as they inched their way down the corridor and up the steps leading to the cell door, a tell-tale shadow preceded them, blocking the light coming through the ventilator holes and giving us plenty of warning. Some guards resorted to standing at one side of the door and making a dive for the slot, but the result was always the same.

Forbidden to move around, we sat in the centre of the cell keeping an eye on the ventilator holes, only too well aware that at any time an eye could peer through the slot, or though the spyhole, checking that we were sitting at attention. Sitting with legs crossed, on a cement floor, was the pits. At least at Kuching the floor had been timber. From sunup until sundown we did nothing but sit. We sat, waiting for food to come. We sat, waiting until was time to lie down. We sat and sat, feeling itchy and trying not to scratch.

I'd been inside Cell 72 for 37 days when, one fantastic morning, a key turned in the lock (was there ever such a welcome sound?) and as the door swung open a gruff voice called out '*Koi*'. In a flash I koied out and down the steps – landing fair on my backside. My legs had gone from under me. They'd become disorientated, and my brain moved too slowly to keep up with them so that I finished up in a heap. Solitary confinement, together with a poor diet, cramps the mind as well as the body, and every thought has to be squeezed out of a constipated brain.

Freedom, however, is an excellent laxative. Freedom from the wall-to-wall confinement and isolation. Freedom from the intimidation of the evil eye and that rotten peephole. How sweet it was to have the door open and to see other human beings come stumbling out, all with the same look of surprised hesitancy on their faces. Then the floodgates opened and speech gushed out like water from a burst main, as we all started talking at the same time.

'KORA! *Bakayaro! Hanasu nai no! Kora! Binta no. Bakayaro!*' The guard, livid with rage, screamed, '*HANASU NAI NO. BAKAYARO. BINTA NO. WAKARU? KORA!*' – his way of telling us that we moronic arseholes were not

The guard checks cell 72

allowed to talk, and threatening to hit us, at the same time actually doing so. He continued on with his '*Kora! Kora!*' and bashing away at us with his metal sword scabbard until he was satisfied that his message had been rammed home. Bruised and battered, we marched in single file through the centre of the prison block, passing hundreds of black, iron-banded cell doors, set into the walls of the three-storey galleries, like giant black dominos ready for a game.

The penetrating light of day fleshed out details that the gloom of our late arrival weeks before had hidden. A timber stairway gave access to the top floor, where a tiled roof and a criss-crossed arrangement of rafters and collar-ties supported heavy timber louvres just below the eaves. The louvres were supposed to create a breezeway.

The blazing sunlight and its reflection off the concrete surface of the courtyard was a shock to the eyes after the gloom of the cellblock. Dazzled, it took us a while to see clearly, and what a sight. Sitting in the shadows against the walls was a mass of creatures scarcely recognisable as human. We'd had a taste of solitary confinement but looking at these living skeletons, matchstick men, was looking into a mirror of what lay ahead. I thought, for a moment, that I was back at the Johor Leper Colony.

About eighty of them were spread along the concrete in the shade of the walls: mad eyes gleaming from deep bony sockets; golf-ball-sized Adam's apples running up and down scrawny necks, like lifts on the outside of a modern office tower; bones wrapped in skin, leftovers on the edge of the plate of life; scabs and festering ulcers, the pus running out. Even the palms of their hands were bubbled with pustules. If it were not for a slight rocking motion, the slow turn of a skull, the roll of an eye, an observer might have wondered if any life lay within. They all looked the same – an assemblage of scarecrows, an overflow from the drains of life; filthy, dirty, skinny, rotten, stinking dregs of humanity. Lumped together, they barely made a decent shadow.

And we were about to join them.

The inmates gathered in the courtyard had only recently been granted this concession, following the attempted murder of a guard in May 1942, shortly after the Kempeitai opened the prison for business. In the very early days prisoners had enjoyed many concessions, such as being allowed out of the cells to eat together at long tables. This came to an abrupt end after a frontline soldier, seconded to guard duty, was escorting the prisoners on a short stroll down the corridor and was hit over the head by a Chinese prisoner, who'd picked up a hammer left on a table by workmen carrying out renovations. The assailant was about to deliver the killer blow when Pen Dean tackled him, saving the guard's life. However, the Japanese who arrived on the double in response to McGregor's calls for help assumed that all the prisoners were involved in a riot as part of a mass escape attempt.

They opened fire, hitting one Chinese. The rest of the prisoners bolted back to their cells and slammed the doors shut. They were not opened again for many months. All privileges were withdrawn and communal dining was a thing of the past. Instead, as Billy correctly surmised from the freshly exposed edges of the timber layer in his door, crude slots were cut just below the spyhole to allow for the delivery of rice bowls. It wasn't just the prisoners who experienced the effects of the all-powerful Kempeitai. The guard whose life had been saved by Dean was found guilty of dereliction of duty and executed.

In the last months of 1942 and well into 1943, conditions in the gaol were horrendous. With the totally inadequate rice diet, complete lack of medical care, poor sanitation, scabies and bed bugs, the physical and mental health of the prisoners plummeted at an alarming rate.

I'd no sooner settled among the 'lepers' when a voice from out of nowhere said 'G'day'. Astonished, I wondered where to look, and how to answer. One of these Stick Men had said something, but who, what? Then with the slightest movement of the jaw next to me, immovable lips said, 'G'day. I'm Ken. Careful now, don't let the bastard hear ya talkin'. Where ya from, which mob were ya with, whatcha in for, got any news?'

Although this was the main street of a ghost town, life was still being lived. Under those piles of skin and bone communication was made, and all around us gossip was being exchanged. A hive of activity, the silent mime of fluttering fingers semaphored messages from neighbour to neighbour. Eyelids, blinking, relayed messages in Morse code; fingers and palms talked the language of the deaf and dumb. Only those who were tuned in to the correct frequency could detect the silent sounds of busy fingers, distributing news from the gaolhouse via the grapevine and beaming the latest world news, all without the guard being any the wiser.

I learnt that my new-found friend and ventriloquist, Kenny Bird, was from South Australia. As I was also to discover, he was a natural-born comedian and brilliant mime artist who had refined his skills over many years while working on tourist boats on the Torrens River. Skinny Kenny Bird was, without a doubt, the funniest man that ever braved the wrath of the Kempeitai. He could still crack jokes when the world around him was at its very worst.

Kenny Bird was in Outram Road Gaol because he and four mates had been dobbed to the Japanese by a senior Australian officer.

In April 1942, a couple of months after Singapore capitulated, they were drafted into a working party to build the shrine to Japanese war dead at Bukit Timah. As the job would go on for months, they were transferred from Changi Camp to new billets in damaged palatial bungalows in a housing estate known as Adam Park.

As the camp was loosely guarded, it was not difficult for prisoners to slip away under cover of darkness on foraging expeditions. One night in early May, while out scrounging for components to build a radio, signallers Chris Neilson and Bob Green met a young Chinese man who had links to guerrilla parties operating behind the lines in Malaya. When the two Australians learned that the guerrillas were in need of wireless technicians, they volunteered their services. Three truck drivers were also on the Chinese wish-list, so they roped in Kenny and two of his Motor Transport cronies, Reg Morris and Bill Goodwin, who also hailed from South Australia.

Arming themselves with a Thomson submachine-gun and pistols, and dressed in sarongs provided by their Chinese contacts, the men made good their escape on the night of 4 May. They headed for the Straits of Johor, where they were to be taken by boat to Malaya, but almost immediately Bob Green became ill with dysentery. As neither they nor their Chinese pals had access to any drugs, the men had no option but to sit tight in the jungle and hope he could ride it out. By the sixth day Green was raving with delirium and the others realised that they could do one of only two things: kill him, or take him back. They took him back.

They arrived back in camp on 10 May, intending to go out again that night and continue with their original plan. However, when the camp's commanding officer, Lieutenant Colonel Oakes, learned that the escapees were back, he immediately informed the Japanese, claiming he was not prepared to risk his life, or the lives of the others in the camp, 'for the sake of a few irresponsible men who try the impossible'. The escapees' argument that it was the duty of every POW to try to escape fell on deaf ears. The five men were placed under guard and handed over to the Kempeitai the following day.

After being interrogated for five days at the Kempeitai's torture house in the YMCA Building on Stamford Road, they were sent to Outram Road and placed in solitary confinement to await trial. A month later they were found guilty of attempting to escape and sentenced to three years' imprisonment, which the court pointed out was extremely lenient. The following day, 17 June, when they returned to Outram Road to begin their sentence, they had the dubious honour of joining the prison's only other Allied inmates, Penrod Dean and John McGregor, and six Britons who had also tried to escape.

After the war, furious that Colonel Oakes had dobbed him and his mates, Chris Neilson tracked Oakes down, intending to shoot him. However, while undertaking a reconnaissance of Oakes' property, he observed a woman and small children playing in the garden. Realising that the colonel had married and had a young family, Neilson did not carry out his plan.

Through Kenny, the blindfolds imposed during our first five weeks of solitary were lifted. Through the patience and virtuoso of Kenny the ventriloquist, I learned the answers to many of the tantalising things – the sounds, the voices, the movements – that I'd heard from my cell. I also discovered why we had been herded into the gaol courtyard. Kenny told me that for the past few weeks they had been coming

The kempetai's interrogation centre in the YMCA Building on Stamford Road

out for an hour to sit in the sun, and to have a disso – a disinfectant bath.

Disinfectant bath?

'Well, yeah', said Kenny. 'Here's the drill. Ya see that hip-bath over there? When his nibs brings out the bottle of disso, make sure you get down there in front of those three Indians. They have the pox, and we're not sure if the disso kills pox germs. So be ready!'

'Good-oh', I answered, not feeling too good about it at all. I was left wondering, and not understanding much of what he'd just told me. The understanding came quick enough. Learn fast, or you don't last.

Scabies mites are not racists. They'll take on any bugger. They'll eat anyone – Aussies, Pommies, Indians, even Jap guards. No discrimination whatsoever. They loved the taste of all of us and a concerted effort was being made to get rid of the little mongrels, which was why we were sitting outside, enjoying the sun and about to take the waters.

The Ceremony of the Bath was a most unpleasant ritual. The bath itself was an old-fashioned ceramic hip-bath, of the kind Cleopatra might have used, ornately decorated with engravings and Egyptian hieroglyphics and probably filched from the home of some wealthy, and most likely now dead civilian. It was half-filled with water. Holding up a Swan Ink bottle that he waved around as if it were magical, our guard paused dramatically before pouring the magic disinfecting potion into the tub. As he stepped back, Kenny whispered, 'Get ready'. Glaring round to make sure no one had moved, the guard growled *'Yoshi!'* (OK!).

The reaction was unbelievable. The heaps of skin and bone took shape and took off in one frantic rush to the bath. All order went by the board as they morphed into human beings, pushing and shoving to get the front of the line ahead of the blokes with the pox. We new chums were not in the race, even though we had been forewarned; not with this well-practised mob of old lags. Within seconds it was all over bar the shouting, and we were left standing at the end of the line, behind the three Untouchables.

By the time our turn came the disso bath was a black, turgid swill, its surface floating with thousands of scabs; the filthy leavings from the infection-riddled skins of 80 diseased blokes. Pox germs be damned. Everything in that water was poxed. So I closed my eyes and, with my mouth shut as tight as a fish's bum, hopped in, hoping that the disinfectant had done its work on all the germs, and scabs, and bits of skin. In time, when the scabies epidemic reached its peak (what we had endured to date was minor compared to later on), we looked forward to the bath.

I emerged from my dip, certain that I was a candidate for a dose of syphilis. I could feel it coming on already, but Kenny reassured me. According to him, the stuff they put in the water killed germs like nothing else; it must work, otherwise everyone would have been dead long ago. To show me just how sure he was of the bath's health-giving qualities, he rose up on his skinny matchstick-legs, saluted, gave the obligatory bow, yelled out his number, got the guard's permission, and went off to have another bath.

Then followed one of the best mime acts I have ever seen.

The snapshots of memory are printed indelibly on my mind, like a negative developing in a wash of hypo. Here was a man I thought was at death's door, a bloke who had spent fifteen long, agonising months in this rotten, filthy hole. Beaten and starved, this scab-covered caricature of skin and bone could still laugh and poke fun at his tormentors.

We sat, open mouthed, as Kenny strutted over to the hip-bath positioned just behind the guard, who was completely oblivious of the performance about to unfold.

Slowly and deliberately Kenny pretended to remove a dressing gown, which he placed with exaggerated care on the back of an imaginary round-backed chair. When it slid to the ground, he frowned in annoyance, and hung it back up – again and again. Kicking it in frustration, he left it on the floor and put a foot into the water. Ouch! It was much too hot, so he turned on the cold tap, and tried again.

CHAPTER 10 ... and into the fire

The disso bath

Ah! Perfect. With a look of great pleasure, he lowered his long thin body into the muck. Sighing with contentment, he reached for his dressing gown, took out his cigarettes, tapped a fag on his fingernail, lit up, drew in a lungful of smoke and coughed. For the grand finale, he took a good puff and blew a series of smoke rings that spiralled above the guard's head. The guard turned just in time to see Kenny rise from the water with a flurry of splashes, bowing and roaring out his number, confirming that had finished bath number two. Saluting the guard, he somehow managed to get his thumb under his nose to create an audible raspberry.

It was a sublime performance, but it was not yet over.

Without warning, Kenny collapsed into a heap, head jerking and arms and legs thrashing. When his eyes rolled back I was convinced he was either about to die or was having some kind of fit, so I grabbed him and laid him on his side. With froth and blood bubbling from his mouth because he'd bitten his tongue, he looked as if he were a goner. If we'd had a priest handy, he'd have administered Last Rites.

The guard ordered MP and me to carry Kenny to his cell, a task that was far from easy. He'd gone completely off his rocker; a struggling bundle, kicking and growling without let-up. As we neared his cell he asked in a voice much too strong for a dying man, 'Where's the guard?'

Surprised, we told him not to worry about the guard, as he was watching the other prisoners. At that, our dying patient leapt from our arms, bounded through the cell doorway and launched into an Irish jig.

Kenny hadn't gone off his rocker – at least, no more than the rest of the blokes. He was simply trying to take advantage of a heaven-sent opportunity. I soon discovered that it was the custom, on important national days, for a Jap doctor to inspect the sickest prisoners. Those deemed to be ill enough were sent out to the hospital at Changi, where they stayed until either they died, or were pronounced 'fit enough' to come back to gaol.

After spending his 37 days in total solitary confinement, Billy had been released to have his first disso bath on 28 September. Around 23 September each year, the Japanese celebrate Shubun No Hi, or Autumn Equinox Day. A day of great significance, it is a national holiday and also the time of year when the ancestors' graves are visited and tended. Kenny, who had been locked up in Outram Road since June 1942, not only knew the significance of the date, he also knew the drill.

Of the five in his group, only Kenny Bird was still in Outram Road at the time of the disso bath. The rest, some at death's door, had already been transferred to Changi, not because it happened to be a special day in the Japanese calendar, but because there was a big chance that they might actually die in Kempeitai hands.

The Japanese offered little or nothing in the way of medical care at Outram Road and usually made the transfer just before the prisoner's condition became critical, to avoid a death in custody at the gaol. If a prisoner died at the POW camp, his death could be blamed on the incompetence of the AIF doctors.

The first of Kenny's group to make the move was Bob Green. After five months in solitary he had suffered a complete mental breakdown that led him to upend his toilet bucket over his head. He was removed from the gaol in November 1942 and managed to stay in Changi for more than a year. Driver Bill Goodwin, transferred at the same time, remained in Changi until 9 August 1945, a week before Japan surrendered. Signaller Chris Neilson, beaten up for telling a Korean guard with a large blubbery mouth why he had been nicknamed Groper, was taken to Changi with broken fingers and a skull fracture in July 1943, along with Reg Morris. Also with them on the July transfer were John McGregor, who was suffering from severe pellagra, and Jack Macalister, an Australian pilot, also extremely ill, who had been captured after his plane was shot down. Although Macalister and two others, who'd tried to escape from Changi in December 1942, were to have been executed, their sentences were reduced to twenty years' penal servitude in April 1943, as an act of clemency on the Emperor's birthday. Neilsen, Morris, McGregor and Macalister had left for Changi before Billy arrived, so he did not meet any of them until 1945, when they returned to the gaol to finish their sentences.

Kenny had played his part to perfection. The doctor gave him a leave pass to Changi, along with five other Australians: Major John Wyatt of 8 Division HQ and

CHAPTER 10 ... and into the fire

Mr Roberts, a Red Cross representative, who had made the escape attempt from Changi with Macalister, and Herb Trackson, Murray Jacka and Norm Shelley, three Sandakan escapees who had been in Outram Road since December 1942, after making a break at the same time as Norm Morris's group. Two others who had escaped with them were dead. Tom Harrington had died in Kuching prison while awaiting transfer to Singapore and Ted Allen had died in Outram Road, about six weeks before Billy arrived.

A day or so before the disso bath, in the early hours of the morning, I had heard explosions that seemed to be coming from down near the harbour, followed by high-pitched air-raid sirens. Those on my side of the cellblock could also see the reflection of what seemed to be searchlights. Whatever had happened was big. For days afterwards, the gaol was alive with the comings and goings of Kempeitai officers, followed by a rash of mass executions.

Death by the state was great entertainment for those who flocked to the Colosseum in Roman times and, like those ancient spectators, the Japs now had plenty to entertain them. Death worked overtime, so much so that the end cells of our block were put aside to accommodate the overflow. Those earmarked for dispatch had their cell doors marked with a cross inside a circle. For those with unmarked doors, the bonus for staying alive was a bowl of burnt rice cake, handed out to inmates on the day of every mass execution. It was an offering we accepted with a degree of satisfaction, if not of delight. Civilisation is always at its best when the fields are ripe, but hunger stirs the beast within. We, in our hunger, began to look forward to the time when the end cells would be full again, for not only would we get our little pieces of rice cake, but the delivery was also a celebration of one undeniable fact: we were still very much alive.

Who the victims were, and why they had been singled out for sudden death, remained a mystery. The chalked circles were drawn above those same cell doors time and again. And, time and again, we received the burnt rice cake offerings. Taking into account the number of burnt rice cakes I ate in the days that followed the explosions, hundreds must have been executed.

The mysterious explosions occurred an hour or so before dawn on 27 September 1943. Six specially trained Australian and British commandos had infiltrated Singapore Harbour and attached delayed-action magnetic mines to the hulls of seven ships. Using a captured Japanese fishing boat renamed Krait, the party had sailed undetected from Australia to the islands off Singapore, where six had transferred to small two-man folboats (collapsible kayaks) for the actual raid. Setting the fuses to explode just before dawn, the raiders paddled off to a hideout on a nearby Indonesian island. After

Marked for death

observing the effects of their handiwork and the chaos it caused, with sirens sounding and searchlights quartering the sky, they returned to their mother ship and sailed for home.

The Japanese had no idea that the saboteurs had come from the outside world, assuming that the attack had been carried out by locals with the help of prominent British civilians interned in Changi Gaol. Determined to discover who had masterminded this audacious and humiliating attack, on 10 October 1943 the Kempeitai swooped on the hapless civilian population in a reign of terror that would go down in history as the Double Tenth Massacre. Had the Japanese known who had actually pulled off the raid, the chances of Kenny and the others being transferred to Changi POW Camp for medical treatment following Autumn Equinox Day would have been negligible.

The disinfecting baths turned out to be an on-and-off affair at the whim of the guards, and as we always returned to our scabies-ridden cells there was no discernible lessening of the infestations. It looked like we were stuck with fattening the mites for the duration. What with scabies, the lousy food and the rotten solitude, we weren't worth two bob, even with our gold fillings included.

Being constantly itchy was a nightmare, but almost as bad was having nothing to hand to cut my nails, or my hair. Over time, my crowning glory would evolve into a tangled mat of accumulated dirt, sweat, scabies and lice. Just when it became an impossible mess, a Jap trusty would come along, armed with a pair of the bluntest hand shears – the kind that were used for shearing sheep a hundred years ago. With this instrument of torture he'd chop away, pulling out clumps of the longest hairs, roots, scalp and all.

Although we still had scabies, the disso treatment provided me with an unexpected windfall. I was hauling myself out of the hip bath one day when the guard, who had been busy writing in his little notebook, glanced up to see his superior officer approaching. As he jumped to attention he dropped the book, and I 'accidentally' stepped on it. I quickly stooped and picked it up and, as I wiped it dry and handed it back, somehow or other three of the back pages got themselves stuck under my arm. Rather than see them wasted, I palmed them and took them to my cell.

I fairly drooled over my luck. Using as a template a small square mosaic tile that I'd found outside among some sweepings, I took one and a half of my precious pages and folded them with exacting care until I had 52 equal shapes, enough to make a deck of playing cards. It took me weeks to turn them into individual cards. I had no scissors, so I rubbed each crease along the sharp edge of a bed-board with the tile until the paper severed, all the while keeping a close watch for any approaching guard. With my pencil I marked each card according to the suits until, finally, my patience was rewarded and I could play patience.

Many a time a guard would look in through the peephole and see me sitting up like the good fellow I was, back straight in the correct manner, a model prisoner, little realising that I was playing patience with a full deck of cards spread out between my crossed legs and feet. The cards were only fingernail sized, and looked more like confetti than playing cards, but they certainly helped to pass the time. But it wasn't all play. I also engaged in some serious study. While I'd been working on my cards, I had used the other half page to learn Morse code. The remaining page I kept in reserve by hiding it in a wall crevice – reserved for what, I had no idea at the time.

I'd been trying finger language to communicate with the others while sitting outside in the courtyard, but I was way too slow. There were no signallers to help – the three who had been in Outram Road had been shipped off to Changi before I arrived. So MP, who knew everything – Morse code, semaphore and sign language – wrote down the entire Morse alphabet in dots and dashes on my half sheet of paper, using my bit of pencil. It was the only pencil in the entire place. He thought he should be allowed to keep it, and I had a devil of a job getting it back so that I could finish my deck of cards.

The Morse chart did the rounds of the cells for a month or so via the benki tobans until the walls at night resounded with so many taps that it seemed they were being attacked by a flock of woodpeckers. Most of us were infantrymen, and our knowledge of Morse, semaphore and sign language was limited. But it's surprising what a spur necessity is to learning, and we amateurs soon became reasonably efficient at all three.

About the middle of November Kenny, fattened up from his two-month holiday in Changi, came back. With him were Norm Shelley, one of the Sandakan escapees, and two blokes I'd never met. One was a mate of Kenny's who'd also been dobbed by Lieutenant Colonel Oakes and had managed to stay in Changi for almost a year. The other was a fella named Bluey Rollason.

Kenny's mate was Bob Green who had tipped the toilet bucket over his head. Their companion was Herbert Rollason, universally known as Bluey because of his red hair, was serving an eight-year stint for an escape attempt from the Changi camp. Placed in 'detention' for two weeks by an Australian officer for trying to steal a radio while on an outside working party, Rollason had become fed up with the way his superiors were seemingly kowtowing to the Japanese – so he left.

Shortly afterwards he met up with two other Australian escapees, Arthur Ross and Mervyn Hughes. The trio created a bush camp in the jungle near Seletar airfield and spent the next six months scrounging food from nearby farms. Their luck ran out when they were spotted by a local and betrayed. As Ross and Hughes had been at large longer than Bluey, they were sentenced to ten years. Ross didn't last long, dying in gaol in May 1943, before Billy arrived.

Bluey Rollason had also managed to fake his way out of gaol with an 'attack' of acute appendicitis. Like most redheads, Bluey had a fair complexion and burned very easily. Covering his skin carefully apart from a small strip on the right side of his abdomen, he exposed himself to the noonday sun with predictable results. The tender skin burned to a crisp bright red and was hot to the touch. When the Japanese doctor pressed the spot, Bluey groaned agonisingly, and achieved the desired result. Of course, when he arrived at Changi supposedly suffering from life-threatening appendicitis, the Australian doctors were obliged to maintain the charade by operating on him. By the time he had recuperated, he had spent six months in Changi.

Less than three weeks after Kenny and Bluey arrived back at the gaol, the Japs executed Sergeant Hatfield, one of our Eighth Division men. We always referred to him as sergeant, but after the war the army classified him as private because he had been promoted during the fighting and no official notification had been received. As far as the army was concerned, he was still a private.

I'd never met him and knew nothing of his trial, so his decapitation, while a gruesome way to die, was of no personal significance to me – until a few months later, when I discovered that the cell I was currently occupying was the one in which Hatfield had been imprisoned in the weeks before his execution.

In 1942 the 2/30 Battalion's Eric Hatfield and two other POWs escaped from Singapore to Malaya, where they joined Chinese guerrillas in a jungle camp near Mandai. Over the next few months they engaged in various acts of sabotage and espionage before being recaptured in May 1943 as they were trying to escape from Malaya in a boat. They were taken to Singapore and tortured by the Kempeitai before being placed in solitary confinement in Outram Road on 12 August. They remained there until 30 November, when they were tried. The Kempeitai had found Hatfield's highly incriminating diary and had ample evidence to support the charges of sabotage, espionage and fighting with Chinese guerrillas with intent to overthrow the Japanese. Escaping, resisting arrest with the use of firearms and being in an armed party with intent to escape were added to the main charge. All three were found guilty and sentenced to death. Ten hours later Hatfield's companions had their sentences commuted to fifteen years' solitary confinement but for Hatfield, who had given the Japanese a great deal of false information, there was no reprieve. He was beheaded at the gaol on 6 December 1943. His remains were recovered postwar, and reburied in Kranji War Cemetery as Private Eric Hatfield, in grave 23 A 10.

A sword swings
An arm flings
In futile defence
As death sings.

I remember the exact moment when Hatfield's death became personal. Sitting on the benki bucket one day, I spotted some writing scratched on the wall. Hatfield had also sat there and, with a nail or wire, had left a signed message, a message I was now reading. Here were his final words, his last hurrah, etched in bold letters, deep into the limewash. Name, rank and the word 'FAREWELL', beneath which, laboriously written and in a clear hand, was his epitaph – in the form of a poem he had committed to memory.

Outram Rd – Eric Hatfield's poem scratched on his death cell wall.

The poem was penned originally by Thomas Bracken, a nineteenth-century poet who had emigrated to Australia from Ireland as a 12-year-old. In 1869, at the age of 25, he had moved to New Zealand where he wrote a great deal of verse, including the words of his adopted country's national anthem, 'God Defend New Zealand'.

Some of the words that Hatfield had inscribed were missing where chunks of the limewash had broken away, but the poem's message of consolation made a huge impression on Billy as he sat, day after day on the toilet bucket, also committing the poem to memory.

Not Understood

Not understood, we move along asunder;
Our paths grow wider as the seasons creep
Along the years; we marvel and we wonder
Why life is life, and then we fall asleep
Not understood.

Not understood, we gather false impressions
And hug them closer as the years go by;
Till virtues often seem to us transgressions;
And thus men rise and fall, and live and die
Not understood.

Not understood! Poor souls with stunted vision
Oft measure giants with their narrow gauge;
The poisoned shafts of falsehood and derision
Are oft impelled 'gainst those who mould the age,
Not understood.

Not understood! The secret springs of action
Which lie beneath the surface and the show
Are disregarded; with self-satisfaction
We judge our neighbours, and they often go
Not understood.

Not understood! How trifles often change us!
The thoughtless sentence and the fancied slight
Destroy long years of friendship, and estrange us,
And on our souls there falls a freezing blight;
Not understood.

Not understood! How many breasts are aching
For lack of sympathy! Ah! day by day
How many cheerless, lonely hearts are breaking!
How many noble spirits pass away,
Not understood.

O God! that men would see a little clearer,
Or judge less harshly where they cannot see!
O God! that men would draw a little nearer
To one another, – they'd be nearer Thee, And understood.

Billy looked further. Right beside the door, where the surface was more stable, Hatfield had scratched another poem called 'The Quitter', evidently to strengthen his resolve prior to his trial. The poet who gave Hatfield the strength to maintain the fight and not fall prey to self-pity and despondency was Lancashire-born Robert Service, who had moved to Canada in 1895, aged 21, where he became known as 'The Bard of the Yukon'.

When you're lost in the Wild, and you're scared as a child,
   And Death looks you bang in the eye,
And you're sore as a boil, it's according to Hoyle
   To cock your revolver and … die.
But the Code of a Man says: 'Fight all you can,'
   And self-dissolution is barred.
In hunger and woe, oh, it's easy to blow …
   It's the hell-served-for-breakfast that's hard.

'You're sick of the game!' Well, now that's a shame.
   You're young and you're brave and you're bright.
'You've had a raw deal!' I know – but don't squeal,
   Buck up, do your damnedest, and fight.
It's the plugging away that will win you the day,
   So don't be a piker, old pard!
Just draw on your grit, it's so easy to quit.
   It's the keeping-your-chin-up that's hard.

It's easy to cry that you're beaten – and die;
   It's easy to crawfish and crawl;
But to fight and to fight when hope's out of sight –
   Why that's the best game of them all!
And though you come out of each gruelling bout,
   All broken and battered and scarred,

> *Just have one more try – it's dead easy to die,*
> *It's the keeping-on-living that's hard.*

Sergeant Hatfield had come out of his corner fighting, aware that under Japan's system of justice the gloves were weighted: something I understood only too well. Yes, they had cut his head off. They had taken his life, but they were powerless against his spirit. Inspired by his courage, I squatted there in that corner on that toilet bucket, day after day, carving the testimony of a brave man word for word onto my mind, in much the same way as Hatfield had engraved them on the walls of his dreary cell.

His execution was just one of many that year. Down at the far end of our corridor the empty cells continued to take the overflow when the Death House was full. As each cell was filled, the guards chalked the circled cross above the door. Lives were then put on temporary hold, waiting until the numbers built sufficiently for a mass execution, when the white-circled crosses would be erased, along with the lives of the occupants. Unlike the story in the Old Testament, when the eldest sons of the Israelites were spared by a cross painted on the door, the marks above these doors always attracted the Angel of Death, and he did not pass over.

> *A circled cross above each door.*
> *The executioners making sure,*
> *Of who and whose head will fall,*
> *A required number, the official score.*

The ghosts of Sergeant Hatfield and the other poor unfortunates have long since gone – gone with the buildings, and the dirty, filthy, dank cell walls with their scratchy epitaphs. Smashed into rubble, the remains lie buried deep under modern Singapore, serving a far more useful purpose now than they had ever served before. The gaol is all so much landfill now, extending the low-lying shoreline to make the island flatter and much bigger. Those smashed-up bricks and mortar, those tiny pockets of memories, lie like unexploded shells of history, ticking away on delayed-action fuses; waiting, with other silent witnesses, to explode when least expected. They can be defused, but the Japanese have yet to reach into the slime of time and set free the ghosts of those monstrous years by acknowledging their nation's collective guilt.

I had no wish to join the ranks of the dead so, no matter what food was passed through the door, I ate it. Once it was eaten, I went back to thinking about food. Thinking of eating, and trying not to think of scratching, were the constants of the day. When 8 pm came, I would put the three timber boards into place, lie down and think about food, and try not to scratch so much as the night's insects came out to feed. And so it went on, all night long, night after night, scratching away, trying to sleep, and constantly pulling at the scrap of cotton blanket to keep the worst of the mosquitoes at bay.

Not knowing anything was also frustrating. Where or what? How or when? Who or why? So many sounds – the mystery voice shouting commands; the reason for the slamming of cell doors; and occasionally a tantalising word of English, like a shaft of sunlight against a storm cloud. Any noise at all was welcome. At least the slamming doors, shouted commands and marching feet helped to break the silence of the cell.

The claustrophobic silence was never ending, countered only by rethinking words I'd heard, by going over the dog-eared pages of thoughts resounding inside my head, by putting faces in place and filling in the blanks. My imagination had been honed on the whetstone of writers like Jules Vern, H G Wells, Robert Louis Stevenson, C S Lewis, and a host of others. I was able to conjure up numerous possibilities for what was happening outside my cell; possibilities I desperately wanted to know about. How I longed to be able to put scenes to the sounds, faces to the voices, to say 'G'day', to escape from my solitary existence.

And then a bowl of rice would come through the hole in the door and all was momentarily forgotten. Is it more or less grub than last time? On some happy days there was a little bit of fish paste, or a piece of yam, but size was really all that mattered: how much rice was in the bowl. Never mind the quality. Whatever there was, it was enough to starve on.

With such a restricted diet, our bodies were vitamin deficient in every letter of the alphabet, not just A, B, C, D and E. Vitamin deficiency caused swollen joints, beriberi, burning feet, loose teeth, scurvy, pellagra, chalky bones and balls as big as footballs. We looked like the soil-eroded paddocks of the outback; skins scarred and cracked with gullies, bodies worn out from overcropping and ringbarked by malnutrition.

The palms of our hands were not exempt from the ravages of pellagra, and our first chore of the day was to pick away at the sores to relieve the pressure of the night's accumulation of pus. We all had our favourite instruments for the job: a bit of wire or a fishbone, hidden away in some crack or cavity in the thick layers of the spongy limewash, ready for the morning's surgery. I had a small length of wire, which I had found pushed into a crack at the base of one of the walls, hidden by a former inmate who had either forgotten about it or had died, bequeathing it to the next bloke who came along.

Once I had made little hole in the blister, I was able to push the muck out and relieve the pressure. Some tough blokes actually slammed their palms against the rough surface of the walls to burst the pustules, leaving impressions like Aboriginal hand paintings in sandstone caves. I never did find out which vitamin shortage caused the nightly eruption over the palms and fingers of each hand, and some days they would be so swollen and tender that I had to balance the rice bowl on my knees, and lap away, like a hungry dog.

Pellagra is caused by a lack of vitamin B3, or niacin, which is found in a variety of food ranging from oily fish such as salmon and tuna, to chicken, turkey and beef, liver, green peas, peanuts and mushrooms – none of which were on the menu at Outram Road. Pellagra not only results in diarrhoea, dermatitis, dementia and death, it also causes a sensitivity to sunlight, hair loss, oedema, insomnia, general weakness, nerve damage, enlarged heart and mental confusion.

Diseased and hungover, unable to sleep because of our itching, burning feet, aching bones and cracked skin, we suffered from the mind-numbing effects of chronic insomnia, or the Big Wake. Sleepless for months, time weighed heavily, minute by minute, hour by hour, day by agonising day. There were only two avenues of escape – finish the sentence or death.

Life in Outram Road was like a poor swimmer taking a dip in the ocean with a punctured inner tube. Some of us managed to keep our chins above the water, while many others sank from the combined weight of malnutrition and disease. With the tube deflated, they no longer had the strength to stay afloat. Those who had plenty of strength when they left were generally the very short-term inmates. For many of the rest it was in one day, gone the next – permanently.

All throughout those first months of solitary confinement, the flame of life fluttered and flickered at the slightest breeze. It burned down to a mere pilot light; the gas was running out, with nothing much left to put in the meter. Here and there, from within a nearby cell, a flame sputtered with a last gasp, and another life dimmed and faded away. Quietly, and without fuss, someone's war had ended. Men died, bit by bit, one by one, to be wrapped up, tied with string, and parcelled out.

They were miserable months, unbelievably so. The cells were a stinking mess, and so were we. Most of the guards left us to our misery, but not from any sense of shame. It was repugnance at the contagion, or the fear of it, that made them keep their distance. They'd roar and curse through the slot in the door, and some of them would grin and whisper '*Gohyaku ju go. Soona mati*' (Number 515. Soon you will be dead) as they drew a finger across their throats. We called them the Urry-Curry Kids. According to them, after they killed us off they would do the honourable thing and commit hara-kiri. In spite of their big talk, they were ever mindful of the scabies infestation in our cells and usually left us alone, giving us a consolation prize – of sorts.

We did have a couple of flies in our particular ointment. One was a big bloke we called The Mopoke, because his oversized glasses made him look like a barn owl. The similarity stopped there. Our Mopoke was a real dunce. There was nothing wise about him, even though he was longest serving of the original Kempeitai guards. He specialised in being capricious. We never knew from one day to the next whether he was wearing his bad hat or his good hat, although we always knew when he was coming. Unlike the other guards, he stomped noisily along the corridor. One day he'd be in rage about something, kicking out at anyone who got in his way, and calling us all a lot of cowardly prisoners as he boasted of how he would commit hara-kiri rather than be taken a prisoner. The next day he'd ask if me if I were thirsty, and would fill and refill my cup through the slot in the door until my thirst was slaked. As the tide of war turned, so too, did The Mopoke – no more talk of suicide.

There was one really nasty piece of work who let nothing interfere with his little pleasures. Everyone knew and feared The Postman. When he knocked on the door, we trembled, for we knew only too well that when he knocked there was going to be a delivery. He knocked only once, for he knew that we were in. We'd listen, hoping with all our hearts that the rap was on someone else's door, or that perhaps it was just the wind blowing. But no, it would be The Postman all right, standing outside the door, enjoying his moment of fun, as he allowed plenty of time for the inmate to wonder which sin of omission he was guilty of. Had legs had been correctly crossed? Back nice and straight? Eyes to the front, not gazing at the ceiling?

If I close my eyes I can still hear him coming. The keys are dangling outside, he's putting one into the lock. The bastard hasn't turned it yet. He waits. The seconds, and even minutes, tick by. When he considers that the exact psychological moment has arrived, he will turn the great key in the lock, and wait some more. He gently pushes the door, which swings silently towards me – just a little. He waits. I sit, still and silent except for my heartbeat, which is racing at a hundred miles an hour and making one hell of a noise. Hopefully, he won't drag it out much longer.

The Postman excels in the art of anticipation, a Black Belt Master in the sport of Sadism. Punishment is a matter of timing. My mind races too, wondering what exactly it is that I have done. I am sitting up, nice and straight, a credit to the establishment. My legs are crossed, just so, and my hands are on my knees, perfect. Everything is perfect, the way it always is, Scout's honour! Hope is my body shield, and it's getting thinner by the second. Whatever strength I may have had has long since drained away. From previous experiences I know only too well what to expect. Even so, I wrap hope's armour about my vulnerable body, just as the door swings completely open to reveal the black silhouette of the man himself.

He's standing beside me. Up until now not a word has been spoken. I'm mute, dumb, my mouth is sealed. Hope has gone, eloped with optimism. This is it. We are about to start on act three, the finale.

'Kora. Gohyaku ju go. Kora.'

For such a hard man, he has such a soft voice. It is almost a whisper. It won't be long now. I hear the keys rattling as they are being lifted high in the air. He waits. I desperately will my hair to magically grow thick and strong, to create a safety helmet. The hope that he will call it off is trying to sneak back into my mind, when Bang! down comes the largest, heaviest bunch of keys on my unprotected skull. I feel the immediate pain of it but, amid the blood and tears, I am thankful it is over. The Postman has made his delivery. I rock back and forth while I watch the bastard depart. As soon as I think it is safe, I lean across and knock on each of the side walls, hopefully in time to warn them that The Postman is on duty. When I'm sure the bugger's really gone, I sit on the toilet bucket and tell God all about it.

The application of pain had been refined to an art form with this bloke: not too much, so that it blunted the message, but enough for the brain to know that the body is being punished. All of us received our fair share of bashings, from all sorts of Jap guards, but by unanimous vote the prize went to The Postman Calling. It wasn't just the pain inflicted by the keys, it was the whole package, from the first knock on the door to the last knock on the head. No one moved an inch once we knew that that he was on duty, which was not until he'd visited his first victim. He slithered around, snake-like, without making any noise at all.

To survive I bunkered down, put the shutters up, and went into storm mode. Apart from constant hunger, loneliness weighed heavily upon me. As a young and gregarious bloke, I suspect that the months of solitary affected me more than the older men. I had thrived on the company of my battalion mates, and now, except for a bird that sometimes came along for a visit, there was nothing to help pass away the lonely hours. So I just sat, and watched the door.

The bird, or birds, had frequented the gaol since goodness knows when. Most flew around the rafters, but mine stood on the ledge of the window, outside the bars. I remember thinking, 'There's a bit of a twist. He's up there looking through the bars at me in a cage, a gaol-bird.' I don't know if it was always the same bird, but it was certainly a nice plump little creature. I'd spend hours figuring on how to get him to fly down. I'd think, 'If only I had some wheat.' Although if I did have some I'd have eaten it – and bugger the bird.

Hunger pangs acknowledge no friends, only food, and for those who could bring themselves to eat them there were plenty of bugs and insects around, including scorpions. Topper Brown, a Pommy bloke, squashed them all up and mixed them in with his rice. He reckoned they were vitamin enriched. But I couldn't come at it. Besides, most of the insects were so small it wasn't worth the effort.

Some of the fellows claimed to have pet spiders who 'really understand me', but we all talked to the insects, and the walls absorbed the words. The walls were our confidants, our bankers. We hid our treasures in the larger cracks. These wall safes held our Crown Jewels – bits and pieces of bone and wire, lumps of charcoal, stones, and my precious little bit of pencil. Like pirates in days of old, we hoarded every gem, every piece-of-eight and, because we often had to change cells, we got to know our treasures intimately and could identify them at a glance.

Like Hatfield, we added personal touches to the walls of our cells – drawings, poems, calendars – and in each new cell we redrew the walls and stowed the bric-a-brac in a new wall safe. The patches and scratches, the marks and stains, were an ever-changing pictureboard: a tapestry of the imagination, an art gallery of the mind, upon which hung the maps, the drawings, the poems, and the last Will and Testament of many an inmate. The history of Outram Road Gaol was scratched on what was left of the whitewashed walls.

The walls remained our only means of proper communication, and were used by anyone who knew basic Morse and had a chip of stone or a fingernail long enough to tap out a message. Night time was when messages were sent and received while we stretched out against the wall pretending to be asleep; one hand tapping, one ear listening, and both eyes watching the peephole in the door. These gossip sessions were a blessing, especially throughout the months of the scabies and the Big Wake. Lying on the boards and staring up at the light globe; thinking about this and that; trying to remember what sleep was all about; and then to have the, dot, dot, dash, dash come through. An urgent message tapping its way from cell to cell: pass to Spike Smith, five cells along, from Topper Brown, three cells the other way.

During the early hours of the morning, when the guards were sleepy and less likely to interrupt, *The News of the World*, our world, was scratched and tapped, stone on stone, tap and a dash, and a tap-tap-tap. This is Outram Gaol Speaking. We were on the air – veritable wailing walls of information. I also scratched and tapped, slow but sure. I was all right at sending, but receiving was another matter. They went too fast, the show-offs. They lost me, and the News Flash would become a News Smash.

Passing on the news

The stories we told, the scoops, the scandals, the highs, the lows, a hundred stories in every cellblock, a tale of woe in every stone. A wall of wishful thinking, fair dinkum facts, vouchsafed as coming straight from the horse's mouth: the Yanks had landed in Penang (a story told so many times that it was barred); the food rations are going to be doubled, trebled, cut back, added to, done away with; on the next Emperor's birthday we are all going to be sent back to Changi, or be beheaded, pardoned, or sent home; to celebrate the next lot of mass executions, we were going to have a party – and this was a well-known, true fact, undeniable in every way because someone from the cookhouse had said so, cross me heart and hope to die.

Heck knows what some of the original messages were, or how or when they'd started, let alone if they ever arrived at their destination. It needed only one cell whose inhabitant had no interest or ability in Morse code to cut the whole line. By the time the dots and dashes got to their destination, they'd often end up like the fabled verbal military message, passed from man to man, which started out as 'Send reinforcements, we're going to advance' and was delivered as 'Send three and fourpence, we're going to a dance'. But who cared? It wasn't the start or the ending, or what happened in the middle that counted – it was the having a go.

The number of stories, in all their various variations and disguises, would have kept a news digest going for years. But for all the bullshit, the one lifesaving bit of news, the most important message to come through, was always the one that warned us that The Postman was on duty. Over and out.

CHAPTER 11

RIDING A RECEDING TIDE

Early 1944 – early 1945

I was still in solitary when The Wall began wailing with news that sounded too good to be true. According to whoever started it, we were going to be given outside work and, of course, with that would come extra rations. Hope was at it again. The Wall, for once, was partly right, and my interpretation was pretty close to the truth: we *were* given outside work, but without the extra rations. Our task was to sit outside making ropes by hand, in quantities more than enough to hang ourselves with.

Every day, roughly, eighty or ninety inmates were mustered for work in a large concreted area between the right-hand side of the cellblock and a steep bank topped by a brick wall and security fence. The labour force was a mixed bag of British, Indians, Dutch and Australians – and also Tasmanians, who the Japs had classified as belonging to a separate, sovereign nation.

Making rope was easy. Just take an armful of tangled manila hemp from the bin, go back to your place, squat down, and then carefully untangle it, thread by thread, from the heap in front of you. When you have separated thirty threads, tie them up nicely at one end, and place the bundle to one side. Repeat the process until all the threads in your pile are untangled. Stand, make a bow, call out your number and when the guard says '*Yoshi*', ask for, and get, permission to go back to the bin for another armful of the tangled mess.

It took a week of combined effort to create enough 30-strand bundles to be woven into a rope. To start the process, the bundles were collected and spun into much longer strings. That was straightforward enough, but the next bit was tricky. I'm only going to explain this once, so pay attention.

When it was considered that there were enough longer strings to make a rope, they were fed onto a machine – a wooden, turning Thingo with horizontal handles, a bit like a capstan on a sailing ship. While three or four blokes pushed the handles, others fed the Thingo with the long strings until we had a rope stretching all the way to the far wall. We started off in a modest way, making one-inch-thick ropes, before working up to ropes of three-inch thickness. By that time we knew all there was to know about entangled weaves. Lord knows just how many threads of hemp we formed into strings before pulling and twisting them into ropes.

At the lunchtime break on the first day we formed into ranks, expecting to be returned to our cells for our usual bowl of rice. However, when we reached the block we saw that trestle tables had been erected all along the corridor, which we had dubbed Broadway. This communal eating was a surprise to us relative newcomers, but Pen Dean, who had been in for a much longer time, assured us that this was how things used to be, before the Chinese prisoner decided to wallop the guard and ensured solitary for everyone.

The meal was the same as always – a bowl of rice. As everyone was eating together, and could see how much the bloke next to him received, the cooks had been very careful to make sure each diner was given exactly the same amount, filling the bowls and levelling each one with geometric precision. Normally, how much was in the bowl pushed through the slot depended on how big a dollop was on the cook's serving spoon – sometimes large, but often smaller, if the rice had stuck to the spoon and had not come off cleanly. Whatever you got was it. However, working outdoors, it didn't take us long to find a way to supplement the lunchtime rice.

When we first started making the ropes, the toilet bucket was up front, near the guard. It wasn't long before the stench, and the inconvenience of having equally smelly prisoners coming to use it, prompted the guards to have the bucket moved. A couple of the fellows volunteered to carry it further away, close to where the Jap prisoners had a pigsty, complete with a food trough into which kitchen scraps were tipped. The pigs were far better fed than we were – and oddly, with the relocation, the requests to take a pee increased. So did the number of prisoners suffering from the trots, as pig food, while helping reduce hunger pains, was a little hard on the digestion.

One day I was taking a leak, stooping low and looking busy at weeing while my fingers raked through the trough. I was sieving the solids from the slops when

I touched a nose that wasn't that of a pig. Well, not a porky pig. It was a human pig. That he was slurping away among the real pigs was no surprise, but I was very surprised to see that the face belonged to an English Civilian Big Shot. I've forgotten his name, but he was a chief secretary or a chief secretary's secretary, or whatever. Anyway, there he was dining out with a litter of pigs. I was so shocked by his unabashed grovelling that I almost dropped the piece of yam my eagerly searching fingers had found.

Apparently this bloke had been working over on the rope-turner Thingo, which was quite close to the sty. He was a big bloke, over six feet, so I guess he needed all the extra rations he could grab and decided to dine with the swine. It wasn't long afterwards that he was released from the gaol and, according to The Wall, went back to England under some kind of exchange agreement. Anyway, good luck to him. As a man who performed in the political arena I figure he lost nothing by the experience gained from having his snout in the trough with the pigs.

Fortunately or unfortunately, depending on the strength of one's stomach, our newfound source of food was not to last. Another of the fellas also made a hog of himself. Reaching too far into the trough in his search for scraps he fell in head first among the grunting and squealing pigs, and the game was up.

We ended our rope-making days on a high note by producing the World's Biggest Hand Made Rope. That one rope took weeks to make, and used the entire production line's worth of hemp. We sat on the concrete, hemmed in by hemp, heads bowed over piles of entanglements, creating strings of strands and spinning them into long thin ropes until they covered the whole prison yard, in some places feet thick. When the Japs thought we had enough strings ready, we got down to the tricky business of making it. We took turns, four in each shift, turning the handles of the Thingo, while dozens of other workers fed it with our offerings.

The World's Biggest Hand Made Rope was easily big enough to have tied up the *Queen Mary*, which was the biggest ship any of us had ever seen. It was our last hooray, and hooray for that. With help from some of the Jap trusties, we carried it out to the front and loaded it onto a truck. We were in two minds about watching it go, because now it was finished we were going back to the cells, and solitary, again.

Whenever I'm down near the docks I compare the big ropes with ours. Nothing comes within a bull's roar of our Outram Road Special. It was some rope, and it just shows what can be done with unlimited access to cheap labour.

Rope making had ceased, but it had left me with an unexpected bonus, a strand of hemp I'd been able to palm. It was long enough to tie to some of my treasures, including the pencil stub that I'd managed to bring with me from Borneo, my pride and joy and my most valued possession. After securing my last sheet of notepaper, the deck of cards, the pencil stub, the mosaic tile and my bit of wire carefully to one end of the hemp, I dropped the little bundle into the cavity created by one of the wall ventilators at the back of the cell. When I felt it hit bottom, I hid the tail of the string by pressing it into a crevice of the soft limewash. To retrieve my little hoard, all I had to do was uncover the end and pull it up.

This pathetic collection of items, my most blessed treasures, illustrates just how vulnerable we are without small, ordinary, everyday things. Our whole world is made up almost entirely of little things – the greatest mountains and the mightiest seas are made from tiny little bits. Real life is about little things, and without them we are great useless blobs of nothing.

When death and starvation were your bedfellows, when freedom, justice and mercy had fled the field, it was not a new car or the latest wind-up record-player that we hankered after. We didn't miss the sumptuous feasts, or the smart suits and shoes. The things I missed were the everyday things – a mirror, a comb, a bar of soap, and toilet bloody paper. How we prisoners longed for these ordinary little things that we had for so long taken for granted.

Two of the stand-out constants in gaol, the deadly twins of hunger and disease, continually dangled like nooses above the cells. Food was always the main topic of conversation, transmitted covertly by Morse-code taps. Always hungry, never getting near enough to eat, we stoked the fires of our appetite with dreams of wonderfully celebratory feasts when the Jap bastards were routed and in retreat. No matter how low the tide was in the bowl, the very thought of what we would eat after liberation was almost enough to keep us going throughout the day. Almost, but not quite. The reality was that no matter how much rice, or dobs of yam or dried fish or blatcham (fish paste) appeared in the bowl, it was never enough.

A scoop of rice, a slice of yam
No wonder I'm the man I am
No sign of flab, and no spare tyre
If they keep this up then I'll expire.

Having no scales, we weighed ourselves by measurement. A circle made by connecting the tips of my thumb and index finger passed easily up the length of my arm. By adding the index finger of my other hand and converting the circle into a D shape, the D passed without effort up and down my thigh, while all 24 of my ribs stood out like a xylophone.

On very rare mornings, the cell door swung open and a call of '*Koi!*' brought us out like a lot of eager puppies, overjoyed by the prospect of being outside. What precious moments: to be with other people and to hear other voices. Each of us would stand in front of a bucket of water, waiting for the command – but not to have a wash. Confined to a cell that was always damp and humid, washing was a secondary consideration. Our primary aim was to have a drink – sticking our heads into the buckets and gulping down as much water as possible before the guards shouted for us to stop. With my belly filled with water, I'd wobble back to the cell, in the hope that, like a camel, it would last me until the next trip to the bucket.

We were able to slake our thirst, but there was nothing we could do to speed up time or the monotonous chain of endless pain and sleepless nights. Seconds dragged into minutes, and minutes into hours, as the day crawled on to a week, and then to a month, with the sands of time trickling from the glass to form sand dunes and then a desert, stretching on, it seemed, forever.

Our days continued to be strictly regulated. A time to sit; a time to stand; a time to eat; a time to lie down and a time to try to sleep. And, while you lay there, plenty of time to think about the next bowl of rice.

> *Rice*
> *If it were more than had come before,*
> *What bliss and joy. Olay! Olay!*
> *But, woe betide, if there was less,*
> *you lay, a wretched sleepless mess*
> *all throughout the night forlorn,*
> *while shadows crept across the walls*
> *waiting for the dawn.*

There was nothing we could do about our gaolers whose behaviour was, at best, erratic. Humour was our only defence against these sweepings of the Orient, and we exploited their ignorance to the full. No matter how black and despairing the days became, if we looked closely enough there was always a funny side to everything, which helped soften the blows and blunt the sharpest edges from the cutting edge of prison life. 'For God's sake, stop laughing, this is serious' is so very true, especially when you're hanging onto life by your fingernails. If you look down, all you'll see is trouble, but if you can manage to look up, you can see if the skies are blue, that the storm has passed, and smile or even laugh.

If you can laugh at yourself, and to yourself, it doesn't matter a tinker's cuss if the world laughs along with you, or not. I often talked to myself during those solitary months and, in so doing, I found out just how ignorant I was. Of all the questions I asked myself, I answered very few. However, as I was both ventriloquist and doll (some might say dummy), one of us always came out on top, and we proved to be good company and conversationalists. Our audience consisted of bugs, spiders, beetles and other fly-ins.

I might look at a bloodsucking visitor and say 'Well, Well! If it isn't old Bugsy Malone. Come to have dinner, have we? But not today, and not on me, thank you very much, so here take this, and that. I'd eat you myself, but I have my principles'. Or to a spider, 'G'day Leggy, how's the wife and kids? What, you ate them? Gee mate, that's cannibalism. What d'yer reckon? It's a case of survival? Guess yer right, at that. How did they taste?'

However, the guards were the chief and unsuspecting targets of our humour. Whenever we counted to four, for instance, it was always 'itchy knees can't see'. And when they boasted 'Nippon number one, the best' our reply would be 'Hai, Nippon itchy bum, goat-o'. The Japanese phrase for 'Pee I have done' became 'You're such a hoary bastard', and the answering '*Yoshi*' (Yes) never failed to give us a lift. So it was silly stuff, juvenile – we all knew that – but it reminded us that we were not much more than kids, and we loved it.

Our keepers had their own endearing characteristics, and we nicknamed them accordingly: a bully-boy with the look of a maniac and who constantly ranted and railed was Little Hitler; the well-mannered fellow, who would explain exactly why you deserved the bashing he had just given, became Attila the Hun. Fat-Gut was the humourist among them and his jelly-like belly would come alive at the sight of one of us in trouble. Himmler, Hitler's offsider, was another. There was also Lughead, the basher, and The Black Bastard. I'd found one of him in every camp. The Japs must have discovered the secret of cloning. And, last but not least, over in the red corner, the middleweight king himself. The one and only, knock 'em down, pick 'em up, and knock 'em down again: The Postman.

Prison staff were known by different nicknames to different groups of prisoners, a factor that made identification difficult for those investigating war crimes after the war. Among the Outram Road guards with multiple names were Hattori Tenji (known as George Formby and The Farmer), Shimoi Maseo (Slippery, Mickey Mouse), Murata Misasuchi (Groper, The Bastard), Haciya Jutaro (The Chimp, Big Boy) and Tsukuda Keiji (Bomber, Bruiser). Sergeant Major Sato Takeo, a chief warder, was known as The Bull or Rubberlips. One of those whose nickname was universal was Sergeant Okuhidra Masanori – Little Hitler. The Postman was never identified, as he was not among those rounded up for trial.

CHAPTER 11 Riding a receding tide

What a rotten lot they were, strutting and swaggering, roaring and yelling, with their hands on the handles of their swords – the 'phalli' of the samurai. Whether Attila, Fat-Gut or Little Hitler, they were just another one of those sadistic, bombastic, peasant bastards who, for all their bows and ah-sos to one another, were nothing more than a bunch of ugly, contemptible little pricks – perfect targets for our sardonic humour, for which they provided us with material galore.

I didn't know it, but the black lonely days of despair and the torment of the long hours spent in a solitary cell were slowly but surely coming to an end. There was no clue that we were turning a corner and that escape, via the ever-beckoning hand of death, would no longer be welcomed as an option.

These had been longest months of my life. My wall calendar, give or take a day or two, was reasonably correct and had so far recorded six months' worth of days, stroke upon stroke – 23/8/1943 to 23/2/1944. And, on every one of them, I'd told myself that surely the Yanks would come along before the close of the year. Until they turned up we would just have to hang on, and hope that in the meantime we could avoid the excesses of the worst of the guards. Most of them were absolute bastards, but there were a few gracious, humane individuals, which the thousand years of the samurai feudal system had failed to cull from the ranks. Humanity, amazingly, was still alive and well within the breasts of a small minority. One, in particular, stands out in my memory.

I first noticed the old Japanese sergeant standing up on a bank where long rows of paw-paw trees enticingly dangled their succulent wares as we sat waiting for our disso bath. It was obvious, from the attitude of the guards, that the old bloke was someone special; more special than the three stars on the brown stripes of his lapels and the brown sword ribbons, which indicated he was a sergeant major.

Among the Japanese, rank or status is highly regarded. Their history is steeped in accounts of its importance and the consequence of its observance. It is a commodity jealously guarded by those who have it, and to a fanatical degree. I once witnessed the punishment meted out to a two-star private by a three-star private for not showing enough respect for the difference in their rank. When it was over, the two-star bloke was a bloodied mess.

The old soldier stood watching for the whole time it took for us to have our bath. He was an elderly man, which was unusual, and this alone made him stand out among the younger members of the Kempeitai. His face was lined and worn, his hair snow-white and his movements slow. I christened him The Old Bloke, but he wasn't an ordinary, everyday, run-of-the-mill old codger. He had a sense of presence that I had never seen in any of the others – dignified, with a natural air of authority and a kind of aura that seemed to be way above the ordinary. There was no arrogance, just a bearing of authority, entirely unforced.

I think we all felt a sense of expectation. Perhaps we were hoping that with him things might improve. For once our feelings were right. From the time The Old Bloke came to Outram Road, things started to change, and change for the better. It was the turning point in our years of imprisonment.

Change came slowly over the next month, almost imperceptibly. It was like having a room repainted the same colour as it was before. Something had changed, but precisely what? The first improvement came immediately after the bath, with the distribution of buckets of disinfectant and short-handled mops to scrub out our cells – walls, floor, bed-boards, the lot. While we were at it, we washed ourselves as well. We did this for week or so, and what a difference it made. The cells were as clean as clean, free of the scabies mites, bugs and god-knows-whatever-else that had infested the place.

Next, fresh vegetables appeared on top of our rice. Even better, we were allowed out at midday to eat together at the long bench, set up in the walkway each day for the very purpose. It is impossible for anyone who hasn't been in prolonged solitary confinement to appreciate how much of a treat that was. We were hopeful that the community dining was an indication that conditions would revert to the earlier, more humane time that Pen Dean told us about. Of course the rules still had to be obeyed – no talking, no this, no that – but the magic of sitting at a table among my own and eating a meal, almost like a civilised person, was there.

Of all our new surprises, the morning we were taken outside the gates was the biggest. We were marched out the front gate and along to a creek bed near the school, where some shrubs grew along the bank. Using a combination of mime and gesture, and a few 'mmmm' sounds, The Old Bloke indicated that we should start eating the foliage, which was apparently rich in vitamin C. Squatting down beside the bushes, we plucked the leaves and began to chew. Heck! They may have been rich in vitamins, but they tasted horrible, like having a mouth full of glue. I happened to look up and see the The Old Bloke, watching us carefully from the opposite bank. On his face was something I'd never expected to see – a look of compassion.

We weren't that far into our leaf-eating days when I lay down on my bed-boards one night, ready for the usual slow-paced hours of chronic insomnia. Next thing, it was morning. Sleep had returned to the cells at Outram Road Gaol.

Whenever I pause to reflect on something that is either too cruel for words, or too sad to relate, I think back to those days in Outram Road, and to the painful and miserable time before the coming of The Old Bloke. It illustrates to me the stupidity, greed and ignorance of human beings. We are the only species who know why things are as they are now, and also know how things were, almost back to the beginning of time. We know what caused the extinction of major species millions of years ago, and what happened when very small objects hit a major planet at high speed. Yet we ignore the suffering and the blight that threatens our world, at our peril: in the same way as the Jap guards discovered that, while the scabies made life hell for us, by ignoring it they also became infected. I suspect that the effort needed to make our planet safer, for everyone, wouldn't be any greater, in comparison, than what the old Jap sergeant major gave us: just a bucket or two of disinfectant, a few leaves off a bush, and a little consideration.

He wasn't with us for very long, not more than a couple of months, and I don't think I ever heard him speak to any of us. He'd appear on the bank above the gaol yard, watch for a while, and then he'd be gone. One day he came walking through the prison, no longer dressed as a sergeant major. The three stars on his shoulder were now on a thin blue line, and the ribbons of his sword were also blue. He was in full dress uniform, his tunic ablaze with medals, and his jodhpur-type trousers tucked into highly polished riding boots. He was now a captain. I never saw him again. Where he went, we didn't know. He just marched out of our lives, a Japanese officer who, through his compassion towards us, had brought credit to himself.

Trying to keep an alert mind was just as important as a bug-free environment. While sitting for days on end on that hard concrete floor at cross-legged attention, I improvised various games: splinters of wood from the edges of the bed-boards made great matchstick puzzles; small pebbles, or tiny rolled-up balls of paper, and some rough lines scratched on the cement floor with my tile created a variety of board games. To add interest, I played myself against myself – checkers, draughts, you name it. My right hand always won, but there was a suspicion that my right hand was inclined to cheat.

Most of the military blokes and ex-Boy Scouts had a Morse sending stone. I kept mine high on the window ledge, tied to a piece of my precious hemp concealed among the flakes of the limewashed wall. One pull, and down it came ready to tap out a vital message to one or the other of the neighbours. Getting the stone back onto the ledge was infinitely harder. First of all, check to see who was on duty. If it were one of the real bastards, the transmitting station was closed for repairs. If not, a gentle twirl of the hemp to guide the stone so that it landed just right. Not too far, or I'd lose it out the window. Too short, and the sharp eyes of the guard might spot it. It had to be just right. When I was completely satisfied, I pressed the hemp into the thick grime of the wall. Following this routine, I managed to remain an undiscovered secret-transmitter of secrets throughout the war.

A few weeks after the rope-making business, I was elevated to the position of benki toban, the gaol's equivalent to the night-cart man. Four of us were on this job. Each morning we'd do a round of the cells, collecting the toilet buckets and stacking them onto a timber carry-all – a tray some six feet long by four foot wide and six inches deep, with a wooden shaft at each corner. When it was fully loaded, each of us would lift one of the handles, and off would go the Outram Road Poo Express.

Benki duty

One of the pros that came with the job was that, after washing the buckets, we were able to leave an inch or so of water in each one. We told the Japs it helped keep down the smell down, and that it was good. 'Ah-so. Hi-jean,' they said. We replied 'Ah-soles', and everyone was satisfied. Thirst was always a problem, so that little inch of water was a blessed bonus for the cell dwellers. Fortunately the cell numbers were still visible on many of the buckets so we were able to ensure that most of the blokes got their own bucket back – an important factor, considering the number of syphilis cases.

CHAPTER 11 Riding a receding tide

Our job was ranked, next in importance, to that of the meicha toban or tea cart men. Unfortunately, we handled the wrong end of the food chain, and there was nothing fattening in it for us. The job, however, does illustrate the truth of 'all things are relative', and while some may have looked on our job as downmarket, in the gaol we were the suits, the businessmen, the movers. Gathering the day's takings and loading them onto the tray was only secondary; giving and receiving the latest gossip and news, as well as relaying messages, was our number one priority. Like honeybees buzzing from flower to flower, we went from cell to cell, pollinating the cells with news while relieving the occupants of their buckets of poo. We cultivated and sustained the hybrids of wishful thinking, of heartfelt longings, and of hopes for the future. We were the vital link, in this Internet of cells.

Our collection services took on many sidelines and sometimes it became necessary to distract our guards' attention. As most of them were ignorant peasants, this wasn't hard. All we'd have to do was draw a map with a small stick or a toe in the dust, and say 'Osutoraria (Australia) – Nippon, boom, boom, boom?' Invariably the guard's eyes would light up, and off he'd go: 'Hai! Osutoraria – Nippon, BOOM, BOOM, BOOM'.

'How about Darwin?' And the twit would answer 'Hai! Darwin – Boom, boom, boom.'

'And Sydney?'

'Hai, hai! Sydney. Boom, boom, boom.'

This line of bullshit would continue until whatever it was that we were after had been accomplished, so we'd sign off with 'How about Shirley Bloody Temple?', which produced the inevitable response. This scam never failed to work, not even once, in over two years of over-use. The little buggers just loved it. BOOM, BOOM, BOOM.

Yet another way of working the angles was to play on their vanity as experts in the martial arts. Many a time, when wanting a long diversion, we'd ask in all innocence, '*Ukeru jujitsu?*' (Jujitsu lesson).

The reply was nearly always '*Kora! Nippon banme ichi koso jujitsu*' (Nippon number one jujitsu for sure), the signal not to attempt to dodge the attack that was sure to come, because if the little creep didn't succeed in his attack the challenger would really be left in pain. If the prisoner won, the guard could not cope with the loss of face, and not only would his victim be belted with a sheathed sword, but his accomplices would lose the opportunity to scrounge, or do whatever it was that they had planned. Playing the Japs at this game, allowing the guard to demonstrate his ability without being killed in the process, was a finely balanced affair. If the challenger could carry it off, the possibilities were enormous, but only if it were handled right.

Spike Smith, who had participated in more fights than I'd had hot dinners, was a former heavyweight champion of his Pommy regiment and was also a Grand Master when it came to guard-baiting. In order to survive the rough and tumble of army in-fighting, he had taken more falls than the Zambezi River and was an expert at spectacular dives. A strong bloke, he was a magnet for every would-be Jap jujitsu expert, so it was easy to set up a guard. To a man, those challenged always reacted the same way.

With a cry of '*Banzai!*', Spike's target-of-the day would run full-pelt towards him. As contact took place the Englishman, in an astonishing display of agility, would go flying into the air. Spike's dives were a joy to behold. Furthermore, they got results. Real gold medal stuff. Spike would come down smack onto the concrete, give a grunt or two and, with an admiring grin, say in a mixture of Japanese and Malay, 'Hai! *Nippon banme ichi koso. Jujitsu, Nippon bunya bagus*' (Nippon number one for sure. Nippon very good).

Spike's exhibition dives were so good that there were times when the guard gave him a taste of his rifle butt to finish off the contest, but in the meantime we would have managed to scrounge everything in sight that was worth scrounging. On one fantastic day, when we were carrying a load of clean toilet buckets past the pigsty, there, standing all by its lonely self, was a drum full of pig-swill. It seemed too good to be true, a mirage sent to taunt us. But the bucket was not only real, it was full to the brim. Somehow it had been left there, forgotten and, furthermore, unguarded with not a soul in sight – other than us and our guard, who was a new bloke and an absolute rookie.

Opportunity not only knocked, it rang the bell, and we answered immediately. Going into emergency mode, we tripped, and the lids and buckets went tumbling all over the place, causing us all to come to an unscheduled stop. As we rushed around like a lot of old hens, chasing after lids and tubs to waste even more time, Spike asked the guard, in all innocence, if he was any good at jujitsu.

Hai! Yes! *Kora!* Was he any good? Such a bloody stupid question! Positively bristling at the insult, the guard took up his stance and lunged at Spike, who took one of his more spectacular dives. Meanwhile, we divided the pig-swill among the toilet buckets. What a day! That night, we enjoyed a smorgasbord of delectable delights. A day like that made us feel good to be alive.

Spike was much better at diversion than carrying out an actual heist. While out in the yard, washing out the benki buckets over the sewer grid, we came across a bucketful of slop rice, awaiting disposal just behind the kitchen. 'Quick', I said to Spike, 'put some in our bucket.' Instead of taking just a bit, he almost filled it. We had reached the corridor on our way back to the cells when another new guard, uncharacteristically watchful, noticed that one of the buckets Spike was carrying looked a bit heavy. 'What's in there?' he barked. 'Just benki', said Spike, as the guard lifted the lid.

Spike had been in the army since about the age of sixteen, and had a well-ingrained and totally unbreakable philosophy: never admit to anything, ever, and never admit to being wrong. 'Billy', he'd say, 'the best way to keep out of trouble, when you're in it, is to deny everything.' So, true to form, he spent the next five minutes arguing with the guard, swearing that he had nothing to do with what was in the bucket. The rest of the gang, just standing around as Spike kept up his denials, was getting a bit fed up. I knew he'd never admit to anything so, as the argument was going nowhere other than to maybe get all of us in strife, I said 'I took it'. The rookie guard was smarter that we thought. Realising at once that I hadn't, it wasn't me who got beaten up, it was Spike. Back in the cells, he had a real go at me. 'What did ya do that for Billy? I've told ya a million times, never admit to anything.'

The Japanese military prisoners remained in the cells above us – colonels, majors, captains, all the way down to one-star privates. What a system they were serving under! If you fail, go to gaol. We in the flats below pondered on their ultimate fate. We rarely saw them, but we could certainly hear them. At various times throughout the day the catwalks came alive with stamping feet and shouted orders, and the responding yells of inmates as they numbered off. This was replaced by the flip-flap of hundreds of thonged feet marching along the walkway, followed by the pitter-patter as they came down the stairs, and on past our cell doors. More flip-flapping, accompanied by stamping boots and the scream of commands, and out they went, the sounds becoming fainter and fainter until there was only the sound of silence. When they were confined to their cells we always listened for the steady slap, slap of boots on the catwalk, warning us where the guard was on his rounds.

On certain days, either early in the morning or later in the afternoon, when we on the lower deck were tucked up safely in our cells, our phantoms from on high were put through their paces in the gaol yard. No one could fail to wonder exactly what was going on and I would have given quids to be out there, just once, to witness whatever it was they were doing. The sounds of marching were followed by patriotic chants and songs and screams of '*Banzai!*' before the final crescendo – some kind of one-on-one fighting, with the sharp rap of wood on wood and the duller thud of wood on flesh. The screams told of the fury and realism that went into the mock sword fights. The chants and songs were always the same, and it always ended with the grand finale, the thump of wood upon wood, the yells of *'Banzai!'* and other bloodthirsty Japanese battle cries.

These blokes practised like it was for keeps and it was not an uncommon sight, in the days that followed a mock fight, to see a number of guards with their arms in a sling, or with heads bandaged, and/or limping. Heck knows just what sort of a mess their prisoner opponents were in, as the injuries to the guards were sustained despite the heavy protective gear they wore. Not that they got any sympathy from us.

Outram Road catered mainly for Allied military prisoners on our floor. They came from all over the conquered lands, in groups and singly. A continuous supply of British, Dutch, Indians, Australians, but also an occasional civilian, with sentences ranging from months to years and, in some cases, life – in the literal sense. There weren't many executions at our end of the block but at the other end the blood ran freely. In the labour camps the Japs also executed POWs who'd been caught while trying to escape. Those sentenced to terms of imprisonment were the lucky exceptions to this rule.

The Japanese rationale for executing prisoners of war for trying to escape was that all POWs were under the command of the Japanese Imperial Army and, as part of it, were subject to the same laws that applied to army personnel. The penalty for any Japanese soldier who left his post without authorisation was death. As POWs who tried to escape were 'deserting', they too were liable to execution, quite often without trial.

Indications that maybe the flood of executions, following the purge that had begun in the months after I arrived, had reached its peak and was on the ebb, came with a lessening of the strictest of the prison rules. We took each little improvement as it came with wonder, along with a grain of salt. Hoping that the improvement would last, but ever mindful of the pitfalls, we knew that fate was always ready to trip up those who banked on hope alone. From the mood of the Japs, we detected that the euphoria of victory had long gone. Evidently the advantages of possessing so much new land, now that they had stripped it and defiled the population, had lost its lustre.

One day, in the first few months of 1944, The Wall announced that a new batch of Aussie prisoners arrived. The influx of any new prisoners was always a great event as it meant fresh news or, at least, fresher news than the stale stuff we had in the cupboard. News of any sort in the gaol was a like a blood transfusion, and Dracula himself couldn't have sought it more eagerly. The Wall ran hot for days with the latest griff, the freshest of facts, the wildest of furphies. Communication from the outside was vital to our existence, and any news was better than no news at all: the Yanks were about to land up at Penang – again; the war was dying, finished, on its last legs. It must be true. These new prisoners had said so.

This latest mob was special to me and to MP. They were all Aussies – even better, they'd come from our old camp at Sandakan, more or less following the same route we'd taken. One of them was Curly Mills. Tall and lanky, he always stood out in a crowd, with his black curly hair standing up like a banner to rally his fellow Tasmanians when blokes from the 'big island' sought to denigrate us. MP and I had shared mutual friendships with many of the newcomers from Sandakan, and now, with a bit of luck, we hoped to find out how things were going back there when we did the rounds on benki toban duty.

Cyril Mills, always known as Curly, was aged 38 and therefore classified as one of the old blokes. Describing himself as a tractor driver and motor mechanic, he had enlisted almost as soon as the war broke out, only to be discharged late the following April as medically unfit. Eight days later, as a lorry driver, he re-enlisted, this time in the militia, but within weeks was discharged on the grounds that his services were no longer required. Undaunted, he lopped a year off his age and enlisted for a third time, in December 1940, as a motor mechanic. He was posted to 2/3 Motor Ambulance Convoy, which had the distinction of being the only Australian unit to be in action in Malaya and Singapore from the day hostilities commenced in December 1941 until the surrender in February 1942. Sent to Sandakan with B Force, Mills had assisted with the making of the camp's radio, which resulted in his arrest and trial when the underground organisation was betrayed in July 1943. Sentenced to two years' hard labour, he arrived at Outram Road Gaol on 11 March 1944, along with eighteen others. Like Billy, his nationality was listed in the gaol register as Tasmanian.

When I eventually met up with Curly Mills face to face, he was shocked to see me, not because I was in gaol, but because I was actually alive. 'You're supposed to be dead!, he said. 'You and MP Brown. You're both supposed to be dead with your eyes gouged out.'

Another bloke in this group was Carl Jensen. I hadn't met him previously, because he came from Western Australia and was with E Force. I'm glad I stayed on the right side of him because it was no secret that he was determined to survive the war so that he could kill one of his officers. He told me E Force's intelligence officer, Charlie Wagner, had done the dirty on him and his mates by promising to include them in an escape attempt. They'd handed over their escape kit material in good faith, but he'd taken off without them. Carl swore that if Wagner survived he would track him down and kill him with his bare hands. I reckon the need for vengeance was the only thing that kept Carl alive.

Lieutenant Charles Wagner, Carl Jensen's intended victim, was an officer with 2/18 Battalion. When E Force had stopped over at Kuching for a couple of weeks, on the way to Sandakan in April 1943, Jensen's mate Don Marshall had crawled over to the civilian men's compound. There he had made contact with senior members of the Sandakan community, recently arrived from the internee camp on Berhala Island at the entrance to Sandakan Harbour. They were only too happy to help. When Marshall wriggled back to the POW compound he had with him maps of British North Borneo, a Forestry Department survey chart, notes of introduction to members of the underground assistance group and information on possible escape routes – one through the Celebes and the other via the Philippines. Using this information and with the help of the trusted contacts, Marshall, Jensen and two other mates, Joe Weston and Ted Keating, hoped to make a break for freedom at the first possible opportunity.

It came when E Force, on arrival at Sandakan, was transferred to the old Quarantine Station on Berhala Island, only a relatively short distance from the southern Philippines. On settling in, Keating approached Wagner, E Force's intelligence officer, to tell him of their escape plans. Wagner was receptive to their proposal and said he would not only join in their attempt, but lead them. As Wagner was to arrange the finer details and date of departure, the group trustingly handed over the material they had obtained at Kuching. Another would-be escapee gave Wagner a precious compass. Using these items Wagner then planned an escape with three fellow officers and four other ranks.

Confident that Wagner would keep his part of the bargain, Keating's party waited patiently to be told it was time to move. In the fifth week of their stay on Berhala, hearing that transfer to the mainland was imminent, they asked Wagner if he were ready to make the attempt. He replied that it would be best to wait until favourable conditions prevailed on the mainland. That night, Wagner's party escaped.

With the help of the underground contacts they reached Tawi Tawi in the Philippines, where they joined an army composed of US military and Filipinos operating behind the lines. Before the escapees could be evacuated by US submarine to Australia, however, Wagner and one of the ORs were killed.

Meanwhile, back at Sandakan, Keating's party, seething over Wagner's duplicity, had become even more determined to escape. They made contact with the local underground network, but were caught in the purge that followed the discovery of the camp radio and taken to Kuching for trial. As there was insufficient evidence for the Japanese to proceed against Joe Weston, he was transferred to the POW camp. Keating died in gaol while awaiting trial, but the other two, Marshall and Jensen, were found guilty of planning to escape and sentenced to four and two years' imprisonment respectively. Marshall died in Outram Road Gaol on 11 August 1944. Jensen survived the war as he had vowed to do, only to discover that Wagner had not. Jensen never forgave Wagner, and remained embittered until his death.

Because of the ever-growing list of rules and regulations to which civilians and POWs in Singapore were subjected, there was need for constant policing. And with the increased surveillance came more arrests, resulting in an increase in the number of gaol inmates, especially civilians: all 'useless mouths' that had to be fed.

Along with the relaxation of rules in our part of the gaol came the gradual introduction of outside work periods. We were supposed to remain within the walls but, with the war situation deteriorating, combined with the cost of paying for our upkeep and the increase in inmates, the Japs considered it only fair that we should undertake gainful employment – market gardening.

To make it easier for the guards to keep an eye on us, and to save them unlocking and locking so many cell doors, we were herded together, two to a cell, and concentrated on the right-hand side of Broadway. This shared accommodation plan, along with outside work, did not go without feigned protest, and reminded me of the story of Brer Rabbit and the Tar Baby, when cunning Brer Rabbit, captured by Brer Fox, got what he wanted by begging *not* to be thrown in the prickly briar patch where he had been born and bred.

'Please, not two to a cell', we begged. 'Oh dear. Please, not outside work.'

Of course, we got both. It was wonderful.

To be outside the gaol on working parties. To have a companion to talk to in the cell. I really could identify with the Count of Monte Cristo, and I understood and shared in his elation on finding a companion after long solitary years in goal. There was plenty of spare land just outside the gaol walls, and within a few months every inch of it would be planted with some kind of veggie crop.

The shared-cell arrangement turned out to be a double blessing. Assigned to my cell was my old mate and benki toban offsider, Spike Smith. What a good bloke he was. A Cockney from the East End of London, he'd joined the permanent army as a youngster, looking for a good feed. The army became his only home, and for years he had been 'soldiering on', travelling throughout the world for God, King and Country, gaining valuable life skills in all manner of lands and in all sorts of conditions.

The prisoner known to Billy as Spike Smith was Lance Sergeant Frederick John Smith, of 9 Coastal Regiment. He and eight others, including Lieutenant Eric Lomax, known to readers and movie-goers worldwide as 'The Railway Man', had been arrested at a camp near Kanchanaburi in Thailand: Smith and Quartermaster Thew for being in possession of a radio, and the officers as a form of reprisal. All those arrested were taken off for 'questioning'. Two of Lomax's fellow officers were so badly beaten they did not survive the subsequent interrogation. Their bodies were dumped in a latrine. The others were sent to trial in Bangkok, where they were found guilty on 22 November. Smith and Thew were sentenced to ten years, Lomax and the other officers to five.

Spike told me about the places he'd been, and of things that he had seen in the course of his ten-year stint helping to underpin the declining years of the British Empire. He and his like were the backbone of the British Army: strong tough blokes, rough as sandpaper, the product of a thousand years of combined experience. These men didn't break, or drop. They had run the course that had been set for them. The Top Brass, crumbling at the first sign of force, had failed them. Confronted with the heat of the fires of war, they had melted like butter on a hot knife.

> *They were drilled, sweated and drained.*
> *For a shilling a day they were trained.*
> *Flying the Flag where the sun never set –*
> *It was the Empire that finally waned.*

However, not long after the arrival of Curly and his mob from Kuching, the Japs changed the rooming arrangements. They shifted Spike to another cell. My companion for the next four or five weeks was one of the new blokes, Rod Wells. He was a lieutenant so, when he moved in, I moved up a few rungs of the prison's social and intellectual ladder.

When Rod, who was a university graduate and an expert in things scientific, came along with his university-gained knowledge, he must have been surprised to find such an empty and enthusiastic vessel ready for the filling. I reckon he would also be surprised to know how much I can still remember of the many lectures he gave me including one, of all things, on 'The structure and nature of the atom'.

As I'd dropped out of school at fourteen and had spent a lot of time wagging it anyway, at first I found the lessons on atoms and valency and electrons and protons and shells a bit heavy going. I'd ask Rod, 'If you can't see the bloody things, how the hell do I know what you're telling me is right?' As he patiently explained the complexities of atomic structure, neither of us knew that Allied scientists were

Rod Wells, who taught Billy the complexities of atomic structure

working flat out to create the atomic bomb, nor just how important the things he was describing would be to our safe and final deliverance.

Later I had Pop Blain, who'd got mixed up in the Sandakan underground organisation, sharing my cell for a while. His real name was Adair Macalister Blain, and he was the Member of Parliament for the Northern Territory. He was a nice old joker full of stories about the Top End – stories, he assured me, that were all fair dinkum, but as Pop was a politician I took this with a grain of salt.

In spite of the improved conditions, some prisoners went completely mad. The Japs put some poor Chinese bloke who'd gone into a mental decline into one of the now empty cells opposite mine. He was desperate for more rice, crying out and bashing his head his head time and again on the sharp corner of his cell wall. The screams of '*Lagi nasi*' (More rice) and the harsh thud each time his head struck the stone finally attracted the attention of the guard, who dragged him into the corridor and tied him to a cross made from two bed-boards. He lay there, moaning away ever so softly, until there was only silence. A couple of trusties then rolled him up in atap matting and tied the bundle with string – just another discarded parcel to be buried somewhere outside the wall.

There was also some weird behaviour from a couple of Pommy officers who had served with the Indian army. They hadn't gone mad, just a bit odd. For some reason they got it into their heads that an Indian bloke called Mankav, who resembled Mahatma Ghandi, was some kind of spiritual guru. They spent hours meditating with him in their cell and took everything he said as gospel.

A couple of days before Rod Wells and the others arrived at the gaol, Bill Fairy, who was in my battalion and one of Norm Morris's escape group, had been moved to Changi. Unlike his dainty name, Bill was a big bloke, and a champion cyclist. We were outside doing odd jobs when we were ordered to remove a tree that was growing in the bank near the rope-making yard. It had its roots firmly embedded in the sewer drain and we were hoeing at it ineffectually when Fairy, who liked a challenge, took over and began chopping at it like a man possessed. The handle of the changkul was rough, and it wasn't long before he had developed some whopping great blisters, just right for the zillions of germs from the sewage-laden tree roots to invade. Infection set in rapidly and when the Japs finally worked out he had blood poisoning, they packed him off to Changi.

It was a one-way trip for poor Bill Fairy. He died four weeks later on 6 April but it wasn't for another nine months, when Neilson, McGregor and Reg Morris returned from their spell in Changi at the end of January 1945, that his mates learned of his death.

Over the next few months quite a few others departed for Changi. Some were gravely ill. Others, like Eric Lomax (The Railway Man), deliberately injured themselves. Once on the mend, they enjoyed a respite from the monotonous rice diet at Outram Road and as their health improved also enjoyed the vastly superior facilities at the POW camp, which they reckoned was 'like heaven'.

With regular entertainment in the form of plays and musicals, social clubs where after-dinner coffee could be bought for a few cents, a well-stocked library, mail deliveries, church services, a proper hospital and infinitely better rations, some Outram Road inmates, such as Jack Macalister, went to extreme lengths to extend their stay. With his return to gaol imminent, Macalister had an Australian doctor at the camp, Charles Huxtable, break his shin bone with a ten-pound sledge hammer, after first administering a small amount of pain killer. The injury enabled Macalister to stay in Changi until April 1945.

The thought of returning to Outram Road was also too much for another inmate, Driver Merricks, an English prisoner who had attempted to escape from a camp in Thailand in July 1942. He arrived at the gaol to serve his four-and-a-half-year sentence the following month, at the time when conditions were about to deteriorate. After six months, he was transferred to Changi in January 1943. Ten months later, with his return evidently imminent, he escaped from Changi, but his freedom was short-lived and he died in the attempt.

The medical staff tried to keep others there as long as possible on one pretext or another, but most, except for a lucky few, had to return at some time or other to Outram Road to complete their sentences. Time out in Changi didn't count. Although the Kempeitai made every effort to avoid deaths on their patch, Sapper Don Marshall, who was involved in the Sandakan underground, did not oblige them. He died in the gaol in August 1944.

As time wore on, the Kempeitai waited until the last minute to transfer the sick to Changi. Roy Davis, another involved with the Sandakan underground, reached the sanctuary of the Changi hospital on 11 October, but died within 48 hours. A fortnight later two other Sandakan men, Arnold Small and Norm Shelley, also became gravely ill. Shelley, who had previously earned two months' respite in September 1943 when he was transferred to Changi with Kenny Bird, lasted four days, Arnold less than a month. It wasn't until the early part of 1945, when some of the other Outram Road inmates returned, that it was learned all three were dead.

Although we were confined to the gaol and the immediate surrounding area, we realised that the war was getting to an interesting stage. It must have been in late October 1944, not long after Norm Shelley went off to Changi, that we noticed a reconnaissance plane circling overhead. A few days later, something happened.

At the time I thought the date was 4 November 1944, my birthday, but my wall calendar was a day out. It was actually the 5th. But that's beside the point. I remember what happened that day, because birthdays, when you are young, are important. I had turned nineteen, and it was the third birthday I had spent as a prisoner of war. In Civvy Street I was now old enough to join the Army, and in another two years I could vote, get married without permission, and even go into a pub and have a beer – unlike Outram Road, where age had no bearing on what we were allowed and not allowed to do.

The day had started ordinarily enough. I held a private birthday party for myself, and sang 'Happy Birthday to Me'. My cellmate at the time, a non-English-speaking Tamil, didn't join in. He thought I was a mad dog of an Englishman. I thought he was as thick as brick as, in the short time that I knew him, all he could ever say, or would ever say, was 'I no understand'. So we came to an understanding that we misunderstood each other, and left it at that.

The first job of the day was to tend to the market gardens on the hillside outside the gaol, above the house belonging to the superintendent. The guard assigned to watch us was Little Hitler, and accompanying him were two Jap trusties. We were hoeing away at rows of vegetables when a flight of B-29 bombers came from out of nowhere, the first indication that this was going to be a far grander birthday than I had ever imagined. The leading aircraft flew right over us, heading towards the north-east and the great naval dockyard, once the pride of the British Empire. One of the first bombs dropped hit the oil storage depot, and what a glorious sight it was to see great black thunderheads of thick oily smoke towering hundreds of feet into the air and nearly blotting out the sky.

The sight of those Yankee planes unleashing their hardware was exhilarating. Shouting to make himself heard above the sounds of the explosions and a few ack-ack guns and machine-guns firing ineffectually into the air, MP Brown yelled, 'How do you like them apples, Nippon?' We laughed and shouted our delight as we helped ourselves to some yams, safe from any retaliation: Little Hitler, our brave and courageous guard, and his two trusties had almost shat themselves with fright and scarpered to a nearby shelter as soon as the first bomb fell. When the planes departed, and things had quietened down a bit, yells of 'Kora! Kora!' rang out as the guards emerged from their hiding places to once more bravely take up the fight against us prisoners.

But the Yanks hadn't finished with us yet. Another wave passed over and caught us with our heads down and arses up. They came in fast from behind the smoke to frighten the life out of us, Japs included. Little Hitler tore off down the hill like a rabbit. Kenny, sheltering in a culvert beside the road leading to the Superintendent's house, was shoved out of the way by one of the trusties, who then promptly went to pieces, his nerves totally shot. The other took off to the steps leading to the house and cowered there, covering his head with his arms.

After the aircraft had passed over we became aware of a sound like the hum of a million bees coming from behind the smoke. Suddenly, the sky was filled with flight after flight of glittering silver planes. Strewth! The noise was terrific, and they had yet to drop their bombs. There seemed to be hundreds of aircraft droning away and, when they were right over their target, they let go. The bombs seemed to twirl, rather than fall straight down, and when they hit the poor old island it fairly shook. Great clouds of thick black smoke arose, twisting and swirling, edged with tongues of red flame and creating a fringe on a black curtain that now obliterated the whole of the eastern side of the island. Some of the explosions were so massive that we felt the shock waves hit the hillside where we were standing. What a way to celebrate my birthday!

Billy was witnessing the first Allied air attack on Singapore. On 5 November, Guy Fawkes Day, 76 B-29 Superfortresses, long-range bombers of the United States XX Bomber Command, took off from their base at Karagpur in north-eastern India, 2000 miles away – a return journey of 4000 miles (6200 kilometres) without refuelling and, on paper, beyond the limit of the aircraft's range. The primary target was the huge King George VI dry dock at the Naval Base, as the Battle of Leyte Gulf had just taken place in the Philippines and the Americans wanted to ensure that no enemy ships could make use of the dock for repairs.

Due to the enormous distance to be travelled, each bomber carried a payload of only two 1,000 pound (450 kilogram) bombs. The pilots were instructed to drop their load from a relatively low altitude while maintaining loose formation. The leading aircraft scored direct hits on the base, putting the dry dock out of action and damaging a 142 foot cargo ship awaiting repairs.

Unfortunately, as the attack took the Japanese by surprise many civilian workers in and around the dock area had no time to escape and were killed. *The response from Japanese anti-aircraft guns and fighter planes was minimal, but two attacking aircraft were lost due to accidents.*

The Japs were still keeping their heads down, but up there on the hill we had a box seat, watching the devastating damage being done by the might of the United States Air Force. It was an awesome and welcome display. We had been alone for so long, and now we had something to yell and cheer about. Open-mouthed, we watched as flurries of bombs continued to flutter to earth, like a New York ticker tape parade. In fact, we were so enthralled by what was going on we failed to notice that our watchdogs had squibbed it yet again, and had left us alone and unguarded, lord protectors of their kitchen garden. While we had been gazing skywards, all those veggies at our feet had been ours for the taking. We could have kicked ourselves. Such was the momentousness of the occasion that, for once in our lives, we had failed to take advantage of a situation.

A bull-horn shout of '*Kora!*' from over near the prison wall brought us back to reality. Our guards, huddled there in a state of high anxiety, were too scared to leave the shelter of the wall to come and get us, so they were they yelling for us to koi. We did, but we took our sweet time about it, to make the bastards suffer. And they were indeed suffering. The nastier of the trusties was crouching down beside a concrete post, terrified. Little Hitler was jumping up and down like a cat on hot bricks, such was his hurry to get inside the safe haven of the prison. When we finally reached him he carried on as if he was about to poop himself. '*Bakayaro! Binta no!*' he screeched, as if it were our fault there had been an attack.

We were halfway along the track leading to the main gate when more B-29s flew past at a much lower level, strafing the side of our hill with their machine-guns as they dropped bombs on factories in the valley just below us. Hugging the ground, we shook our fists at them as they flew on. With friends like that, who needed enemies!

When the dust settled, we got to feet to discover that this time we had been completely deserted by Little Hitler and his two offsiders. With complete disregard for our welfare, they had turned tail and left us to our fate which, as it turned out, was to tramp down to the prison entrance, knock on the big door, and ask to be let in through the small postern door.

I know this seems farfetched, but it is all perfectly true. At the time I began to record all this, there were at least three in the outside working party still alive, apart from myself: Bluey Rollason, Alan Minty and Herbie Trackson. We stood alongside the wall for a while, weighing up our options. Deciding that the safest place was back inside the prison, we continued on to the gate, only to find it shut tight, and unattended. Fair dinkum, there was no one on duty. We had to knock not once, but several times, and quite hard at that. Finally the postern door opened and a guard peeped out. He glared at us for moment before growling '*Kora! Kochie koi*', and we were permitted to come back inside, away from the nastiness outside. I could hardly credit it. Prisoners, free on the outside after being locked up for more than a year, asking to be let back in!

Later in my cell I relived the day's events, realising that, even if I lived to be a hundred, the odds of ever experiencing a day like it would be a zillion to one – about as much chance as of discovering a priceless painting by Van Gogh tucked away in a corner of the attic. I've had many birthdays since then, but none of them have been anywhere near as exciting, or as exhilarating, as that one in November 1944. I tried to explain how I felt to my Tamil cellmate, but he didn't understand.

Not long afterwards, we noticed a reconnaissance plane whose observers seemed to be very interested in the nearby Queen Victoria docks. Later, while on another outside working party I made it my business to find out what the attraction was. It was the Japanese heavy cruiser IJN *Takao*, which had been torpedoed by USS *Darter*, an American submarine hunting Japanese shipping near the Balabec Strait, just off Borneo's north-western tip. Having limped back to Singapore, *Takao* lay wounded and powerless while engineers assessed the damage.

Years afterwards, when I read of the tremendous land, sea and air battles that had taken place over and around the Philippines and North Borneo, and of the attack on *Takao*, my imagination soared into orbit, and transported me to the Balabec Strait and to nearby Banggi Island, that beautiful oasis where we had drunk coconut milk with the island's kids on the way to Kuching to stand trial. It was also the place, on board the ex-sultan's yacht, where I had dreamed about the American fleet steaming to our rescue from across the blue horizon.

As it turned out, although Takao *was of interest to the reconnaissance plane, it was not yet a target. Hit by two torpedoes, the ship had arrived back at Singapore in November 1944, shortly after the first air raid. Decreed too badly damaged to be sent back to Japan for repairs, the vessel was shored up and later towed into the Straits of Johor, where it was moored alongside the hulk* Myoko *to be used as floating anti-aircraft batteries for the defence of the now-vulnerable naval base.*

Months later, on 31 July 1945 and with the war almost over, the two ships were targeted for attack by a party of Royal Navy sailors, undertaking a mission code-named Operation Struggle. Unaware that the vessels were unseaworthy, and their guns bereft of ammunition, the saboteurs approached in two midget submarines, HMS XE1 and

XE3. When XE1 was unable to reach Myoko, its designated target, being delayed by the presence of enemy surface craft, the limpet mines were laid alongside XE3's prey, Takao. The ship was anchored in shallow water, leaving hardly any clearance for XE3 to manoeuvre beneath it. With only one foot separating the two vessels, Acting Leading Seaman James J Magennis nevertheless managed to partially open the submarine's hatch and squeeze out to access Takao's hull. After scraping away barnacles and seaweed to attach six delayed-action magnetic limpet mines, Magennis and the submarine's commander, Lieutenant Ian Fraser, made a successful getaway.

Some of the mines exploded, tearing a hole in the hull. The ship did not sink, but Magennis and Fraser were awarded a Victoria Cross for their efforts. After the war it was also discovered that Takao was manned only by a skeleton crew and had no ammunition on board for the eight-inch guns. In October 1945, after Japan surrendered, Takao was towed to the Straits of Malacca where it was finally sunk after being used for target practice by HMS Newfoundland.

Until the November bombing raid, our guards would often taunt us for having been taken alive. Unlike the dishonourable prisoners it was their misfortune to guard, they boasted that they would all commit hara-kiri rather than surrender. Although the writing was on the wall, we didn't notice any entrails messing up the floor but because they were such a touchy lot we refrained from mentioning it at the time.

The complacency of the conquerors had now been replaced by nervous tension. By this time most of the older guards had moved on, their places taken by a much younger mob, mostly Koreans. We old lags welcomed the change, as the seasoned guards had begun to wake up to most of our schemes. We were able to recycle the Osutoraria-Boom-Boom routine to much better effect and with a greater degree of success.

Even so, it didn't always work out as planned. On day, while some of our mob were keeping a new guard busy recounting how Nippon was bombing the hell out of Australia, I and a few others nipped inside a shed to look around for anything that might be edible. Spotting what appeared to be a bag of almond nuts, I shovelled a couple of handfuls down my throat before the guard came in. Thank God he appeared when he did. The nuts, as I found out later, were not almonds but castor oil seeds, one of the most effective purgatives known to mankind. Crook! Was I crook! I sat anchored to the toilet bucket for days, with the most violent attack of the runs, ever. The memory stayed with me, and it was years before I could look at an almond.

It didn't stop us swiping food at every opportunity. Not long afterwards, in order to cover up for a mate who was busy pinching sweet potatoes from the guards' kitchen garden, one of our blokes told The Mopoke what marvellous fellows they were, and it was no wonder that they were all *dai ichi* (first). Turning to me for verification, he asked 'Isn't it true that the guards are number one, Youngie?' Whereupon the Jap enquired '*Anata no namae Youngey, ka?*' I agreed that 'Yes, my name is Youngie'.

From then on, the guards called me Youngie instead of Prisoner 515. It was '*Youngie kochie koi*' (Youngie come here), '*Youngie madotte koi*' (Youngie come back here), and Youngie this and that, and I thought 'Crikey! What charisma I must have. I'm on first name basis with the bloody Japs'. It was some time before I was to discover the reason for my newfound popularity. To the Japanese ear, Youngie sounded a bit like *yagi*, the Japanese word for goat.

CHAPTER 12

OUT OF THE SHADOWS

Early 1945 – 19 August 1945

With the November air raid of 1944, which was followed by several others in the first months of the New Year, the tempo of our work increased and the pressure was on – for us to make a greater effort towards winning their war. We'd already converted every available inch of ground into vegetable gardens, but we certainly weren't getting a fair share of the fruits of our labour. So it was with a most unpatriotic feeling that we set to work clearing old ammunition dumps and clearing the ground prior to digging defence tunnels into the nearby hills.

We were driven to our various work sites each morning in the back of an old ex-British Army truck, into which eighty or so of us somehow fitted. One morning the dilapidated vehicle broke down on an almost equally dilapidated wooden bridge spanning the Singapore River, which was nothing more than an open sewer. Squashed in the back of the truck with the hot, humid air sponging our faces, we faced a dilemma. Should we pray for the truck to be fixed, and get us off the bridge and out of the boiling heat, or hope that it wasn't, and save us from a day's backbreaking work. We were still pondering this weighty conundrum when our nostrils were assailed by the most tantalising, mouth-watering aroma imaginable.

I sniffed the air like a bloodhound to determine the source. My nose told me it was coming from a flotilla of Chinese junks and sampans where pots of delectable food were being cooked and stirred over small open fires, ready for the next meal.

The thought suddenly struck me that I had been this way before, but a long time ago and under entirely different circumstances. During our first leave in Singapore, Herb 'Crooky' Cruickshank and I had hired a couple of rickshaws for a tour of the town. Partway through our tour, just for a lark, we had swapped places with our drivers. As we had neared this same hump-backed bridge, a revolting smell had hit us. 'Stone the crows', we cried, 'What a stench', and hightailed it back the way we had come.

What little Lord Jims we were back then with our privilege, pomp and pedigree – so secure in our superiority. We couldn't get back to camp fast enough to tell our mates about the adventures we'd had in Singapore, extolling the highlights but also describing the lowlights, especially the dirty, smelly, stinking river. How we decried the disgusting habits of the boat people, who actually cooked and ate their food in such filthy surroundings.

Now, not much more than two years later, with Crooky long gone, I was back at the bridge. It was definitely the same bridge but, I wondered, where had the Bad Smell got to? The bridge was now the most beautiful, mouth-watering, aromatic bridge in the whole world. And as for the river and all those lovely boats ...!

The aromatic bridge

Hunched down in the truck, trying to quell the rumbles in my stomach, I wondered about the amazing transformation of my sense of smell, and in so short a time. It was a miracle. It was then I realised that I had accidentally discovered the most powerful deodorant of all – poverty. There's nothing quite like being poor and hungry to keep things in perspective.

At that moment the truck's dicky engine burst into life and off we went, left with only the memory of the fragrant hour spent on top of a fleet of Chinese cooking pots.

CHAPTER 12 Out of the shadows

Poverty Spray – The Balm
A little squirt under your arm
Removes all smells.
It works like a charm.

After we finished clearing the ground for one of the tunnels, the Japs sent us to clean up one of our own long-abandoned ammunition dumps. As the shells had been lying around since February 1942, we handled those with care, but were more blasé about the bundles of unstable cordite the Japs had carelessly tossed into the dump. Unfazed by the danger and to speed up the process, we threw clumps of it onto the fire while boiling the billy – until an English prisoner was badly burnt when the flames followed a carelessly left cordite trail and he ignited.

As the Japs intended to dig in, big time, tunnels were dug at key defensive places, including Johor Bahru on the other side of the causeway. Once we'd finished cleaning out the ammo dumps, a gang of us was sent to Johor. It was hairy, scary work. The Japs didn't believe in occupational health and safety, and there was more than one collapse.

I figured that this might be a good time to be elsewhere, so I had a go at getting sent to Changi. To date, MP and I, and Bluey Rollason's mate Merv Hughes, who came from Tasmania and was in my battalion, were the only Aussies not to have had some respite in Changi. As I had spent every rotten day of my sentence banged up in the gaol, I thought it was time I had a bit of the good life. But my timing was dreadful, and the results were worse. I deliberately took a tumble off a heap of dirt, biting my tongue to create a good show of blood. Unfortunately,

A respite from digging tunnels in Johor

in my enthusiasm for realism I nearly bit my tongue in half. I was taken back to Outram Road where I lay in my cell moaning and groaning, but nothing happened. The doctor had given up house calls. I had a sore tongue for weeks.

Another inmate who had not been off for a holiday in Changi was a Pommy bloke, Jack Sharpe. He was in the gaol when I arrived. I saw him quite often in the yard, and had yarned to him when we were making the rope. He'd tried to escape from Thailand, with a couple of others I think. He was a chirpy, cheeky little cove, and must have had a ton of resilience, because he was still alive, despite being almost skin and bone from his long imprisonment.

Corporal John 'Jack' Sharpe, of the Leicestershire Regiment, also answered to the name of Becky, after Becky Sharpe, the spunky heroine in William Thackeray's classic novel, Vanity Fair. *In June 1942, Sharpe attempted to escape from the poorly guarded Ban Pong Camp in Thailand, along with two mates, Corporals J P Smart and E H Armstrong. They stayed at large for two days, when they were rounded up by a band of armed Thais who handed them over to the Japanese. Paraded before a firing squad, they were facing what they believed was certain death when a colonel strode out of the jungle and struck the officer in charge of the execution, effectively bringing proceedings to a halt. After a heated argument, the colonel beat Sharpe with his sheathed sword, kicking him repeatedly each time he fell to the ground.*

Hands bound behind his back, Sharpe was marched back to the camp where he was handed over to a guard, a former front-line soldier who loosened the bonds, thereby saving the prisoner's hands. Then he gave Sharpe a Three Castles brand cigarette, informing his captive that it would be the last cigarette he ever smoked. After being confined to a cage measuring five feet by eight feet, Sharpe was court-martialled for his attempted escape and sentenced to two years imprisonment in Outram Road.

When the president of the court asked the infuriated prisoner if there was anything he wished to say, Sharpe let fly with a torrent of curses and abuse that saw his sentence extended to four-and-a-half years. The final straw came when the judge added that no Japanese as fit as Sharpe would ever have surrendered.

Even more furious, Sharpe replied, 'I am going to live, not only to see you surrender, but the whole Japanese nation, and I will walk out of prison on my own two feet.'

He arrived at Outram Road on 5 August 1942 and spent the next fourteen months in solitary, kept alive by the thought of home and the sting of the judge's insult. Although his fellow escapees, just as weak and sick as he was, were sent to Changi camp in early 1943, and remained there for almost two years, Sharpe refused to leave the prison. When they were returned to Changi after being back at Outram for only a month or two, his friends entreated him to go with them this time but Sharp was determined to carry out the vow made at his court martial and stayed put.

By the new year of 1945, Becky Sharpe was looking pretty crook, and conditions in the gaol were deteriorating. As the war started to go against the Japs, the Korean guards really started to take it out on us. Treated as second-class citizens in their own country, which had been under Japanese occupation for decades, these bullies now had someone below them in the pecking order. Just to let us know they were alert and on the job they'd come darting into the cell on any pretext, shouting and roaring, trying hard to imitate their masters; hitting away with their great bunches of keys, throwing the bedboards and blanket around the cell, then forcing us to restore order. For all their carrying on and shows of efficiency, when they conducted body searches they, too, failed to look in our hands.

I reckon their general ill-temper was not improved in the slightest by the air raids, which continued at fairly regular intervals. At first, focus was on the naval base, but the nearby Empire docks were also targeted in an attack that included incendiary bombs.

This raid, which focused on the docks and was the eighth since November, took place on 24 February, when 116 B-29s armed with incendiaries burnt out almost 40 per cent of the nearby godowns. Because of poor visibility caused by the smoke, 26 of the planes dropped their bombs 'blind', causing huge damage to commercial and residential areas. According to the Japanese, 396 people were made homeless by the raid. No planes were shot down, and the only casualty was one aircraft that ran out of fuel on its way back to base. While the damage to property was great, there was no reported loss of life.

Not long after this raid, The Wall passed on the news that a number of Allied pilots who had been shot down were being held in the cells at the end of our block. We assumed that they must have been crews from one of 'our' air raids, but we didn't really care why or how they had ended up in Outram Road, only that they had. New prisoners meant fresh news and, as gathering news was the specialty of the benki tobans, we regarded them as a professional challenge.

At that time, my cell was the last in our section. Normally we were not allowed to go any further, as the cells beyond held people we were not supposed to see. For some reason, however, the Japs had placed one of the airmen in the cell just two along from mine. I didn't know he was there, as we had an empty cell between us acting as a buffer. As luck would have it, we had a new guard accompanying us on the benki rounds and he ordered us to collect the new bloke's bucket.

Realising that this was a heaven-sent opportunity to get some news, the others went into the now well-rehearsed Boom! Boom! caper, allowing me to duck back to my cell and grab my pencil and my last sheet of paper. While the guard was engrossed in telling the gang how much of Australia was not left, I was able to sidle past and slip into the pilot's cell, where I found him curled up in the corner. I can't adequately describe the look of bewilderment on the poor bloke's face as I shoved the pencil and paper into his bandaged hands, saying, 'I-can't-stay-long-I-haven't-gotta-moment-gotta-take-your-toilet-bucket.-Now-here's-a-little-bit-of-paper.-For-God's-sake-don't-lose-it.-Quick-write-the-news-and-anything-else-and-I-will-come-back-and-get-it-when-I-bring-your-tub-back.' And with that I grabbed his toilet bucket and was off.

What a surprise it must have been for the poor fellow, lying in a dirty, stinking cell, his arms and neck wrapped in filthy bandages and probably suffering agonising pain from his burns and crash injuries, not to mention the inevitable Jap inquisition, to have a dirty, skinny apparition suddenly rush in and thrust pencil and paper at him, gabble something about writing news, grab the toilet bucket, and go. In the few seconds that I was there, he went from open-mouthed surprise to incredulous delight and then to disappointment when I rushed away, leaving him only with the promise that I would be back to collect the news.

Hours later, I returned his bucket. The new guard had started to get suspicious of our goings on and was shouting '*Kora!*' all over the place, so as we neared the cell Alan Minty dropped the stack of tubs he was carrying. 'Great clumsy bugger!' everyone yelled, and while the others were going crook at him I had just enough time to collect the mail, shake the pilot's hand, wish him luck and say that I would try to get back again. I didn't. My lasting memory is of a big dark-haired man crouching in the corner and giving me a wave with his bandaged hand as I hurriedly left.

Back in my cell I unfolded the scrap of paper and digested the hard-won news. It was difficult to read – a hurried painful scrawl, as the pencil stub was so small. The scrap of paper was also tiny, but he had managed to squeeze quite a bit onto it. I don't remember all the words, but his note went something like this:

'My name is Habi ... [I couldn't remember the rest of the name]. My friends call me Habby. I am a Kiwi Pilot and was flying a Hellcat Fighter off an Aircraft Carrier on a raid on Pelambang when I was shot down. The news is as follows ...'

For prisoners who had been starved of information from the outside world for months, Habby's report, even though the news was old, was sensational: the D-Day invasion, the fighting going on in Europe, the Allied victories in Africa and Russia and the destruction of the German battleship *Tirpitz*.

In November 1944 KMS Tirpitz, the pride of the German Fleet, had been in port undergoing repairs when it was attacked and sunk by two massive 12,000-pound bombs dropped by Lancaster bombers. Several previous attempts to sink this battleship had

Habby the pilot

failed, so this major coup, along with the D-Day invasion of Normandy on 6 June 1944, was big news.

The pilot Billy met was Lieutenant John Kerle Tipaho Haberfield of the Royal New Zealand Air Force, who was part-Maori. On 24 January 1945, flying his Hellcat fighter plane in Operation Meridian against Palembang in Sumatra, Habby was shot down. He was transferred to Singapore, where he was most likely held for prolonged interrogation at the Kempeitai's torture house in the YMCA building. With the interrogations over, Haberfield and eight other airmen were transferred to Outram Road Gaol to await trial for 'indiscriminate bombing'.

The Wall ran hot that night transmitting the latest bulletins, and for the next few days our backs were straighter, our steps firmer.

The large cracks that had already appeared in Nippon's Far Eastern Co-Prosperity Sphere expanded considerably at the end of March when the night suddenly erupted with a violence that shook the very foundations of the building. At first I thought the explosions were rumbles of thunder from one of the frequent electrical storms. But then the sirens began, and we knew it was an Allied air raid. Although the raids so far had occurred in daylight, we always hoped that night-time rolls of thunder were the sounds of exploding bombs, only to have our hopes dashed. When we realised this was indeed an air raid, that the Yanks were striking again, and at night, we were momentarily struck dumb. Having sound but no vision, we could only sit on the floors of our cells, listening to what we hoped were the death throes of the war.

Having only the soundtrack reminded me of the Depression, when I was a kid with no money and wanted to go to the pictures. I could either cadge a pass-out at interval, or sneak in under the legs of the ingoing patrons. On the rare occasions that either of these methods failed, I would sit on the doorstep of the stage exit and listen to the show. This was intensely frustrating. A pistol shot, followed by a long silence. What the hell is happening? Then the sound of footsteps, and spurs clinking. Silence. Dramatic music. More footsteps. A gunshot breaks the tension, only to be followed by more silence. By the time a voice says 'Good shooting Hoppy, I think you got the varmint', I am almost peeing myself with excitement.

Once again I am that little boy sitting on the doorstep. But this time I'm sitting on a concrete floor at the World Theatre, with a long-running show and a million cowboy heroes running the gauntlet. A dramatic, death-defying enactment, a battle of titans fought in the shadows, is happening just the other side of the wall. With only the soundtrack to go on, the story so far is a mite distorted, transmitted only in snatches through the steel bars of a small window, in dribs and drabs; a leaking tap of a war.

The cell light goes out for the first time in memory, along with the corridor and perimeter lights. After so many months of constant illumination, it is great being in the dark. I stick my tongue out at the door, and my cellmate and I lean against the walls and talk. The Jap guards don't like the darkness at all, and come along the corridor with torches, shouting and ranting.

As the urgent screams of sirens pierce the darkness, we stand and look up at the half-inch of sky we can see, and wait. It seems ages before the guns open up and the steady drone of aircraft can be heard overhead.

Then, from outside the gaol walls comes the sound of fury, as the planes attack with a vengeance. 'You little bloody bewdy!' we chorus.

Three cheers for the Yanks. We hope they know exactly where to drop their bombs, which is anywhere other than on top of us. They seem to be attacking the dock areas and oil storage facilities on the southern side of the island. With the lights off, we can see the reflected glow of huge fires burning. The rhythmic crump-crump and flashes of light from the exploding bombs, the guards rushing round like a lot of chooks with their heads off, make this a night to remember.

More silence follows until the aircraft reach their secondary target. The crump of distant explosions, followed by the whine of the 'all clear', and the lights are back on. It's interval.

After agreeing with The Wall that the show wasn't too bad tonight, we have just settled down when the lights go off again, and the sirens wail afresh. It must be a double feature tonight, with a blockbuster for the main event, judging from the intensity of the sirens. The action opens with the heavy breathing of approaching planes. Brr-mmm, brr-mmm, brr-mmm, they come, pushing through the air until the single brr-mmms join together to make one continuous, and mighty, B-R-R-M-M-M. No wonder the sirens are going ballistic. The attack is right on top of us.

We can read the entire action purely by sound: the sharp wispy snaps of answering ack-ack, rapping my eardrums like the crack of a rawhide stock whip. The pom-pom guns jumping and snarling, whosh-crack, whosh-crack. The outpourings of war stream through the bars, filling the cell with the rattle of machine-guns and all the other paraphernalia of air defence.

Finally, drowning out all else come the thundering crashes of exploding bombs, shaking the walls in their rage. The earth trembles, and the island seems to tilt. Then the 'all clear' sounds and the lights come on. The war has packed up and gone and we are left – but not alone. '*Kora! Hanashi nay no, bito no, bakayaro, wakaru ka.*' The Theatre Ushers are coming down the aisle with their torches to make sure that all is in order. Although death and turmoil are on the outside, life inside returns to normal.

The eleventh and final air raid using B-29s based in India, prior to these aircraft being relocated to the Mariana Islands, took place on the night of 29–30 March, when 29 Superfortresses attacked Pulau Bukom, the large oil storage island just off Singapore's southern coast. In order to train aircrew for the low-level tactics to be used in air raids against Japan itself, on this particular raid the bombers homed in on their targets at a very low altitude – between 5000 and 7000 feet. Seven of the 49 oil storage tanks were destroyed, and another three were damaged. All aircraft returned safely to base.

That the night raid came as a big shock to the Japs was obvious from their sullen, deflated looks. There was also a very marked decrease in their boasting and swaggering – the horror of finding themselves on the receiving end was all too much. It was a mighty psychological blow, as well as a physical affront. The Invincibles of 41–42 were coming up against The Incredibles of 44–45.

One of our first outdoor jobs after Cracker Night was very close to home. Just before the gaol's previous owners had so hurriedly vacated the premises they had dug a line of air-raid shelter trenches along an earth bank, just inside the perimeter wall near our cells. The shelters were covered with roofing of coconut-tree trunks onto which earth had been piled for added protection.

The new owners, being practical types, had planted the rows of paw-paw trees in this ready-made raised garden bed. But now, having second thoughts in regard to their personal safety, they decided to resurrect the shelters. And who better to do the job but the hapless inmates? The work itself was okay, but working up on the bank, with dozens of great long golden paw-paws dripping from the tree trunks, was sheer psychological torture.

Something had to done to ease the pain, so Spike went into the Osutoraria-Boom-Boom-Boom routine while I reached up and grabbed the largest paw-paw I'd ever seen. It was a beauty. I'd managed to take just one huge bite before my ears were shattered by the roar of '*Kora!*' coming from the roof of the cell block. A guard was on the parapet spying on us. Never before had we known any of the mongrels to be up on the walkway that provided access to the huge louvred ventilators and could only be reached by a rusting condemned staircase. The guards were dumb, but it didn't take Einstein's brain for this one to figure what was going on.

Kenny Bird, as luck would have it, was on his way down the steps leading to one of the air-raid shelters, armed with his little bucket and broom. In one swift single-arm movement I lobbed my prize into his can.

All hell broke loose when our guard realised that one of his charges was being accused by the lookout on the roof of stealing, and in a gaol too. Furious, he almost broke his scabbard on my shoulder as he emphasised his displeasure. 'Where's the bloody paw-paw?' he yelled at me in Jap. 'I haven't got none' is what I would've answered if I could've but, because he had grabbed me by the jaw, I couldn't. He looked into my mouth for any sign of the golden fruit, and finding no trace, worked himself into a frenzy. Thoroughly enraged, he screamed '*Kora, bakayaro, binta no!*'

There was nothing like the promise of a potential beating to rally the troops. Japs came from everywhere, guards and trusties, all shouting and carrying on. Tipped off by the cockatoo guard, they ran down the steps to the shelter where Kenny, despite his terror of the scorpions that inhabited the darkness, had managed to stay out of sight. Yelling and screeching, the posse dragged him out, along with his bucket and broom.

They searched high and low for any sign of Exhibit A. They looked in every corner of the shelter and in his bucket; they opened his mouth and examined every tooth. The search was so thorough it's a wonder they didn't look up his backside. It wasn't long before light began to dawn: there was not going to be any Exhibit A.

Kenny, far from being beaten to a pulp for receiving stolen goods, was the centre of an admiring throng of Jap guards and their pack of trusties. If they'd found just a trace of that paw-paw we would've been done for. But in not finding anything they had saved face. Like fishermen recounting a tale, the size of the paw-paw grew with each telling until its dimensions were more in keeping with a watermelon.

The time lapse, from when the guard had screamed out from the rooftop until they dragged Kenny up from the shelter, couldn't have been more than a couple of minutes and yet, there he stood, a bundle of skin and bone, a matchstick of a man, suggesting that somehow or other, in that impossibly short time he's managed to swallow the whole bloody thing.

The Japs would believe anything, but I thought it was a big con. So I sidled up beside him and out of the side of my mouth, muttered, 'Come clean, Kenny. What did you do with me paw-paw? And don't give me any bullshit.'

'I ate it.'

'What! All of it?'

'Yep.'

'Seeds and all?'

'Yep.'

'Greedy little bugger!'

At about this time I was paired with a new cellmate – Private Alan Minty, who'd been in gaol with me in Kuching. He'd not long returned from a ten-month visit to Changi, so he was refreshing company. He was also a good ventriloquist. Poker-faced, he could sit with his legs crossed and his back straight, a picture of innocent attention while he relayed the latest gossip, all without moving his lips. He had a deadpan look that never gave anything away, so he could relate the news of the world right in front of the watchful eyes and ears of the guard.

There was a secret radio at Changi but there was no up-to-date hard news, of course, because it was a couple of months since Alan had been there. Frequent air-raid alarms told us that the Allies must be coming closer but, although the flood was receding, we were mindful that the storms could return, roaring and raging, ready to torment us again. In the past, false hope had left us stranded on the hard pebbly beach of bitter disappointment, when the rumble of artillery we'd thought we heard was only the sound of distant thunder, and the flashes of light were lightning, not the flickering signs of a distant battle. Wisely, we now examined each new furphy carefully before placing it in our hope chest.

By this time my shrunken corner of the world was becoming more multicultural. After Alan moved on, I had a Sikh cellmate for a few weeks. He was a bit of a weirdo. I never found out what he was in for, or for how long, but by the time he moved into my cell he'd already suffered his most severe punishment, bar decapitation. The Japs had shaved his entire head. Spiritually, he was lost. His hair, like Samson's, was vital to his salvation, and he went downhill fast. He didn't get any sympathy from any of us, though, because many of the Sikhs, who'd switched sides when Singapore fell, had become POW guards and were worse than the bloody Japs. As far as we were concerned, they had made their beds and now they could lie on them.

Apart from sharing my cell with the Sikh, only one thing of note happened in the next few weeks. One day, as we went in and out of our block, we spotted a Jap soldier upstairs, standing at attention by a cell door on the corner. We didn't take much notice at first but as the days wore on we realised he was still there on guard duty, in full battle dress and shouldering his rifle. Finding this very odd, we paid closer attention. Whoever was in that cell, we decided, was someone of great importance. A very big Mr Big. Not only were all his meals brought to him on a covered tray, but he received frequent visits from none other than Colonel Mikizawa, the Kempeitai commandant, who was Mr Trouble himself and never made cell calls.

Keeping tabs on this special bloke upstairs took the combined efforts of The Wall's management, coupled with our personal observations and whatever else we could glean from talkative guards. With nothing much else to occupy our minds it was amazing how interesting this little drama in the Jap hierarchy became, an unfolding serial on the life and times of a Japanese military prison.

I only ever got to see the prisoner once, and that was only for a fleeting moment, when they were carting him off to his court martial. He was a big wheel all right, dressed to the nines in his best uniform, with the red tabs of a field officer and a load of golden fruit salad dripping from his jacket and cap. The guard detachment escorting him was also impressive. The Wall concluded that he must have been a very big wheel indeed, so we decided to dub him 'The General'.

Not having any secret radios we were restricted to some degree in our general newsgathering. However, The Wall was exceptional when it came to the home-town grapevine. Whatever happened in the gaol, whether it was hard fact, an educated guess, or just a thought, would be relayed by the dit-dit, dah-dah of The Wall, Outram Road's *News of the World*.

Even so, The Wall never came to an understanding of what The General had done to land himself in a high-security military prison. The Nip guards were close-mouthed, such was the seriousness of the crime of their VIP inmate; a crime so heinous that, while we did not know what it was, was so bad that the court had sentenced him to death – not by the sword, the more honourable method of dispatching those suffering capital punishment, but by firing squad.

One evening, shortly after this news came through, a squad of Jap prisoners started digging into the bank outside my cell. The sharp commands of the guards, mingling with the grunts of hard-working men, aroused my curiosity. What in the blue blazes was going on outside, and at this time of day? Had they had decided to construct more dugouts in anticipation of an air attack? Or were they digging up the retaining wall to grow more veggies? Finally, the tone of the commands told me that whatever was being done had been done and the workers were packing up for the day, leaving me and the blokes in nearby cells to face a long night of answering questions coming through The Wall.

Before daybreak the next morning I heard the sharp sound of hobnailed boots stamping in unison in the concrete yard. It was very early, much too early to be part of another ordinary day. If I were another four or five feet taller, I could have looked out the window and seen what was going on for myself. Alas, all I could do was tap on The Wall and see if it knew anything. But it was a dumb, know-nothing wall, and no help at all.

By this time the cell light had gone out, officially heralding the start of another day. The day may have begun, but it was a morning unlike any other. We insiders read sound in the same way as the blind read Braille. Every whisper and bump, any and every unusual noise, was examined and read accordingly. The sounds coming through the window told me that the situation outside had changed, had become more military in tone. The cry of '*Ki-wo-tsuki!*' resulted in the usual sound effect of boots coming to attention but, with each new call I perceived a greater sense of urgency. The effect all this had on the inmates, locked up and unable to see, was intensely dramatic. Certain something was about to happen, I crouched down, an ear to the outside wall and an eye on the door lest The Postman or some other guard catch me at it.

The sudden crack of a volley of rifle fire gave me a start. Light suddenly dawned. My brain went into overdrive. 'It's a firing squad! Eureka! So that's what it's all about. They've gone and shot their bloody General.' Of course they'd shot him, I told The Wall. It had happened right outside my cell window and if I'd have been another five feet taller I would've been an eyewitness.

The Wall agreed.

Later that morning, going outside on a working party we saw with our own eyes the trouble the Japs went to when they shot one of their Big Boys. The noises I'd heard the day before had been made by a special detail removing part of the sloping retaining wall. The workers had then dug into the bank to create a straight-sided shooting gallery. Out in front and to the left of the alcove was a row of stools – the front stalls – and off on the other side, in the dress circle, stood two throne-like armchairs. Later that afternoon, when we returned from work, the shooting gallery had disappeared. The only sign of the early morning drama was in the newly cemented bricks and freshly rammed dirt.

Not long after The General was dispatched, the best cellmate I ever had moved in with me. He was a Dutch Eurasian, an infantry army captain called Pieter. A captain! I'd just moved up another rung on the ladder. Alan Minty was a private. So was Spike Smith, although he had been a sergeant on several occasions. Pop Blain was a parliamentarian (but politicians don't count for much). Rod Wells was a lieutenant. And now I had Pieter the Infantry Captain.

Billy's new cellmate was 40-year-old Captain Pieter Lodewijk van Hemert, who was born in Sumenep, on Madura Island off the north-eastern tip of Java, not far from the city of Surabaya. His well-to-do family had interests in sugar mills and made sure he received a good education. After graduating from the Royal Academy in Holland, he had joined the Royal Netherlands East Indies Army (Kokinkliijk Nederlands Indisch, or KNIL) where he served as a military policeman in Sumatra. When the Dutch East Indies fell to the Japanese in March 1942, he became a POW.

In May he was transported on Kyokusei Maru, along with 500 British and 1500 Dutch POWs, to Tavoy in Burma, where they worked on an airfield with Australian prisoners sent from Singapore. They were all then marched to Thanbyuzayat to start work on the notorious Burma-Thai Railway.

One evening in October 1942, while Pieter's working party was camped at Wagale, the Dutch commander arrived in a very poor state. He had spent the past few days being beaten into submission to sign a no-escape agreement, the same agreement that those at Sandakan had been forced to sign, and he had been ordered to ensure that his men did likewise.

On the evening of 4 October, the day before the prisoners were to sign the agreement, a 26-year-old Dutch-Javanese artilleryman serving with the KNIL, Ernst Ferdinand Portier, decided to escape and invited three of his comrades to go with him. As he hoped to reach the coast, the first person he sounded out was Pieter van Hemert, who could sail a boat, and whom Portier described as 'a real Indies guy, a fine man and a military police officer'.

The other two would-be escapees were also Dutch Indonesians – a man named Schuurman and another called Hoffmann, a self-sufficient bloke who could find his way in the jungle. Escape itself was easy. Since the camp was surrounded by dense jungle full of malarial mosquitos, the Japanese did not post guards, believing that the likelihood of escape was minimal.

Pieter and his companions were in no doubt as to their fate should they be recaptured. In early June 1942, while working on the airstrip at Tavoy, eight Australian POWs who'd tried to escape, and been betrayed by locals for a few rupees, were shot by firing squad. Despite this, the Dutchmen were willing to give it a go.

Taking an axe and a machete, and some rice they'd scrounged, they slipped away from the camp, walking along a stream to avoid leaving any tracks before turning into the jungle and following what they hoped was a south-easterly route. The sun could not penetrate the thick foliage, so they had no idea which way they were going as they had no other method of determining their direction. Portier recalled: 'We were terribly afraid. By God, you really didn't know what to do. The first two weeks were absolute misery. It was the rainy season and we couldn't make a fire, because the smoke could be smelt from a great distance. So we kept on walking, hoping for the best.' To make matters worse, three of them became sick.

By following the waterways downstream, they hoped to reach the coast – but their efforts were in vain. After fifteen days of privation they discovered they had walked in a huge circle and were back again at Wagale. Setting course in a more southerly direction, they plodded on and about two weeks later spotted a hut, where a Malay from a forced labour camp gave them some rice before guiding them to a village inhabited by pro-British Karen tribespeople. After being provisioned they were led by six guides deep into Karen territory, but being constantly on the run was a precarious existence. Often there was nothing to eat and there was constant danger from wild animals, including tigers, bears and poisonous snakes. After a while the group split up temporarily, and Portier and Schuurman found themselves at an elephant camp, deep in the wilderness.

In July 1943, the four men were reunited at the village of Bisakah. In September, after learning that the Japanese were on their trail, they decided to join a band of 200 undisciplined brigands in a jungle camp, most of them runaways from the military. As members of the gang they carried out an attack against Japanese who had been enacting atrocities, including rape, looting, murder and arson, against the local population. In this action, which saw Portier manning a Bren gun, fifty of the enemy were killed. After this they returned to Bisakah where Pieter, who was suffering from malnutrition, was able to recuperate.

In mid-October, the headman suggested that they return to the brigands' camp by ox-cart but Hoffmann elected to remain behind in the village. Pieter's health was by now much improved. Seizing the initiative, he suggested that they train the gang to form a guerrilla fighting force to harass the Japanese and be in a state of readiness should the Allies attack. During the next month the guerrillas attacked a police station, making off with weapons and cash; a seven-vehicle convoy belonging to the Burmese security forces, which yielded clothing and fifteen guns; and a Japanese police boat, which added a Bren gun and rifles to the growing haul. After these hit-and-run raids, the guerrillas split up and dispersed into the jungle. In mid-November, the three Dutchmen returned to Bisakah.

Hoffmann by this time had left the village, preferring to go it alone as he believed it would be safer. It wasn't. He was betrayed and killed.

Shortly after his departure Quartermaster C Knoester, a Dutch Indonesian, had joined Pieter, Portier and Schuurman. He and three white Dutch officers – Captains Johan Hendrik Wilhelm de Rochemont and Frederik Anton Marie Harterink, and Lieutenant Gerard Arnold Hermans – had escaped from Wagale on 25 November 1942. Five days later, lured into a trap by treacherous locals, the three officers were recaptured. At 8.25 am, on 13 December, they were shot. Knoester, who had somehow managed to escape from the trap, was taken in by Karen tribespeople.

The four remaining escapees stayed with the Karen villagers until February 1944, working with them in the rice fields. During this time they raided a police station, securing guns and money and killing six Japanese, but on discovering that the Japanese were on their trail they rejoined the brigands. Shortly afterwards they raided Mubon village in Thailand, killing sixty Japanese and Thais and adding fifteen more guns to their arsenal. During this engagement Saw Koo, the brigand who had led the raid, was killed.

The Japanese, enraged by the boldness of the gang, introduced drastic countermeasures. Village headmen were tortured and killed; anyone found in possession of a British gun was gruesomely murdered, and their homes and property torched. Fully aware that the consequences of harbouring outlaws would be a hideous death, the headman of the village where the four men were based suggested they move to a safer place – Bisakah village.

Of course, not everyone could be trusted and in July of 1944, after surviving for the best part of two years in the jungle, the four men found themselves being hotly pursued by a posse of Japanese and bounty-hunting locals, accompanied by dogs. Portier had a rifle with four bullets in it. Realising that the search party was closing in, he floated the idea of shooting Knoester, whom he considered useless, and Schuurman, who had lost his night vision due to malnutrition. 'Pieter', he said, 'you and I are going to make it. But not if those two stay with us! Shall I shoot them?' 'No', his companion replied. 'In for a penny, in for a pound.' Portier threw the rifle away.

The posse, armed with rifles, machetes and sabres, began to close in. Running towards the Dutchmen, a Burmese collaborator fired at Portier. Nothing happened. So he fired again. Another misfire. Dropping the weapon, he fled. Portier picked up the rifle. It was his. Two of the four bullets had been duds.

Capture was inevitable. Tied up with split bamboo, they were brutally beaten and interrogated. The Japanese refused to believe they were the prisoners who had escaped from Wagale two years before, and concluded they were spies sent in from India. The Kempeitai also brought in suspects from among the Karen people, including the village chief who had given them shelter. No one gave any sign of recognition. Although severely tortured, the chief remained stoically silent throughout his terrible ordeal. Unable to extract from him anything of value, the Japanese doused him with kerosene and set him alight. As the flames took hold, they saluted his burning corpse.

All apart from Knoester considered suicide a better option than further interrogation. Portier, who had come close to taking his own life shortly after their capture, still had a piece of a razor blade hidden in his sarong, but the prisoners were too tightly trussed to use it.

Two days later they were walked fifteen kilometres to the village of Sikh before being taken by canoe to Moulamein. They endured a month of heavy treatment at the hands of the Kempeitai before they were transferred to Bangkok for trial, via Kanchanaburi. All were tried and sentenced to death. This was subsequently mitigated to twenty years' hard labour for Pieter, and fifteen for the others, probably because the end of the war was already in sight. In early October 1944 they were transferred to Outram Road Gaol.

Pieter and I got along famously. He was that sort of a bloke, a marvellous character. He'd travelled the world, been there, done that, and still managed to come across as a nice, modest fellow. He was also an expert on fine dining and food in general. We would sit beside each other, legs crossed, keeping an eye on the door, while he talked and I just listened, mouth agape, drooling over the banquets created by his imagination.

Together we partook of the world's finest culinary achievements, including the best that the Chinese had to offer: Fried Rice with Foo Yong Hie; Peking Duck; Hundred-Year Eggs; Bird's Nest Soup. By way of a change we'd then slip across to France. Crikey! What a culinary tour that was. Frogs' Legs, Snails, Jugged Hare in Red Wine, the lot. Oh, and the famous Pea Soup of Holland, a mouth-watering delight chock-a-block with lumps of smoked ham and bacon. After all that gourmandising, what a letdown it was when our bowls of rice arrived.

Pieter was a combination of the best of his two cultures: intelligent, calmly self-assured, with a firm politeness that never left him. He would look across at me and say, 'Billy, when the war is over I want you to come and be my guest in Surabaya and to share a meal with me and my family. We just have to wait the war out and that shouldn't be too long now'.

Alas, it was too far away for Pieter, who became ill with beriberi. The result of a constant rice diet completely lacking in vitamin B, beriberi causes severe oedema or fluid retention. At the onset of the disease, the joints begin to swell, making them almost impossible to bend, then the arms and legs puff up until they resemble fat sausages. Sometimes the testicles swell to the size of large melons, making it impossible for the sufferer to walk without the aid of a harness to support the weight. These outward signs are obvious. The real danger is hidden – a build-up of fluid around the heart or in the lungs.

In the early hours of one morning I realised from Pieter's laboured breathing that he was in real trouble. He was drowning in his own fluids. As I sat beside him, unable to do anything to ease his suffering, I had never experienced such a sense of utter helplessness . Not knowing what else to do, I lifted his head and cradled it on my lap as I worried the hours away.

After a while the gurgling noises and the troubled breathing seemed to ease, and it was then that Pieter spoke, quite clearly. 'Ah Billy', he said. 'The war will soon be over and you will come to Surabaya to visit me and have that meal.'

'Yes Pieter', I answered. 'It won't be long now, and we'll all be able to go home.'

I looked down and Pieter was gone. His war was over. Death must have worn slippers – I hadn't heard a thing. I kept a silent vigil until morning, when our breakfast bowls of rice arrived. I placed the one that looked the biggest beside Pieter. I ate mine, and then ate his. It was the only real banquet that we had ever had together.

Later that morning, I called the guard and told him about Pieter. It was Little Hitler. He thought it was a great joke, so much so that he waved his finger at me and laughed, telling me in Malay 'Chuckup chakap tida bully na' (Cukup capak tidak boleh na – 'enough talking'). The very thought of ordering me to cease talking to a corpse made him double up with laughter and he went off chortling to himself: 'Chuckup chakap tida bully na – chuckup chakap tida bully na'.

Later in the day the guard brought the atap matting and string and I wrapped Pieter up like a parcel, wishing that I could somehow send him home to his family. Pieter was a good bloke. A great mate.

Pieter Lodewijk van Hemert died on 17 June 1945. Post-war, his body was recovered from the gaol cemetery and taken home to Java. He now lies in the Dutch War Graves Cemetery at Kembang Kuning in Surabaya, in Section B, Grave 377. Ernst Portier, who had initiated the escape, died in Holland in 2008.

One night, shortly after Pieter's death, The Wall broke silence with the terrible news that our friend Habby had been found guilty of indiscriminate bombing, and that both he and his friends had been sentenced to death.

As I recall these sad happenings from out of the long-ago, how can mere words be made to shape my thoughts in such a way to convey a picture of the pilot we knew as Habby? He'd been shot down in flames, interrogated for days by the Kempeitai and lain for weeks in a stinking rotten cell, so badly injured that he had to be carried on a stretcher to face the military court. Some trial! Indiscriminate

Pieter's grave in Surabaya. The flowers and message are from Billy

bombing? Pig's bum!! Habby flew a Hellcat fighter plane that didn't carry bombs. However, the Japs had no interest in justice, especially in the case of pilots, who were routinely condemned to death.

The Wall was outraged. 'The trouble with the Japs was that they just couldn't stand the thought of losing. Indiscriminate bombing! Just look at their track record', The Wall ranted. 'China and Korea for a start, and don't forget Pearl Harbor!'

At the war's end our military blokes gave us a form to fill in, asking for information about any of the inmates. At that time, most of us were only interested in one thing – going home – but I did write down what I knew of the Kiwi Fighter Pilot, Habby. I don't know if any action was taken as I wasn't asked anything further. It was not for almost fifty years that I finally discovered exactly who Habby was.

In 1993, I was invited to a lunch in Sydney by the Burma Star Association. Sitting opposite was an old friend, Stan Bryant-Smith, of 2/29 Battalion, who had suffered greatly as a POW with F Force on the Burma-Thai Railway. Beside him was another ex-POW, also from his unit. With so few members of the battalion, which was composed mostly of Victorians, living in Sydney, Stan and his friend attended functions together.

Stan introduced me to his mate – whose name was Billy Young.

We struck up an instant rapport, which intensified when Billy discovered I knew a great deal about Sandakan and the inmates of Outram Road Gaol. As the lunch progressed, Billy told me about a New Zealand pilot identified only as Habby, and wondered if I possibly identify him. As I had come across the story of the New Zealand pilots held at Outram Road in my research I was able to tell Billy his name.

A week or so after Pieter died, the Japs decided to concentrate us further by putting three to a cell. I discovered later that this was not because the Japs were short of room, but so that we would be easier to handle when the time came to carry out the Japanese version of the Final Solution: a solution that they expected to put into effect in these last months of our imprisonment. The guards were more surly and bad-tempered now, and often drew their fingers across their throats. We figured that there had been some very bad news from their war front. What it was, they weren't saying.

On 22 June 1945, at about the time the prisoners were moved three to a cell, the Japanese island of Okinawa fell into American hands, after a ferocious battle that took the lives of 110 000 Japanese, or about 90 per cent of their troops. As most had dug in, they were burnt alive with flame-throwers. Another 7400 Japanese were captured. The Okinawa action virtually eliminated Japanese home defences as almost 8000 planes were destroyed, or lost in kamikaze attacks. About 180 Japanese ships, including IJN Yamamoto, the largest battleship in the world, were sunk. Terrified civilians, certain from Japanese propaganda that anyone taken prisoner would be subjected to a terrible death, committed suicide in droves by jumping from high cliffs onto the rocks below.

That same day, US planes dropped 3000 tons of bombs onto munitions plants in Kobe, Osaka, Nagoya and Okayama.

The three of us who now shared the cell couldn't possibly have been more different in appearances and outlook, but we got on famously. Quartermaster Beech was British Army, right down to his toenails. Known to everyone as Q, he was an artilleryman. A big man, and big-boned with it. When he first came into the cell, I'd looked up at him and thought 'Gawd! Another bloody Pommy, and get a load of the size of this bloke'.

CHAPTER 12 Out of the shadows

Billy's new cellmate, Ernest Edward Beech, of the British 18th Division's 135 Field Regiment, was almost 41 years old. In August 1943 he'd been sent to Tamarkan in Thailand to work on the railway. His commanding officer was Colonel Philip Toosey, the British officer responsible for building the railway bridge over the River Kwai. *The Bridge on the River Kwai*, a completely fictionalised account of the bridge construction and its destruction, supposedly by an eccentric colonel named Nicholson, became a bestseller for writer Pierre Boulle in 1952. In 1957 a film of the same name, starring Alec Guinness as the colonel, won seven Oscars and was a smash hit at the box office. Believing the story to be true, tourists still flock to the River Kwai to see where the action took place.

Ernest Beech had arrived at Outram Road from Tamarkan on 19 August 1944, following his trial in Bangkok, to serve a four-year sentence for reading a newspaper. He was more fortunate than Lieutenant Colonel P W Parker, of the Indian Army, and two soldiers from 2 Loyal Battalion, R Hunt and I Willcocks, who were all convicted in January 1945 for committing the same offence. The colonel received five years. The other three men were sentenced to life.

After a lifetime spent on army parade grounds, Q was fairly set in his ways. His back, even then, was ramrod straight and with his chin tucked in I could almost see a swagger stick stuck under his arm. Whenever his number was called, his bare feet quivered and clicked to attention, purely out of habit, but once I managed to decipher the rapid, machine-gun delivery of his Yorkshire-cum-Parade-Ground diction he proved to be a first-rate bloke. Like breaking the Jap navy code, once the accent was deciphered I was able to tap into a wealth of information. The only problem was to make sure that there were no guards within coo-ee, as Q's whisper was equal to anyone else's roar.

Charlie, the other lodger, was Chinese. I don't remember who he had served with, but he must have been in one of the Pommy Volunteer outfits. As an English-speaking Chinese, Charlie was singled out very early for Japanese corrective measures and he had been in various detention centres on and off, stretching from Burma to Singapore Island. Short, plump and bubbling with optimism when he first arrived, Charlie brought a breath of fresh air to our jaded, war-weary cell. He'd been given ten years for whatever he'd done, but it didn't faze him. 'Not to worry', he said. 'The British will be back again, in no time at all.' However, like food, hope was in short supply, and it wasn't long before most of his exuberance evaporated, diminishing in proportion to his weight loss.

Preparations for the defence of the Island were escalating by the day, and we had become important cogs in the works, gainfully employed in the war effort.

Every day was now a 'work-hard day', with groups of stick men and sick stick men digging tunnels and clearing old, very old, ammo dumps. When we were not cleaning out neglected air-raid bunkers, we were clearing and cultivating every spare plot of ground that had not already been claimed. Planting seeds, digging holes, loading bombs and cutting trenches: the hills were alive with the sound of us making preparations to face the foe, working on Tojo's defences.

Digging defences

These blokes weren't going to let go, not without a fight. They obviously intended to hang on to their conquered lands, their fledgling Empire, and to fight with might and main. You had to give the buggers their due; they fought like a threshing machine, cutting and slashing at anyone and anything that got in its path.

The Allied forces, poised ready for the kill, were also busy, either fighting or consolidating their positions. The net was tightening, and this didn't augur well for us cave-dwellers, or for the thousands of other POWs on the island. Our future lay in jeopardy, as did the lives of millions of civilians throughout the entire Far East.

Unbeknown to the Allies, a terrible bloodletting was being planned by a frightened and cowardly enemy. With the Allied armies steadily and assuredly closing in, hundreds of POWs and thousands of civilian slaves, trapped in outlying camps, were destined to die. They were to perish with no regard for their wellbeing, in circumstances of unimaginable suffering.

Back in Outram Road we were still safe enough, if apprehensive, as we hadn't been out of our cells for some time and there was nothing coming through The Wall at all. The guards were just as quiet. They never told us why we were being ignored and had been sent to Coventry, but we knew from the looks on their faces that the Japs were getting their backsides kicked. They didn't like it, any more than we did in 1942.

The guards continued their regular beats but occasionally they'd stop and look through the slot, to threaten us with the old taunt '*Soona mati*'. Locked up and under the control of the Urry-Curry Mob, things could get decidedly crook, so we figured that it was not a good idea to yell 'Yah. Ha. You're getting licked'. No indeed, this was not the moment for such behaviour. It was a time for great diplomacy. So we sat quietly in our cells and crowed – softly. 'Drop dead, too', we'd whisper back. 'Go to hell', which of course, many of them did.

The Death House, just behind our cell block, had now become a haven for the Grim Reaper. Inside the building were several large holding cages, and it was in these that we learned that groups of very special Allied prisoners were being held: ten who had tried to blow up Japanese shipping, and a number of airmen, captured after their aircraft had been shot down.

The ten saboteurs were Australian and British commandos who had infiltrated Singapore waters on a second covert mission, Operation Rimau, following the success of the Jaywick raid the previous year. In October 1944 they had penetrated the waters off Singapore in a junk, intending to blow up or damage sixty enemy ships. The 23-man team had been within hours of executing the plan when they were spotted by a collaborator and forced to flee. All were either killed or captured. After preliminary interrogation, ten of the Rimau men, caught in and around the islands to the south-east of Singapore, were taken to Outram Road in mid-February 1945, where further 'investigations' were carried out. As the Kempeitai wished to keep them isolated from the other inmates during this time, they were placed two to a cell, according to rank, in the far end of the ground floor of Billy's block, in a special section reserved for 'spies' and airmen.

On 3 July, they were taken to Raffles College for trial, where all were found guilty of espionage and perfidy and sentenced to death. On their return to Outram Road, the commandant granted a request for them to be together, by transferring them to a large cell on the upper floor of the Death House. To prevent any contact with other prisoners, the front of the cell, composed entirely of bars, was draped with blankets.

Now that they had been condemned to death, their treatment changed dramatically, with the formerly meagre rations assuming feast-like proportions. They were also given cigarettes, tins of condensed milk, and blankets to make their bed-boards more comfortable.

Despite the attempt to prevent any contact with other prisoners, Bluey Rollason, on benki duty, managed to snatch a few words with them as he passed by. The last time he spoke to them was on 6 July, when they told him they were to be executed the following day.

The next morning the rest of the inmates were alerted that something was up by the huge kerfuffle that erupted as the guards tried to prevent anyone from seeing the men as they were led away. But as they were loaded into the van they were seen fleetingly by Bluey, whose guard was less than vigilant. He reported that if any of them were frightened, or even nervous, that they were about to keep an appointment with Death, they certainly did not show it, putting on an outstanding performance for the Japanese, laughing and joking as if they didn't have a care in the world.

The prisoners were beheaded on a piece of wasteland close to what is now the intersection of Clementi and Dover Roads, by lowly guards from the gaol, whose expertise with the sword left a great deal to be desired.

Colonel Mikizawa points out the Rimau graves to War Crimes investigator Major Wild, at the execution site

I didn't see the Rimau men in their cell or when they were taken away. Although we often worked near the building where they were held, and walked past it every day on our rounds with the toilet buckets, I had never been inside. On the day the ten were executed, however, the guards had been distracted and failed to ensure that the benki bucket in a cell holding a number of the airmen was emptied. While a couple of blokes were sent upstairs to clean out a couple of large cells, one of the new guards ordered our two Jap trusties to send me and MP to attend to the airmen's cell on the ground floor.

The Death House was very different from our block. The ground floor had several iron-barred holding cells, one of which held eight or nine American airmen, looking very much the worse for wear. A couple must have been wounded, as arms and legs were bandaged, and at least one other was lying down, looking very crook. The floor was in a mess, awash with overflowing sewage from the single, entirely inadequate toilet barrel. The place was flooded with it.

We rushed around like mad things. The Yanks must have thought that we were stark raving mad – and we were, but not in the way they assumed. We were just implementing our news-gathering routine; first of all create confusion, and then get the information. As mops swished and buckets sploshed, we learnt all that we could from them. Unfortunately, it wasn't much. With the guard and the two trusties yapping constantly at our heels, our opportunities were somewhat limited. We did manage to come up with the fact that they'd been in two B-29s that had been hit. A circled cross, chalked above their steel enclosure, the mark of death, told us of their intended fate. Obviously they didn't realise its significance, and for some reason or other the Japs hadn't told them.

The death cell

Execution was par for the course for many who fell into the hands of the Kempeitai. While it was especially true for pilots, the Kempeitai seemed to make very little distinction between military and civilian prisoners. In fact, the way in which local people were treated was almost unbelievable. Numbers were not a consideration – ones, twos, tens, hundreds or even thousands – it didn't make any difference. Anyone caught in their all-encompassing net was in big trouble.

Most of the atrocities carried out were by ordinary, everyday looking Japanese. Some looked innocent, as if butter wouldn't melt in their mouths. There really is no special training needed to make sadists out of ordinary people, once all sense of decency and fair play have been culled. On many occasions I overheard our guards boasting of their prowess with the sword, telling of how they had chopped the head off this one, or that one, and laughing about some other guard who had taken two or three swipes to get the job done. Yet they often described themselves as being honourable followers of Bushido.

For many years I winced when I heard remarks about honourable Japanese businessmen – comments made, as a rule, by people dazzled by the lure of the dollar bill. Greed was the common denominator for most of our enemy entrepreneurs, who have today evolved into multinational companies. I have often wondered what our reaction in Australia would have been if a German automobile manufacturer had come out with an Adolph Hitler sedan or a Marshall Goring four-wheel drive or, for the more discerning and fastidious driver, a Himmler sports car. Or perhaps, from Toyota or Mitsubishi – two firms that made fortunes using POW slave labour in Japan – a Tojo convertible or a Kempeitai coupe.

Finishing the defences was now a top priority. How the heck we matchsticks managed to get through the workload is a testament to the strength of the human frame. Now and again one or two of the older blokes keeled over, but generally speaking Death kept his distance. It was a Jap boot, or a sword stick, that we had to look out for.

Finally, the trench systems that criss-crossed the landscape and the tunnels dug into the hillsides were ready for occupation by the 60 000 fanatical Japanese troops who were prepared to die for their God Emperor, and to take us with them. We all knew we were in a no-win situation, irrespective of who won the war. If they won, we still had to survive long enough to finish our sentences; if our side won, the chances of survival were just as slim, because the Japs had indicated time and again that they no intention of allowing us to live, and with good reason. Dead men tell no tales.

Our one and only hope lay in a quick and decisive Allied victory. If the Allies attempted to invade Singapore, we figured it would be curtains for all of us. While there were no circled crosses chalked above our doors, we all knew we were marked down for extermination.

There is no shadow of a doubt that if the Allies had been forced into making a landing we would not have survived. The orders issued through the occupied areas showed that retaliation would have been swift, and final – and not only for us. Singapore could so easily have ended up like the Chinese city of Nanking, when Japanese troops raped and murdered tens of thousands of civilians over a six-week period in 1937–38.

The entire island was in a state of anxiety as people wondered where, and when, and what. Speculation and rumour abounded. We all trembled on a knife-edge of uncertainty, praying for a quick and resounding victory. Nothing less would do, and nothing else would save us. The Allies had to win.

Although caught up in the maelstrom of war, we were frustrated by our ignorance of its exact whereabouts. No prisoners had come in from Changi since April, so all we had to go on was the boasting of the guards. The war was never far from our minds and, as it became more strung out, survival became paramount. We were not at the front line, but we were under attack from the guns of time, from the crushing weight of the great stone walls, and from the battering-ram of hunger. Our only defence was the will to live; our only counterattack a sense of humour, along with the fortitude to keep going.

We humans manage to survive in times of great hardship because we are stronger than we think, and we suffer because we are weaker than we suppose. On this planet we are veritable gods. We can create and destroy at will, and at whim. The future is in our hands; it is entirely dependent upon our actions. We can blow the lot on one roll of the dice.

We have the power, but can we afford the price? During those dark days in Outram Road, I often thought of the time when we had we come across those sad remains near the Convent of the Little Sisters of the Poor.

The soldier on the stretcher and the bearers paid the fees
As did all those other dead, lying crushed beneath the trees.
Death came knocking loudly, beside the Convent's walls,
To collect his toll in payment for mankind's bloody sprees.

The one good thing about this particular time was that the Allied planes had complete control of the skies. The Jap Zeros no longer tried to intercept, and it was only every now and again that we'd hear the snap, crackle and pop of anti-aircraft fire. The war was drawing to a close and, while this is what we had hoped and prayed for, we had put our faith in rumours for so long that now it was actually happening we couldn't bring ourselves to believe it. While we were cheered by the thought that perhaps there were not many more laps to go, we were acutely aware of the hurdles that had to be overcome. For a start, there was a huge, iron-banded door standing between us and freedom. We wanted to throw our caps into the air and laugh, but were sobered by the knowledge that it was not yet over, and we could die laughing. It is all so long ago now, seventy years in fact, that only the few of us still alive know what the consequences may have been had the Yanks not dropped those atomic bombs in time.

As hostilities entered their sixth year, the Allies had prepared for the inevitable invasion of Japan by firebombing Tokyo and other major cities. The war in Europe ended on 8 May, but the Japanese refused to accede to Allied demands for unconditional surrender. A further demand on 26 July was also rejected, despite the threat of 'prompt and utter destruction'. Consequently, on 6 August, an American B-29 bomber, flying from the United States Air Force Base on the Mariana Islands, exploded an atomic bomb over the city of Hiroshima, killing well over 100 000 of the inhabitants. With the Japanese still refusing to surrender, a second bomb was dropped over Nagasaki three days later, wiping out an estimated 40 000–80 000 people. Many more died in the days that followed from the effects of radiation sickness and burns, exacerbated by malnutrition. It took the combined effect of these two bombs, plus a declaration of war on Japan by the Soviet Union, to finally bring an end to Japanese hostilities.

Then came the morning all of Asia, Australia and the South Pacific remember. The fifteenth day of August, 1945. In Outram Road it was early morning, a normal hot and muggy morning just like any of the other one thousand hot and muggy mornings we had so far spent as guests of the Emperor.

I was sharing my cell with two Tamil Indians. Both were mean, dirty buggers. One of them was riddled with the pox and clinging precariously to life. The relationship between me and the other one was strained, as he had a real chip on his shoulder about white-skinned people. One day, while pointing at my legs, tanned and brown from working in the gardens and outdoors generally, he sneered 'And you say you white man'. I don't really know why I reacted, but I pulled up the leg of my shorts to expose a thigh so lily-white that it even surprised me. The Tamil never said another word. The loss of face was too great.

From the scratches on my wall, I knew the date. It seemed just like an ordinary day, but two events were to unfold that were to make it anything but ordinary. When our bowls of water were delivered after the noon meal they contained not water, but milk! This was not entirely unheard of, because the whole gaol including the Japs upstairs had been given milk several times before, on what we assumed must be the Emperor's birthday or to celebrate some special event.

However, as it had been a long time since our last drink of milk, we wondered what had prompted today's issue. As usual, it was only milk from a can, but it was still milk, and by Crikey, this time it tasted wonderful. Pure nectar of the gods. I lapped at mine like a cat to make it last as long as possible. We were still digesting this amazing treat when The Wall came to life with something equally amazing, and also very significant: the upstairs mob had missed out!

The next extraordinary event came by airmail. A plane flew over, and across, and around the island, time and time again, buzzing like a bumblebee, but there was no response from the Jap defences. Nothing at all. Not a peep. Not a sound. The Wall, realising the implications, went frantic and our spirits soared in anticipation. My Indian companions also realised the implications and I suddenly went from White Bastard to Sahib.

With a high like that, whatever follows is sure to be a letdown, and it was. It was a colossal anticlimax, for nothing further happened. The steady flip-flop of the guards' thongs as they slapped their way along the concrete passageway was the only sound. No aeroplanes, no cannons, no guns. Just Bloody Thongs. Cell politics were also badly affected and I slipped from Sahib back to White Bastard.

Three days passed by. Three more scratches on the wall soured any memory of the milk. The prison was quiet, so quiet that when I heard the sound of raised voices and multiple footsteps, curiosity overtook me and I looked through the slot in the door. A prison warden, a big bloke with moustache and glasses, appeared to be engaged in some kind of heated discussion with several Japanese, distinguishable as Kempeitai officers by their black uniforms. With them were a number of European prisoners. As they passed by, one who had a Maori look about him caught my eye. Was it Habby, the Kiwi flier? It looked like him. I didn't get a chance to make up my mind for sure because at that point the Tamil who spoke English pushed me aside. By the time he had finished gawking, the group had passed out of my range of vision. In any case, it was too risky to linger at the slot, in case a guard came along.

Although Billy cannot swear to it, it seems almost certain that the prisoner whom he saw that day saw was Habby. The war was definitely over, but the story of Habby and his companions did not have a happy ending.

After the nine British and New Zealand airmen were shot down and captured, several junior Japanese officers had unsuccessfully pressed for their immediate execution, but their superiors had sent the pilots for trial, a decision that was not well received.

On 18 August, following the news that atomic bombs had been dropped on Japan, and that the Emperor had unconditionally surrendered, it appears that smouldering resentment among the junior officers had erupted into fury. It also seems that, over what appear to be the protests of the warden, all nine airmen were removed from the gaol by the Kempeitai and taken to Changi Beach, where they were beheaded and their bodies sunk in a weighted boat in deep water.

When senior officers learned of the illegal executions they decided it would be prudent to keep the matter quiet. Subsequently, the official Japanese report accounting for the deaths stated that 'a boat sailed from Singapore carrying these nine British airmen to Japan and the boat met aerial bombings off Cam Ranh [Vietnam] and was lost, together with the entire personnel on board'.

The three officers responsible for the executions, Lieutenant Mayashita, Captain Ikeda and Major Kataoka, later committed suicide after admitting that the airmen had been beheaded on Changi Beach. Evidently in an attempt to conceal the fact that the beheadings had taken place three days after their Emperor had capitulated, they stated the atrocity had taken place on 15 August, the day of the surrender.

The story has been muddied somewhat by reports that gaol inmates, sent to clean one of the large cells at about the same time as the Rimau men were executed, had said that it was awash with blood and the floor strewn with blood-soaked clothing. Other prisoners reported that they had observed shrouded bodies, placed on boards, being removed from the gaol. The dates on which these various events took place are not clear. From the available evidence it now seems that, on the day the Rimau men were executed, three large cells were cleaned: the cell Billy cleaned that was awash with sewage; the cell holding the Rimau men; and a third cell in which several men seem to have been beheaded. It is possible that the third cell held a group of Chinese who had been found guilty of carrying out the Jaywick raid in 1943. Although the Rimau men who had taken part in that raid confessed that they were the culprits, it did not save the Chinese. The Japanese insisted that the executions be carried out, rather than admit that the Japanese judicial system was flawed.

The next morning, the 19th day of August, a key turned in the iron lock and the door swung silently inwards, just an inch or two. Cautiously, I opened it wider and took a look. Something was out of whack. The two guards, standing on the opposite side of Broadway, were not wearing their usual swords. The only things they had with them were keys.

'Koi!' The command that we had heard so often, and for so long, rang out along the passageway. 'Koi!'

Out from the cells we came, stumbling and shuffling, uncertainty making us timid and fearful; afraid to believe, afraid to accept the evidence. Wanting and hoping, and yet afraid. We had hoped for this day for so long and, now it had finally come, we were petrified that it might not be true, after all.

I went over to MP and said, for the umpteenth time, 'I think this is it. This is the real thing.' Always the super pessimist, MP replied, 'Now then Billy, don't give me another one of those old cock and bull stories about the Yanks landing at Penang.'

Further conversation was interrupted by the well-known cry of '*Kora! Hanashi nay no, binta no*', as we were herded to a table near the exit door. Behind it sat the Commandant. Speaking through an interpreter, he announced, 'Today we are sending you back to Changi Prisoner of War Camp.' To which he added the face-saving 'But you must come back later, to complete your sentence'.

And that was how we received the momentous news that the war was over. We were free at last. But for so many of my mates it had come too late.

We'd actually been free for four days, but who was counting? One minute we were prisoners, with years left to serve. The next we were being told we were free, and in such an oblique manner that it took a while to sink in that the war was really over. It was finished, ended, and we were free, let loose, out of bondage, slaves no longer. No drum rolls, no trumpets blaring. Just a few bland words.

One of the guards opened the outer door of the cell block, and we filed out into the courtyard that had witnessed so much. My eyes were like magnifying glasses, taking in every little detail: the concrete slab where we had so often sat, scratching away while waiting for the disso bath; the powerline that the two Jap prisoners had supposedly climbed down in their escape attempt, and which we had seen lying dangling and broken the next day. I'd often thought about that wire. Did it break on their way down and, if not, did they get away?

I looked over to the retaining wall, along which we had worked for so many months making ropes. All those ropes, where are they now? And there, way up on the bank, the golden fruit of the paw-paw still tempted. I did grab one as we moved further along, but a guard took it from me, the rotten sod. There was one spot along the bank that still stood out – the scar that marked the filled-in shooting gallery where they had executed The General.

As we moved on, we were joined by the group of American airmen, saved from death by the sudden end to the war.

It seems that the ten who were liberated that day were among the few aircrew to beat the death sentence. All other US airmen captured near Singapore were executed, including the crew of a B-29 shot down by a Kamikaze-class destroyer. Beheaded at the Nee Soon Rifle Range on about 4 August 1945, they were buried alongside fourteen other airmen, including eight shot down in a PBY 4 plane, executed at the same spot earlier in the year. On 20 August, five days after Japan surrendered, the remains of the 22 victims were exhumed, incinerated on the parade ground and thrown into the Straits of Johor in a futile attempt to cover up the atrocity. Post-war, as war crimes investigators were unable to determine who had given the orders to execute, those found guilty were sentenced to imprisonment ranging from just two to eight years.

I have often wondered what those Yanks must have thought when they saw us coming towards them: skinny sticks of humanity chattering in a multitude of tongues, ears flapping, eyes popping and arms waving, all yelling 'It's over, it's over, the bloody war is over!'

By now the guards had given up trying to contain our excitement and, except for a last *'Kora!'* or two, that was it. It was a big temptation, but we thought it best not to remind them about the Urry-Curry bit.

We stopped off at the gaol office where, to my surprise, I was handed my battered old haversack, which I had not seen since Sandakan and which must have followed me from prison to prison. I checked the contents. Everything was there: my blue-striped pyjama top and the shorts made by cutting two holes in a kit bag for my legs, both spattered with the dried blood of the hundreds of bedbugs I had squashed in Kuching; the Log Cabin tobacco tin containing the inch-long sliver of shrapnel that had given me my war wound; and a couple of Malay coins.

As we finally passed through the gate I looked at Charlie the Chinese bloke and said, 'Well Charlie old mate, at last it's over'. 'Yes', he replied, adding in his most hangdog manner, 'and with the bloody Japs still owing me eight years of free board and lodging.' Then the creases in the skin of his face quadrupled into the greatest smile as the natural optimism of a born-again fatalist shone through, as the main gates swung open to let in the light of a free country. We were out of the dark age, out from under the feet of the tyrant, finally free.

Another inmate who had made it out alive was Becky Sharpe. Bloated with beriberi, his actual weight was less than 25 kilograms, and he was so weak that his mates were carrying him. As the group passed through the archway of the main gate, Becky saw the sign Outram Road Prison above it, and demanded that his friends put him down. He then fulfilled the vow he had made three years before, and took his faltering steps to freedom.

How could anyone begin to describe that first new day and give it its full due? To convey what it meant to be back among the living, to be reunited with one's own, and to revel with them in the joy of being free. The emotions were many and varied. Relief was there, along with exhilaration and joy, tempered by the sadness of so many spaces among the ranks and the ghostly images of absent friends who would never come back. It was all too much to assimilate, but we greedily grabbed at it all. Gorging ourselves with freedom, we needed time to let the day digest.

We were loaded onto a bus for the drive out to Changi: not to Selarang Barracks, but to the gaol! Well, it wasn't really a gaol any more. It had been full of civilian internees when we left for Sandakan, but they had been moved in May 1944. Since then, the gaol and its surrounding area had been converted into a large POW camp, with dozens of atap huts outside the actual walls supplying additional accommodation.

Riding in the bus with us to Changi was a ring-in – Becky Sharpe. He had been about to board the Pommy bus taking the British Outram Road blokes to a POW hospital at Woodlands, out near the causeway, when MP and I stopped him. 'Come with us, Becky', we said. 'Come with us to Changi. The food will be a bloody sight better there than at any Pommy camp.' He didn't need persuading. All the Poms knew that Aussie tucker was superior by far to any rations they might expect. So Becky came with us, an honorary Aussie.

Most of the route from Outram Road to Changi retraced the path the blokes had taken on that long walk to captivity in February 1942. Not a lot had changed. The girls who plied their trade in Lavender Street were back in business, and there didn't seem to be a great deal of damage to this part of the island, despite the recent bombing. St Patrick's College, where I had been taken in the ambulance for treatment, had survived, seemingly without a scratch.

After what seemed an age, the truck finally ground to a halt, and there was Paddy O'Toole, with his great loveable face beaming with joy. I will never forget the look of compassion as he lifted me gently to the ground and welcomed me back home, to what was left of the battalion. The ambulance men wanted to cart me off to the hospital ward, but I wouldn't have a bar of it, not just yet. I had mates to see, yarns to swap, old friendships to reignite.

Paddy told me had been sent to Thailand with F Force to work on the railway. They'd had a dreadful time, the worst experience of all the work parties there. We both mourned the loss of many good friends who died on that railway of death. They reckon it was a life for every sleeper. So many faces missing. Too many.

In the months that we had been imprisoned in Outram Road, MP had reflected on our predicament many times. 'If only we hadn't gone outside the wire that day, Billy', he'd lamented. 'We'd be back with all our mates at Sandakan, having a great time.'

We had had no idea that Dobbo, Bob Shipsides, Jimmy Finn, Harry and the other Dead End Kids were all gone; that nothing we had endured at Outram Road could possibly compare to what had happened in Borneo. Sandakan was not a bad camp when we left, so MP and I were sure most of them would have made it. It was not for some weeks that we began to learn the awful, devastating truth.

Of the almost 2500 POWs at Sandakan, only six, all Aussies, would come out alive. A whopping 1400 had died at the main camp, murdered outright or killed indirectly from the effects of disease, starvation and neglect. Another 1000 had been sent to Ranau on a series of marches across 250 kilometres of crocodile-infested swamps and mountainous, jungle-covered terrain. Anyone who could not keep up, Jap and POW alike, was killed. The rest died in appalling conditions at various sub-camps. The last fifteen, including Doc Oakeshott, who had played cards with me at Tampoi when I was hospitalised with tinea, were shot dead near Ranau, twelve days after the war ended. Not one of the Poms made it.

But MP and I had survived, and so had Paddy, and now here he was at this special time of celebration and jubilation, to meet and greet, and see to the needs of a mate.

On that first magical evening of freedom we wandered over to the barbed-wire fence that separated the camp from the beach. After strolling along the water's edge, feeling the warm, gentle waves tickle our feet, we made our way back to the dry sand and sat. We sat there all through that night, beneath the light of a huge moon and millions of stars, marvelling at the beauty of the tropical heavens, and listening to the soft, lapping sounds of an ocean at peace.

No one said a word.

We were far too busy.

Looking, and smelling, and feeling.

EPILOGUE

AFTERWARDS

After a spell in the POW hospital at Changi, where he received treatment for his multiple ailments and was placed on a nourishing diet, Billy was well enough to be repatriated to Australia. On 15 September an ambulance took him to the harbour, where his stretcher was deposited on the deck of the hospital ship Oranje, along with a brand-new American kitbag containing an aircraft compass and presents for his family. Noticing the bag at Billy's feet, a passing seaman removed it, saying it had to be fumigated. It was a con. Billy never saw his beautiful new bag, or its contents, again.

Luckily, he did have some souvenirs left to take home to show Nana. Still safely tucked beneath his head was his old haversack with the tobacco tin holding his precious shrapnel splinter, the bug-and-blood-stained pyjama jacket, and his POW card 515 retrieved from outside his cell.

After a tumultuous welcome in Darwin, and a picnic by the beach for the returning POWs, Oranje sailed to Sydney via Brisbane. Waiting for Billy at Pyrmont wharf with a leave pass organised was Aunty Ilma, who whisked him away for lunch at Romano's, a top restaurant in the city.

The ship's next and final port of call was Melbourne. As soon as the vessel docked on 30 September, the POWs were besieged by the media, which included an outside broadcast unit equipped for live transmissions. As Billy was carried down the gangplank, the radio journalist shoved a microphone the size of a football under his nose, asking his name and how old he was. Learning that he was only nineteen, and assuming that the patient was a member of the ship's crew, the reporter was about to move onto a more interesting target when Billy put him right, explaining he was definitely a POW and that he had joined up at the age of fifteen. Fifteen! The reaction from the public was immediate. For the five days he was in hospital, being treated for hookworm and beriberi, Billy was something of a celebrity, receiving visits, cards and letters from complete strangers.

Homecoming

Discharged from Heidelberg Repatriation Hospital, he was flown to Launceston, and then to Hobart for further treatment there. Finally, six days before Christmas, he was discharged from the army and allowed to go home to the family at New Town. Displaying uncharacteristic solicitude, Nana asked what Billy would like for dinner. Remembering the pact made with Pieter in Outram Road Gaol, there was only one possible answer – home-made pea and ham soup.

Billy remained in Hobart for the immediate post-war period, but made occasional trips interstate, visiting Big Bill's former fiancée Marie and the now very elderly Pop Jepson in Sydney, and also travelling to Melbourne for battalion reunions with old mates like Paddy O'Toole. On one of these trips, in late 1948, Billy met up with fellow Sandakan and Outram Road inmate Norm Morris. Now a proud father, Norm had brought along his baby son, who was giving a fine demonstration of how powerful his lungs were. Billy and his mates teased Norm unmercifully about the racket, unaware that in the 1960s and 70s the bawling baby, Russell Morris, would become such a successful songwriter and singer that he would be inducted into the ARIA Hall of Fame in 2008.

After qualifying as a carpenter in Hobart, Billy married in the early 1950s and fathered four children. But the trauma of his imprisonment played havoc with personal *relationships and he and his wife eventually parted company. Unlike many ex-POWs who suffered at the hands of the Japanese, Billy was able to work through his post-traumatic grief and torment to some extent, by writing poetry to honour his dead mates and painting pictures depicting some of his experiences. Looking back on his long and productive life, Billy has never forgotten just how fickle was the finger of fate that allowed him to survive, against all odds, when his comrades did not.*

> *Where jungle canopy blocks sunlight from the ground*
> *Where towering mountain peaks lie covered in cloud*
> *Where foul black swamp and deadliness abound*
> *There, falling leaf and twig became their shroud.*
>
> *From Sandakan they came away, stumbling on until they fell.*
> *There along the track they lay, leaving only six to tell.*
>
> *That track is silent now, their voices stilled*
> *Those scars at Ranau the years have filled.*
> *The signs of massacre have all but gone*
> *Leaving those of us who mourn*
> *To reflect upon.*

One of those left to mourn with Billy was MP Brown. He had reached Changi from Outram Road in such poor physical condition that he was not allowed to return home immediately. Two days before Billy sailed, MP found himself on board the hospital ship Manunda, bound for a large army field hospital in Labuan and three weeks of further rest and recuperation before tackling the long voyage back to Australia. MP's legs never fully recovered from his tropical ulcers or the battering he had received at the boiler house. When he and Billy met up again, some years later, Billy reminded his friend that MP owed him a beer.

'What for?' he asked.

'For saving your life.'

Remembering the countless times that he had bemoaned their fate in Outram Road, regretting bitterly that he had ever tried to leave Sandakan, MP thought for moment, before grudgingly conceding that Billy had indeed saved his life.

Inadvertently.

Not long after this meeting MP met with a fatal accident. After surviving the horrors of POW imprisonment, his life ended at 8.40 on the morning of 23 October 1954 when he was electrocuted, the result of touching exposed live wires on the switch of an electric mower while mowing the lawn of the boarding house in which he lived with his wife, Valeria, in Highgate Hill, Brisbane.

Twenty-four of the thirty Australians sent to Outram Road from Sandakan survived the ordeal. Two (Private E Allen and Sapper D Marshall) died in the gaol. The other four (Sapper R Davis, Corporals W Fairy and A Small, and Driver N Shelley) died after being transferred to Changi Camp.

Jimmy Darlington, after serving his six-month imprisonment at Outram Road, was liberated from Changi Camp with the others in early September 1945 and returned home to Barraba, in country New South Wales. In 1976 he fell asleep while smoking in bed and, with his wife, perished in the fire that gutted his caravan home.

One Outram Road inmate who survived against all odds was Englishman Becky Sharpe. He was admitted to hospital on arrival at Changi and was too sick to leave his bunk to go down to the beach with Billy on the first night of liberation. The next morning Billy and the other Outram Road inmates were also admitted to hospital.

Shortly after admission, while paying a visit to the latrines, known as 'boreholes', Becky collapsed. The fluid trapped in his tissues, which had inflated his limbs like little fat sausages, now began to pour from his body. When Billy and the others from the ward arrived at the latrine, Becky was sprawled on the ground, as deflated as a limp balloon.

During the 48 hours that he was unconscious, the doctors worked feverishly to save his life. When he came to, he saw a padre sitting at the end of the bunk and he thought he'd died and gone to heaven. Later, a corporal arrived with 38 letters from his mother. Refusing to believe that her much-loved son was dead, she had written to him every month for more than three years. It was only now, on reading her letters, that Becky, who had endured so much without wallowing in one skerrick of self-pity, allowed himself the luxury of weeping.

When Billy was allowed to visit the patient, he could hardly believe his eyes. Becky was little more than a skin-coated skeleton. But his eyes burned with passion, leaving no one in any doubt that here was a true survivor.

His cheeky grin and indomitable spirit were captured for posterity by a press photographer, who snapped the emaciated but stoic Englishman on his bunk, propped against Billy's pillow. The photograph was flashed around the world and remains, to this day, one of the most powerful images of World War II.

It is also one of the most misleading. This photograph, along with those of other Outram Road survivors and prisoners recently returned from the horrors of the Burma-Thai Railway, were certainly taken in Changi. However, the skeletal creatures depicted in the newspapers and on newsreels were not representative of Changi inmates, and have resulted in the camp being universally described as a notorious hellhole, with the very word Changi synonymous with unimaginable suffering. As those who were fortunate enough to remain in Changi for the whole of the war readily admit, compared to other POW camps, 'Changi was like heaven'.

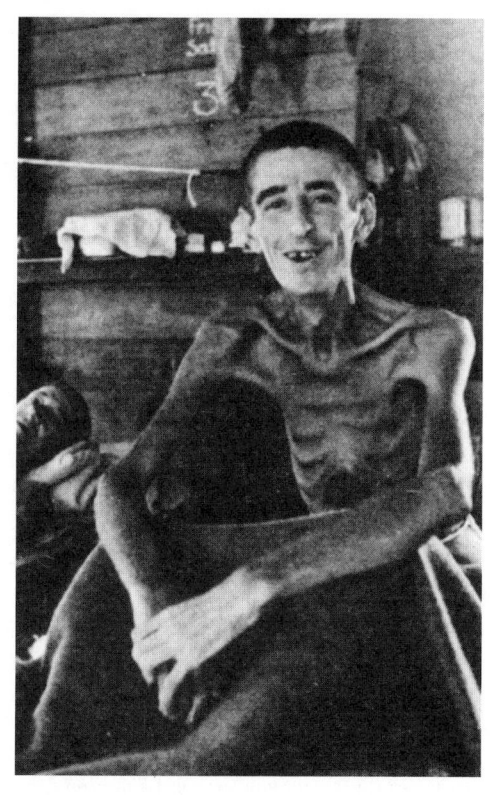

Changi – Becky Sharpe

When Billy last saw Becky Sharpe he was extremely thin. It therefore came as no surprise to hear that Becky had died on a ship somewhere in the Indian Ocean, en route to England, and had been buried at sea. Saddened by the loss of his plucky friend, Billy penned a few lines in his memory.

He always had a smile,
No matter what.
A friendly nod,
A cheeky grin.
He never made it home.
Buried at sea.
Canvas shrouds.
My friend within.

So it was with a feeling of absolute joy and amazement that in 2002, almost sixty years later, Billy learned that Becky was not dead after all. I was delighted to report, on returning from a visit to Singapore, that not only was Jack 'Becky' Sharpe alive and well, but that he had been to Changi in February that year while on a pilgrimage to commemorate the 60th Anniversary of the Fall of Singapore.

Outram Road Gaol had long been demolished, but Becky visited the museum at Changi Gaol to have his photo taken alongside the famous 1945 image, on display in the Museum's gallery. This was to be Becky's only return visit to Singapore. He died the following August at the age of 88 in his home town of Leicester, just two days shy of the 57th anniversary of the end of World War II.

To Billy's dismay, none of the Dead End Kids who remained at the Sandakan Camp were alive at war's end. Annihilation there was absolute. Of the more than 1000 POWs forced overland to Ranau on three separate death marches, just six Australians who escaped, including Bill's mate Keith Botterill, lived to tell the tale. The escapees owed their lives to Dusun villagers, who harboured them at huge risk to themselves and, indeed, their entire community. The final death toll from the Sandakan camp and the marches was 2428 – 1787 Australians and 641 British.

In late June 1945, Billy's best mate, Harry Longley, had arrived at Ranau with 183 survivors from the 500-plus second death march, after a trek that had lasted four weeks. Wracked with malaria, and close to starvation, he collapsed at a jungle camp five miles south of the village on 5 July while working as a coolie labourer for the Japanese. Survivor Keith Botterill, who was with him, propped him against a tree and placed the stub of a cigarette in the mouth of his nicotine-addicted friend before moving on. Not long afterwards, shots were heard.

In June 1943, Joey Crome and Wally 'Henry' Ford were in a group of five Dead Enders transferred for disciplinary reasons to the Kuching camp, where the chances of survival were infinitely better than at Sandakan. Hilton 'Terry' Risley, Sid Outram, Eric 'Mo' Davis and all but five of the 150 Australian officers survived.

Unlike Sandakan, Kuching's Batu Lintang Camp was large, with reasonable facilities. Prisoners and internees suffered varying degrees of hardship, and food became scarcer in 1945 but for anyone not required to work conditions were much better than at any other camp, apart from Changi.

With nothing to do other than tending a vegetable garden near their huts, Australian officers alleviated their boredom by joining debating and social clubs, forming a most professional concert party, borrowing books from a 2000-volume library and attending lectures at a 'university' run by highly qualified officers who offered courses in a large range of subjects. The tuition was of such a high standard that the 'students', who sat for exams marked by their lecturers, received signed certificates attesting to their

Kuching – Mo Davis and others

competence, enabling them to enter the next year of university when they reached home.

Although the food ration was depleted towards the end of their imprisonment, Major Rayson, the senior Australian medical officer, recorded that the calorie count for his fellow officers in mid-1945 was 2600 calories per day, well above starvation level. The rice ration was about 170 grams: two-and-a-half times the amount issued at Sandakan in 1945. To do their cooking, and carry out general duties, officers appointed some of the AIF's rank and file to act as their batmen.

The first Australian death in Kuching was not until July 1945, when Lieutenant Peter Stewart succumbed to beriberi. Three other officers died in August-September, just prior to liberation, from dysentery, tuberculosis and a heart attack. The official cause of death on 27 July of the fifth officer, a captain aged 27, was malaria. However, his fellow officers admitted later that, along with one or two others, he had been severely ostracised for arranging to obtain extra food from the camp kitchen. By the time his persecutors desisted with their tormenting, it was too late. Overcome with remorse and shame, he deliberately starved himself to death.

Another Australian officer, a 25-year-old captain, who proudly declared himself to be the fittest and strongest man in the Kuching camp, had no such qualms. As he freely disclosed in a personal account of his experiences, his vastly superior physical condition was due to the fact that he had managed to secretly gain admission into Kuching's black market: the only Australian officer to do so.

Having struck up a friendship with the Dutch officer supplying food to the ring, the officer was given a favourable exchange rate of $10 to the Australian pound, instead of the usual $3. As he candidly recorded, 'My worries were over from the food point of view, as I was obtaining more than double the normal ration. The Dutchman would cook the food and pass it under the fence after lights out and I had to eat it, maintaining the strictest secrecy.'

This particular captain, who was posted to the Australian Army Service Corps, had been well supplied with food for most of his imprisonment. Before the long march out to Changi following Singapore's fall, he had loaded his suitcase, filled with clothing and 4000 cigarettes, onto an AASC truck ferrying food supplies to the camp. With cigarettes in huge demand, it appears that he had no trouble procuring additional food, and in such quantities that, while the medical staff was predicting serious health consequences for the prison population unless the ration was improved, he and four fellow officers were 'living like fighting cocks' – so much so that they had 'all put on a lot of weight and were literally rolling in fat'.

Some of the surviving officers. The fittest man in the camp is easily identifiable

At Sandakan, his batman Jim Warren, who was heavily involved in the black market there, had supplied his boss with food throughout his period of imprisonment. These extra rations, and the excellent officers' canteen at the B Force camp, allowed the officer and several friends, from their monthly incomes of $10–$15, to live well during the last nine months they were at Sandakan. Unlike other officers who had a good rapport with their men, even to the extent of providing them with food purchased with their own money from the officers' canteen, this particular officer experienced no guilt, then or later. In an interview in May 1996 he declared: 'My men didn't care about me, and I didn't care about them'. Such behaviour was not limited to Sandakan. A study carried out some years ago by Professor Joan Beaumont revealed that abuse of officer privilege was common in Japanese POW camps – a conclusion endorsed by Billy Young, who had experienced it first-hand.

Joey Crome

Although no Australian 'other ranks' died in Kuching, in the latter part of 1944 Dead Enders Joey Crome and Wally Ford were among 300 POWs (mainly British) transferred from Sandakan and Kuching to Labuan Island to build an airstrip. Both died of starvation and malaria. Not one of the prisoners placed on this draft survived.

Another Dead Ender, Trevor 'Dobbo' Dobson, whose rendition of the nonsensical ditty 'The Ringle-Rangle Ram' had so entertained his hut mates, died at the Sandakan camp on 10 June 1945, from malaria and starvation, which also claimed the life of Bob Shipsides, Billy's much-loved mentor, on 3 April, and boxer Snowy Bryant in March. Keith 'Shearer' Gillett, Snowy's trainer and bankrupt promoter of the 'Big Fight', survived the rigours of the first death march. He reached Ranau in February 1945, but died from beriberi the following month.

Gunboat Simpson, who had run the gambling den beneath the hut, perished on the second march to Ranau, but not at the hands of the killing squad ordered to dispose of anyone, Japanese or prisoner, who faltered. True to form, he wandered away into the jungle on 2 June, near Mile 20, to die on his own terms.

Two of Billy's other hut mates, Bill 'Cookee' Cooke and the good-natured George Plunkett, both of whom had survived attempts by Japanese troops to behead them in Singapore, were too ill to go on the marches. Left behind at Sandakan after the second march departed for Ranau on 29 May, they died in June 1945 within four days of each other: Bill on the 10th from malaria and George on the 14th from dysentery.

George Plunkett

Australian investigators actively pursued those responsible for these, and hundreds of other deaths, with dogged persistence. At least 444 of the 898 Japanese on the Borneo 'wanted list' were rounded up and arrested. Of the remaining 545, 36 had died, 16 had left Borneo, 33 could not be traced and 131 had gone underground, using false identities. Of those tried specifically for crimes against Sandakan POWs, eight were executed and at least 55 sentenced to terms of imprisonment ranging from two years to life.

Facing an inevitable death sentence, Colonel Suga, Commandant of All the Borneos, tried to take the 'honourable' course of action, but was only partially successful in an attempt to commit suicide by cutting his throat with a table knife. His batman finished him off by hitting him over the head with a sand-filled waterbottle before lighting a mosquito bomb in place of the fragrant, but unprocurable, incence that his superior had requested. At least Suga had the courage of his convictions. Despite their constant boasting that they would kill themselves rather than surrender, no Japanese soldier or guard connected to the Sandakan story did so.

Captain Hoshijima, who had reduced the rations at Sandakan to starvation level, withheld medical supplies, sanctioned the first death march and permitted many acts of brutality to take place, was found guilty of murder at a war crimes trial held in Labuan. Sentenced to death, he was hanged at Rabaul in New Britain in April 1946. Defiant to the end, as he mounted the scaffold he bit the hand of the Australian provost marshal escorting him, drawing blood. The last words Hoshijima heard as the trapdoor opened

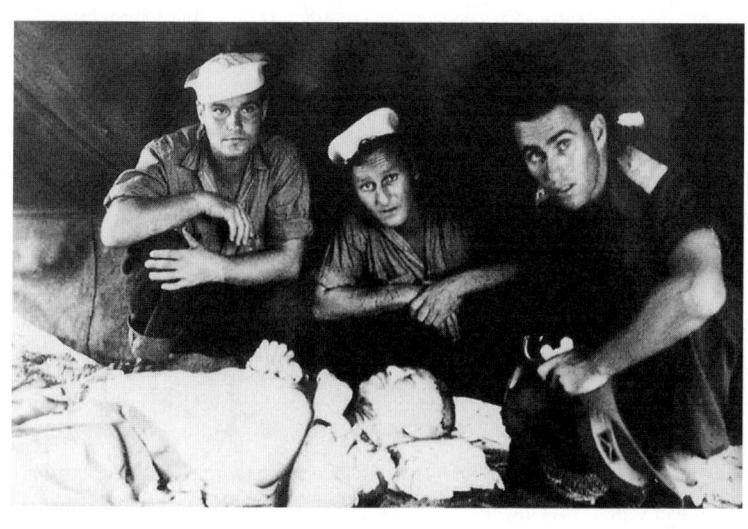

Mo Davis' American hut mates from USS *Houston*, Harry McManus (left) and Harry Stone, inspect the body of Colonel Suga, shortly after his suicide

were those of his executioner: 'This is for the Aussies you killed at Sandakan'.

Even though Hoshijima had bashed him severely, Billy was surprised to learn that the commandant had been hanged, as he found it hard to reconcile the Hoshijima he had known with someone who had gouged out the eyes of two prisoners. If the accusations were true, Billy thought, Hoshijima certainly deserved to be executed – until he discovered from Keith Botterill that Billy himself and MP Brown were the supposed victims. Worried that this 'evidence' had played too big a part in bringing down the death penalty, Billy was relieved to learn that Hoshijima had been found guilty of multiple crimes, including cutting the rations to zero, condoning the first death march, and withholding lifesaving drugs and medicines as well as Red Cross parcels.

Billy's personal tormentor, Second Lieutenant Moritake, who had orchestrated the terrible beating at the boiler house, and inflicted pain and death on many other prisoners, died from malaria at the Japanese barracks at Sandakan in July 1945. Dressed in full ceremonial uniform, he was buried in the compound, not far from the administrative office.

Fukishima Maseo, The Black Bastard, who had made the lives of POWs a misery at the airfield, was sentenced to fifteen years for the murder of POWs at Ranau. Survivors Keith Botterill and Bill Moxham, furious that he had not received a death sentence for this crime, failed in an attempt to have him found guilty of the murder of another POW, on the grounds that there was insufficient evidence regarding actual cause of death. Determined to see him hang, the pair recruited Bill Sticpewich to their cause. Although he was not there at the time, Sticpewich declared that he was, and a retrial was ordered so he could give his 'evidence'. A powerful performer in the witness box, Sticpewich convinced the Tribunal of Fukishima's act of murder, which carried the death penalty. The sentence was never promulgated. As the reviewing legal authorities in Australia pointed out, it was a case of 'double jeopardy' – no one can be tried twice for the same crime. Like all Japanese war criminals sentenced to terms of imprisonment, including those with life sentences, Fukishima was out of gaol by 1958.

Forty-three Japanese from Outram Road Gaol were tried in Singapore between August and October 1946 for causing the deaths of at least seventeen prisoners of war and 22 civilians. Four of the accused were acquitted. Five were sentenced to death by hanging, five to life imprisonment and the remainder to terms ranging from fifteen years to twelve months. All those sent to gaol were released by 1958.

No one was brought to trial for executing the ten Rimau men held in Outram Road Gaol. A war crimes investigation concluded that they had been legally beheaded after being found guilty on spying charges. In any case, those involved had already been hanged or were serving gaol terms.

The bodies of the Australians involved in the Sandakan underground plot and who died while at Outram Road Gaol or after transfer to Changi were recovered and buried in Kranji War Cemetery, Singapore. The remains of Billy's cellmate, Pieter, were also recovered and taken home to Surabaya for burial. By this time, his family members were all dead or had moved to Holland, following the fight for independence by the Indonesian people. No one who was close to Pieter had ever visited the grave until in 2015, Robbert van de Rijdt, Director of Dutch War Graves Commission (Oorlogsgravenstichting) in Indonesia, made a special pilgrimage from Jakarta to the grave in Kembang Kuning cemetery in Surabaya to lay a floral tribute for Billy, in memory of his friend and 'of the wonderful meals of your imagination that we shared during those dark days of long ago.'

Billy has outlived all his comrades and all his persecutors. Now the last soldier from Sandakan and the only one from Outram Road Gaol still alive, Billy lives in contented retirement in suburban Sydney, painting, writing and recording his experiences for posterity and to keep the torch burning for his mates.

Passing years do not erase
Scars from horrendous days
Of black-hearted samurai
With barbarous ways.

Yet time's layered swirl
Flowed to encurl
Such bitter memories
Within a priceless pearl.

Hardened in the fires of war
Prison camps from Singapore
A jewel is shaped.

It shines for men

Who are no more.

THE AUSTRALIAN DEAD OF SANDAKAN

The following lists have been compiled by collating and comparing thousands of records, in Japanese and English, held in archival repositories and supplemented by information from survivors. No definitive lists exist.

At Sandakan Camp (1007)

ABBOTT, E A	BAILEY, N E	BELL, R M
ABFALTER, P J	BALDING, H M	BENNETT, A D
ADAIR, J	BALLARD, G M	BENNETT, H C
ADAM, J C	BANCROFT, E D	BENNISON, R J
ALLAN, L B	BARBER, G K	BENSON, G E
ALLINGHAM, M A	BARKER, D T	BETTS, J
ALLNUTT, S G	BARKLA, E A	BETTS, J M
AMBROSE, G	BARNES, K G	BEVES, E N
ANDERSON, A	BARNES, Reginald	BICE, C J
ANDERSON, J F	BARNES, Ronald	BIGGS, F
ANDERSON, W O	BARNIER, J N	BILLS, W R
ANDREWS, S	BARRATT, R H	BINSTEAD, A H
ANNAND, D	BASTIN, J C	BIRD, B S
ANNEAR, L J	BATES, A E R	BIRD, J E
ARCHIBALD, G R	BATESON, D F	BIRD, J K
ARGO, D M	BAXTER, M P	BLACK, J
ARMSTRONG, F	BAYLEY, A E	BLACKIE, J W
ARMSTRONG, R W	BEARD, W H	BLACKWOOD, L C
ARNOLD, J H	BEASLEY, H C	BLAIR, W F
ARTHUR, H A	BEAUMONT, F J	BLEWETT, C B
ASHBY, F R	BEAZLEY, J D	BLOOM, E
AVICE, S	BEDFORD, R D E	BLUFORD, E H
AYRES, C H	BEER, N P	BLUNDEN, A J
BACCUS, A A	BEER, W H	BOARD, W E
BACON, S T	BEETSON, G J	BOLLARD, J T
BADGERY, B L	BEHRENDORFF, C	BOLTON, E D
BAGUST, R H	BELFORD, N T	BOND, F T

At Sandakan Camp

BONIS, R T
BOOTH, C L
BOTT, J E
BOUGOURE, O W
BOURNE, P J
BOUSIE, G
BOUSTEAD, M G
BOW, W N
BOWE, J M
BOXHORN, K
BOYD, J W
BOYD, J W
BOYD, R
BOYES, W E
BRABHAM, V G
BRACK, D
BRACKEN, C N
BRETT, N F
BROOKER, W
BROOMHAM, C F
BROUGHTON, W E
BROWN, C
BROWN, E G
BROWN, F
BROWN, J E
BROWN, S W
BROWN, V M
BROWNING, J H
BRUCE, R C
BRYANT, F L
BRYANT, J C
BUCKLEY, L F
BULLEN, E F
BUNDEY, G W
BURCHNALL, F R
BURGESS, L
BURGUN, G
BURKE, W J
BURLEY, K B
BURLING, J H
BURNES, F C
BURNS, T
BURROWS, J
BURTON, E G
BURTON, G
BURZACOTT, M
BUTLER, T L
BYCROFT, A B
BYRNE, N B

CAIN, C J
CAMERON, C M
CAMERON, D T
CAMERON, J K
CAMPBELL, D A
CAMPBELL, D S
CAMPBELL, M L
CAMPBELL, R
CAMPBELL, W R
CANDLISH, G A
CAPPER, G H
CARLETON, R V
CARLEY, F A
CARLSON, A R
CARLSON, R D
CARNIE, R M
CARR, B
CARROLL, M
CARTER, G C
CARTHEW, J A
CATERSON, K R
CHAMBERLAIN, J P
CHANDLER, M A
CHAPMAN, A W
CHAPMAN, B B
CHAPMAN, E F
CHAPMAN, W P
CHARLES, G F
CHENHALL, N J
CHILVERS, H A
CLARK, G W
CLARK, R P
CLARK, W B
CLARKE, A
CLARKE, L A
CLAYTON, J H
CLEAR, J A
CLEMENT, A W
CLEMENTS, T
CLISSOLD, J J
CLUCAS, J B
CLYNE, P J
CLYNE, E F
COCHRANE, E A
CODE, L J
COFFEY, M J
COGHLAN, R V
COKER, R H
COLE, E H

COLE, T W
COLEMAN, W J
COLLINS, A C
COLLINS, C R
COLLINS, R B
COLLS, L W
COLYER, G W
COMBER, C O
COMMINS, J S
CONDON, L J
CONLEY, H S
CONNELL, F
CONNELL, J F
CONNOR, H F
CONNOR, J C
CONSTABLE, W A
COOK, A J
COOK, J T
COOK, L C
COOKE, W
COOLING, M W
COOMBE, R J
COOPER, T S
COPE, W G
COPELIN, H V
COPP, E F
CORBETT, J W
CORCORAN, F L
CORDY, F
CORNISH, F
COSTELLO, K
COUGHLIN, C J
COUSINS, S J
COWLEY, M C
COX, A H
COX, L
CRAGO, G
CRAIG, A C
CRAIG, R F
CRAPP, H S
CRAWFORD, V O
CRIBB, T B
CRIGHTON, R S
CRILLY, R J
CRIPPS, W G
CROSS, A H
CROUCH, A G
CROWTHER, G G
CRUMPTON, R F

At Sandakan Camp

CUMMING, D A	DUNN, C H	FORRESTER, C H
CUMMINGS, A L	DUNNE, J J	FORSTER, W C
CUNDY, M H	DURAND, G P	FOX, E H
CUNNINGHAM, J M	DYSON, F A	FRAME, C W
CURREY, J E	DYSON, R R	FROST, E I
CURROW, R W	EARLE, L H	FULLGRABE, A C
DALTON GOODWIN, C R	EARNSHAW, W H	FUSS, C R
DALTON, W J	EASTON, H	GALE, P R
DAUGHTERS, J S	EASTWOOD, G E	GALLARD, R F
DAVEY, C W	EDWARDS, G H	GARDE, H G
DAVIDSON, R R	EDWARDS, H J	GARDNER, A W
DAVIES, D T	ELDERTON, W J	GARDNER, C A
DAVIS, H R	ELLIOTT, S W	GARDNER, I L
DAVIS, J A	ELLIOTT, W G	GARNER, G C
DAVIS, J T	ELLIS, K E	GARVIN, J T
DAVIS, R	ELSLEY, G L E	GASKIN, J
DAVIS, R J	EMMETT, G	GAULD, G T
DAVISON, J	ERNST, J A	GAULT, H R
DAWES, L A	ESSEX, R F	GAY, A P R L
DAWSON, A B G	ETCHELL, A E	GAYNOR, B G
DAWSON, T	EVANS, E C	GIBBS, S H
DAY, A T	EVANS, L M	GILL, H M
DE FAYE, C L	EVANS, R B	GILLEN, P P M
DE FAYE, J	EVANS, W G	GILLESPIE, W G
DEAGAN, M	EVANS, W R	GILLIES, A J
DELAHANT, C W	EWERS, C E	GILLIGAN, C A
DELL, W C	EZZY, A J	GLADWIN, F J
DEMAS, H J	FALCO, J	GLENNIE, J T
DENGATE, A J	FARRELL, A R	GLOAG, D
DENNEHY, A C	FELDBAUER, T A	GLOVER, C R (twin)
DICKIE, G O	FERGUSON, J	GODE, H
DICKMAN, F H	FERGUSON, K D	GODSON, C H
DICKSON, L H	FERRIS, G R	GOLDFINCH, S C
DIXON, T F	FEWER, J R	GOLDING, R S
DOBSON, T R	FIELD, G L C	GOULD, A R
DOHERTY, L L	FIELD, S A	GOULD, R G
DOOLEY, F E	FILEWOOD, A A	GOW, A W
DORIZZI, G	FINDLAY, J G	GOWER, E H
DOUGLAS, W E	FINGHER, R E	GRAF, P F
DOWN, T H	FINN, W M	GRAHAM, G A
DOWNARD, N L	FISHER, P L	GRAHAM, J L
DRINKWATER, J R	FISHER, R J	GREEN, E A
DUCKWORTH, S	FITZGERALD, J D	GREEN, T W
DUDDINGTON, H	FLEMMING, A C	GREENFELD, F R
DUFFY, L J	FLETCHER, B A	GREENUP, C R
DUNCALF, V A	FLETCHER, F G	GREGORY, G E
DUNCAN, J W	FLOYED, A E	GRIFFIN, T M
DUNDAS, R C	FOGARTY, J M	GRIFFITHS, E R
DUNHILL, M R	FOGARTY, M J	GRILLS, V E

GRIMWOOD, J R
GRINTER, C A
GRONO, P R
GROSVENOR, R J
GRUBB, D
GUINEA, J D
GULLIDGE, H E
HACKLAND, E C C
HADDON, T
HAGSTON, G
HALDEN, W J
HALES, R A
HALL, T B
HALLFORD, M E
HALLS, R S
HAMALAINEN, F E
HAMILTON, H
HAMILTON, J
HAMS, N T
HANCOCK, M J
HANCOCK, W J
HANKIN, P E
HANNAN, M E
HANSELL, H N
HARCOURT, R B
HARDY, A A
HARDY, L E
HARGRAVE, C H
HARGRAVES, J V
HARPER, B G
HARPER, H C
HARRINGTON, R E
HARRIS, C
HARRIS, J O
HARRISON, W R
HARSTORFF, D P
HARVEY, G E
HARVEY, H F
HASLUCK, L N
HASTED, J J
HAY, C G
HAYES, J W
HAYES, W C
HAZLEGROVE, M B
HELLIWELL, K J
HENLEY, J B
HENLEY, K H
HENSBY, H
HENWOOD, E J

HEWITT, H F(Turk)
HEWITT, N L
HEYWOOD, A McC
HEYWORTH, W
HIBBERT, S E
HIGGISON, F M
HIGGS, J A
HIGHAM, G E
HILL, W
HINCHCLIFF, W H
HINE, V M
HITCHENS, R
HOBBS, J S
HODDER, W J
HOGAN, D
HOGBIN, C W
HOGG, W
HOLDAWAY, L J
HOLDEN, N N
HOLLAND, J
HOLLIER, H F
HOLMES, R F
HOLST, E J
HONOR, B
HOOD, R J
HOOPER, W R
HOPKINS, A G
HORNE, G D
HOTCHIN, D P
HOTSTON, L
HOW, V K
HOWARD, E
HOWSON, H R
HUBBARD, E A F
HUCKLE, R A
HUGHES, A P
HUGHES, K G
HUGHES, R R
HUMBLER, B P
HUMFREY, P C
HUMPHREYS, P G
HUNT, N F
HUNTER, H D
HURLEY, E T
HURST, R E
HUTCHINSON, J N
HUTCHISON, C E
HUTCHISON, G E
HUTTON, A C

HUTTON, J K
HYETT, R G
I'ANSON, W L
ILES, C
INGRAM, C E
INGS, E H
IRVING, R F
JACKES, W K
JACKS, R J
JACKSON, F P
JACKSON, J
JACKSON, L E
JACOBS, F W
JACOBSON, A
JAMES, G L
JAMES, J R
JAMES, R W
JANKTE, R J
JARRETT, P
JENYNS, N W
JESPERSON, T F
JOHNSON, A E
JOHNSON, H L
JOHNSON, H V
JOHNSON, S H
JOHNSTON, A B
JOHNSTON, C S
JOHNSTON, S
JONES, D H
JONES, F J
JONES, K
JORDAN, W A
JOSELAND, K A
JOYNES, C
JUBELSKI, C W M
JURY, S H
JUSTICE, A J
KANE, G F
KEARNEY, J
KEATING, P M
KEATING, W M
KEAY, V A
KELLY, B H
KELLY, H A
KEMP, H A
KEMP, M W
KERRIS, J L
KILMINSTER, E G
KILPATRICK, C H

At Sandakan Camp

KILPATRICK, J
KING, R A
KIRBY, E A
KLINE, J
KNAPP, W G
KNIGHT, H E
KNIGHT, H R
KNIGHT, V
KNOWLES, J
KNOX, E G
KNOX, J W
KOHLER, L G
KRIEGER, L C
KROSCHEL, E M
KYTE, H G
LAIDLAW, A J
LAKE, G
LAKE, W T
LAMBERT, G
LANE, D R
LANE, T H
LANG, J A
LANGTON, C G
LARNER, V G
LAUNDER, F A
LAW, A W
LE FEVRE, R
LEA, R
LEAR, H B
LEARMONTH, R G
LEBEAU, W H
LEE, D H
LEEDHAM, C A
LENNON, V J
LEVER, A L
LEWIS, C W
LEWIS, F A
LEWIS, J
LEY, P
LILLYMAN, J A
LINDQVIST, L R
LINDSAY, R L
LISTER, A W
LIVINGSTONE, H H
LOADER, K M
LOAN, J B
LOCKE, J
LONGBOTTOM, H
LOURAY, F L

LOVE, W H
LOVERIDGE, A A
LOWE, A J
LOWE, J T
LUDBEY, R B
LUMBY, V A
LUPTON, L
LUPTON, S J
LYNE, G N
LYNTON, R L M
MACADAM, S J
MACAULAY, W A
MACDONALD, R H
MACKAY, F J
MACKAY, T R B
MacKENZIE, C
MacKENZIE, D
MACKIE, A G
MacKINNON, D C
MACKLIN, K G
MACMEIKAN, D J
MADDEN, W
MARR, S
MARSH, C K
MARSH, H A
MARSHALL, A
MARSHALL, J L
MARSHALL, L F
MARTIN, M F SAN 3
MAWHINNEY, G B
McCALL, K B
McCALLUM, H D
McCARDLE, P E
McCARTHY, J F
McCLINTOCK, W A
McCONVILLE, J H
McCORMACK, R A
McCRACKEN, W E
McCULLOCH, C R
McCULLOUGH, W
McDONALD, A
McDONALD, C H
McDONALD, F R
McDONALD, G A
McDONOUGH, J B
McEWEN, G A
McGEARY, E D
McGILL, L
McGRATH, P J

McGREGOR, J A
McGREGOR, R
McIVER, C A
McKEAN, I
McKELVIE, M
McKENNA, C R
McLENNAN, L H
McLEOD, C J
McLEOD, J R
McMAHON, J
McMANUS, S J
McNAUGHTON, D
McSWEENEY, J M
MEEK, E L
MENZIES, H W
MERCER, R L
MEREDITH, D H
MIDGLEY, J J
MILLER, A M
MILLER, S B
MILLIKEN, W E
MILLS, J K
MILNE, G W H
MITCHELL, E E
MITCHELL, W E
MITCHELL, W G
MOLAN, D T
MOLONY, S W
MONAGHAN, H J
MONGAN, D
MONRO, W
MOORE, A C
MOORE, A W
MOORE, C G
MOORE, E G
MOORE, E J
MOORE, J E
MOORE, L C
MOORE, M F
MOORE, S L
MORAN, J P
MORAN, R K
MORGAN, H A
MORGAN, L C
MORGAN, N L
MORRIS, R W
MORRISS, G B
MORTIMER, C H
MORTIMER, H W

MORTON, H A
MOTLEY, L
MOULE-PROBERT, J
MULLIGAN, R P
MUNFORD, F A
MUNRO, J F
MURNANE, W J
MURRAY, G B
MURRAY, L W
MURRAY, R J
MYERS, C D
NAGLE, M J
NAZZARI, F
NEAL, C S
NEAL, F W
NEAL, K T
NEAL, R
NEALE, D M
NEALE, T S
NEGRI, P J
NEILSON, R R
NEWHOUSE, F
NEWLANDS, T S
NEWMAN, C W
NEWSON, J A
NEY, W C
NICHOLLS, S T
NICHOLSON, E C
NICHOLSON, G
NINK, L
NIXON, J H
NOBLE, F R
NOON, J T
O'BRIEN, F
O'BRIEN, W M
O'CONNELL, J T
O'CONNOR, A H
O'CONNOR, J H
O'DONNELL, T E
O'HARA, R T
O'LOUGHLAN, G J
O'MEARA, J J
O'NEALE, J T
O'NEIL, L
O'NEILL, C F
OAKLEY, J H
OBEE, A L
OGILVIE, D J
OHLSON, F J

OLIVE, E R
OLIVER, J
OLLIS, J N
OLVER, K F
ORR, J S
ORTLOFF, F C
OSBORNE, S A
OSGOOD, A
OTTER, L T
PALMER, A
PALMER, H W
PALMER, S J
PANTON, O W
PARHAM, A G
PARTRIDGE, N E
PASHEN, J W
PASSMORE, E W
PATERSON, S
PATTERSON, T B
PATTERSON, R A
PATTESON, E
PAWSON, C
PAXMAN, C
PEACOCK, C K
PECK, F
PEDERSON, P M
PEGNALL, C W
PEOPLES, D J
PERCIVAL, E J
PERROTT, C E
PERRY, J C
PERRY-CIRCUITT, E
PETERSON, J W
PHELAN, M J
PHILLIPS, B
PHILLIPS, W A
PICKERING, J A
PILE, E N
PIPER, R
PLATFORD, J
PLATT, S H
PLEWES, K A
PLUNKETT, G W
PLUNKETT, J
PONTIN, R W
POPE, J G
PORRITT, N A
PORTEOUS, A A
POTTER, N

POWER, R G
PRAETZ, N H
PRIDE, V H
PRIEST, H E
PRINGLE, F W R
PURCELL, J S
PURDON, T
PURSELL, A L
QUINTAL, E A
RADFORD, C
RAE, J
RALPH, B D
RALPH, W D
RAMSAY, G A
RANKIN, C F
RANKIN, C W
RANKIN, G H
RANKIN, J R
RAWLINGS, B A
RAYMOND, K M
REDMAN, W H
REED, E A
REID, D A
REID, W
RENAUD, E C
RICHARDS, E M
RICHARDSON, J
RICHARDSON, J G
RICHMILLER, K J
ROBBINS, T H
ROBERTS, F
ROBERTS, H E
ROBERTS, L J
ROBERTS, Sydney
ROBERTS, W F
ROBERTSON, E E
ROBINS, C W
ROBINSON, B A
ROBINSON, F G B
ROBINSON, H
ROCHFORD, F
ROLLS, W F
ROSS, D
ROSS, W
ROUSE, M H
ROWAN, H J
RUDD, W T
RUMMELL, V C
RUNDLE, C A

RUSSELL, A W	SORBY, W T	THOMPSON, W
RYAN, J G	SOTHERON, B E	THOMSON, A
RYAN, J J	SOUTER, G A	THOMSON, E F
SAMPSON, H R	SPEAKE, C R	THORLEY, I E
SANDERCOCK, H A	SPEARS, N	THORNEYCROFT, C
SANKOWSKY, R H	SPURLING, T	THORPE, H
SAWFORD, B G	ST LEON, G	THURSTON, H W
SCAMBREY, W E	STAGGS, F L	TICKLE, W
SCHIPHORST, A	STANLEY, R	TINNING, R J
SCOTT, C	STANTON, E	TOLLIDAY, A S
SCOTT, J	STANWELL, O M	TOMKYNS, E A
SCULLY, J S	STAPLETON, T N	TOMS, H
SEFTON, B L	STARKIE, J D	TOOMBS, R E
SHAW, A D	STARKY, C B	TRAVIS, J H
SHAW, G	STEELE, A R	TREVILLIEN, R G
SHAW, R	STEEN, W S	TRIGWELL, A G
SHEEDY, R H	STEVENS, J J	TRODD, R J
SHELVOCK, C B	STEVENSON, T S	TUCKERMAN, J H
SHERMAN, M O	STEWART, B P	TURNER, H Ray
SHIELDS, E J	STEWART, H J	TURNER, K M
SHIELDS, R	STEWART, H T	TURNER, R E
SHIPSIDES, R A	STEWART, S K	TYRES, K H
SHIRLEY, A F	STEWART, W	TYRRELL, Ronald
SHORT, E R	STIRLING, D H	VEAL, R J
SHORT, M N	STIRLING, G McB	VOGELE, G L
SIMPSON, Herbert	STOCKLEY, R R	VOLLHEIM, E C
SIMPSON, S A	STONE, H D	WADDINGTON, G
SINCLAIR, I A	STRACHAN, G	WALKER, E T
SINCLAIR, I McD	STRANG, P	WALL, R H
SKINNER, G T	STROUT, E A	WALLACE, H W
SKINNER, J F	STUCHBURY, I	WALLER, T
SLIGO, N K	SULLIVAN, D	WALSH, F V
SLIP, E C	SWAN, W A	WALSH, L J
SMALL, R D	SWIFT, D S	WALTERS, L E
SMALL, R P	SYMES, A V	WAPLING, J H
SMALLDON, H J	TAIT, R	WARD, R
SMITH, A A	TANNER, V G	WARREN, H J
SMITH, A J	TAYLOR, G C	WASTNIDGE, R
SMITH, E I	TAYLOR, G W	WATERHOUSE, A
SMITH, Ernest	TAYLOR, H B	WATERS, A J
SMITH, F A O	TAYLOR, I	WATSON, Clarence
SMITH, F S	TELFORD, G F	WATSON, F W
SMITH, G A	TEMPLE, R J	WATSON, T N
SMITH, G J	TENNYSON, B G	WATSON, W J H
SMITH, R E	THOMAS, J O	WATTERS, L L
SMITH, R J V	THOMAS, M G	WATTS, D L
SMITH, T E	THOMPSON, F	WEEKS, F N
SMITH, W H	THOMPSON, R J	WEHL, F G
SOMMERVILLE, A C	THOMPSON, V R	WEIR, S J

WEISSEL, G	WILLIAMS, J C	WOOD, R B
WELCH, W A	WILLIAMSON, L R	WOODCROFT, K R
WELLARD, C J	WILLMOTT, K W	WOODLEY, E G
WELLS, H G	WILSON, A	WOODLEY, F E
WESTWOOD, Bert	WILSON, A E	WOODS, F H
WHEELER, J E	WILSON, C B	WOOLARD, A I
WHEREAT, M C	WILSON, C W	WRIGHT, C
WHITE, Bernard	WILSON, G E	WRIGHT, T J
WHITE, C H	WILSON, L A	WRIGLEY, K G
WHITE, L A	WILSON, R M	WYNN, W E
WHITE, S H	WINKS, A K	YOUNG, A D
WHYMAN, H A	WINTER, S C	YOUNG, D
WILKIE, J	WISEMAN, E W	YOUNG, J S
WILKINS, G H	WITT, K C	YOUNG, T O
WILKINS, K	WOLTER, G J	

Escaped from Sandakan Camp and died at Sandala Estate (3)

LEDWIDGE, F B	RADNEDGE, G	TRESEDER, H A

On the Death March Track (424)

ADAMS, H	BEXTON, S O	BUSHELL, R F
ADAMS, T	BIGNELL, K W	CADWGAN, A D
ADLINGTON, N C	BILLS, L	CALLANDER, H M
AINSWORTH, T L	BLATCH, W G	CAMERON, F
ALBERTS, W*	BOWERMAN, H F	CAMPBELL, C
ALBRESS, A S	BOWMAN, H R	CAMPBELL, J
ALLEN, S J	BOYLE, C R	CARSON, W J
ANDERSON, E R	BOYLEY, W A	CARVETH, A J
ARNOLD, L R	BRADY, W P	CASSIDY, L A
ARTHUR, R G	BRAY, E W	CAVENAGH, C R
ASGILL, C C	BRAY, J	CHANT, J R
AULD, R J	BREDBURY, I	CHAPMAN, S
AYTON, A C	BRODY, L	CHILD, F T
BAGNALL, N W	BROWN, A A	CHIPPERFIELD, R
BAILEY, E G	BROWN, M	CHISHOLM, H F
BAILEY, I S	BROWN, W F	CHISOLM, R S
BALGUE, D N	BRUCE, F W	CHRISTENSEN, H G
BALL, C G	BUCKLEY, H W	CHRISTIANSEN, W
BARKER, J H	BUCKLEY, J J	CHRISTIE, N McN
BARLOW, W J	BUNCH, N H	CLACK, J P
BARRIE, J	BURCHNALL, F A	CLAIR, T E
BARTILS, G H	BURKE, F J	CLARK, D S
BEER, W J	BURNS, C E	CLARKE, L B
BELL, M C	BURNS, R N	CLARKSON, J M
BENDALL, B A	BURNS, S A	CLIFFORD, E T
BENNETT, H P	BURRIDGE, F R	COGGINS, P R

COLLINS, H W	EVANS, W C	HARDING, L C
COLLINS, S G	EWING, H	HARRIS, C H
COLUMBINE, R E	FARREY, L W	HARRIS, L A
COMMERFORD, G F	FARROW, H	HARRIS, R C
CONQUIT, G D	FERGUSON, N J	HARRIS, S N
COONEY, J	FERGUSSON, N W	HAWKINS, C A
CORE, S R	FINCH, W H	HAYE, L J
COSTELLO, J	FITZGERALD, G S	HEDLEY, G W
COSTIN, K H	FLANAGAN, W J	HEWITT, H
COUGHLAN, T	FLAVELL, R R	HICKS, V O
COULTER, W J	FLETCHER, J S	HILL, C S
COULTON, G L	FLINT, A E	HILL, E T
COX, R C	FOLKARD, S B	HODGES, D
COY, F T	FOOTE, P N	HODGES, G H
CRANE, A B	FOSBURY, B J A	HODGES, R E
CRANNEY, R T	FOSTER, D	HOLLAND, H W
CREES, R J	FOTHERINGHAM, T	HOLME, C
CREWDSON, A J	FRANKLIN, F G	HOWELL, D W
CROCKETT, E R	FRAZIER, J W	HUGHES, R
CROSS, J R	FRY, V J	HUMPHRIES, D
CROSSMAN, E R	FULLER, E J	HUNT, R P
CULL, A	GANNON, W J	HUSTLER, F E
CUMMINGS, N G	GARRARD, J H	HUTCHINSON, V
DALE, A	GEMMILL, S C	INCE, J W
DARRAGH, L A	GENTLE, T R	INGS, J
DAVEY, B A	GHANANBURGH, C	JACKAMAN, G E
DAVIDSON, G L	GIBSON, J B	JACOBS, C J
DAVIS, R V	GIBSON, N A	JEFFREY, V A
DE COSTA, G F	GLOVER, F M (twin)	JILLETT, R E
DEMPSTER, C	GLOVER, S	JOHNSON, C G
DESHON, F H	GOLDIE, J McL	JOHNSON, S R
DEZIUS, F C	GOLDSWORTHY, T	JOHNSTON, C 'Vic'
DIXON, J	GOODEAR, N F	JONES, A F
DORAN, P M	GOOUD, L	JONES, H B
DORIZZI, H	GRAHAM, R	KELLY, F W
DOWNEY, H A	GRAHAM, R J	KELLY, S J
DOYLE, E A	GRANT, F M	KERR, J R
DOYLE, P J	GRANT, J J	KING, E
DUNHILL, E G	GRAVE, R L	KING, J S
DYER, W	GREEN, A A	KING, P C
EBZERY, T	GREENWAY, A C	KINGSLEY, C M
EGEL, R C	GREENWOOD, R J	KINNON, V R
ELLIS, A G	GRIFFIN, K C	LANCASTER, W J
ELY, T H	GRIGSON, A G	LARCOMBE, C T
EMMETT, E V	HACK, A M	LARKINS, M J
ENGELHART, N	HALLIGAN, J	LAWRENCE, A S
ERWIN, L R	HALY, S O'G	LE CLERCQ, A E
EVANS, B H	HANKINSON, R F	LEAR, J
EVANS, J W	HANSON, K D	LEITH, F A

LESTER, J B	NOLAN, G N	ROSS, J H
LEVEY, R E	NUNN, J O	ROUSE, J F
LEVIS, H	O'BRIEN, M V	ROWE, C H
LIGHT, J W	O'CONNOR, R M	RUANE, R M
LLOYD, H G	O'HARA, M T	RUSCOE, G
LYNCH, J J	O'MALLEY, G F	RUSH, M J
MABEN, R R	O'ROURKE, T J	RYAN, R T
MABIN, D W	OVENS, H	RYAN, W A
MacDONALD, L	PALLISTER, R	SADLER, R E
MACKAY, T	PALMER, D	SALTER, P J
MacKENZIE, D H	PALMER, N W	SAVAGE, E C
MACONACHIE, R D	PARFREY, T H	SAVAGE, T
MADDISON, J W	PARKER, N L	SCHIBECI, D
MAGUIRE, J	PARNELL, R J	SCHMUTTER, W J
MAHONEY, G	PATTERSON, H A	SCOLLEN, T P
MAHONY, K P	PAYNE, H J	SCOTT, J M
MAIN, C D	PEARCE, J S	SEARLE, L E
MAKIM, G J	PEARCE, K J	SEELEY, J W
MALIN, W M	PERRY, K G	SEVIER, J
MANKS, E F	PETERS, C J	SHEARD, W A*
MANTON, L C	POGSON, C R	SHEPHERD, W P
MARTIN, F J	POWELL, C A	SHERRING, F
MARTIN, J W	POWELL, K N	SIMPSON, Henry
MATHEW, A W	PRENDERGAST, J J	SIMPSON, L P
McAPPION, H E	PRIOR, L	SINNAMON, F
McCARTHY, J F	PROSSER, W R	SKEWS, R
McCLOUNAN, R L	PURVIS, R C	SKINNER, E K
McCONNELL, A	QUAILEY, A C	SLIGAR, G W
McFARLANE, J	RAISON, V R	SMEETON, B L
McHENERY, L G	RAPHAEL, H N	SMITH, A W L
McILHAGGA, W J	REA, E H	SMITH, G
McLACHLAN, K J	REARDON, F W	SMITH, H V
McLAGHLAN, T D	REAY, S V	SMITH, J B I
McLEENAN, L A	REID, F C	SMITH, M H
McLELLAN, A P	REILLY, V A	SMITH, W S
McLEOD, N P	RENDALL, D	SOLOMON, J H
MEAGHER, G F	RENNIE, O A	SPENCE, R H
MERRITT, R L	REYNOLDS, C	SPROUL, L J
MIDLANE, D L	RICHARDS, Evan	STACE, R A
MILDENHALL, J S	RICHARDS, R M	STANDRING, H C
MILNE, R A	RICHARDSON, J L	STEEL, J A
MITCHELL, A L	RICHARDSON, L W	STEVENS, C C
MITCHELL, R J	RICKERBY, K W	STEVENS, Charles
MOLDE, K C	RING, R	STEWART, A B
MORRIS, H	ROBERTSON, R J	STIRLING, C
NEALE, S E	RODGERS, E A	SULLIVAN, Ronald*
NEAVES, G M	RODRIQUEZ, J F	SULLIVAN, Roy H
NICHOLSON, J F	ROGERS, J S	SYME, A J
NOAKES, A H	ROOKE, R G	TANKO, V K

At Ranau Number 1 Camp (146)

TANZER, H J	TYRRELL, A R	WILMOTT, A J
TAYLOR, G J	VARRIE, G B	WILSON, E W
TAYLOR, G L	WALKER, N G	WILSON, G
TAYLOR, H T	WALTER, R W	WILSON, R S
TAYLOR, J A	WALTON, D R	WILSON, S C
TAYLOR, N H	WARD, J A	WINNING, H
TAYLOR, W C	WARDMAN, J	WINTERBOTTOM, A
THOMAS, A D	WARNER, Bertie	WOLFE, G
THOMPSON, A H	WARREN, J McK	WOODALL, J
THONDER, W C	WATTS, E R	WOODS, C J
THOROUGHGOOD, H	WEBBER, S A	WOOLNOUGH, A W
TIERNEY, J E	WEBSTER, A G	WORBY, R P
TIERNEY, M J	WEST, J S	WORLAND, N C
TRINDER, L G	WHITE, J A	WRAIGHT, D C
TURNER, A J	WHITEHEAD, W	WRIGHT, F P
TURNER, E H	WHYTE, R J	YOUNG, D G
TURNER, H Robert	WILKES, H R	
TWISS, R T	WILLIAMS, G E	

At Paginatan Camp (32)

BARAGWANATH, W	JONES, J W	ROBERTS, H A
BOCK, H J	LEINSTER, V P	ROBINSON, G B
BRINKMAN, J H	MACPHERSON, S D	ROWLEY, B
BROWN, W	MAINSTONE, C D	SMITH, J D
CAPON, W A	MANN, C N	STOLARSKI, C
DOCWRA, G A	MARSH, W R	TAYLOR, A A
DUFFY, S D	MARTIN, J T	THOMAS, E
GARLAND, A W	McCARTHY, L	TURNER, N
GRANT, E T	MORGAN, E	WILSON, H
GRAY, R S	MUMME, L W	WYE, F R C
IZZARD, C H M	PATTEN, C E	

At Ranau Number 1 Camp (146)

Three POWs (Alberts, Sheard and Sullivan – see the listing for On the Death March Track, page XXX) have been definitely identified as among the fifteen or so prisoners whom Botterill confirmed died while carrying rice to Paginatan. The names of the POWs below, marked with an asterisk, may be among the remaining twelve, as their death dates coincide with rice-carrying duties).

ALEXANDER, E C	BOYD, R T*	CHANDLER, R K
ANDERSON, P A*	BRADY, C	CLARK, F H
ATTENBOROUGH, A	BRIEN, D H	CLARK, J C
BARKER, G J*	BROWN, N N*	CLEARY, A N
BARNARD, L G*	BURNETT, E R*	CLYDSDALE, T J*
BOESE, R J*	BYRNE, B*	COOPER, J A
BOVEY, A R	CANNING, B C	CORNEY, L C
BOYCE, A R	CARTER, P W*	COX, G K

At Ranau Number 1 Camp (146)

CRAZE, R
CREASE, W
DIGBY, G H*
DIXON, K A
DORIZZI, T H
DOWLING, E
DOWNES, I G
DUGGAN, S J
DWYER, J
ELLIOTT, S
ELLIOTT, T A
FERGUSON, R P*
FITZGERALD, H R*
FRANCIS, F C
FRASER, T W
GAVEN, J
GILLETT, K B
GILLHAM, A J*
GRAHAM, W H
GROSVENOR, L L
HALES, L J
HARDSTAFF, R A
HARRIS, C M
HARRIS, W L
HARWOOD, F
HASTIE, L J
HEADFORD, F W
HICKMAN, C
HORNE, N
INGHAM, A E
IRELAND, G A*
ISBEL, C E
JACKSON, L W
JACOBS, G W
JONES, V
JONES, W N
KAVANAGH, L M
KEAYS, D C
KENT, E J
LE CUSSAN, E W
LIVET, V L
LOBEGEIGER, J
LOCK, B C
LOGAN, R W B*
MARSHALL, P O
MAUNSELL, J F
McCRUM, A*
McGEE, H A
McGEE, W A
McGOWAN, W J
McIVER, G D
McKENZIE, W J
McKINNON, V H
McLAUGHLIN, B L
McLAUGHLIN, R G
McLEOD, W
MEEK, D R*
MITCHELL, J W
MONLEY, F J
MOORE, T A*
MORGAN, H C
MORGAN, L G
MORLAND, R G
MULRAY, W P
MULVOGUE, R H
MURRAY, D A
NASH, C O
NOAKES, A W
O'CONNOR, G*
ORR, E J K
PAGE, R A
PARKINSON, D S
PEARCE, W H
PEPPER, G D*
PHELPS, R L
PHILLIPS, E J
PRIESTER, F*
PRYOR, D R
PURTILL, J F
REID, R D
RIDLER, C J
RIGHETTI, L J
ROBERTSON, G C
ROBINSON, F
ROOKE, D R
SCHUTT, L V
SEFTON, I G
SEWELL, A E
SHACKELL, J H
SHARP, W
SHAW, D R
SHEARMAN, S G
SHERWOOD, S
SINCLAIR, W
SKINNER, T R
SLATTER, A J
SMITH, C T
SMITH, J S
SMITH, W J
SPENCER, H F
SPURWAY, R S
STONE, R D
STOREY, G J
SUTTON, J E
SWAN, C W
SYMONS, G H
TAPPER, S ('James')
TAYLOR, D*
VICTORSEN, L M*
WACHNER, E C*
WALKER, J S
WALTERS, A F
WARD, S W
WATSON, C Y
WATTS, T J*
WESTON, W E
WILLIAMS, H P
WILSON, D G
WILSON, E
WOODS, M P
WREN, C R
YATES, G

At Ranau Number 1 Jungle Camp (28)

ADDISON, P R	JEFFREY, R L	PLAYER, G C
ALLIE, N R	KINDER, J W	RATCLIFF, R B
ARMSTRONG, T E	LEADBEATTER, W	REITZE, H
CANTERBURY, L C	LYTTON, H	ROEBUCK, J T
CHAPMAN, S H	MOLLOY, J	SMYTH, C G
DONOHUE, J A	MUNRO, L A	STANLEY, J R
DUNKINSON, J L	MURRAY, R	WARRINGTON, C W
FITZPATRICK, D A	PEPPER, C D	WOODFORD, C A
FOXWELL, C A	PERRY, W G	
HARDY, G R	PETERS, K A	

At Ranau Number 2 Jungle Camp (145)

ALLEN, J M	EVANS, G J	JUKES, C G H
ARCHARD, C	EVANS, O R	KEALEY, J V
ARMSTRONG, J W	FAHEY, A M	KING, C H
BENNETT, W D	FARRELL, V H	KOPANICA, J F
BEXTON, T	FERGUSON, A J	LAST, A B
BIRD, A W	FINN, A H	LETHBRIDGE, T C
BIRD, C R	FINN, J A	LONGLEY, H
BOBBIN, R J	FITZGERALD, L N	LUTON, H W
BOLTON, G A	FITZPATRICK, F J	LYSAGHT, H W
BOWE, W J	FLOOD, L A	MADDOCK, N L
BROWN, R G	FRENCH, R F	MAIZEY, C W
BROWN, S	FROST, H T	MANN, W R
BROWNLEE, G F	GAGAN, L A	MASKEY, L W
BURGESS, J	GALTON, D	MATCHETT, H D
BURKE, J E	GARDNER, E J	MAY, D J
BURNELL, A D	GELLATLY, R A	McCORLEY, K
BUTHERWAY, J H	GOOD, G	McDONALD, W B
CHAPMAN, C K	GORDON, T	McEWAN, R I
CHAPMAN, J J	GRIMWOOD, H	McGLINN, A J
CHARLTON, R J	GRIST, N S	McGUIRE, A D
CODLIN, J M	HALL, R W	McILROY, K A
CONNOLLY, T W	HARPLEY, J C	McKERROW, E A
COOK, G R	HEASLOP, J E	McMARTIN, J
CRAWFORD, J O	HERD, B	MUNRO, E L
CURREY, W J	HICKS, H R	NEWLING, R W
DAVIDSON, F G	HODGES, J D G	NOONAN, E G
DAVIES, E D	HOLLAND, L U	NOONAN, W A
DAVISON, E	HOPKINS, W R	O'CONNOR, H B
DAY, G	HORDER, R J	O'DONOHUE, E J
DOYLE, A G	HUNTER, A C	O'KEEFE, H J
DOYLE, L H	JEAVONS, J A	OAKESHOTT, J B
EDWARDS, G E	JEWISS, A C	OWER, W J
ETHERIDGE, J O	JUCHAU, R F	PARSONS, J W

At Ranau Number 2 Jungle Camp

PAULETT, L	SMITH, E S	GREENWOOD, H
PEACH, J T	SMITH, O	WEATHERBY, W S
PHILLIPS, R	STACY, R L	WELLS, G D
PICONE, D G	STANTON, A J	WHITEHEAD, B C
POWELL, L V	STEINBECK, W J	WHITELAW, J R
POWER, C G R	SYKES, R W	WHITING, W G
RALEIGH, J	TAYLOR, T C	WHYBIRD, J A
READ, W G	TERRETT, E	WILKINSON, D L
READING, T A	THISTLEWAITE, V	WILLIAMS, A T
RICHARDS, E R	THORNS, A S	WILLMOTT, A C
ROBERTS, S	TIPPING, N A	WILSON, R J
ROBERTSON, F H	TULLY, N McK	WISEMAN, R H
ROBINSON, J F	TYRRELL, R	WOLFE, E J
SCHOLEFIELD, R	VAUGHAN, W J	WRIGHT, C L
SHEPHERD, G A	WALKER, R G	WRIGLEY, K H
SLEEP, J	WARDALE-	

Escaped from Ranau 2 Jungle Camp and died near Ranau (2)

ANDERSON, F D
REITHER, H

Summaries for Sandakan, Ranau and the Three Death Marches

Died on the track, including three known rice carriers	424
Died at Paginatan village	32
Died at Ranau 1 Camp or rice carrying	146
Died at Ranau 1 Jungle Camp	28
Died at Ranau 2 Jungle Camp (The Last Camp)	145
Escaped from The Last Camp and died	2
Total	**777***
Died at Sandakan 1 Compound	784
Died at Sandakan 2 Compound (incl. one E Force and 23 shot at the airstrip)	223
Escaped and died at Sandala	3
Total	**1010****
FINAL TOTAL	**1787**

Notes

* 314 (out of 316) who went on the first march died; 406 (of 410) who went on the second march died; 57 who went on the third march died: total 777

** 1007 died at Sandakan; 3 who escaped from Sandakan died at Sandala: total 1010

Outram Road Gaol Inmates from Sandakan (30)

ALLEN, E A*
BLAIN, A McA
BROWN, M P**
CARR, M J
DARLINGTON, J
DAVIS, R G*
DAVIS, S G
FAIRY, W F*
JACKA, M E
JAMES, J H
JENSEN, C E
MacMILLAN, J A
MARSHALL, D G*
MARTIN, F J
McDONAGH, W J
McWILLIAMS, B J
MILLS, C C
MINTRY, A R
MORRIS, N S
NEW, F T
RICKARDS, J H
ROFFEY, W G
RUMBLE, T H
SHELLEY, J N*
SMALL, A L*
STEVENS, A
TRACKSON, H R
WELLS, R G
WEYNTON, A G
YOUNG, K W**

Notes

* Died in captivity (6)

** K W 'Billy' Young and M P Brown were the only prisoners from Sandakan not to obtain relief at Outram Road Gaol by being transferred to Changi

In Kuching Gaol (2)

HARRINGTON, T
KEATING, E

Other Australian Outram Road Inmates (34)

BARTLETT, C E
BIRD, K J
BLEE, S W
CAREY, W G**
DEAN, P V
FALLS, W G**
FLETCHER, R B**
GOODWIN, W C
GOOLEY, D P**
GREEN, R H
HARDY, J T**
HARRIS, R B
HART, H J
HARVEY, T J
HATFIELD, E E**
HOLM, G
HUGHES, M R
MACALISTER, J L
MCFALL, J
MCGREGOR, J A
MICHELL, A K
MORRIS, R L
NEILSEN, C H E
PAGE, R C**
PRICE, W B
ROBERTS, W E
ROLLASON, H
ROSS, A*
SARGENT, A L**
SMITH, G H
STEWART, C M**
WARREN, A**
WILLIAMS, P H
WYETT, J W C

Notes
* Died
** Executed

BIBLIOGRAPHY

Selected Bibliography

All autobiographical material in this book has been compiled from direct interviews conducted by Lynette Silver with Billy Young and from his various written records and memoirs.

The additional narrative has been drawn from various sources.

Official records

Australian National Archives
    ASIO records

Outram Road Gaol records
    War Crimes Files, various
    War Graves Registration Cards
    WW1 Dossiers
    WW2 Dossiers

Australian War Memorial Collection, Canberra
    Official Records
    Photographic Collection
    Private Records

Australians at War Film Archives

Birth, Death and Marriage Records, NSW

Birth, Death and Marriage Records, Tasmania

Commonwealth War Graves Commission Records

Department of Health and Human Services, Victoria

Department of Veteran Affairs World War 2 Nominal Roll

Divorce Records, NSW Archives

Dutch War Graves Records

Electoral Rolls for NSW, Victoria and Tasmania

National Film and Sound archives

Police Records, NSW Archives

Rookwood Cemetery Records

Singapore National Archives
Singapore National Library Collection
United States Archives, Washington DC

Published books

Australian Dictionary of Biography

Chilstrom, John S, Mines away! The Significance of Us Army Airforces Minelaying in World War II, 1993

Christie, R W (ed), A History of the 2/29th Battalion – 8th Australian Division AIF, 2/29 Battalion Association, 1985

Craven, Wesley Frank and Cate, James Lea, The Pacific: Matterhorn to Nagasaki June 1944 to August 1945, Vol 5, 1953.

Cunningham, Michelle, Defying the Odds, Lothian Books, 2006

Gould, Bob, Irish Catholics and the Labour Movement in Australia, (pamphlet) 1999

Hogan, Michael, A History of the Labour Party in Glebe, 1891-2003

Kirby, S. Woodburn, The War Against Japan Volume IV: The Reconquest of Burma, 1965

McGregor, John, Blood on the Rising Sun, circa 1980

Michno, Gregory F, Death on the Hellships, 2001

Middlebrook, Martin and Mahoney, Patrick, Battleship: The Sinking of the Prince of Wales and the Repulse, 1979.

McPhillips, Jack, Penal Powers (pamphlet, nd)

Moran, Stan, Reminiscences of a Rebel, 2008

Nelson, Hank, Prisoners of War, Australians Under Nippon, 1985

Pieris, Anoma, Hidden Hands and Divided Landscape, 2010

Post Office Directories (various)

Royal Navy, War with Japan. Volume IV, The South-East Asia Operations and Central Pacific Advance, 1995

Sands Directories (various)

Silver, Lynette Ramsay, Blood Brothers. Sabah and Australia 1942-1945, 2010

Silver, Lynette Ramsay, Deadly Secrets. The Singapore Raids 1943-45, 2009

Silver, Lynette Ramsay, Sandakan A Conspiracy of Silence, Revised 4th edition, 2010.

Silver, Lynette Ramsay, The Bridge at Parit Sulong, 2004

Silver, Lynette Ramsay, The Heroes of Rimau, 1990.

Tamura, Keiko, 'Triumphant Return', in Wartime, Journal of the Australian War Memorial, Issue 45

Toh, Boon Kwan, 'The American Strategic Bombing of Singapore, 1944–45', The Journal of Military History, July 2009

Wigmore, Lionel, The Japanese Thrust, Australian War Memorial, 1957

Newspapers, journals etc.

Advocate (Burnie): 24/3/1947

Argus: 8/10/1910, 19/11/1928, 9/12/1928, 30/5/1941, 30/8/1941,

Burnie Advocate: 24/3/1947

Cairns Post: 14/9/1936

Courier Mail: 24/10/1954

Daily News Perth: 30/8/1930, 14/3/1932

Daily Express (Malaysia): 7/8/2015

Green Left Weekly: Issue 153

Illawarra Mercury: http://www.illawarramercury.com.au/story/1881006/watch-port-kembla-wharfs-wonder-woman/

Independent (UK): 15/8/2002

Evening News (Sydney): 22/1/1885, 9/10/1889, 16/1/1891, 30/11/1891, 4/9/1903, 20/6/1906, 17/7/1907, 11/9/1907, 20/12/1908, 28/9/1910, 10/4/1912, 5/6/1913, 16/11/1920, 17/11/1920, 10/12/1920, 25/9/1930, 6/12/1930

Mirror, Perth: 8/9/1934

National Advocate, Bathurst: 26/9/1910

Nepean Times: 31/1/1952

Newcastle Morning Herald and Miners' Advocate: 7/10/1910, 15/4/1925,

Northern Star (Lismore): 9/11/1920

Police Gazette: 26/1/1891, 15/10/1910

Scone Advocate: 7/4/1925

South Coast Times and *Wollongong Argus*: 28/10/1938

Sunday Times, Perth: 31/8/1930, 4/3/1934, 9/9/1934, 14/9/2934,

Sydney Morning Herald: 19/9/1895, 11/11/1903, 4/6/1906, 20/6/1906, 21/6/1906, 26/1/1907, 17/7/1907, 11/9/1907, 4/10/1907, 12/10/1907, 23/10/1907, 24/10/1907, 25/11/1907, 26/11/1907, 24/12/1907, 4/6/1908, 3/8/1908, 9/10/1909, 12/10/1909, 5/10/1910, 7/10/1910, 15/10/1910, 19/11/1911, 10/4/1912, 17/4/1912, 24/4/1912, 4/5/1912, 27/5/1912, 1/6/1912, 11/6/1912, 28/6/1912, 12/8/1912, 13/8/1912, 15/8/1912, 21/8/1912, 5/10/1912, 8/10/1912, 30/11/1912, 3/12/1912, 15/12/1912, 4/6/1914, 5/6/1913, 21/2/1914, 22/7/1918, 16/11/1920, 17/11/1920, 10/12/1920, 9/4/1921, 30/6/1921, 22/3/1922, 25/5/1922, 8/8/1923, 15/4/1925, 29/9/1926, 10/11/1926, 2/8/1928, 9/6/1929, 7/9/1929, 1/3/1930, 10/7/1930, 13/10/1930, 14/10/1930, 15/10/1930, 30/12/1930, 18/2/1931, 20/4/1931, 21/4/1931, 4/5/1931, 16/5/1931, 18/5/1931, 19/5/1931, 22/7/31, 23/8/1931, 25/8/1931, 3/9/1931, 7/9/1931, 10/9/1931, 119/9/1931, 15/10/1931, 16/10/1931, 22/10/1931, 23/10/1931, 23/12/1931, 18/5/1932, 19/5/1932, 10/11/1932, 11/11/1932, 25/11/32, 9/2/1933, 11/2/1933, 16/3/1933, 14/9/1933, 15/6/1934, 30/6/1934, 23/7/1936, 18/9/1939, 23/4/1983, 26/1/2004

The Mercury, Hobart: 2/4/1918, 12/11/1920, 22/5/1922, 9/7/1924, 17/6/1925, 19/6/1925, 14/11/1925, 17/6/1926, 17/6/1927, 9/7/1927, 24/10/1927, 1/12/1927, 14/9/1928, 14/11/1928, 10/9/1929, 13/10/1930, 15/10/1930, 30/5/1932, 8/4/1933,

2/5/1936, 4/5/1936, 2/5/1938, 10/7/1943, 21/9/1943, 1/10/1946, 24/3/1947, 3/4/1947, 2/11/1950, 15/2/1954, 18/2/1954

The Straits Times (Singapore): 29/3/1950, *Truth* (Perth): 31/8/1931

Truth (Sydney): 18/8/1912, 22/7/1922

West Australian: 26/8/1930, 30/8/1930, 5/3/1932, 14/3/1932, 5/3/1934, 14/3/1934, 16/3/1934, 8/9/1934, 11/9/1934, 14/9/1934, 15/9/1934

Workers' Weekly: 29/9/1937, 26/11/1937, 21/12/1937, 25/1/1938, 18/2/1938, 8/7/1938, 23/8/1938, 26/8/1938, 30/8/1938, 13/9/1938, 11/10/1938, 14/10/1938, 28/10/1938, 1/11/1938, 9/12/1938, 13/12/1938, 16/12/1938, 20/12/1938, 3/1/1939, 6/1/1939, 10/1/1939, 20/1/1939, 3/2/1939, 24/2/1939, 17/2/1939

Private papers

Young Family papers
Silver Papers
Wells Papers

Memoirs

Millner, James

Roderick Wells

Young, William, *Long Ago in Borneo*; *My Little Book of Poems*; *My War in Pictures*; *My Thoughts in Verse*; *Return to a Dark Age*, (manuscript begun in 1970s, various revisions)

Website articles and websites

Banning, Jan, *Traces of War: Dutch and Indonesian Survivors*, 10/8/2005 (www.opendemocracy.net)

Mallory, Greg, *The 1938 Dalfram Pig-iron Dispute and Wharfies Leader, Ted Roach* (http://asslh.org.au/hummer/vol-3-no-2/dalfram-pig-iron/)

http://www.emelbourne.net.au

http://www.findandconnect.gov.au

Interviews

Keith Botterill, John Campbell, Owen Campbell, Carol Collidge, Eric Davis, Frank Gavan, Karl Jensen, James Millner, Ken Mosher, Paddy O'Toole, Bert Rollason, Nelson Short, Herbert Trackson, Roderick Wells, Keith William Young